AA

y Pubs

CW00376005

Credits

Cover Photo: AA World Travel Library / Alex Kouprianoff

All other photographs in this book come from the AA World Travel Library and were taken by Tom Mackie.

Design by Jamie Wiltshire
Typeset/Repro: iCandy Design Ltd, Basingstoke
Printed by Everbest, China
Editor: Denise Laing

Pub descriptions have been contributed by the following team of writers: Phil Bryant, Neville Chalkley, Nick Channer, Alice Gardner, David Halford, Judith Hope, Julia Hynard, Denise Laing, Philip Moss, Derryck Strachan.

Published by AA Publishing, a trading name of Automobile Association Developments Limited, whose registered office is Southwood East, Apollo Rise, Farnborough Hampshire GU14 OJW. Registered number 1878835.

A CIP catalogue for this book is available from the British Library.

ISBN 074952691
A0 2039

Welcome to the Guide

This pocket guide is intended to help you find pubs that actively welcome children. There are country pubs and city pubs, some very well known, some in breathtaking locations, and many offering wonderful food and a good choice of beer for the grown ups.

How to Use this Guide

Explanation of entries and notes
on abbreviations

Sample Entry

NEWTOWN   **SP05** — ②

① **The Red Lion**   ★ ⑳ ⑳ ⑳ — ③

④ High Street SGXX 9XX
☎ 01284 567890 📠 01234 567890

⑤ **Dir:** Off B658 SW of Weston

*Unspoilt inn, featuring intimate, quarry-tiled
rooms with latched doors and panelled walls,
Real ales are served and a straightforward
menu includes home-made cottage pie*

⑥ **OPEN:** 12-3 6-11 (Sat 12-4, Sun 12-4)
BAR MEALS: L served all week 12-2.30
D served Mon-Sat 7-9 — ⑦
⑧ **RESTAURANT:** L served all week 12-2.30
D served Mon-Sat 7-9.3
BREWERY/COMPANY: GREENE KING — ⑨
⑩ 🍺 :Greene King Abbot Ale, IPA & Ruddles
County **ROOMS:** 10 en suite (2 family)s£65 — ⑬
⑪ d£80 **CHILDREN'S FACILITIES:** Fam room
Play area (Outside Play Area) Portions/Menu
High Chairs Food Warming
⑫ **NOTES:** Dogs Allowed Garden Food Served
Outside 12 tables on patio, lawn area
Parking 30 Coach parties welcome No credit
cards

4

---

① **GUIDE ORDER** Pubs are listed
alphabetically by name (ignoring The)
under their village or town. Towns and
villages are listed alphabetically within
their county. County names appear
down the side of the page. The guide
has entries for England, Channel
Islands, Isle of Man, Scotland and
Wales in that order. Some village pubs
prefer to be initially located under the
nearest town, in which case the village
name is included in the address and
directions.

② **MAP REFERENCE** The map
reference number is based on the
National Grid.

③ **SYMBOLS** See symbols in the
column on page 6.

④ **ADDRESS AND POSTCODE**
Street name plus the postcode. If
necessary the name of the village is
included (see 1 above). This may be up
to five miles from the named Location.

5 *DIRECTIONS* Directions are supplied by the proprietor. Please telephone for directions where none are supplied.

6 *OPEN* The opening times and closed dates of the establishment.

7 *BAR MEALS* indicates the times and days when bar food can be ordered, and may show the average price of a main course as supplied by the proprietor. Please be aware that last orders could vary by up to 30 minutes.

8 *RESTAURANT* indicates the times and days when food can be ordered from the restaurant, and may show the average cost of a 3-course á la carte meal and a 3- or 4-course fixed-price menu as supplied by the proprietor. Last orders may be approximatley 30 minutes before the times stated.

9 *BREWERY/COMPANY* The name of the Brewery or Company to which the pub is tied. Free house indicates an independently owned pub.

10 The beer tankard symbol indicates the principal beers sold by the pub. Many pubs have a much greater selection, with several guest beers each week.

11 *CHILDREN'S FACILITIES* as listed

12 *NOTES* We indicate whether dogs are welcome, information about the pub garden, parking and credit cards. We only indicate places which do not take credit cards.

13 *ROOMS* Only accommodation that has been inspected by The AA, RAC, VisitBritain, VisitScotland or the Welsh Tourist Board is included. AA Stars and Diamonds are shown at the beginning of an entry. Small Stars and Diamonds appearing under ROOMS indicates that the accommodation has been inspected by one of the other organisations. Please see page 6.

Symbols

◉ Rosettes
The AA's food award.

★ Stars
The rating for Hotel
accommodation.

🏠 Restaurants with
Rooms
Category of inspected
accommodation

◆ Diamonds
The rating for
Bed and Breakfast
accommodation.

🐷 Indicates that a pub
serves a minimum of
four main course
dishes with sea fish as
the main ingredient.

♀ Indicates the number
of wines available by
the glass

◧ Denotes the principle
beers sold.

AA Classifications and Awards

Establishments in the guide that have Stars or Diamonds shown next to their name have been inspected and rated by the AA. The Star system for Hotels ranges from 1 to 5. The Diamond system for B&Bs also ranges from 1 to 5. The best of both types of establishment are shown in red. A Rosette award is shown where the food is particularly good. Restaurants with Rooms are local or national destinations for eating out which also offer accommodation. For more detailed explanations of our ratings please see the AA website **www.theAA.com.**

BROOM

The Cock

23 High Street SG18 9NA
☎ 01767 314411 📠 01767 314284

Dir: Off B658 SW of Biggleswade

Unspoilt to this day with its intimate, quarry-tiled rooms with latched doors and panelled walls, this 17th-century establishment is known as 'The Pub with no Bar'. Real ales are served straight from casks racked by the cellar steps. A straightforward pub grub menu includes home-made cottage pie, casseroles and chilli. There is a camping and caravan site at the rear of the pub.

Open: 12-3 6-11 (Sat 12-4, Sun 12-4)
Bar Meals: L served all week 12-2.30
D served Mon-Sat 7-9
Restaurant: L served all week 12-2.30
D served Mon-Sat 7-9.30
Brewery/Company: GREENE KING
🍺: Greene King Abbot Ale, IPA & Ruddles County **Children's Facilities:** Fam room Play area (Outside Play Area) Portions/Menu High Chairs Food Warming
Notes: Dogs Allowed Garden Food Served Outside 12 tables on patio, lawn area Parking 30 Coach parties welcome

KEYSOE

TL06

The Chequers 🦢

Pertenhall Rd Brook End MK44 2HR
☎ 01234 708678 📠 01234 708678
📧 Chequers.keysoe@tesco.net

Dir: On B660 N of Bedford

In a quiet village, a 15th-century inn characterised by original beams and an open stone fireplace. Take a ridge-top walk for fine views of Graffham Water in anticipation of a warm welcome, good real ale and some fine pub food. Food served in the bar includes chicken curry, fried scampi, steak in a grain mustard cream sauce, chicken breast stuffed with Stilton in a chive sauce, or salads, sandwiches and ploughman's. Good wine list. A play area in the garden, overlooked by a rear terrace, is an added summer attraction.

Open: 11.30-2.30 6.30-11 **Days closed:** Tue
Bar Meals: L served Wed-Mon 12-2 D served Wed-Mon 7-9.45
Brewery/Company: FREE HOUSE
🍺: Hook Norton Best, Fuller's London Pride
Children's Facilities: Fam room Play area (Play tree in garden) Portions/Menu Cutlery High Chairs Food Warming
Nearby: Beds Butterfly Park, Grafham Water
Notes: No Dogs (except Assist Dogs) Garden Food Served Outside Patio & grassed area fenced off from car park Parking 50 Coach parties welcome

SOUTHILL   TL14

The White Horse ☜ ♀

High Street Biggleswade SG18 9LD
☎ 01462 813364
✉ jack@ravenathexton.f9.co.uk

A village pub retaining traditional values, yet happily accommodating the needs of non-smokers, children and those who like sitting outside on cool days (the patio has heaters). Locally renowned for its chargrilled steaks from the Duke of Buccleuch's Scottish estate. Other main courses include Cajun chicken, chargrilled pork loin steaks, Whitby Bay scampi, and stuffed breaded plaice. Greene King beers, with London Pride up from Chiswick. Old Warden Park and its Shuttleworth Collection of old planes is nearby.

Open: 11-3 6-11 (Sun 12-10.30, all day BH's) **Bar Meals:** L served all week 12-2 D served all week 6.10-10 (Sun 12-9) Av main course £7.50 ◖: Greene King IPA, London Pride, Speckled Hen, Flowers
Children's Facilities: Play area (Climbing frame with swings and slides) Cutlery Games High Chairs Food Warming Changing
Nearby: Woburn, Gullivers Land
Notes: Dogs Allowed in garden, water Garden Food Served Outside Large grassed area with trees & seating Parking 40 Coach parties welcome

TILSWORTH   SP92

The Anchor Inn ☜ ♀

1 Dunstable Road LU7 9PU
☎ 01525 210289 📠 01525 211578
✉ tonyanchorinn@aol.com

The only pub in a Saxon street village, the Anchor dates from 1878. The restaurant is a recent addition to the side of the pub, and the whole building has recently been refurbished. The licensees pride themselves on their fresh food and well-kept ales. Hand-cut steaks are particularly popular (they buy the meat at Smithfield, butcher it and hang it themselves). An acre of garden includes patio seating, an adventure playground and a barbecue.

Open: 12-11
Bar Meals: L served all week 12-2.30 D served 6-10 (Sun 12-4) Av main course £9
Restaurant: L served all week 12-2.30 D served 6-10 (Sun 12-4) Av 3 course · à la carte £25 **Brewery/Company:** GREENE KING ◖: Green King IPA, Abbot Ale, Wadworth 6X
Children's Facilities: Fam room Play area (Adventure playground) Portions/Menu Cutlery Games High Chairs Food Warming
Nearby: Mead Open Farm, Woburn Safari Park, Whipsnade Zoo
Notes: No Dogs (except Assist Dogs) Garden Garden Food Served Outside 1acre+ of garden, seats, BBQ, patio Parking 30 Coach parties welcome

ALDWORTH   SU57

The Bell Inn ☺

Reading RG8 9SE
☎ 01635 578272

Dir: Just off B4009 (Newbury-Streatley rd)

*One might be surprised to discover that an
establishment not offering even egg and chips
can hold its own in a world of smart dining
pubs and modish gastropubs. Well, be
surprised. The Bell not only survives, it
positively prospers and, to be fair, it does
serve some food, if only hot, crusty,
generously filled rolls. The Bell is old, very old,
beginning life in 1340 as a five-bay cruck-built
manor hall. It has reputedly been in the same
family for 200 years: ask Mr Macaulay, the
landlord-he's been here for thirty of them, and
he has no plans to change it from the time
warp it is.*

Open: 11-3 6-11 Closed: 25 Dec, Mon (ex
BHs) **Bar Meals:** L served Tue-Sun 11-2.50
D served Tue-Sun 6-10.50
Brewery/Company: FREE HOUSE ◁:
Arkell's Kingsdown, 3B, West Berkshire Old
Tyler & Maggs Magnificent Mild, Guest Beer
Children's Facilities: Portions/Menu Food
Warming
Nearby: Wyld Court Rainforest, Child Beale
Park, Berkshire Downs
Notes: Dogs Allowed On leads Garden Food
Served Outside Peaceful, old fashioned
Parking 12 No credit cards

ASHMORE GREEN   SU56

The Sun in the Wood ♀

Stoney Lane Newbury RG18 9HF
☎ 01635 42377 📠 01635 528392
📧 suninthewood@aol.com

Dir: A34 Robin Hood rndbt, L to Shaw, at
mini rndbt R then 7th L into Stoney Lane,
1.5m, pub on L

*Standing in the shadow of tall trees, this
popular, extensively refurbished pub occupies
a delightful woodland setting and yet is only a
stone's throw from the centre of Newbury.
Stone floors, plenty of wood panelling and
various prints by Renoir and Monet add to the
appeal. The extensive choice of food includes
fillet steak Rossini, pan-fried calves liver, and
sea bass fillets. Freshly baked baguettes are
available in the bar from Tuesday to Saturday.*

Open: 12-2.30 6-11
Bar Meals: L served Mon-Sun 12-2 D served
Mon-Sat 6.30-9.30 Av main course £11.50
Restaurant: L served Mon-Sun 12-2 D served
Mon-Sat 6.30-9.30 Av 3 course · à la carte
£20
Brewery/Company: WADWORTH
◁: Wadworth 6X & Henrys Original IPA,
Badger Tanglefoot
Children's Facilities: Play area (Swings,
slides, climbing frame) Portions/Menu Games
High Chairs Food Warming Changing
Notes: No Dogs Garden Food Served Outside
Lovely country garden among national
woodland Parking 60

CURRIDGE SU47

The Bunk Inn 🐾 ♀

Nr Hermitage RG18 9DS
☎ 01635 200400 📠 01635 200336
📧 alison@thebunkinn.co.uk

Dir: M4 J13/A34 N towards Oxford then 1st
slip rd then R for 1m. R at T-jct, 1st R
signposted Curridge

Not so long ago local builders used to bunk
off to this now smart, considerably extended
inn with beams, brasses, log fire and
attractive bar. There are starters such as
carrot and coriander soup; deep-fried Brie
with apple and cider chutney; and dim sum
with dips. Recent main courses include
Mediterranean vegetable crumble; half
shoulder of lamb with Singapore noodles,
chilli and plum sauce; and grilled fillet of
organic salmon with fennel and saffron sauce.
Nine blackboard specials daily.

Open: 11-11
Bar Meals: L served all week 12-2.30 D
served all week 7-10 Av main course £13
Restaurant: L served all week 12-2.30 D
served all week 7-10 Av course fixed price £25
Brewery/Company: FREE HOUSE ◀: Arkells
3B, Wadworth 6X, Fuller's London Pride
Children's Facilities: Play area
Portions/Menu Cutlery Games High Chairs
Food Warming Changing
Nearby: The Living Rainforest, Bucklebury
Farm Park
Notes: Dogs Allowed Garden Food Served
Outside Parking 38

KNOWL HILL SU87

Bird In Hand Country Inn ♀

Bath Road Twyford RG10 9UP
☎ 01628 826622 & 822781 📠 01628 826748
📧 sthebirdinhand@aol.com

Dir: On A4, 5m W of Maidenhead, 7m E of
Reading

A fascinating old inn that has remained in the
same family for three generations. Dating
back to the 14th century, its features include a
main bar whose oak panelling came from a
Scottish castle. In the building that is now the
Forge Bar, George III stopped in the late
1700s and granted a royal charter to the
landlord in gratitude for the hospitality shown
him. This tradition of warm welcome and
friendly service lives on to this day. Bar snacks
are available, whilst a more serious restaurant
menu offers an appealing mix of modern and
classic dishes.

Open: 11-3 6-11 (Sun 12-4, 7-10:30)
Bar Meals: L served all week 12-2.30 D
served all week 6.3-10 Av main course £9.95
Restaurant: L served all week 12-2.30 D
served all week 7-10
Brewery/Company: FREE HOUSE
◀: Brakspear Bitter, Fuller's London Pride,
Pedigree **Rooms:** 15 en suite 1 family room
£60 d£70 (★★★) **Children's Facilities:**
Portions/Menu High Chairs Food Warming
Changing **Nearby:** Legoland, Coral Reef
Notes: Dogs Allowed Garden Food Served
Outside Garden next to patio with fountain
Parking 86 Coach parties welcome

The Wheatsheaf 🐾 ♀

Main Street Maids Moreton MK18 1QR
☎ 01280 815433 📠 01280 814631

Dir: From M1 jct 15A, take A43 towards Oxford, take A413 towards Buckingham, follow signs for Maids Moreton.

Old world village pub serving real ales, quality bar snacks and an à la carte menu in the spacious conservatory overlooking the secluded beer garden. Options include chicken breast in a cream and Stilton sauce, mushroom and brandy strudel, duck breast with Madeira sauce, or Stilton and broccoli pasta. Fish specialities include breaded Whitby fish and chips, smoked haddock topped with prawns and cheese, and salmon steak in a lemon and lime sauce.

Open: 12-30 6-11 (Sun 7-10.30)
Bar Meals: L served Mon-Sat 12-2.15
D served Tue-Sat 7-9.30 Av main course £6
Restaurant: L served Mon-Sat 12-2.15
D served Tue-Sat 7-9.30
Av 3 course · à la carte £22
Brewery/Company: FREE HOUSE
🍺: Hook Norton, Black Sheep, John Smiths, Side Pocket For A Toad
Children's Facilities: Fam room Play area Portions/Menu Food Warming
Nearby: Stowe Landscape Gardens, Gullivers Land, Silverstone Race Track
Notes: No Dogs (except Assist Dogs) Water Garden Food Served Outside Large secluded garden, chairs on lawn/patio Parking 15 Coach parties welcome

The Old Thatched Inn ♀

Adstock MK18 2JN
☎ 01296 712584 📠 01296 715375

Licensed since 1702, this thatched and beamed 17th-century inn has come through a refurbishment with its traditional beams and inglenook fireplace intact. A modern conservatory and the timbered lounge provide a choice of eating place where the menu plus specials and light bites is offered. Pork and sage sausages; Imam Bayildi aubergine with apricot, onions and pine nuts; fresh oven-baked cod; Caribbean chicken; steak and kidney pudding; and rod caught rainbow trout are all part of an interesting menu. Desserts include blood orange mousse torte and apple and rhubarb crumble.

Open: 12-30 6-11 (open all day bank holidays & weekends)
Bar Meals: L served all week 12-2.35 D served all week 6-9.30 (Sat 12-9.30, Sun 12-9) Av main course £10.95
Restaurant: L served all week 12-2.30
D all week 6-9.30 Av 3 course · à la carte £20
🍺: Hook Norton Best, Bass, Hook Norton Seasonals
Children's Facilities: Licence Portions/Menu Games High Chairs Food Warming
Nearby: Stowe Gardens, Claydon House & Milton Keynes
Notes: Dogs Allowed Water provided Garden Food Served Outside Floral terrace with tables, lawned area Parking 20

MARLOW SU88

The Kings Head ☺ ♀

Church Road Little Marlow SL7 3RZ
☎ 01628 484407 🖨 01628 484407

Dir: M40 J4 take A4040 S 1st A4155

This flower-adorned pub, only 10 minutes from the Thames Footpath, dates back to 1654. It has a cosy, open-plan interior with original beams and open fires. From sandwiches and jacket potatoes, the menu extends to the likes of sea bass with ginger, sherry and spring onions; lamb shank with rich minty gravy, mash and fresh vegetables; pheasant casserole; tuna and Mozzarella fishcakes; and stir-fry duck with plum sauce.

Open: 11-3 5-11 (Sat-Sun 11-11)
Bar Meals: L served all week 12-2.15 D served all week 6.30-9.30 (Sunday 12-8) Av main course £8.25
Restaurant: L served all week 12-2.15 D served all week 6.30-9.30 Sunday 12-8 Av 3 course · à la carte £14
Brewery/Company: ENTERPRISE INNS
🍺: Brakspear Bitter, Fuller's London Pride, Rebellion IPA, Timothy Taylor Landlord
Children's Facilities: Portions/Menu High Chairs Food Warming Changing
Nearby: Odds Farm
Notes: No Dogs (except Assist Dogs) Garden Food Served Outside Safely behind pub, lots of tables & chairs
Parking 50 Coach parties welcome

WEST WYCOMBE SU89

The George and Dragon Hotel ♀

High Street HP14 3AB
☎ 01494 464414 🖨 01494 462432
📧 enq@george-and-dragon.co.uk

Dir: On A40, close to M40

Built on the site of a 14th-century hostelry, this 18th-century former coaching inn in a National Trust village has welcomed generations of visitors. The hotel is a delightful jumble of whitewashed, timber-framed buildings offering a good range of real ales, and a varied menu. At lunchtime you'll find chicken and mushroom pie, wild boar and apple sausages, and barbecued chicken wings. In the evening, expect beef Wellington, slow-roasted lamb, even more-slowly-roasted pork (four hours!), as well as cassoulet and curries.

Open: 11-2.30 5.30-11 (Sun 12-30, 7-10.30, Sat 12-30, 5.30-11)
Bar Meals: L served all week 12-2 D served all week 6-9.30 Av main course £8
Brewery/Company: UNIQUE PUB CO LTD
🍺: Scottish Courage Courage Best, Wells Bombardier Premium, Greene King Abbot Ale, Adnams Broadside, Marston's Pedigree
Children's Facilities: Fam room Play area (Climbing frame, swings) Portions/Menu Cutlery High Chairs Food Warming
Nearby: West Wycombe Caves
Notes: Dogs Allowed Water Garden Food Served Outside Large garden adjacent to car park Parking 35

ELTON   TL09

The Black Horse 🐾 ⚌

14 Overend nr Peterborough PE8 6RU
☎ 01832 280240 🖷 01832 280875

Dir: Off A605 (Peterborough/Northampton rd)

Although the Black Horse is within easy lunching distance of the Peterborough business park, this is a genuine village inn. Its warm country atmosphere is somewhat at odds with parts of its history: Harry Kirk, the landlord here in the 1950s, was an assistant to Tom and Albert Pierrepoint, Britain's most famous hangmen; Harry's son is now said to haunt the bar. During the summer a tapas menu is available if ever the kitchen is closed. Traditional set Sunday lunch menu. The delightful one-acre rear garden overlooks Elton's famous church and rolling open countryside.

Open: 12-3 6-11 open all day summer
Days closed: Sun eve
Bar Meals: L served all week 12-2 D served Mon-Sat 6-9 Av main course £9.95
Restaurant: L served all week 12-2
D Mon-Sat 6-9 Av 3 course · à la carte £20
Brewery/Company: FREE HOUSE
🍺: Bass, Everards Tiger, Nethergate, Archers
Children's Facilities: Fam room Play area Portions/Menu Cutlery High Chairs Changing
Notes: Dogs Allowed in the garden only. Water provided Garden Food Served Outside Food served outside. Patio area Parking 30 Coach parties welcome

FORDHAM   TL67

White Pheasant 🐾 ⚌

Nr Newmarket CB7 5LQ
☎ 01638 720414
✉ whitepheasant@whitepheasant.com

Dir: From Newmarket. A142 to Ely, approx 5 miles to Fordham. On L as you enter village

Named after a protected white pheasant killed by a previous landlord, this white-painted, 17th-century free house is set in a Fenland village between Newmarket and Ely. Rug-strewn wooden floors, tartan fabrics, soft lighting and scrubbed, candlelit tables characterise the interior. Food ranges from sandwiches and salads to a restaurant carte. Home-cured meat and fish is a speciality, alongside mussels steamed in Norfolk beer, and pan-fried fillet of gilthead bream with roasted aubergine and tomato dressing.

Open: 12-3 6-11 (Sun 7-10.30) Closed: 25-30 Dec, 1 Jan
Bar Meals: L served all week 12-2.30
D served all week 6-9.30 Av main course £12
Restaurant: L served all week 12-2.30
D all week 6-10.30
Av 3 course · à la carte £25
Brewery/Company: FREE HOUSE
🍺: Woodforde's Nelson's Revenge, Norfolk Nog, Admirals Reserve, Wherry
Children's Facilities: Portions/Menu Cutlery Games High Chairs Food Warming
Nearby: Anglesey Abbey, City of Ely
Notes: No Dogs (except Assist Dogs) Garden Food Served Outside Pleasant area, Parking 30

GOREFIELD TF41

Woodmans Cottage 🐾 ♀

90 High Road Wisbech PE13 4NB
☎ 01945 870669 🖷 01945 870631
✉ magtuck@aol.com

Dir: 3m NW of Wisbech

Popular pub run by a hard-working brother and sister team. Their efforts have paid off, and Woodmans Cottage remains a successful local with well-kept beers and a good choice of locally-sourced food. Established favourites include seafood platter, Chinese rack of ribs, lamb and mushroom with red wine, minty lamb shank, nut roast, the mega mix grill, and Cajun chicken. There is also an award-winning sweet trolley.

Open: 11-2.3 7-11 **Closed:** 25 Dec
Bar Meals: L served all week 12-2.30 D served all week 7-10 Av main course £7.50
Restaurant: L served all week 12-2.30 D all week 7-10 Av 3 course · à la carte £20
Brewery/Company: FREE HOUSE
🍺: Greene King IPA & Abbot Ale, Interbrew Worthington Bitter
Children's Facilities: Play area Portions/Menu Games High Chairs Food Warming
Nearby: Play Today and Bowling Alley Park
Notes: No Dogs (except Assist Dogs) Garden Food Served Outside walled patio area Parking 40 Coach parties welcome

HUNTINGDON TL27

The Old Bridge Hotel ★★★⊚ ♀

1 High Street PE29 3TQ
☎ 01480 424300 🖷 01480 411017
✉ oldbridge@huntsbridge.co.uk

Dir: Signposted from A1 & A14

Ivy covers almost every square inch of this handsome 18th-century façade. Décor throughout acknowledges its original character, with the panelled dining room and main lounge with their fine fabrics, quality prints and comfortable chairs. Walls in the more informal Terrace dining area are all hand-painted. Look out for fresh fish from Cornwall. Lighter dishes include risotto of the day; and bangers and mash with onion and Dijon mustard sauce.

Open: 11-11 (Sun 12-10.30)
Bar Meals: L served all week 12-2.30 D served all week 6.30-10.30 Av main course £10 **Restaurant:** L served all week 12-2.30 D served all week 6.30-10.30 Av 3 course · à la carte £25 Av 2 course fixed price £12
Brewery/Company: HUNTSBRIDGE 🍺: Adnams Best, Hobsons Choice, Bateman XXXB
Rooms: 24 en suite 1 family room s£85 d£125 **Children's Facilities:** Portions/Menu Cutlery Games High Chairs Food Warming
Nearby: Wimpole Hall Home Farm, Grafham Water, Cambridge
Notes: No Dogs (except Assist Dogs) Garden Drinks served only Parking 60

BURWARDSLEY   SJ55

The Pheasant Inn ★★◉◉ ♀

Nr Tattenhall CH3 9PF
☎ 01829 770434 📠 01829 771097
✉ reception@thepheasant-burwardsley.com

Dir: From Chester A41 to Whitchurch, after 4m L to Burwardsley. Follow signs 'Cheshire Workshops'

A delightful old sandstone inn tucked away in a beautiful rural setting with lofty views over the Cheshire plain. This traditional country inn is cosy indoors with reputedly the largest log fire in the county, while outside a flower-filled courtyard is ideal for summer evening drinks. The half-timbered former farmhouse makes a great setting for a bar that boasts sophisticated cooking and well-kept ales. Home-cooked specialities kick off a meal splendidly in the stone-flagged conservatory. The old outbuildings have been tastefully converted to provide a range of comfortable modern en suite bedrooms.

Open: 11-11 **Bar Meals:** L all week 12-2.30 D all week 6.30-9.30 Av main course £9
Restaurant: L all week 12-2.30 D all week 6.30-9.30 Av 3 course · à la carte £18
Brewery/Company: FREE HOUSE
🍺: Weetwood Old Dog, Eastgate, Outhouse, Best **Rooms:** 10 en suite 2 family rooms s£65 d£80 **Children's Facilities:** Licence Play area (Swings, slide, climbing frame) Cutlery High Chairs Food Warming Changing
Nearby: Candle Factory **Notes:** No Dogs (except Assist Dogs) Garden Food Served Outside, Parking 40 Coaches welcome

CHOLMONDELEY   SJ55

The Cholmondeley Arms ♦♦♦ ◌ ♀

Malpas SY14 8HN
☎ 01829 720300 📠 01829 720123
✉ guy@cholmondeleyarms.co.uk

Dir: On A49, between Whitchurch & Tarporley

This former school closed in 1982, re-opening as a pub six years later. Specialities include fillet steakburger with hot tomato relish, and steak and kidney pie. Seafood is represented by hot baked prawns in sour cream and garlic; grilled king prawns with a chilli and garlic mayonnaise; and fillets of sea bass grilled with butter and herbs. Home-made puddings include the likes of Pavlova, Bakewell tart and chocolate roulade.

Open: 11-3 7-11 **Closed:** 25 Dec
Bar Meals: L served all week 12-2.30 D served all week 7-10 Av main course £15
Restaurant: L served all week 12-2.30 D served all week 7-10
Brewery/Company: FREE HOUSE
🍺: Marston's Pedigree, Adnams Bitter, Banks's, Everards Tiger Best
Rooms: 6 en suite 1 family room s£50 d£65
Children's Facilities: Play area (Climbing frame & swing) Portions/Menu High Chairs Food Warming Changing
Nearby: Cholmondelay Castle Gardens, The Croccy Trail, Beeston Castle
Notes: Dogs Allowed Garden Food Served Outside Lrg lawns Parking 60

CONGLETON   SJ86

The Egerton Arms Hotel ◆◆◆◆ 🕭 ♀

Astbury Village CW12 4RQ
☎ 01260 273946 📄 01260 277273
📧 egertonastbury@totalise.co.uk

This 16th-century village inn is situated in the picturesque village of Astbury, adjacent to the 11th-century church. The mainly traditional menu includes, roast topside of beef; steak, kidney and mustard pie; fresh halibut grilled with lime and coriander butter, but also very hot chilli seafood linguine. Among the bar snacks are, jacket potatoes, baguettes and sandwiches. As well as Robinson's ales there is a large selection of malt whiskies and gins. Bedrooms are attractive and well equipped.

Open: 11.15-11 (Sun 11-3, 7-10.30)
Bar Meals: L served all week 11.30-2 D served all week 6.30-9 Av main course £5.99
Restaurant: L served all week 11.30-1.45 D served all week 7-8.45 Av 3 course · à la carte £14 Av 3 course fixed price £13.95
Brewery/Company: ROBINSON'S
🍺: Robinsons Old Stockport, Double Hop, Robinson Best Bitter
Rooms: 6 en suite s£45 d£60
Children's Facilities: Fam room Play area (Slide, climbing frame, fort) Portions/Menu Games High Chairs Food Warming
Nearby: Little Merton Hall, Biddulph Grange Gardens
Notes: No Dogs (except Assist Dogs) Water, Gravy Bone Garden Food Served Outside Large grassed area with tables Parking 100

PLUMLEY   SJ77

The Golden Pheasant Hotel 🕭 ♀

Plumley Moor Road Knutsford WA16 9RX
☎ 01565 722261 📄 01565 722125

Dir: From M6 J19, take A556 signed Chester. 2m turn L at signs for Plumley/Peover. Through Plumley, after 1m pub opposite rail station.

In the heart of rural Cheshire, the hotel has a large restaurant, bar area (that also serves food), public bar, children's play area and bowling green. The menu offers a wide choice, from sirloin steak to crab and coriander fishcakes, and from bangers and mash to penne arabbiata. Real ales are pulled from handpumps installed by J.W. Lees, one of the country's few remaining independent family breweries, with its own cooperage.

Open: 11-11 (Sun 12-10.30)
Bar Meals: L served all week 12-2.30 D served all week 6-9.30 (Sat 12-9.30, Sun 12-8.30) Av main course £6.95
Restaurant: L served all week 12-2.30 D served all week 6-9.30 (Sat 12-9.30, Sun 12-8.30) Av 3 course · à la carte £18
Brewery/Company: J W LEES 🍺: J W Lees Bitter, GB Mild & Moonraker
Children's Facilities: Licence Play area (Play area in large garden) Portions/Menu Games High Chairs Food Warming Changing
Nearby: Tatton Park, Chester Zoo
Notes: No Dogs (ex Assist Dogs) Garden Food Served Outside Seating front and back of pub Parking 80 Coach parties welcome

BOLVENTOR SX17

Jamaica Inn 🐾 ♀

Launceston PL15 7TS
☎ 01566 86250 🖷 01566 86177
✉ enquiry@jamaicainn.co.uk

With its cobbled courtyard, beamed ceilings and roaring log fires, this mid-eighteenth century former coaching inn set high on Bodmin Moor is steeped in the atmosphere that inspired Daphne du Maurier to write her famous novel of smuggling and intrigue; the Smugglers Museum houses one of the most extensive collections of smuggling artefacts in the UK. Today the inn offers the traveller a warm welcome and a large range of home-cooked food from bar snacks and cold food to steak, fish, and vegetarian meals that can be washed down with a selection of real ales.

Open: 9-11
Bar Meals: L served all week 12-2.30
D served all week 2.45-9 Av main course £7
Restaurant: L all week 2.30-9 D all week 2.45-9 Av 3 course · à la carte £16.50
🍷: 4x, Doombar, Budweiser, Stella, Carlsberg
Rooms: 6 en suite s£45 d£60 (♦♦♦)
Children's Facilities: Licence Play area (Pirate Boat with rope, swings, slide) High Chairs Food Warming Changing
Nearby: Flambards, Trethorn Farm
Notes: No Dogs (except Assist Dogs) Garden Food Served Outside Lawn area with tables Parking 6 Coach parties welcome

CONSTANTINE SW72

Trengilly Wartha Inn ★★ ◎ 🐾 ♀

Nancenoy TR11 5RP
☎ 01326 340332 🖷 01326 340332
✉ reception@trengilly.co.uk

Dir: SW of Falmouth

The Cornish name means 'settlement above the trees' and the old family-run free house with six acres of gardens and meadows lies in the wooded valley of Polpenwith Creek, off the Helford River. The river supplies the oysters that appear on the menu during the season, while the sea and surrounding farmland supply much else. The bar menu includes crab cakes, wholetail scampi, Cornish pasty, and butternut squash gratin. Restaurant main courses include prime Cornish fillet steak on horseradish rösti; and baked John Dory.

Open: 11-3 6.30-11 RS: 25 Dec No Food
Bar Meals: L served all week 12-2.15 D served all week ex 25 Dec 6.30-9.30 (Sun 12-2, 7-9.30) Av main course £8
Restaurant: D served all week except 25 Dec & 1 Jan 7.30-9.30 Av 3 course fixed price £27
Brewery/Company: FREE HOUSE
🍷: Sharps Cornish Coaster, St Austell HSD, Skinners, Exmoor Gold **Rooms:** 8 en suite 2 family rms s£49 d£78 **Children's Facilities:** Fam room Play area (High chairs, toys, changing room) Portions/Menu High Chairs Food Warming **Nearby:** National Seal Sanctuary, Flambards **Notes:** Dogs Allowed Garden Food Served Outside Walled garden, Parking 50

CRACKINGTON HAVEN   SX19

Coombe Barton Inn ◆◆◆ ☜ ♀

EX23 0JG
☎ 01840 230345 🖷 01840 230788
✉ info@coombebartoninn.com

Dir: S from Bude on A39, turn off at Wainhouse Corner, then down lane to beach

Originally built for the 'Captain' of the local slate quarry, the Coombe Barton (it means 'valley farm' in Cornish) is over 200 years old and sits in a small cove surrounded by spectacular rock formations. Local seafood is a feature of the menu and includes sea bass, lemon sole, plaice, salmon steaks, and halibut. The kitchen is also known for its vegetarian specials, steaks and Sunday carvery. Bedrooms are comfortable and one suite is suitable for families.

Open: 11-11 (Winter weekdays closed 3-6)
Bar Meals: L served all week 11-2.30 D served all week 6.30-9.30 Av main course £8.75
Restaurant: L served all week 11-2.30 D served all week 6-10
Brewery/Company: FREE HOUSE
🍺: St Austell Dartmoor Best & Hick's special Draught, Sharp's Doom Bar Bitter
Rooms: 6 bedrooms 3 en suite 1 family room s£30 d£25
Children's Facilities: Fam room Games Portions/Menu High Chairs Food Warming
Nearby: Ten Pin Bowling, Treethorne Leisure Park **Notes:** No Dogs Garden Patio Parking 25 Coach parties welcome

CUBERT   SW75

The Smuggler's Den Inn ☜ ♀

Trebellan Nr Newquay TR8 5PY
☎ 01637 830209 🖷 01637 830580
✉ hankers@aol.com

Dir: From Newquay A3075 to Cubert x-rds, then R, then L signed Trebellan, 0.5m

Two miles from the coast in an attractive valley, this thatched 16th-century pub features a long bar, an inglenook wood-burner, and barrel seats. Among other features are a family room, beer garden and well-kept real ales tapped from the cask. Fresh fish is always available. Other options range from chicken burger to lamb cutlets. Rich hot chocolate fudge cake and hot pecan pie are among the puddings.

Open: 11-3 6-11 (Winter 12-2) RS: Mon, Wed Closed Lunch Winter **Bar Meals:** L all week 12-2 D all week 6-9.30 Av main course £10 **Restaurant:** L all week 12-2 D all week 6-9.30 Av 3 course · à la carte £20
Brewery/Company: FREE HOUSE
🍺: Skinner's Smugglers Ale, Betty Stogs Bitter, Sharp's Doom Bar, St Austell Tribute & HSD
Children's Facilities: Fam room Play area (Climbing frames, rope nets, slide, seesaw) Portions/Menu Games High Chairs Food Warming **Nearby:** Holywell Bay Fun Park, Dairyland, Newquay Zoo
Notes: Dogs Allowed Water Garden Food Served Outside Small fenced beer garden, tables & chairs Parking 50 Coach parties welcome

DUNMERE SX06

The Borough Arms

Bodmin PL31 2RD
☎ 01208 73118 📠 01208 76788
✉ Borougharms@aol.com

Dir: From A30 take A389 to Wadebridge, pub approx 1m from Bodmin

Popular with walkers, cyclists, anglers, families and local businesses, this large pub is situated directly on the Camel Trail. Traditional pub fare includes a light menu of sandwiches, ploughman's and jacket potatoes; typical pub dishes like grills, a daily curry, lasagne, and jumbo cod, plus daily specials and a fill-your-own-plate carvery.

Open: 11-11 (Sun 12-10.30)
Bar Meals: L served all week 12-2.15 D served all week 6.30-9.15 Av main course £5.50 **Restaurant:** L served all week 12-2.15 D served all week 6.30-9.15
Brewery/Company: SCOTTISH & NEWCASTLE 🍺: Sharp's Bitter, Skinner's, Scottish Courage John Smith's Smooth
Children's Facilities: Fam room Play area (Highchairs, baby changing facilities) Portions/Menu Cutlery Games High Chairs Food Warming Changing
Notes: Dogs Allowed Water Garden Food Served Outside Large with kids play area Parking 150 Coach parties welcome

GOLDSITHNEY SW53

The Trevelyan Arms ◆◆◆◆

Fore Street TR20 9JU
☎ 01736 710453
✉ georgecusick@hotmail.com

Dir: 5 miles from Penzance. A394 signed to Goldsithney

The former manor house for Lord Trevelyan, this 17th-century property stands at the centre of the picturesque village just a mile from the sea. It has also been a coaching inn and a bank/post office in its time, but these days is very much the traditional family-run Cornish pub, recently refurbished. Food is fresh and locally sourced, offering good value for money. Typical dishes are rib-eye steaks, home-made lasagne and chicken curry.

Open: 12-11
Bar Meals: L served all week 12-2 D served all week 6-9 (L Sun 12-2.30) Av main course £6.50
Restaurant: L served all week 12-2 D served all week 6-9
Av 2 course fixed price £10
🍺: Morland Speckled Hen, Sharps Doombar, Flowers IPA, Guinness, Carlsberg
Rooms: 2 en suite s£25 d£50
Children's Facilities: Portions/Menu Cutlery Games High Chairs Food Warming
Nearby: Cheney Mill Farm, Flambards, Paradise Park
Notes: Dogs Allowed water Food Served Outside Front patio Parking 5

GWEEK   SW72

The Gweek Inn

Helston TR12 6TU
☎ 01326 221502 📠 01326 221502
✉ info@gweekinn.co.uk

Dir: 2m E of Helston near Seal Sanctuary

A traditional family-run village pub at the mouth of the Helford River with a great reputation for quality service and value-for-money food. Extensive menu offers starters and snacks, jackets and salads, traditional roasts, and children's meals; the chalkboard lists locally-caught seafood and other specials. A good selection of real ales.

Open: 12-2.30 6.30-11 (Sun Eve 7-10.30)
Bar Meals: L served all week 12-2 D served all week 6.30-9 (Sun 7-9) Av main course £6.50 **Restaurant:** L served Sun & by reservation 12-2 D served all week 6.30-9 (Sun 7-9) Av 3 course · à la carte £15
Brewery/Company: PUNCH TAVERNS
🍺: Interbrew Flowers IPA, Old Speckled Hen, Sharps Doom Bar, 2 guest beers
Children's Facilities: Play area (Screened garden area) High Chairs Food Warming Changing
Nearby: Flambards, National Seal Sanctuary
Notes: Dogs Allowed on lead Garden Food Served Outside BBQ, food served outdoors Parking 70 Coach parties welcome

HAYLE   SW53

The Watermill ☺

Old Coach Road Lelant Downs TR27 6LQ
☎ 01736 757912
✉ watermill@btconnect.com

Dir: From the A30 take the A3074 towards St Ives take L turns at the next two mini Rdbts

The old watermill here was in use until the 1970s. Today the building is a family-friendly free house offering fine Cornish ales and an excellent selection of meals. There is an extensive bar menu, and Upstairs at the Watermill is a separate restaurant, open every evening. Expect ham hock glazed in honey and cider; grilled whole lemon sole; or roasted vegetable pancakes with lemon and lime sauce served with saffron rice.

Open: 11-3 6-11 (Jul-Sept 11-11)
Bar Meals: L served all week 12-2.30 D served all week 6.30-9.30 Av main course £6.95 **Restaurant:** D served all week 6.30-9.30 Av 3 course · à la carte £17.50
Brewery/Company: FREE HOUSE
🍺: Sharp's Doombar Bitter, Dreckley Ring 'o' Bells, Skinners Betty Stogs
Children's Facilities: Play area (Large lawned area) Cutlery Games Highchairs Changing
Nearby: St. Ives, Flambards
Notes: No Dogs (except Assist Dogs) Garden Food Served Outside, stream, pergola, ample seating, lawn Parking 35 Coach parties welcome

HELFORD PASSAGE   SW72

Ferryboat Inn 🐾 ♀

Falmouth TR11 5LB
☎ 01326 250625 📠 01326 250916
📧 ronald.brown7@btopenworld.co.uk

Dir: From A39 at Falmouth, towards River
Helford

*Beautifully positioned on the north bank of
the Helford River, this 300-year-old pub
overlooks a safe beach and stands bang on
the Cornish coastal path. Enjoy the views from
the nautical-themed main bar, whose French
windows open onto a spacious terrace. Well-
kept St Austell ales are backed by a good
range of wines, available by the glass. Food
includes chicken salad, ploughmans, daily-
changing fish specials and Ferryboat ocean
pie.*

Open: 11-11 Sun 12-10.30
Bar Meals: L served all week 12-2.30
D all week 6.30-9 Av main course £6.25
Restaurant: L served all week 12-2.30
D served all week 6.30-9 Av 3 course · à la
carte £10.95 **Brewery/Company:** ST
AUSTELL BREWERY 🍺: St Austell HSD, Tribute
Children's Facilities: Games High Chairs
Food Warming Changing
Nearby: Trebar Gardens, Glendurgan Maze,
Flambard's Theme Park (30min)
Notes: Dogs Allowed Garden Patio, food
served outdoors Parking 80
Coach parties welcome

MANACCAN   SW72

The New Inn ♀

TR12 6HA
☎ 01326 231323
📧 penny@macace.net

*Thatched village pub, deep in Daphne du
Maurier country, dating back to Cromwellian
times. Attractions include the homely bars and
a large, natural bars full of flowers. At
lunchtime you might try a locally made pasty
or moules marinière, and in the evening
perhaps sea bass and chive fishcakes with
tomato coulis and sautéed vegetables, or
slow-roasted lamb shank with red wine and
redcurrant gravy.*

Open: 12-3 6-11
(Sat-Sun all day in summer)
Bar Meals: L served all week 12-2.30
D served N all 6-9.30 (Sun 12-2, 7-9)
Av main course £9.50
Brewery/Company: PUBMASTER
🍺: Flowers IPA, Sharps Doom Bar
Children's Facilities: Portions/Menu Cutlery
Games High Chairs Food Warming
Nearby: St Anthony Beach
Notes: Dogs Allowed Very welcome, Water
Garden Food Served Outside Large, natural,
lots of flowers Parking 20
Coach parties welcome

PERRANUTHNOE SW52

The Victoria Inn ♦♦♦ 🛏 🍷

TR20 9NP
☎ 01736 710309 📠 01736 719284

Dir: Take the A394 Helston- Penzance road and turn down to the village following all the signs for Perranuthnoe

This 12th-century inn is mentioned in the Domesday Book and is reputed to be the oldest hostelry in Cornwall. The pub is idyllically situated close to a sandy beach and the coastal footpath. With its Mediterranean-style patio, good food and en suite accommodation, the Victoria makes a pleasant stopover. Expect daily fresh fish, as well as dishes like braised venison in Burgundy jus; or home-made ratatouille with cheese topping and salad.

Open: 11.30-2.30 6.30-11 July & Aug open at 6pm **Bar Meals:** L all week 12-2 D all week 6.30-9 No bar meals 25-26 Dec
Restaurant: L served all week 12-2 D served all week 6.30-9
Av 3 course · à la carte £18
Brewery/Company: INNSPIRED
🍺: Bass, Doom Bar, Abbot Ale
Rooms: 3 en suite s£35 d£55
Children's Facilities: Portions/Menu Cutlery High Chairs Food Warming
Nearby: Flambards, Seal Sanctuary, Paradise Park **Notes:** Dogs Allowed Water provided; in bar only Garden Food Served Outside Paved Mediterranean-style Parking 10 Coach parties welcome

PORT GAVERNE SX08

Port Gaverne Hotel ★★ 🛏

Port Isaac PL29 3SQ
☎ 01208 880244 📠 01208 880151

Dir: Signed from B3314, S of Delabole via B3267 on E of Port Isaac

Just up the road from the sea and a beautiful little cove, this delightful 17th-century inn is a magnet for locals and holidaymakers alike. It is a meandering building with plenty of period detail, evocative of its long association with both fishing and smuggling. Bread is home made and locally supplied produce is to the fore. The bar menu offers seafood pie and deep-fried plaice with chips and peas, while at dinner you might try crab soup, or vegetable curry with rice pilaff. Walkers from the Heritage Coast Path can pause for a pint in the small beer garden, or at a table in front of the hotel.

Open: 11-2.30 6-11 (Summer 11-11) **Closed:** Early Jan-Mid Feb **Bar Meals:** L all week 12-2.30 D all week 6.30-9.30 Av main course £7 **Restaurant:** D served all week 7-9.30 Av 3 course fixed price £25
Brewery/Company: FREE HOUSE
🍺: Sharp's Doom Bar, Bass, Greene King Abbot Ale **Rooms:** 15 en suite 2 family rooms s£35 d£70
Children's Facilities: Portions/Menu Cutlery Games High Chairs Food Warming
Notes: Dogs Allowed Water provided Garden Food Served Outside Parking 15 Coach parties welcome

SEATON   SX35

Smugglers Inn

Tregunnick Lane Nr Torpoint PL11 3JD
☎ 01503 250646 📠 01503 250646

Dating back to the 17th century, The Smugglers is idyllically located opposite the beach. Inside, the atmosphere is warm and friendly, and the décor is in keeping with the pub's age. Local ales are served, and the menu offers such dishes as chargrilled halibut steak; fillet of beef medallions with brandy and wild mushroom cream; and field mushrooms stuffed with wild rice and topped with slivers of smoked cheese. There is an extensive bar menu, and a good choice of children's dishes.

Open: (Times vary, ring for details)
Bar Meals: L served all week 12-2.30
D served all week 6-9.30
Restaurant: L served (Varies to season)
12-2.30 D served all week 7-9.30
Av 3 course · à la carte £22.50
Brewery/Company: FREE HOUSE
🍺: Real ales from local brewery
Children's Facilities: Fam room High Chairs Changing
Nearby: Monkey Sanctuary, Dobwalls theme park, Seaton Beach & Country Park
Notes: Dogs Allowed Water Garden Food Served Outside Patio area Parking 10 Coach parties welcome

ST BREWARD   SX07

The Old Inn 🐕 ♈

Church Town Bodmin Moor PL30 4PP
☎ 01208 850711 📠 01208 851671
✉ darren@theoldinn.fsnet.co.uk

Dir: 4 miles from A30 near Bodmin, or signed from B3266. Pub next to landmark St Breward church

The Old Inn is located high up on Bodmin Moor in a village surrounded by spectacular scenery. It was constructed in the 11th century by monks who built the parish church next door, and retains its slate floors, wooden beams and log fires. Real ales and home-made dishes are served in the bar and restaurant, including fish, steaks, roasts, venison, and Moorland Grill. Wedding receptions and other functions can also be catered for.

Open: 11-3 6-11
(Summer open all day Fri-Sun)
Bar Meals: L served all week 11-1.50
D all week 6-8.50 Av main course £6.95
Restaurant: L served all week 11-1.50
D served all week 6-8.50
Av 3 course · à la carte £22
Brewery/Company: FREE HOUSE
🍺: Bass, Sharp's Doom Bar Bitter, Sharps Special, Guest Ales
Children's Facilities: Fam room High Chairs Food Warming Changing
Notes: Dogs Allowed Water Garden Food Served Outside Garden & decking area Parking 35 Coach parties welcome

ST MAWES   SW83

The Victory Inn 🐾

Victory Hill TR2 5PQ
☎ 01326 270324 📄 01326 270238

Dir: In centre of village close to the harbour

Close to St Mawes Harbour on the Roseland Peninsula is this friendly fishermen's local, named after Nelson's flagship. These days it doubles as a modern dining pub, offering the freshest of local seafood, harbour views, and overnight accommodation in one en suite bedroom. The blackboard specials change daily according to the catch, with dishes such as pan-fried monkfish with ginger and mango salad. There's also a choice of pub grub dishes-fresh mussels with fries, pasty and gravy, sausage and mash-while lunchtime snacks include white Cornish crab sandwiches.

Open: 11-11 (Sun 12-10.30)
Bar Meals: L served all week 12-2.15
D served all week 6.30-9 Av main course £7
Restaurant: L served Mon-Sun 12-2.15
D served Mon-Sun 6.30-9 Av 3 course · à la carte £20
🍺: Sharps, Bass, Ringwood, IPA, Tetley Smooth, Speckled Hen
Children's Facilities: Play area (Darts, Various games) Portions/Menu Cutlery Games High Chairs Food Warming
Nearby: Eden Project, Falmouth Maritime Museum **Notes:** Dogs Allowed Biscuits, water and toys Food served outside

ST MAWGAN   SW86

The Falcon Inn ♦♦♦♦ 🐾 ♀

Nr Newquay TR8 4EP
☎ 01637 860225 📄 01637 860884
📧 enquiries@falconinn.net

Dir: From A30 8m W of Bodmin, follow signs to Newquay/St Mawgan Airport. After 2m turn R into village, pub at bottom of hill

Taking its name from a falcon which, at the time of the Reformation, flew over the village to indicate a secret Catholic church service was being held, this 15th-century pub lies in the sheltered Vale of Lanherne. The dazzling gardens have won many awards and there are attractive terraces and wisteria-covered walls. Comprehensive menu and daily specials range from monkfish in coconut curry, or salmon en papillette, to hearty sirloin steaks, and steak and kidney pie.

Open: 11-3 6-11
Bar Meals: L served all week 12-2 D served all week 6.30-9.30 Av main course £7
Restaurant: L served all week 12-2
D served all week 6.30-9.30 Av 3 course · à la carte £14 **Brewery:** ST AUSTELL BREWERY
🍺: St Austell HSD, Tinners Ale & Tribute
Rooms: 3 bedrooms 2 en suite s£26 d£54
Children's Facilities: Fam room Play area (Outdoor slide, swing bridge, climbing rame) High Chairs Food Warming Changing
Nearby: Dairyland, Shire Adventure Park
Notes: Dogs Allowed Water Garden Food Served Outside Lrg garden, sheltered, safe Parking 25

TINTAGEL — SX08

The Port William ◆◆◆◆ ♀

Trebarwith Strand PL34 0HB
☎ 01840 770230 🖷 01840 770936
✆ theportwilliam@btinternet.com

Dir: Off B3263 between Camelford
& Tintagel

*Occupying one of the best locations in
Cornwall, this former harbourmaster's house
lies directly on the coastal path. The inn is 50
yards from the sea and the building dates
back about 300 years. Smuggling was also a
regular activity in these parts. There is an
entrance to a tunnel at the rear of the ladies'
toilet! Focus on the daily-changing specials
board for such dishes as artichoke and roast
pepper salad, grilled sardines, warm smoked
trout platter, or spinach ricotta tortelloni.*

Open: 11-11 (Sun 12-10.30)
Bar Meals: L served all week 12-2.30
D served all week 6.30-9.30
Restaurant: L served all week 12-2.30
D served all week 6-9.30
Brewery/Company: FREE HOUSE
🍺: St Austell Tinners Ale & Hicks, Interbrew
Bass **Rooms:** 8 en suite s£55 d£75
Children's Facilities: Fam room Play area
(Beach) Portions/Menu High Chairs Food
Warming Changing
Nearby: Beach
Notes: Dogs Allowed Water Garden Patio
overlooking sea, food served outside
Parking 75 Coach parties welcome

TORPOINT — SX45

The Edgcumbe Arms ◆◆◆◆ ♀

Cremyll PL10 1HX
☎ 01752 822294 🖷 01752 822014
✆ edgcumbearms1@btopenworld.com

*The inn dates from the 15th century and is
located right on the Tamar estuary, next to
the National Trust Park, close to the foot ferry
from Plymouth. Real ales from St Austell and
quality home-cooked food are served in a
series of rooms, which are full of character
with American oak panelling and stone
flagged floors. Fresh local seafood and
Cornish beef steaks are a feature of the
menus alongside a daily curry and steak and
ale pie. A good choice of bar snacks is also
offered.*

Open: 11-11 (Sun 12-10.30) RS: 6 Jan-28
Feb closed from 3-6
Bar Meals: L served all week 12-2.30 D
served all week 6-9 Av main course £6.95
Restaurant: L served all week 12-2.30 D all
week 7-9 Av 3 course · à la carte £16
Brewery: ST AUSTELL BREWERY
🍺: St Austell HSD, Tribute HS, IPA, Cornish
Cream **Rooms:** 6 en suite 2 family room s£35
d£50 **Children's Facilities:** Fam room High
Chairs Food Warming
Nearby: Mount Escombe Park, Monkey
Sanctuary
Notes: Dogs Allowed Water Garden Food
Served Outside Large picnic area with tables
Parking 12 Coach parties welcome

TREBURLEY SX37

The Springer Spaniel ⓭ ♀

Nr Launceston PL15 9NS
☎ 01579 370424 📠 01579 370113

Dir: On the A388 halfway between Launceston & Callington

This unassuming roadside hostelry dates from the 18th century, and the old creeper-covered walls conceal a cosy bar with high-backed wooden settles, farmhouse style chairs, and a wood-burning stove. Blackboards in the bar list the lighter snack options-freshly filled sandwiches and rolls, soups and daily specials-as well as the more serious choices that are also served in the separate beamed dining room where the setting is more formal. Children's meals are available, along with a vegetarian selection.

Open: 11-3 6-11
Bar Meals: L served all week 12-2 D served all week 6.30-9 Av main course £8.50
Restaurant: L served all week 12-2 D served all week 6.30-9
Av 3 course · à la carte £20
Brewery/Company: FREE HOUSE
🍺: Sharp's Doom Bar, Eden & Cornish, Springer Ale
Children's Facilities: Fam room Portions/Menu Cutlery Food Warming Changing **Nearby:** Hidden Valley, Tamar Otters, Launceston Castle
Notes: Dogs Allowed Water & Biscuits Garden Food Served Outside Landscaped with seating Parking 30

TRESCO SV81

The New Inn ★★ ⓢ ⓭ ♀

New Grimsby Isles of Scilly TR24 0QQ
☎ 01720 422844 📠 01720 423200
📧 newinn@tresco.co.uk

Dir: By New Grimsby Quay

'The Best Pub on Tresco'-well the only one actually, although once there were thirteen. Tresco's day job is tourism, and most people's itineraries include The New Inn. In the evenings it becomes the island's social centre, locals and visitors enjoying each others' company. Maritime artefacts abound: walls panelled with exotic woods jettisoned by a freighter, a mahogany bar top from a French wreck, the pub's signboard salvaged from The Award, wrecked in 1861. Lunch is speciality or open sandwiches, fresh fish, a few meat dishes, pasta or something vegetarian. Dinner might be pizzas, home-made seafood lasagne, vegetable Thai-fry, rack of lamb, and more.

Open: 11-11 **Bar Meals:** L all week 12-2 D all week 6-9 (limited menu available all day Apr-Sept) Av main course £8.95 **Restaurant:** D all week 7-9 Av 3 course fixed price £27
Brewery/Company: FREE HOUSE
🍺: Skinner's Betty Stogs Bitter, Tresco Tipple, Ales of Scilly Maiden Voyage, St Austell IPA, Ales of Scilly Natural Beauty
Rooms: 16 en suite d£138 **Children's Facilities:** Games High Chairs Food Warming Changing **Notes:** No Dogs (Assist dogs by arrangement) Garden Food Served Outside Patio area with sub-tropical plants

The Burnmoor Inn ♀

Eskdale Valley CA19 1TG
☎ 019467 23224 ▤ 019467 23337
✉ stay@burnmoor.co.uk

The whole family is welcome at this traditional 16th-century free house nestling at the foot of Scafell Pike-and that includes the dog! In cooler weather a log fire burns in the beamed bar, and, naturally enough, the pub attracts many hill walkers. The restaurant dates back to 1578, but there's also a new conservatory and dining area with spectacular all-year-round views of the western fells. Menu options might include venison red wine casserole or a vegetarian cottage pie.

Open: 11-11
Bar Meals: L all week 11-5 D all week 6-9 (Sun 11-5, 6-8.30) Av main course £7.50
Restaurant: L all week 11-5 D all week 6-9 Sun 11-5, 6-8.30 Av 3 course · à la carte £17.50 **Brewery/Company:** FREE HOUSE
◖: Jennings Cumberland, Bitter, Worthingtons, Roosters Brewery, Great Gable Brewery
Rooms: 9 en suite 2 fam s£30 d£60 (♦♦♦)
Children's Facilities: Licence Fam room Play area (Swings, ropes, climbing frame, slide) Portions/Menu Cutlery Games High Chairs Food Warming Changing **Nearby:** Muncaster Owl Centre, Ravenglass & Eskdale Railway
Notes: Dogs Allowed blankets, water Garden Food Served Outside part paved part grassed Parking 30 Coach parties welcome

Brook House Inn ☜ ♀

Eskdale CA19 1TG
☎ 019467 23288 ▤ 019467 23160
✉ stay@brookhouseinn.co.uk

Family-run inn located in the heart of Eskdale with glorious views and fabulous walking country all around. The owners take great pride in the quality of their food, beer and accommodation, and they make all their own bread, marmalade, jams, desserts and sauces. Fresh, seasonal produce is the basis of the dishes-local where possible. Specials include baked Esthwaite water trout wrapped in pastry, and braised leg of local organic mutton with Armagnac and prune sauce.

Open: 11-11 Closed: 25 Dec
Bar Meals: L served all week 12-5.30 D served all week 5.30-8.30 Av main course £8
Restaurant: L served all week pre-booked 12-4.30 D served all week 6-8.30
◖: Theakstons Best, Timothy Taylors Landlord & up to 4 guest ales
Rooms: 7 en suite s£40 d£60 (♦♦♦♦)
Children's Facilities: Licence Fam room Portions/Menu Cutlery Games High Chairs Food Warming Changing
Nearby: Boot Corn Mill, Muncaster, Ravenglass & Eskdale Railway
Notes: Dogs Allowed Garden Food Served Outside Terrace with seating; views across valley Parking 25

CUMBRIA

BOUTH   SD38

The White Hart Inn ♀

Ulverston LA12 8JB
☎ 01229 861229 ▤ 01229 861229
✉ nigelwhitehart@aol.com

The Bouth of today reposes quietly in the Lake District National Park, although once it had an occasionally noisy gunpowder factory. When this closed in 1928 villagers turned to woodland industries and farm labouring instead, and some of their tools now adorn this 17th-century coaching inn. Ever-changing specials may include pork medallions in port and mushroom sauce; homemade lamb and apricot pie; or fresh haddock in light beer batter. The upstairs restaurant looks out over woods, fields and fells, while the horseshoe-shaped bar offers six real ales, including Cumbrian brews.

Open: 12-2 6-11
Bar Meals: L served Wed-Sun 12-2 D served Mon-Sun 6-8.45 Av main course £7.45
Restaurant: L served 12-2 D served Wed-Sun 6-8.45 Av 3 course · à la carte £17
Brewery/Company: FREE HOUSE
◀: Black Sheep Best, Jennings Cumberland Ale, Tetley, Yates Bitter, Timothy Taylor Landlord
Children's Facilities: Licence Fam room Play area (Playground Opposite) Games High Chairs Food Warming Changing
Notes: No Dogs (except Assist Dogs) Garden Food Served Outside West facing terrace Parking 30

BRAMPTON   NY56

Abbey Bridge Inn

Lanercost CA8 2HG
☎ 016977 2224 ▤ 016977 42184
✉ info@abbeybridge.co.uk

The pub is located by the bridge over the River Irthing, 400 metres from Lanercost Priory (1166), a mile from Hadrian's Wall and half a mile from Naworth Castle. In the 19th century the Naworth family were deeply involved in the Temperance Movement, so the Black Bull, as it was then, lost its licence until the 1960s. Now the pub has three bar areas, one specifically for walkers where dogs are welcome, a main bar area and a restaurant/lounge. The menu offers local and British favourites using locally supplied produce. Look out for flaky fish pie, and chicken and apricot casserole.

Open: 12-3 6-11
Bar Meals: L served all week summer, Sat-Sun Winter 12-2 D served Wed-Sun 6-9
Restaurant: L served all week summer, Sat-Sun Winter 12-2 D served Wed-Sun 6.30-9 Av 3 course · à la carte £15
◀: Black Sheep Special, Yates Bitter, Coniston Bluebird XB, Carlsberg-Tetley Tetley Smooth
Rooms: 5 en suite 1 family room s£37 d£55
Children's Facilities: Portions/Menu Cutlery Games High Chairs Food Warming Changing
Nearby: Birdoswald Museum, Tulliehouse Museum, Talkin Tarn Country Park
Notes: Dogs Allowed Garden Food Served Outside Terraced garden, bridge & grass area Parking 20 Coach parties welcome

BUTTERMERE   NY11

Bridge Hotel ★★★ ☺ ♀

Cockermouth CA13 9UZ
☎ 017687 70252 📄 017687 70215
✉ enquiries@bridge-hotel.com

Dir: Take B5289 from Keswick

Spend a weekend at this 18th-century former coaching inn and enjoy its stunning location in an area of outstanding natural beauty between Buttermere and Crummock Water. Main courses from the restaurant include sliced duck breast served with a confit of leg with a honey and orange glaze; or poached plaice roulade. The bar menu offers Cumberland hotpot, Cumberland sausage and a good range of vegetarian choices. For smaller appetites there's a good selection of salads, sandwiches and toasties.

Open: 10.30-11 (open all day in summer)
Bar Meals: L served all week 12-2.30
D served all week 6-9.30 Av main course £6
Restaurant: D served all week 7-8.30 Av 5 course fixed price £21
Brewery/Company: FREE HOUSE
🍺: Theakston's Old Peculier, Black Sheep Best, Interbrew Flowers IPA, Tirrell Old Faithfull, Boddingtons
Rooms: 21 en suite s£60 d£60
Children's Facilities: Licence Portions/Menu Cutlery High Chairs Food Warming Changing
Notes: Dogs Allowed Garden Food Served Outside Parking 60 Coach parties welcome

CARTMEL   SD37

The Cavendish Arms

LA11 6QA
☎ 015395 36240 📄 015395 36243
✉ jmsmcwh@aol.com

Dir: M6 J36 take A590 follow signs for Barrow-in-Furness, Cartmel is signposted. In village take 1st R.

Cartmel's oldest hostelry, and the only one to be built within the village walls, dates from the 15th century. Now managed by new owners who welcome families with children and dogs, the pub's oak beams, log fires, low ceilings and uneven floors create a traditional cosy atmosphere. Bar food also follows traditional lines, ranging from soup and sandwiches to bangers and mash. Locally bought and freshly cooked produce feature in typical restaurant dishes such as fillet steak, sea bass and local ostrich.

Open: 11.30-11 (Sun 12-10.30)
Bar Meals: L served all week 12-2 D served all week 6-9 (Sun 12-6) Av main course £7.25
Restaurant: L served all week 12-2 D all week 6-9 Av 3 course · à la carte £18
Brewery/Company: FREE HOUSE
🍺: John Smiths, Cumberland, Bombadier, Theakstons **Children's Facilities:** Portions/Menu Cutlery Games High Chairs Food Warming **Nearby:** Cartmel Priory, Newby Bridge Visitor Centre, Beatrix Potter Museum **Notes:** Dogs Allowed Garden Food Served Outside Tree lined adjoining & overlooking stream Parking 25 Coach parties welcome

COCKERMOUTH — NY13

The Trout Hotel ★★★ @ 🐾 ♀

Crown Street CA13 0EJ
☎ 01900 823591 📠 01900 827514
✉ enquiries@trouthotel.co.uk

Dating from about 1670 and once a private house, the Trout became a hotel in 1934. The hand-carved oak staircase and marble fireplace are among the many striking features. Interesting range of starters, old favourites and snacks. Main courses include sea bass, Thai green curry, and grilled sirloin steak, while flaked salmon open sandwich, minute steak baguette, and tuna and cheese melt feature among the lighter options.

Open: 11-11
Bar Meals: L served all week 9.30-9.30
D served all week
Restaurant: L served Sat & Sun 12-2
D served all week 7-9.30
Brewery/Company: FREE HOUSE
🍺: Jennings Cumberland Ale, Theakston Bitter, John Smiths, Marston's Pedigree
Rooms: 43 en suite 1 family room s£59.95 d£109 **Children's Facilities:** Portions/Menu Cutlery Games High Chairs Food Warming
Nearby: Maryport Aquarium, Sheep & Wool centre **Notes:** No Dogs Garden Food Served Outside Riverside garden, food served outside Parking 50 Coach parties welcome

CONISTON — SD39

Black Bull Inn 🐾 ♀

1 Yewdale Road LA21 8DU
☎ 015394 41335 📠 015394 41168
✉ i.s.bradley@btinternet.com

Built at the time of the Spanish Armada, this old coaching inn has a lovely village setting, by the beck and in the shadow of the Old Man. Real ales are brewed on the premises, and excellent food is served in both the bar and restaurant. Fish dishes include fresh whitebait, Morecambe Bay shrimps and a daily special; meat courses range from straightforward Cumberland sausages to the more complex pheasant and chicken breast stuffed with haggis and black pudding, wrapped in bacon and served with a red wine sauce.

Open: 11-11 (Sun 12-10.30) **Closed:** 25 Dec
Bar Meals: L served all week 12-9.30
D served all week
Restaurant: L served by appointment only
D served all week 6-9
Brewery/Company: FREE HOUSE
🍺: Coniston Bluebird, Old Man Ale, Opium, Blacksmith & XB
Children's Facilities: Licence Fam room Portions/Menu Cutlery Games High Chairs Food Warming Changing
Notes: Dogs Allowed Dog beds and meals Garden Food Served Outside Riverside patio outside Parking 12 Coach parties welcome

GRANGE-OVER-SANDS   SD47

Hare & Hounds Country Inn ⌂ ♀

Bowland Bridge LA11 6NN
☎ 015395 68333 ▤ 015395 68993

Dir: M6 onto A591, L after 3m onto A590, R after 3m onto A5074, after 4m sharp L & next L after 1m

This 17th-century coaching inn is 10 minutes from Lake Windermere. The traditional atmosphere is enhanced by flagstone floors, exposed oak beams, and ancient pews warmed by open fires. The bar menu has the usual ploughman's, baguettes with various fillings, salads and hot plates such as chicken curry, Cumberland sausage and mash, or home-made pies in shortcrust pastry. The full menu is concise but comprehensive. Children have their own menu, or portions served from the adult version.

Open: 11-11 (Sun 12-10.30)
Bar Meals: L served all week 12-2.30
D served all week 6-9 Av main course £7.50
Restaurant: L served all week 12-2.30
D served all week 6-9 Av 3 course · à la carte £15 Av 3 course fixed price £8.50
Brewery/Company: FREE HOUSE
◀: Black Sheep, Jennings, Boddingtons
Children's Facilities: Fam room Play area (Swings, Tables, Grassed Area) Portions/Menu Cutlery Games High Chairs Food Warming Changing **Notes:** No Dogs (except Assist Dogs) Garden Food Served Outside Orchard with tables and hard area with tables Parking 80 Coach parties welcome

GRASMERE   NY30

The Travellers Rest Inn ♀

Keswick Road LA22 9RR
☎ 015394 35604 ▤ 017687 72309
✉ stay@lakedistrictinns.co.uk

Dir: From M6 take A591 to Grasmere, pub 0.5m N of Grasmere

Originally three miners' cottages, the inn dates back over 500 years and has been owned and run by the same family for the past 13. It's full of character inside and surrounded by beautiful scenery outside, with stunning views from the beer garden. A good range of beers and an extensive menu of traditional home-cooked fare is offered, ranging from sandwiches and cold platters to mixed Cumberland chargrill, and Borrowdale trout stuffed with prawns.

Open: 12-11 (Sun 12-10.30)
Bar Meals: L served all week 12-3
D served all week 6-9.30 (Mar-Oct, 12-9.30)
Av main course £8
Restaurant: L served all week 12-3
D served all week 6-9.30 (Mar-Oct, 12-9.30)
Av 3 course · à la carte £16
Brewery/Company: FREE HOUSE
◀: Jennings Bitter, Cumberland Ale, & Sneck Lifter, Jennings Cocker Hoop, Guest Ales
Children's Facilities: Fam room Play area Portions/Menu Cutlery Games High Chairs
Notes: Dogs Allowed Water bowls provided Garden Food Served Outside beer garden, stunning views, picnic tables Parking 60 Coach parties welcome

HEVERSHAM   SD48

Blue Bell Hotel ⌂

Princes Way LA7 7EE

☎ 015395 62018 📄 015395 62455

✉ stay@bluebellhotel.co.uk

Dir: On A6 between Kendal & Milnthorpe

Originally a vicarage for the old village, this hotel dates back as far as 1460. Heversham is an ideal base for touring the scenic Lake District and Yorkshire Dales. The charming lounge bar, with its old beams, is the perfect place to relax with a drink or enjoy one of the meals available on the menu, including potted shrimps, sirloin steak, Cumbrian game pie and Isle of Man crab.

Open: 11-11
Bar Meals: L served all week 11-9 D served all week 6-9 (Sun 11-8) Av main course £7.95
Restaurant: L served all week 11-9 D served all week 7-9 (Sun 11-8) Av 3 course · à la carte £17
Brewery/Company: SAMUEL SMITH
🍺: Samuel Smith Old Brewery Bitter
Rooms: 21 en suite 4 family rooms s£39 d£79 (★★)
Children's Facilities: Fam room Portions/Menu Cutlery Games High Chairs Food Warming Changing
Nearby: Wildlife Oasis, Lake District
Notes: Dogs Allowed Garden Food Served Outside Quiet garden, Parking 100 Coach parties welcome

KENDAL   SD59

The Gilpin Bridge Inn ♦♦♦ ⌂

Bridge End Levens LA8 8EP

☎ 015395 52206 📄 015395 52444

Good food is the chief attraction at this convivial pub. A garden with tables, chairs and children's play area has been added by the landlord. Located just off the A590, it offers the likes of home-made steak and ale pie, roast duckling, 16oz T-bone steak, and 'The Gilpin Grill'-a true meat feast-served in both the bar and restaurant at reasonable prices. There is a large selection of single malts and lunch is now available in the restaurant throughout the week.

Open: 11.30-2.30 5.30-11 (Open all day Summer, BHs) **Bar Meals:** L served all week 11.30-2 D served all week 5.30-9 (Sun 12-9) Av main course £5.50 **Restaurant:** L served all week 11.30-2 D served all week 6-9 Sun 12-9 Av 3 course - à la carte £13.50 Av 2 course fixed price £4.95
Brewery/Company: FREDERIC ROBINSON
🍺: Robinsons Best Bitter, Old Stockport Hartleys XB **Rooms:** 10 en suite 2 family room s£40 d£55
Children's Facilities: Licence Fam room Play area (Wooden play equipment) Portions/Menu Cutlery Games High Chairs Food Warming
Nearby: Grange Over Sands Resort, World of Beatrix Potter
Notes: Dogs Allowed Garden Food Served Outside Parking 60 Coach parties welcome

KESWICK NY22

The Horse & Farrier Inn ☜ ♀

Threlkeld Village CA12 4SQ
☎ 017687 79688 📠 017687 79824
✉ enquiries@horseandfarrier.com

Ever popular with hosts of fell walkers, this stone inn has stood in an idyllic position below Blencathra for over 300 years. There's a relaxed, welcoming atmosphere in the traditional-style bars and non-smoking restaurant, decorated with hunting prints and warmed by a cheerful log fire. Diners can expect menus packed with seasonal and local produce, and all meals are freshly prepared to order. Lunchtime brings an appealing selection of platter sandwiches and hot dishes, whilst the dinner menu might include lamb shoulder in red wine; or grilled Cumberland sausage on chive mash.

Open: 11-11 (Sun 12-10.30)
Bar Meals: L all week 12-2 D all week 6-9
Restaurant: L all week 12-2
D all week 6-9 **Brewery/Company:**
JENNINGS BROTHERS PLC
🍺: Jennings Bitter, Cocker Hoop, Sneck Lifter, Cumberland Ale & Guest Ale
Rooms: 9 en suite 1 family room s£35 d£70 (♦♦♦♦) **Children's Facilities:** Fam room Portions/Menu Cutlery Games High Chairs Food Warming **Nearby:** Cars of the Stars, Regheed Visitor Centre, Rookin House
Notes: Dogs Allowed Garden Food Served Outside Long garden with views of Blencathra Mountain Parking 60 Coach parties welcome

RAVENSTONEDALE NY70

The Fat Lamb Country Inn ★★

Crossbank Kirkby Stephen CA17 4LL
☎ 015396 23242 📠 015396 23285
✉ fatlamb@cumbria.com

Dir: On A683 between Sedbergh and Kirkby Stephen

Dating from the 1600s, this is a sprawling country inn with solid grey stone stone walls and its own nature reserve. Don't be surprised to see horses waiting in the car park, as this inn hosts pony trekkers holidaying in the area. From the bar come home-made lasagne, mixed sausage platter, and chilli bean pot. The carte offers seared supreme of salmon with roast vegetables; rack of lamb with a mint and honey jus; and rich casserole of beef in Guinness. From the set menu expect the likes of macaroni and tomato bake, and oven roast ham with parsley sauce.

Open: 11-2 6-11 **Bar Meals:** L served all week 12-2 D served all week 6-9 Av main course £6.50 **Restaurant:** L served all week 12-2 D served all week 6-9 Av 3 course à la carte £16 Av 4 course fixed price £20
Brewery/Company: FREE HOUSE
🍺: Cask Condition Tetley's Bitter
Rooms: 12 en suite 4 fam room s£44 d£36
Children's Facilities: Play area (Garden with sandpit & playhouse) Portions/Menu Cutlery High Chairs Food Warming Changing
Notes: Dogs Allowed Garden Food Served Outside Open grassed area surrounded by shrubs Parking 60 Coach parties welcome

CUMBRIA

SEATHWAITE SD29

The Newfield Inn

Duddon Valley LA20 6ED
☎ 01229 716208
✉ paul@seathwaite.freeserve.co.uk

Dir: A590 toward Barrow, then R onto
A5092, becomes A595, follow for 1m,
R at Duddon Bri, 6m to Seathwaite

*Located in Wordsworth's favourite Duddon
Valley, this early 17th-century building has
been a farm and a post office in its past. The
interior boasts a real fire, oak beams and a
stunning slate floor. The menu encompasses
homemade cuisine, including shortcrust steak
pie, lasagne, local beef steaks, and an ever-
changing specials board. The garden offers
some stunning views of the fells and there is
an enclosed children's play area.*

Open: 11-11 (variations at Xmas & New Yr)
Bar Meals: L served all week 12-9 D served
all week 12-9 Av main course £6
Restaurant: L served all week 12-9
D served all week 12-9 Av 3 course · à la carte
£14 **Brewery/Company:** FREE HOUSE
🍺: Scottish Courage Theakston Old Peculier,
Jennings Cumberland Ale, Coniston Bluebird
Children's Facilities: Play area (Large
enclosed grass area) Portions/Menu Cutlery
Games High Chairs Food Warming
Nearby: Dalton Wildlife Park, Barrow Dock
Museum, Raven Glass Railway
Notes: Dogs Allowed Water Garden Food
Served Outside Sheltered, seating for 40,
Parking 30 Coach parties welcome

TEBAY NY60

The Cross Keys Inn ◆◆◆

Penrith CA10 3UY
☎ 015396 24240 📄 015396 24240
✉ www.stay@crosskeys-tebay.co.uk

Dir: Just off M6 J38. Along A685 to Kendal

*A little gem of a free house, allegedly haunted
by the ghost of Mary Baynes, the Tebay
Witch, still looking for her black cat which
was savagely disposed of by a former
landlord. An extensive lunch and evening
menu-available in both the restaurant and
bar-offers steak and mushroom pie,
Cumberland sausage, Catalan chicken,
chicken and ham pudding, smoky bacon
pasta, smoked haddock and spinach bake,
and salmon and broccoli mornay.*

Open: 12-3 6-11 (Open all day Fri-Sun)
Bar Meals: L served all week 12-2.30
D served all week 6-9 Av main course £6.75
Restaurant: L served all week 12-2.30
D served all week 6-9

Brewery/Company: FREE HOUSE
🍺: Black Sheep Cask, Carlsberg-Tetley Cask,
Smooth & Imperial
Rooms: 6 bedrooms 3 en suite s£25 d£45
Children's Facilities: Licence Play area
(Large grass play area) Cutlery Games High
Chairs Food Warming Changing
Notes: Dogs Allowed Garden Food Served
Outside Large patio area, large lawned area
Parking 50 Coach parties welcome

White Horse Inn ☜ ♀

Badger Lane Woolley Moor DE55 6FG
☎ 01246 590319 ▤ 01246 590319
✉ info@the-whitehorse-inn.co.uk

Dir: From A632 (Matlock/Chesterfield rd)
take B6036. Pub 1m after Ashover.
From A61 take B6036 to Woolley Moor

*This 18th-century inn has outstanding views
over the Amber Valley. The bar food menu
offers such dishes as Thai fish cakes as well as
an extensive range of sandwiches. From the
main menu, expect Moroccan chicken tagine;
winter game casserole; or sweet pepper,
mushroom and Mozzarella bruschetta.*

Open: 12-3 6-11 (Sun 12-10.30, all day
summer wknds)
Bar Meals: L served all week 12-2
D served Tues-Sat 6-9 (Sun 12-5.30/6) Av main
course £7.50
Restaurant: L served all week 12-2
D served Tues-Sat 6-9 Sun 12-5.30/6 Av 3
course · à la carte £16 Av 3 course fixed price
£14.95
Brewery/Company: FREE HOUSE
◀: Jennings Cumberland, Adnams Broadside,
Blacksheep, 1744, Worthington Cask
Children's Facilities: Licence Play area
(Adventure playground, football pitch, sand
pit) Portions/Menu Games High Chairs Food
Warming
Notes: Dogs Allowed Water Garden Food
Served Outside Large patio with picnic
benches Parking 50 Coach parties welcome

Dog & Partridge Country Inn
★★ ☜ ♀

Swinscoe DE6 2HS
☎ 01335 343183 ▤ 01335 342742
✉ dogpart@fsbdial.co.uk

*This pub was extended in 1966 to
accommodate the Brazilian World Cup
football team, who practised in a nearby field.
Its extensive menus offer such dishes as
halibut in Pernod, alongside all the traditional
favourites. Vegetarians are well catered for,
and a local speciality is a Staffordshire
oatcake with a choice of fillings accompanied
by red cabbage, beetroot and salad.*

Open: 11-11
Bar Meals: L & D served all week 11-11
Restaurant: L & D served all week 11-11
Brewery/Company: FREE HOUSE
◀: Greene King Old Speckled Hen & Ruddles
County, Hartington Best, Wells Bombardier,
Scottish Courage Courage Directors
Rooms: 29 en suite 16 family room s£50
d£75 **Children's Facilities:** Fam room Play
area (Board games, sandpit, highchairs,
change area) Portions/Menu High Chairs Food
Warming Changing
Notes: Dogs Allowed Garden Food Served
Outside Good patio area with lovely views
Parking 50 Coach parties welcome

BAMFORD · SK28

Yorkshire Bridge Inn ★★

Ashopton Road Hope Valley S33 0AZ
☎ 01433 651361 ▤ 01433 651361
✉ mr@ybridge.force9.co.uk

Dir: A57 from M1, L onto A6013,
pub 1m on R

The inn dates from 1826 and takes its name from an old packhorse bridge. In winter the bars provide a cosy sanctuary, with their plentiful beams and attractive chintz curtains. Food is available in the bar and dining room from a comprehensive menu ranging through sandwiches, filled jacket potatoes, grills and salad platters. You will also find the likes of lasagne verde, lamb steak sizzler, pot-roasted lamb with minted gravy and three cheese filo art.

Open: 11-11
Bar Meals: L served all week 12-2 D served all week 6-9 Av main course £7.25
Restaurant: L served all week 12-2 D served all week 6-9.30
Brewery/Company: FREE HOUSE
🍺: Blacksheep, Old Peculier, Stones Bitter, Worthington Creamflow, Timothy Taylors Landlord
Rooms: 14 en suite 3 family s£47 d£64
Children's Facilities: Play area (room, play area) High Chairs Food Warming Changing
Nearby: Gullivers Kingdom, Chatsworth House & Farm, Donkey Sanctuary
Notes: Dogs Allowed Garden Food Served Outside Walled courtyard, numerous seating areas Parking 40 Coach parties welcome

DOE LEA · SK46

Hardwick Inn 🐾 ♉

Hardwick Park Nr Chesterfield S44 5QJ
☎ 01246 850245 ▤ 01246 856365
✉ Batty@hardwickinn.co.uk

Dir: M1 J29 take A6175. 0.5m L (signed Stainsby/Hardwick Hall). After Stainsby, 2m L at staggered junction. Follow brown Tourist Board signs.

Built in 1607 from locally quarried sandstone, the pub has been in the same family since 1928. All meals are freshly prepared, with a menu offering a choice of steaks and roasts. There'll probably be trout, salmon, cod, haddock, home-made pies, lasagne and a specials board featuring casseroles, and fish dishes based on that day's delivery. Mixed grills, ploughman's, various salads and sandwiches are also available.

Open: 11.30-11
Bar Meals: L served all week 11.30-9.30 D all week-(Mon 11.30-9) Av main course £6.50
Restaurant: L served Tues- Sun 12-2 D served Tues-Sat 7-9 Sun 12-2 Av 3 course · à la carte £16.50 Av 3 course fixed price £13.20
Brewery/Company: FREE HOUSE
🍺: Scottish Courage Theakston Old Peculier & XB, Greene King Old Speckled Hen & Ruddles County, Marston's Pedigree
Children's Facilities: Fam room Play area (Extensive garden & lawns) Portions/Menu High Chairs Food Warming
Nearby: Hardwick Hall, park & lakes
Notes: No Dogs (except Assist Dogs) Garden Food Served Outside Lrg garden, pond & picnic table, lawns Parking Coach parties welcome

GREAT HUCKLOW   SK17

The Queen Anne ◆◆◆ ♀

Great Hucklow nr Tideswell SK17 8RF
☎ 01298 871246
✉ mal@thequeen.net

Dir: A623 turn off at Anchor pub toward
Bradwell, 2nd R to Great Hucklow

*A warm welcome awaits at this traditional
country free house with its log fires, good
food, and an ever-changing range of cask
ales. The inn dates from 1621, and a
licence has been held for 300 years. Bar food ranges
from freshly-made sandwiches to grills, and
includes favourites like steak and ale pie, beef
stew and Yorkshire pudding, and chicken
jalfrezi.*

Open: 12-2.30 6-11 (Sat 11.30-11, Sun
7-10.30)
Bar Meals: L served Mon-Sun 12-2 D served
Mon-Sun 6.30-8.30
Brewery/Company: FREE HOUSE
🍺: Mansfield Cask Ale, Shaws, Storm Brewery,
Kelham Island, Phoenix Brewery
Rooms: 2 en suite d£55
Children's Facilities: Portions/Menu Games
High Chairs Food Warming
Notes: Dogs Allowed Garden Food Served
Outside Lawn overlooking the hills
Parking 30 Coach parties welcome

HAYFIELD   SK08

The Royal Hotel ♀

Market Street High Peak SK22 2EP
☎ 01663 741721 📠 01663 742997
✉ enquiries@royalhayfield.co.uk

Dir: Off the A624

*A fine-looking, 1755-vintage building in a
High Peak village that itself retains much of
its old-fashioned charm. The oak-panelled
Windsor Bar has log fires when you need
them, and serves a constantly changing roster
of real ales, bar snacks and selected dishes,
while the dining room usually offers sausage
and mash, vegetable chow mein, grilled
gammon steak, glazed lamb hock, T-bone
steak, mixed grill, and wholetail scampi in
breadcrumbs. Kinder Scout and the fells look
impressive from the hotel patio.*

Open: 11-11
Bar Meals: L served all week 12-2.15 D
served all week 6-9.15 Av main course £7
Restaurant: L & D served all week
Av 3 course · à la carte £16
Brewery/Company: FREE HOUSE
🍺: Hydes, Tetleys, San Miguel
Rooms: 9 en suite s£45 d£60
Children's Facilities: Fam room
Portions/Menu Cutlery Games High Chairs
Food Warming Changing
Nearby: Chestnut centre, swimming,
playpark, skate park
Notes: No Dogs Patio, seats 80 Parking 70
Coach parties welcome

LONGSHAW   SK27

Fox House ♀

Hathersage S11 7TY
☎ 01433 630374 🖷 01433 637102

Dir: Leave M1 at J29 and follow Chesterfield. Travel towards Baslow & Bakewell. At Baslow rdbt turn R onto A621 towards Sheffield, after 5m onto B6054 towards Hathersage. The pub is at jct of B6954/A625

A delightfully original 17th-century coaching inn and, at 1,132 feet above sea level, one of the highest pubs in Britain. There was a time when, during particularly hard winters, the tap room would be covered in straw and the sheep given its shelter. The Longshaw dog trials also originated here, after an argument between farmers and shepherds as to who owned the best dog. A simple menu lists sandwiches, starters, Sunday roasts, and mains like chicken and ham pie, ground Scottish beefsteak burger, and lamb cutlets.

Open: 11-11 (Sun 12-10.30)
Bar Meals: L served all week 12-5 D all week 5-10 (Sun 12-9.30) Av main course £7
Restaurant: L served all week 12-5 D served all week 5-10 Sun 12-9.30
Brewery/Company: VINTAGE INNS
🍺: Cask Bass, Cask Stones, Cask Blacksheep
Children's Facilities: Licence Portions/Menu High Chairs Food Warming Changing
Nearby: Chatsworth, Longshaw, Castleton
Notes: No Dogs (except Assist Dogs) Garden Food Served Outside Patio area Parking 80

WARDLOW   SK17

The Bull's Head at Wardlow 🐾 ♀

Buxton SK17 8RP
☎ 01298 871431

Located in the heart of the National Park, this pub has stood next to one of the country's oldest drovers' routes for over 300 years. Largely unaltered inside, it is decorated with antique prints, clocks, coach lamps, brass and copperware. Expect lamb shanks with creamy onion sauce; halibut; trout; vegetarian lasagne; and a selection of steaks. To follow, try profiteroles, or Bakewell pudding with cream.

Open: 11.30-3 6.30-11
Bar Meals: L served Sat-Sun 11.30-3 D served all week 6.30-9.30
Restaurant: L served Sat-Sun 11.30-3 D served all week 6.30-9.30
Brewery/Company: FREE HOUSE
🍺: Scottish Courage John Smith's, Carlsberg-Tetley Tetley's Smooth
Rooms: 3 en suite 2 family d£45
Children's Facilities: Fam room Play area Portions/Menu High Chairs Food Warming
Nearby: Old House Museum, Playground, Cable Cars
Notes: No Dogs (except Assist Dogs) Water Garden Food Served Outside Grassed area, tables, seating Parking 50 Coach parties welcome No credit cards

ASHBURTON   SX77

The Rising Sun ◆◆◆◆ 🕭 ⚤

Woodland TQ13 7JT
☎ 01364 652544 📠 01364 653628
✉ mail@risingsunwoodland.co.uk

Dir: E of Ashburton from the A38 take lane
signed to Woodland and Denbury pub is on
the L approx 1.5m

*The sun rises directly opposite the main building-
hence the pub's name. For a typical starter look
no further than monkfish, crayfish and red pepper
terrine, whole baked Torbay sole with citrus herb
butter and almond and broccoli risotto with salad
are great choices. The kitchen is also known for
its pies and monthly Pie Evenings.*

Open: 11.45-3 6-11 (Sun 12-3, 7-10.30,
Closed Mon lunch in Summer except BHs)
Closed: 25 Dec, all day Mon in Winter
Bar Meals: L served Tue-Sun 12-2.15 D
served Tue-Sun 6-9.15 Av main course £7.95
Restaurant: L served Tue-Sun 12-2.15 D
served Tue-Sun 6-9.15 Av 3 course · à la carte
£16.50 **Brewery/Company:** FREE HOUSE
🍺: Princetown Jail Ale, IPA, Teignworthy Reel
Ale & guest ales **Rooms:** 2 en suite 1 family
s£38 d£60 **Children's Facilities:** Fam room
Play area (Toys, childrens books, swings, old
tractor) Portions/Menu Games High Chairs
Food Warming Changing
Nearby: Otter Sanctuary & Butterfly Farm,
Pennywell Farm, S Devon Steam Railway
Notes: Dogs Allowed Water Garden Food
Served Outside Patio and lawn with seating
Parking 30 Coach parties welcome

BICKLEIGH   SS90

Fisherman's Cot ⚤

Tiverton EX16 8RW
☎ 01884 855237 📠 01884 855241
✉ fishermanscot.bickleigh@
eldridge-pope.co.uk

*Well-appointed inn by Bickleigh Bridge over
the River Exe with food all day and large beer
garden, just a short drive from Tiverton and
Exmoor. The Waterside Bar is the place for
snacks and afternoon tea, while the
restaurant incorporates a carvery and à la
carte menus. Sunday lunch is served, and
champagne and smoked salmon breakfast
is optional.*

Open: 11-11 (Sun 12-10.30)
Bar Meals: L & D served all week 12-9.30
Av main course £7.50
Restaurant: L & D served all week 12-10
Brewery/Company: ELDRIDGE POPE
🍺: Wadworth 6X, Bass
Rooms: 21 en suite 3 family s£49 d£59
Children's Facilities: High Chairs Changing
Nearby: Digger Land, Crealy Park, Woodlands
Notes: Dogs Allowed Garden Food Served
Outside Food served outside. Parking 100
Coach parties welcome

DEVON

BUTTERLEIGH   SS90

The Butterleigh Inn 🌀

EX15 1PN
☎ 01884 855407 📠 01884 855600

Dir: 3m from J 28 on the M5 turn R by The Manor Hotel in Cullompton and follow Butterleigh signs

Dating back 400 years, this was a cider house until the turn of the last century. Today, still tucked away in a sleepy village amid glorious countryside south of Tiverton, the Butterleigh is worth seeking out for its excellent Cotleigh Brewery ales and good food. You can eat and drink outside in two beer gardens, or in the homely bars with their comfortable furniture and open fires. Locally caught fish is served as starters or mains, and the traditional meat courses (pork and cider casserole, game pie, lamb shank, chicken with Brie and bacon) are all home made.

Open: 12-2.30 6-11
Bar Meals: L served all week 12-2 D served all week 7-9.15 Av main course £9.95
Brewery/Company: FREE HOUSE
🍺: Cotleigh Tawny Ale, Barn Owl Bitter, O'Hanlans Yellow Hammer, Otter Ale
Children's Facilities: Licence Play area (Lunch times only) Portions/Menu Cutlery Games Food Warming Changing
Nearby: Crealy Park, Bickleigh Mill, Diggar Land
Notes: Dogs Allowed Garden Food Served Outside Seating available for 30 plus Parking 50 Coach parties welcome

CHERITON BISHOP   SX79

The Old Thatch Inn 🌀 🍷

Nr Exeter EX6 6HJ
☎ 01647 24204 📠 01647 24584
📧 mail@theoldthatchinn.f9.co.uk

Dir: Take A30 from M5 in about 10m take turn on L signed Cheriton Bishop

Listed chocolate box inn with plenty of old world charm and modern comforts. Licensed as a pub in 1974, it is close to Fingle Bridge, described by RD Blackmore as 'the finest scene in all England'. Meals range from light snacks to fillet of smoked haddock, wild mushroom and pepper risotto, and West Country lamb shank with a rosemary and garlic jus.

Open: 11.30-3 6-11 Closed: 25 Dec
Bar Meals: L served all week 12-2 D served all week 7-9.30 Av main course £8.50
Restaurant: L served all week 12-2 D all week 7-9.30 Av 3 course · à la carte £20.50
Brewery/Company: FREE HOUSE
🍺: Sharp's, Otter Ale, Adnam's Broadside, Doombar, O'Hanlon's Firefly
Children's Facilities: Fam room Play area (High chairs, toy box) Portions/Menu Cutlery Games High Chairs Food Warming Changing
Nearby: Crealy Adventure Park, Woodlands Venture Centre, Country Life World
Notes: No Dogs Garden Food Served Outside South facing patio garden Parking 30

CLYST HYDON ST00

The Five Bells Inn

Cullompton EX15 2NT
☎ 01884 277288 📠 01884 277693
✉ rshenton@btclick.com

Dir: B3181 3m out of Cullompton,
L to Clyst Hydon then R to Clyst
St Lawrence. Pub on R

*This traditional inn originally stood close to
the village church, a century ago, the rector
of the day objected to having the pub on his
doorstep. As a result, the business was moved
to its present home in a 16th-century Devon
longhouse at Thinwoods Farm, where the
Symonds family had sold ale and cider since
the 19th century. Over the years, careful
modernisation has left its old-world
atmosphere intact. Bar lunches include steak
and onion sandwiches with French fries. In the
non-smoking restaurant, a decent selection
of grills, specials, vegetarian and fish dishes is
offered.*

Open: 11.30-3 6.30-11 Closed: Dec 26 &
Jan 1 RS: Dec 25 & Dec 31 closed eve
Bar Meals: L served all week 12-2 D served
all week 7-10 Av main course £8.95
Restaurant: L served all week 12-2 D served
all week 7-10
Brewery/Company: FREE HOUSE
🍺: Cotleigh Tawny Ale, Otter Bitter, O'Hanlon's
Children's Facilities: Fam room Play area
(Ropes, climbing frame) Cutlery High Chairs
Food Warming
Notes: No Dogs (except Assist Dogs) Water
Garden Food Served Outside Parking 40

EXETER SX99

Red Lion Inn 🐾 ♀

Broadclyst EX5 3EL
☎ 01392 461271

Dir: on the B3181 Exeter to Culompton.

*At the centre of a National Trust village, close
to Killerton House and Gardens, this
renowned 15th-century inn features original
beams and antique furniture inside, and a
cobbled courtyard outside. Among the
kitchen's dishes you may find fisherman's pie;
baked aubergine stuffed with Mozzarella,
tomatoes and pesto; butternut squash
crumble; Moroccan lamb tajine; or old
favourites such as steak and ale pie or fish
and chips. Special occasions are catered for
with impressive buffets.*

Open: 11-3 5.30-11 (Sun 12-3, 7-10.30)
Bar Meals: L served all week 12-2.30
D served all week 6-9.30 (Sun 12-2.30, 7-9)
Av main course £5
Restaurant: L served all week 12-2.30 D
served Mon-Sat 6-9.30 Sun 12-2.30, 7-9
Brewery/Company: FREE HOUSE
🍺: Bass, Fullers London Pride, O'Hanlons
Local Blakelys Red, Old Speckled Hen
Children's Facilities: Portions/Menu Cutlery
Games High Chairs Food Warming Changing
Notes: No Dogs (except Assist Dogs) In
garden only. Water & biscuits provided Garden
Food Served Outside Small garden with three
tables Parking 70 Coach parties welcome

DEVON

IVYBRIDGE SX65

Anchor Inn

Lutterburn Street Ugborough PL21 0NG
☎ 01752 892283 🖹 01752 897449
✉ enquiries@anchorugborough.co.uk

Owner Tim Martin has brought international flavours like ostrich, kangaroo and crocodile to this village free house. Nevertheless, beamed ceilings, open fires and real cask ales maintain the traditional welcome, and the Anchor is ideally located for exploring Dartmoor or the South Devon beaches. Food is served everyday with bar menu choices or full a à la carte. The pub's trademark dishes are 'Hot Rocks' - steaks cooked at your table with a selection of sauces.

Open: 11.30-3 5-11 (Fri-Sat 11.30-11 Sun 12-10.30)
Bar Meals: L served all week 12-2.30 D served all week 7-9 Av main course £5
Restaurant: L served all week 12-2 D served all week 7-9
Brewery/Company: FREE HOUSE
🍺: Bass, Courage, Directors, local ales
Children's Facilities: Portions/Menu Cutlery Games High Chairs Food Warming
Nearby: Dartmoor National Park, Plymouth National Marine Museum, Paignton Zoo
Notes: Dogs Allowed Water & biscuits provided Garden Food Served Outside Small walled area with two tables Parking 15 Coach parties welcome

KINGSBRIDGE SX74

The Crabshell Inn ☺

Embankment Road TQ7 1JZ
☎ 01548 852345 🖹 01548 852262

Located on Kingsbridge estuary with its good sailing, this historic pub was originally a bathing hut for the local barracks. Crab-catching competitions take place along the quay and in the summer there is always plenty of boating activity. Extensive menu with an array of fresh fish detailed on the display boards. Expect oven-baked fillet of salmon and grilled whole lemon sole, as well as the likes of half roast duck, mixed grill, and local pasty. A wide vegetarian choice and a helpful takeaway and picnic menu.

Open: 11-11 (Sun 12-10.30)
Bar Meals: L served all week 12-2.30 D served all week 6-9.30 Av main course £5.50
Restaurant: L served all week 12-2.30 D served all week 6-9.30 Av 3 course · à la carte £11.75
Brewery/Company: FREE HOUSE
🍺: Bass Bitter, Crabshell Bitter, Wadworth 6X
Children's Facilities: Fam room Play area (room, game machines, pool table) Portions/Menu Cutlery Games High Chairs Food Warming
Nearby: Crab catching on Quayside, Adventureland Parks
Notes: Dogs Allowed Water Garden Food Served Outside Patio area with tables & seats Parking 40 Coach parties welcome

KINGSTON SX64

The Dolphin Inn 🐾

Nr Bigbury TQ7 4QE
☎ 01548 810314 📠 01548 810314

Built as somewhere to live by stonemasons constructing the neighbouring church, this 16th-century inn retains all the beams, inglenooks and exposed stonework one would hope to find. A mile from the sea, and only a few to Bigbury Bay where offshore Burgh Island is reachable at high tide only by tractor transport. Homemade dishes making good use of locally caught or grown produce include fisherman's pie, crab bake, liver and onions, bangers and mash, lasagne and steaks.

Open: 11-3 6-11 (Sun 12-3, 7-10.30, Jan-Feb Mon-Fri 12-3)
Bar Meals: L served all week 12-2 D served all week 6-9.30 (Sun 7-9; closed Mon in winter)
Brewery/Company: INNSPIRED
🍺: Ushers, Four Seasons Ale, Courage Best, Sharps Doom Bar, Wadworth 6X
Children's Facilities: Fam room Play area (Swings and climbing frame) Portions/Menu Cutlery Games High Chairs Food Warming Changing
Nearby: Woodlands Adventure Park, Plymouth Marine Aquarium
Notes: No Dogs (except Assist Dogs) Water provided Garden Food Served Outside Small patio area, lrg garden, seating Parking 40

LIFTON SX38

The Arundell Arms ★★★ ⊛⊛ ♀

PL16 0AA
☎ 01566 784666 📠 01566 784494
📧 reservations@arundellarms.com

Dir: 2/3m off the A30 dual carriageway, 3m E of Launceston

This creeper-clad 18th-century coaching inn is a favourite with country sports enthusiasts, and the owner's passion for angling is shared by many guests who appreciate the 20 miles of private fishing, plus local shooting, riding and golf. The bar menu offers upmarket sandwiches; and light dishes such as sweet pepper salad with Parmesan and pesto. Hot dishes include fillets of fresh red mullet in a light beer batter served with a leaf salad, chips and a green mayonnaise. In the renowned restaurant à la carte dining of considerable class features top quality locally-sourced produce.

Open: 11.30-3 6-11
Bar Meals: L served all week 12-2.30 D served all week 6-10 Av main course £12.50
Restaurant: L served all week 12.30-2 D served all week 7.30-9.30 Av 3 course · à la carte £40 Av 5 course fixed price £34
Brewery/Company: FREE HOUSE
🍺: Guest beers
Rooms: 27 en suite s£52 d£104
Children's Facilities: Portions/Menu High Chairs Food Warming Changing
Nearby: Trethorne Leisure Park, Otter Park
Notes: Dogs Allowed Garden Food Served Outside Terraced garden Parking 70

LUSTLEIGH SX78

The Cleave ♀

Nr Bovey Tracey TQ13 9TJ
☎ 01647 277223 📠 01647 277223
📧 alisonperring@supanet.com

Dir: Off A382 between Bovey Tracy and Moretonhampstead

Originally a Devon longhouse, this 15th-century thatched inn, is a perfect pit-stop for walkers. The cosy lounge bar has granite walls and a vast inglenook fireplace; the bigger Victorian bar has an impressive collection of musical instruments. The menu includes breast of chicken stuffed with Stilton and wrapped in bacon; and a volcanic chilli con carne.

Open: 11-3 6.30-11 (summer 11-11)
Closed: Mon Nov-Feb
Bar Meals: L served all week 12-2.30 D served all week 6.30-9 Av main course £6.95
Restaurant: L served all week 12-2 D all week from 6.30-Av 3 course · à la carte £18
Brewery/Company: HEAVITREE
🍺: Interbrew Flowers Original Bitter, Interbrew Bass, Wadworth 6X, Otter Ale
Children's Facilities: Fam room Play area (Books, crayons & games in family room) Portions/Menu Cutlery Games High Chairs Food Warming Changing
Nearby: Minature Pony Centre, House of Marbles
Notes: Dogs Allowed Water Garden Food Served Outside Traditional cottage style garden Parking 10 Coach parties welcome

MOLLAND SS82

The London Inn

South Molton EX36 3NG
☎ 01769 550269

Just below Exmoor lies peaceful Molland, and to find its church is to find this 15th-century inn. Historic features abound, but try and picture today's spacious dining room as the original inn, and the bar as the brewhouse. Every so often the frequently-changing menu will feature guinea fowl with red wine sauce and black cherries, grilled salmon with parsley butter, and tarragon chicken breast with wine sauce and grapes. Bar snacks lunchtime and evenings. No credit cards, though.

Open: 11.30-11 (Sun 12-3, 7-10.30)
Bar Meals: L served all week 12-2 D served all week 7-9 Av main course £6.50
Restaurant: L served all week-D served all week-Av 3 course · à la carte £12
Brewery/Company: FREE HOUSE
🍺: Exmoor Ale, Cotleigh Tawny Bitter
Children's Facilities: Fam room Play area (Box of toys in family room) Portions/Menu Cutlery Games High Chairs Food Warming
Nearby: Exmoor National Park
Notes: Dogs Allowed Water Garden Food Served Outside Parking 12 No credit cards

PETER TAVY   SX57

The Peter Tavy Inn ♀

Tavistock PL19 9NN
☎ 01822 810348 📠 01822 810835
✉ Peter.tavy@virgin.net

Dir: Off A386 NE of Tavistock

A 15th-century inn at the end of a long lane, surrounded by lovely countryside on the edge of Dartmoor. Home-made dishes prepared from fresh local produce are offered from a regularly changing blackboard menu. At lunchtime options range from filled baguettes and ploughman's to dishes such as game casserole with Stilton dumplings, or Greek aubergine bake with feta cheese. Adopting a more sophisticated tone for the evening are the likes of seafood gâteau; and leek, wild mushroom and chestnut pie.

Open: 12-2.30 6-11 (Sun Eve 6.30-10.30)
Closed: 25 Dec
Bar Meals: L served all week 12-2 D served all week 6.30-9 Av main course £10
Restaurant: L served all week 12-2 D all week 6.30-9 Av 3 course · à la carte £19
Brewery/Company: FREE HOUSE 🍺:
Princetown Jail Ale, Summerskills Tamar, Tavy Tipple, Blackawton Brewery, Sharps Doom Bar
Children's Facs: Licence Fam rm Portions/Menu Games High Chairs Food Warming
Nearby: Morwelham Quay, Tamar Donkey Sanctuary, Trethorne Leisure Park
Notes: Dogs Allowed Water Garden Food Served Outside Small garden Parking 40

RATTERY   SX76

Church House Inn ☺ ♀

South Brent TQ10 9LD
☎ 01364 642220 📠 01364 642220
✉ ray12@onetel.net.uk

Dating from 1028, Devon's oldest inn is also one of the oldest in the UK. Large open fireplaces, sturdy oak beams and loads of nooks and crannies. Traditional English food includes snacks, light meals, sandwiches, lasagne, chicken and cranberry curry, and rump steak. Moussaka features as a special, as do duck, guinea fowl, venison and rabbit. Plaice, sea bass, brill, halibut, lemon and Dover sole are usually available. Always at least three real ales.

Open: 11-3 6-11 (Winter 11-2.30, 6.30-10.30)
Bar Meals: L served all week 12-2 D served all week 7-9
Restaurant: L served all week 12-2 D served all week 7-9
Brewery/Company: FREE HOUSE
🍺: St Austell Dartmoor Best, Greene King Abbot Ale, Morland Speckled Hen, Otter Ale
Children's Facilities: Licence Portions/Menu Cutlery High Chairs Food Warming
Nearby: Pennywell Farm, River Dart Country Park, Dale Devils Adventure Park
Notes: Dogs Allowed Water Garden Food Served Outside Lrg lawn, seating, benches Parking 30 Coach parties welcome

ROCKBEARE   SY09

Jack in the Green Inn

London Road Nr Exeter EX5 2EE
☎ 01404 822240 🖹 01404 823445
✉ info@jackinthegreen.uk.com

> **Dir:** From M5 take old A30 towards Honiton, signed Rockbeare

Named after the Green Man, associated with fertility in ancient pagan tradition, the pub is set in four acres of grounds and gardens overlooking East Devon countryside. The imaginative bar snack menu might offer toasted ciabatta with red pesto and Mozzarella. The restaurant menu offers the likes of roast squab pigeon with potato pancakes, or pan-fried sea bass with peas and pancetta.

Open: 11-2.30 6-11 (Sun 12-10.30)
Closed: Dec 25-Jan 2 inclusive
Bar Meals: L served all week 11-2 D served all week 6-9.30 Av main course £10.25
Restaurant: L served all week 11-2 D served all week 6-9.30 Av 3 course · à la carte £25 Av 3 course fixed price £23.45
Brewery/Company: FREE HOUSE
🍺: Cotleigh Tawny Ale, Thomas Hardy Hardy Country, Otter Ale, Royal Oak, Branscombe Vale JIG
Children's Facilities: Fam room Portions/Menu Food Warming Changing
Nearby: Crealy Adventure Park, Bicton Park
Notes: No Dogs (except Assist Dogs) Garden Food Served Outside Benches Parking 120 Coach parties welcome

SLAPTON   SX84

The Tower Inn 🛏 ♟

Church Road Kingsbridge TQ7 2PN
☎ 01548 580216 🖹 01548 580140
✉ towerinn@slapton.org

> **Dir:** Off A379 south of Dartmouth, turn L at Slapton Sands

A charming 14th-century inn tucked away in a delightful historic village, approached down a narrow lane and through a rustic porch. Lunchtime main courses might be smoked salmon and asparagus risotto or oven roasted vegetables with tagliatelle finished with a hot tomato and basil dressing and fresh Parmesan flakes. At dinner you will find some of the lunchtime dishes, plus others like pheasant supreme on a diced potato, smoked bacon, spinach and mushroom salad in a red wine sauce.

Open: 12-3 6-11 (Sun 7-10.30) Closed: 25 Dec
Bar Meals: L all week 12-2.30 D all week 6-9.30
Restaurant: L all week 12-2.30 D all week 7-9.30 Av 3 course · à la carte £25
Brewery/Company: FREE HOUSE
🍺: Adnams Southwold, Badger Tanglefoot, St Austell, Tower, Guest
Children's Facilities: Fam room Portions/Menu Games High Chairs Food Warming
Nearby: Woodlands Activity Centre, Slapton Sands Beach, Dart Valley Steam Railway
Notes: Dogs Allowed Water, biscuits Garden Food Served Outside Beautiful walled garden Parking 6

DEVON

SPREYTON   SX69

The Tom Cobley Tavern

EX17 5AL
☎ 01647 231314

Dir: From Merrymeet roundabout take A3124 N. Turn R off the Post Inn, the 1st R again over bridge

From this pub one day in 1802 a certain Thomas Cobley and his companions set forth for Widecombe Fair, remembered in the famous song. Today, this traditional village local offers a good selection of bar snacks, lighter fare and home-made main meals, including pies, salads, duck and fish dishes, as well as a good vegetarian selection. Finish off with one of the great ice creams or sorbets.

Open: 12-2 6-11 (Mon open Summer, BHs) Days closed: Mon
Bar Meals: L served Tue-Sun 12-2 D served Tue-Sun 7-9 Av main course £8
Restaurant: L served Sun 12-2 D served Wed-Sat 7-8.45
Brewery/Company: FREE HOUSE
🍺: Cotleigh Tawny Ale, Interbrew Bass, Tom Lobely Bitter, Doom Bar Tribute
Rooms: 4 en suite 1 family s£22.50 d£22.50 (♦♦♦)
Children's Facilities: Portions/Menu Games High Chairs Food Warming Changing
Nearby: Miniature Pony Center & Creley Fm
Notes: No Dogs (except Assist Dogs) Garden Food Served Outside Wooden seated area, Parking 8 Coach parties welcome

STOKE FLEMING   SX84

The Green Dragon Inn 🍺 ♀

Church Road nr Dartmouth TQ6 0PX
☎ 01803 770238 🖷 01803 770238
✉ pcrowther@btconnect.com

A smugglers tunnel is said to connect this 12th-century pub to Blackpool Sands. Certainly the landlord is drawn to the sea: he's famous for his voyages across the Atlantic. Inside, you'll find a warm atmosphere and deceptively simple cooking. Lunchtime snacks include fresh baguettes and locally made beefburgers, whilst dinner menus allow you to order starters as light bites. Main courses include Italian meatloaf, venison pie and lamb shanks.

Open: 11-3 5.30-11
Bar Meals: L served Mon-Sun 12-2.30 D served Mon-Sun 6.30-9 Av main course £6.50
Restaurant: L served Mon-Sun 12-2.30 D served Mon-Sun 6.30-9 Av 3 course · à la carte £15
Brewery/Company: HEAVITREE
🍺: Otter, Flowers IPA, Bass 6x
Children's Facilities: Play area (Garden, climbing frame, swing) Portions/Menu Games High Chairs Food Warming
Nearby: Blackpool Sands, Woodlands Leisure Park, Dart Steam Railway
Notes: Dogs Allowed Garden Food Served Outside Small at rear; covered patio at front Parking 6 No credit cards

D E V O N

TUCKENHAY SX85

The Maltsters Arms 🐾 ⚲

Totnes TQ9 7EQ
☎ 01803 732350 📠 01803 732823
🌐 pub@tuckenhay.demon.co.uk

In secluded, wooded Bow Creek off the River Dart, this splendid 18th-century pub is accessible only through high-banked Devon lanes, or by boat for about three hours either side of high tide. It is noted for real charcoal barbeques in the summer, live music events on the quayside, and a daily changing menu of good local produce imaginatively cooked. This may feature seafood soup with mussels and clams; wild Dart salmon in a fennel crust; and pot roasted local mallard.

Open: 11-11 (Sun 12-10.30)
Bar Meals: L served all week 12-2.30 D served all week 7-9.30 Av main course £10
Restaurant: L served all week 12-2.30 D all week 7-9.30 Av 3 course · à la carte £18
Brewery/Company: FREE HOUSE
🍺: Princetown Dartmoor IPA, Young's Special, Teignworthy Maltsters Ale, Blackawton Special
Children's Facilities: Fam room Play area (Highchairs, comics, games) Portions/Menu High Chairs Food Warming
Nearby: Pennywell Farm, Painton Zoo, Woodlands Adventure Park
Notes: Dogs Allowed Dog Bowl, Biscuits, lots of pals Garden Food Served Outside Riverside paved quay with seating & tables Parking 50 Coach parties welcome

WIDECOMBE IN THE MOOR SX77

The Old Inn

TQ13 7TA
☎ 01364 621207 📠 01364 621407
🌐 oldinn.wid@virgin.net

Dating from the 15th century, the Old Inn was partly ruined by fire but rebuilt around the original fireplaces. Two main bars and no fewer than five eating areas offer plenty of scope for visitors to enjoy the home-cooked food. From several menus plus blackboard specials, options range from filled Widecombe granary sticks through salads and steaks to lamb with gin sauce, organic fillet steak, paella and chicken breast filled with soft cheese with a tomato and basil sauce. No under 16s in the bar.

Open: 11-3 7-11 (Summer 6.30-11)
Closed: 25 Dec
Bar Meals: L served all week 11-2 D served all week 7-10 Av main course £7
Restaurant: L served all week 11-2 D served all week 7-10 Av 3 course · à la carte £15.50
Brewery/Company: FREE HOUSE
🍺: Interbrew Flowers IPA & Boddingtons
Children's Facilities: Fam room Portions/Menu High Chairs Food Warming Changing
Nearby: Horse riding & Pony Trekking on Dartmoor
Notes: Dogs Allowed Water Garden Food Served Outside Streams, Ponds, Gazebos Parking 55 Coach parties welcome

BRIDPORT — SY49

Shave Cross Inn 🐾 ♀

Shave Cross Marshwood Vale DT6 6HW
☎ 01308 868358 📠 01308 867064
📧 roy.warburton@virgin.net

> **Dir:** From Bridport take B3162 2m turn
> L signed 'Broadoak/Shave Cross' then
> Marshwood

*With its thatched roof and cob and flint walls,
the friendly, family-run 13th-century inn looks
every inch the typical Dorset pub. The restaurant
has wonderful old beams, plain wooden tables
and wheelback chairs. The chef's Caribbean
influence is plain to see from a menu featuring
jerk chicken salad with plantain, bacon and aioli.
Traditional British tastes are met with freshly
battered haddock and chips, rump steak,
ploughman's, and fresh crab sandwiches.*

Open: 10.30-3 5-11 (all day Sat-Sun in
Summer, BHs) Days closed: Mon (ex BHs) RS:
25 Dec closed eve
Bar Meals: L served Tue-Sun 12-3 D served
Tue-Sun 5-9.30 (Sun 12-3, 6-8)
Restaurant: L served Tue-Sun 12-3 D served
Tue-Sat 7-9.30 Sun 6-8 (summer) Av 3 course ·
à la carte £25
Brewery/Company: FREE HOUSE
🍺: Local guest beers, Branoc (Branscombe
Valley), Quay Brewery Weymouth
Children's Facilities: Licence Play area
Portions/Menu Cutlery Games High Chairs
Food Warming
Notes: Dogs Allowed On leads,water
available,not in restaurant Garden Food
Served Outside Cottage garden Parking 30
Coach parties welcome

BURTON BRADSTOCK — SY48

The Anchor Inn 🐾 ♀

High Street DT6 4QF
☎ 01308 897228 📠 01308 897228
📧 sleepingsat@hotmail.com

> **Dir:** 2m SE of Bridport on B3157 in the
> centre of the village of Burton Bradstock

*In keeping with its name, the Anchor is full of
marine memorabilia. Seafood is the house
speciality with sometimes as many as twenty
different main fish courses on the menu,
especially fresh local scallops, crab and
lobster. You can choose between lobster
thermidor or armoricaine, grilled plaice with
lobster and prawn sauce, or stuffed crab.
Meat eaters are not ignored with platters like
Barbary duck, beef Stroganoff, and peppered
pork fillet among others.*

Open: 11-11 Sun 12-10.30
Bar Meals: L served all week 12-2 D served
all week 6.30-9 Av main course £14.50
Restaurant: L served all week 12-2 D all
week 6.30-9 Av 3 course · à la carte £25
Brewery/Company: INNSPIRED
🍺: Ushers Best, Flowers IPA, Hobgoblin,
Winter Storm, Boddingtons
Children's Facilities: Licence Fam room Play
area Portions/Menu Cutlery High Chairs Food
Warming
Nearby: Fresh Water Caravan Park,
Abbotsbury Swannery, Jurassic Coastline
Notes: Dogs Allowed Water Food Served
Outside Patio Parking 24 Coach parties
welcome

CERNE ABBAS — ST60

The Royal Oak ♀

23 Long Street Dorchester DT2 7JG
☎ 01300 341797 📠 01300 341797
✉ royaloak@cerneabbas.fsnet.co.uk

Dir: M5/A37, follow A37 to A352 signed
Cerne Abbas, midway between Sherborne
& Dorchester. Pub in centre of village

*Thatched, creeper-clad, 16th-century inn,
formerly a coaching inn and blacksmiths,
situated in a picturesque village below the
Dorset Downs. Home-cooked food is served in
the cosy, traditional interior. An imaginative
menu includes halibut fillet with cream,
tomato and chive sauce, and venison
sausages and belly pork with hoi sin apple
and mushroom sauce.*

Open: 11.30-3 6-11 Summer close 3.30
Closed: 25 Dec
Bar Meals: L all week 12-2 D all week 7-9.30
(Summer 2.30, Sun 9) Av main course £9
Restaurant: L served all week 12-2.30 D
served all week 7-9.30 Sun last orders 9
Av 3 course · à la carte £18
Brewery/Company: FREE HOUSE
🍺: St Austell Brewery, Tribute, Tinners,
Butcombe, Weymouth Best, Old Speckled Hen
Children's Facilities: Play area (Books &
games provided before meals) Portions/Menu
Cutlery Games Food Warming Changing
Nearby: Sealife Centre, Sherborne Castle
Notes: Dogs Allowed Water bowl in garden
Garden Food Served Outside walled garden,
decking, furniture Coach parties welcome

CORFE CASTLE — SY98

The Greyhound Inn 🐾 ♀

The Square BH20 5EZ
☎ 01929 480205 📠 01929 481483
✉ mjml@greyhound-inn.fsnet.co.uk

Dir: W from Bournemouth, take A35,
after 5m L onto A351, 10m to Corfe Castle

*Corfe Castle forms a dramatic backdrop to the
16th-century inn and probably furnished the
stones to build it. Seafood platters, chargrilled
meat baskets and steaks are features of the
menu, plus there's a weekend carvery and a
10-dish buffet feast, based on local
ingredients. There's a coffee and panini deli
bar, with a salad buffet and a create-your-
own-sandwich section. Beer festivals,
barbecues and hog roasts in summer.*

Open: 11-3 6-11.30 Summer open all day
Bar Meals: L served all week 12-2.30 D
served all week 6-9 (Jul-Aug food all day) Av
main course £12.95
Restaurant: L served all week 12-2.30 D
served all week 6-9 Jul-Aug food all day Av 3
course · à la carte £17.95
Brewery/Company: ENTERPRISE INNS
🍺: Fuller's London Pride, Adnams, Timothy
Taylor Landlord, Black Sheep, Ringwood Best
Children's Facilities: Fam room Play area
(Games, Colouring books, mini football)
Games High Chairs Food Warming
Nearby: Monkey World, Farmer Palmers,
Putlake Adventure Farm
Notes: Dogs Allowed Water Garden Food
Served Outside Coach parties welcome

DORSET

GILLINGHAM ST82

The Kings Arms Inn

East Stour Common SP8 5NB
☎ 01747 838325
✉ rayandjannattka@aol.com

Dir: 4m W of Shaftesbury on A30

A 200-year-old country inn, the Kings Arms makes an excellent base for exploring the delights of Dorset's countryside and coast, with plenty of well-loved attractions within reach, including nearby Shaftesbury and the famous Golden Hill. The pub is under family ownership, offering accommodation and meals from a single menu plus daily specials in the bar or restaurant.

Open: 12-2.30 5-11 Longer hrs summer Closed: 25 Dec
Bar Meals: L served Tue-Sun 12-2 D served Tue-Sat 6-8.45 Av main course £7
Restaurant: L served Tue-Sun 12-2 D served Tue-Sat 6-8.45
Brewery/Company: FREE HOUSE
🍺: Cools Worthington's Bitter, Ringwood Best Bitter, Quay Weymouth Best Bitter, Butcombe Ales & Wye Valley Ales
Rooms: 3 en suite (♦♦♦♦)
Children's Facilities: Fam room Play area Portions/Menu Cutlery Games High Chairs Food Warming Changing
Notes: No Dogs (except Assist Dogs) Water Garden Food Served Outside Patio & Sitting area Parking 40 Coach parties welcome

MOTCOMBE ST82

The Coppleridge Inn ♦♦♦♦ 🐕 ♀

Shaftesbury SP7 9HW
☎ 01747 851980 📠 01747 851858
✉ thecoppleridgeinn@btinternet.com

A working farm until 15 years ago, this traditional, family-run country inn is full of character, with flagstone floors, stripped pine and delightful views. Wide-ranging menus offer dishes cooked to order from fresh local ingredients, with typical specials ranging from turkey and bacon pie and beef lasagne to pork, bacon and cider casserole, and home-made crepe stuffed with spinach and Stilton. Extensive choice of snacks.

Open: 11-3 5-11 All day Sat & Sun
Bar Meals: L served all week 12-2.30 D served all week 6-9.30 Av main course £7.50
Restaurant: L served all week 12-2.30 D served all week 6-9.30 Av 3 course · à la carte £17.50
Brewery/Company: FREE HOUSE
🍺: Butcombe Bitter, Greene King IPA, Wadworth 6X, Fuller's London Pride
Rooms: 10 en suite 3 family s£42.50 d£75
Children's Facilities: Fam room Play area (Garden, swings & slide) Portions/Menu Cutlery Games High Chairs Food Warming
Nearby: Haynes Motor Mus, Stourhead Gds
Notes: Dogs Allowed Garden only, water provided, 15 acres Garden Food Served Outside Parking 60 Coach parties welcome

NETTLECOMBE   SY59

Marquis of Lorne ♦♦♦♦ ⌂ ♉

Nr Bridport DT6 3SY
☎ 01308 485236 📠 01308 485666
✉ julie.woodroffe@btinternet.com

Dir: 3m E of A3066 Bridport-Beaminster rd.
From Bridport North to Beaminster after
1.5m turn right signed Powerstock,
West Milton & Mill after 3m at a T Jct,
pub up hill on left

A 16th-century farmhouse converted into a pub
in 1871, when the Marquis himself named it to
prove land ownership. Membership of the
Campaign for Real Food means that much local
produce is used. Daily menus offer such dishes
as home-made curry, fresh cod fillet, and
mushroom and pepper Stroganoff. Superb
gardens with beautiful views.

Open: 11.30-2.30 6.30-11 (Sun all day)
Bar Meals: L served all week 12-2 D served
all week 6.30-9 (Sun 12-9) Av main course £8
Restaurant: L served all week 12-2 D served
all week 6.30-9 (Sun 12-9) Av 3 course · à la
carte £15
Brewery/Company: PALMERS
🍺: Palmers Copper, IPA, 200 Premium Ale
Rooms: 7 en suite s£45 d£70
Children's Facilities: Play area
Portions/Menu Cutlery Games High Chairs
Food Warming Changing
Nearby: The Swannery Abbotsbury
Notes: Dogs Allowed Water Garden Food
Served Outside play area Parking 50

OSMINGTON MILLS   SY78

The Smugglers Inn ♉

nr Weymouth DT3 6HF
☎ 01305 833125 📠 01305 832219

Located bang on the coastal path, with a
stream running through the garden and a play
area for children, it's a good stop on a sunny
day. The interior is cosy, with bare beams and
flagstone floors. Food includes seasonal fresh
fish in the summer, scrumpy chicken,
chargrilled rump steak, stuffed peppers, and
steak and Tanglefoot pie.

Open: 11-11 Sun 12-10.30 RS: Nov-Mar
Closed Mon-Fri 3-6
Bar Meals: L served all week 12-9.30 D all
week 12-9.30 Sun 12-9 Av main course £6.95
Restaurant: L&D all week 12-9.30
Brewery/Company: WOODHOUSE INNS LTD
🍺: Badger Best, Tanglefoot
Children's Facilities: Licence Fam room Play
area (Swings, slide & assault course)
Portions/Menu Cutlery Games High Chairs
Food Warming
Nearby: Monkey World, Dinosaur Museum,
Teddy Bear Museum, Sealife Centre
Notes: No Dogs (except Assist Dogs) Water &
Treats Garden Food Served Outside Large lawn
with picnic benches & BBQ Parking 70 Coach
parties welcome

PIDDLEHINTON SY79

The Thimble Inn

Dorchester DT2 7TD
☎ 01300 348270

Dir: A35 westbound, R onto B3143, Piddlehinton 4m

Good food, open fires and traditional pub games make this friendly village local a favourite spot with visitors. The pub stands in an unspoilt valley on the banks of the River Piddle, and the riverside patio is popular in summer. The extensive menu caters for all tastes, from sandwiches, jacket potatoes and children's meals, to grilled duck breast with pink grapefruit and ginger sauce; game pie which, the menu advises, may contain shot; and a range of fish specials, including fresh Poole plaice.

Open: 12-2.30 7-11 (Sun 12-2.30 7-10.30) Closed: 25 Dec
Bar Meals: L served all week 12-2 D served all week 7-9
Restaurant: L served all week 12-2 D served all week 7-9
Brewery/Company: FREE HOUSE
🍺: Badger Best & Tanglefoot, Palmer Copper Ale & Palmer IPA, Ringwood Old Thumper
Children's Facilities: Portions/Menu Cutlery High Chairs Food Warming Changing
Notes: Dogs Allowed Garden Food Served Outside Parking 50 Coach parties welcome

POWERSTOCK SY59

The Three Horseshoes ♦♦♦♦ ♀

Bridport DT6 3TF
☎ 01308 485328 🖨 01308 485229
✉ info@threehorseshoesinn.com

Dir: E of A3066 (Bridport/Beaminster rd)

Powerstock is popular with walkers and cyclists, and visitors can enjoy glorious coastal views from the Pub garden. Those seeking warmth will find the traditional bar or cosy wood-panelled restaurant, both with open fireplaces, perfect. Boasting a reputation for excellent cuisine, the inn makes extensive use of fresh local produce for its light lunch menu and evening carte. Avocado and seafood Thermidor for a starter, or for a main course, whole roasted partridge with apple and Calvados jus.

Open: 11-3 6.30-11.30 (Sun 12-3 6.30-11.30)
Bar Meals: L served all week 12-2.3 D served all week 7-9 (Summer 7-9.30, Sun 12-3, 7-8.30) Av main course £8 **Restaurant:** L served all week 12-2.30 D served all week 7-9 Summer 7-9.30, Sun 12-3, 7-8.30 Av 3 course · à la carte £17 **Brewery/Company:** PALMERS 🍺: Palmer's IPA, Copper Ale
Rooms: 3 en suite 1 family s£50 d£70
Children's Facilities: Fam room Play area (Large garden with swings & climbing frame) Portions/Menu Cutlery Games High Chairs Food Warming **Nearby:** Dinosaur Museum, Dorchester **Notes:** Dogs Allowed Water, food, toys, blankets Garden Food Served Outside Patio leading to terraced garden Parking 30

SHERBORNE ST61

White Hart

Bishops Caundle DT9 5ND
☎ 01963 23301 📄 01963 23301
(by arrangement)

Dir: On A3030 between Sherborne & Sturminster Newton

Walkers who come to pretty Bishops Caundle owe a debt of thanks to whoever waymarked the route to start and end here. The 16th-century pub was once a monks' brewhouse, and later used by the notorious Judge Jeffreys. An extensive menu ranges through snacks, children's and vegetarian dishes, steaks and chef's specialities. Favourites include grilled duck with port and orange, and spicy sizzling pork. There's also a six-activity play trail and two sunken trampolines.

Open: 11.30-3 6.30-11 (Sun 12-3, 7-10.30)
Bar Meals: L served all week 12-2 D served all week 6.45-9.30 Av main course £6.10
Restaurant: L served all week 12-2 D served all week 6.30-9.30

Brewery/Company: HALL & WOODHOUSE
🍺: Badger Best, Tanglefoot, Golden Champion, Sussex Golden Glory
Children's Facilities: Fam room Play area (Activity play trail, 2 trampolines) Portions/Menu High Chairs
Notes: Dogs Allowed Water provided Garden Food Served Outside Patio area, 6 benches Parking 32 Coach parties welcome

SHROTON OR IWERNE COURTNEY ST81

The Cricketers ◆◆◆◆◆ ☺ ♈

Blandford Forum DT11 8QD
☎ 01258 860421 📄 01258 861800

Dir: Off the A350 Shaftesbury to Blandford

A classically English pub, built at the turn of the 20th century. The Cricketers comprises a main bar, sports bar and den, all light and airy rooms leading to the restaurant at the rear. This in turn overlooks a lovely garden, well stocked with trees and flowers. Inside, the cricket theme is taken up in the collection of sports memorabilia on display and the hand pumps for the real ales, shaped like cricket bats. An extensive menu, serving both the bar and restaurant, offers a good choice of interesting dishes featuring unusual combinations.

Open: 11.30-2.30 6.30-11 Winter Sun eve 7
Bar Meals: L served all week 12-2 D served all week 6.30-9 (Sun from 7) Av main course £5
Restaurant: L served all week 12-2 D served all week 6.3-9 Sun from 7 Av 3 course · à la carte £16

Brewery/Company: FREE HOUSE
🍺: Ringwood 49er, Butcombe Bitter, Shepherds Neame Spitfire, Timothy Taylor
Rooms: 1 en suite s£45 d£65
Children's Facilities: Portions/Menu Cutlery Games High Chairs Food Warming Changing
Notes: No Dogs (except Assist Dogs) Water in garden Garden Food Served Outside Bordered by trees and hedges, herb garden Parking 19

TOLPUDDLE   SY79

The Martyrs Inn ♀

Nr Dorchester DT2 7ES
☎ 01305 848249 📠 01305 848977
✉ martyrs@scottz.co.uk

Dir: Off A35 between Bere Regis
(A31/A35 Junction)

*Tolpuddle is the somewhat unlikely birthplace
of the Trades Union Congress. Its seeds were
sown in 1834 by six impoverished farm
labourers who tried to bargain with local
landowners for better conditions. Their
punishment was transportation to Australia.
Martyrs' memorabilia abounds in the pub.
Main courses include Tolpuddle sausages with
mash and onion gravy, country vegetable
pasta bake, and spicy chicken curry with rice
and naan bread. There is a play area to keep
the children amused.*

Bar Meals: L served all week 12-3 D served
all week 6.30-9
Restaurant: L served all week-D served
all week
Brewery/Company: HALL & WOODHOUSE
🍺: Badger Dorset Best & Tanglefoot
Children's Facilities: Play area (Large
garden) Portions/Menu Cutlery Games High
Chairs Food Warming Changing
Nearby: Monkey World, Tank Museum
Notes: Dogs Allowed Garden Parking 25
Coach parties welcome

WEST BEXINGTON   SY58

The Manor Hotel ★★ 🛏

nr Dorchester DT2 9DF
☎ 01308 897616 📠 01308 897035
✉ themanorhotel@btconnect.com

Dir: On B3157, 5m E of Bridport

*Just 500 yards from spectacular Chesil Beach
and the clear waters of Lyme Bay lies this
16th-century manor house, featuring Jacobean
oak panelling and flagstone floors. It makes
an excellent base for exploring Dorset's
numerous delights and enjoying stunning
coastal walks. The menu offers starters such
as Thai style fish balls cooked in coconut milk;
or air dried Dorset ham with fresh figs;
perhaps followed by baked lemon sole with a
pale sherry sauce; or stir-fried loin of lamb
with ginger, garlic and sesame.*

Open: 11-11 (Sun 12-10.30)
Bar Meals: L served all week 12-2 D served
all week 6.30-9.30 Av main course £9.95
Restaurant: L all week 12-2 D all week
7-9.30 Av 3 course fixed price £19.50
Brewery/Company: FREE HOUSE
🍺: Butcombe Gold, Harbour Master
Rooms: 13 en suite 3 family s£70 d£110
Children's Facilities: Fam room Play area
(Playing Field) Portions/Menu High Chairs
Food Warming
Nearby: Chesil Beach
Notes: No Dogs Water Bowls Garden Food
Served Outside Large garden with sea views
Parking 40

WEST LULWORTH   SY88

The Castle Inn 🕸 ♀

Main Road BH20 5RN
☎ 01929 400311 📠 01929 400415

Dir: on the Wareham to Dorchester Rd,
L approx 1m from Wareham

Picturesque thatched and beamed inn with a delightful setting near Lulworth Cove, close to plenty of good walks and popular attractions. Prize-winning gardens packed with plants, garden furniture and a water feature are an additional attraction. The wide-ranging menu offers a number of mouth-watering dishes, including chicken, ham and mushroom pie; fillet steak with oysters; liver and bacon casserole; seafood stew; sesame chicken with ginger and onion sauce; plus a variety of flambé dishes cooked at the table.

Open: 11-2.30 6-11 (Winter 12-2.30, 7-11)
Closed: 25 Dec
Bar Meals: L served all week 11-2.30 D
served all week 6-10.30 Av main course £6
Restaurant: D served Fri & Sat 7-9.30 Av 3
course · à la carte £15
Brewery/Company: FREE HOUSE
🍺: Ringwood Best, Gales, Courage,
John Smith, Fosters, Kronenburg
Children's Facilities: Licence Fam room Play
area (Outside chess/draughts, board games)
Portions/Menu Cutlery Games High Chairs
Food Warming Changing
Notes: Dogs Allowed Water/Food Garden
Food Served Outside Large tiered garden lots
of plants flowers Parking 30 Coach parties
welcome

WEST STAFFORD   SY78

The Wise Man Inn ♀

Dorchester DT2 8AG
☎ 01305 263694

Dir: 2m from A35

Set in the heart of Thomas Hardy country, this thatched 16th-century pub was originally the village shop and off-licence. It is now a regular stopping off point for those on the Hardy trail. The menu makes full use of good local produce, fresh fish and vegetables, and organic meat. There is a children's menu, and a large secluded garden with ample seating.

Open: 11-3 6.30-11 (Summer 6-11)
Days closed: Mon (winter)
Bar Meals: L served all week 12-2.30
D served Mon-Sat 7-9.30 Av main course £7
Restaurant: L served all week 12-2.30
D served Mon-Sat 7-9.30
Brewery/Company: PUBMASTER
🍺: Ringwood, 3 casked ales each week
Children's Facilities: Fam room Play area
Portions/Menu Cutlery Games High Chairs
Notes: Dogs Allowed Water & biscuits
provided Garden Food Served Outside Large
secluded garden, with plenty of seating,
Parking 25 Coach parties welcome

BARNARD CASTLE   NZ01

The Morritt Arms Hotel
★★★ @ ♀

Greta Bridge DL12 9SE
☎ 01833 627232 ▤ 01833 627392
✉ relax@themorritt.co.uk

Dir: At Scotch Corner A66 towards Penrith,
9m turn at Greta Bridge. Hotel on L

*The present building began life in the 17th-
century as a farmhouse. In coaching days The
Morritt was an important overnight stops for
the London-Carlisle service. Charles Dickens
researched 'Nicholas Nicklelby' here in 1839.
Gilroy's Restaurant offers starters of smoked
haddock and potato chowder; main courses
include rump of Teesdale lamb with garlic
mash, cassoulet; and risotto of wild
mushrooms and artichokes.*

Open: 11-11 **Bar Meals:** L served all week
12-3 D served all week 6-9.30 Av main course
£8 **Restaurant:** L served all week 12-3
D served all week 7-9 Av 3 course · à la carte
£26 Av 4 course fixed price £21
COMPANY: FREE HOUSE ◧: John Smith's,
Timothy Taylor Landlord, Black Sheep Best,
Rooms: 23 en suite s£59.50 d£87.50
Children's Facilities: Licence Fam room Play
area (Swings, slide, grass area) Portions/Menu
Games High Chairs Food Warming Changing
Nearby: Otter Trust, Raby Castle, Hackworth
Railway Museum **Notes:** Dogs Allowed Water
Garden Food Served Outside Terraced,
traditional garden with walk ways Parking 100
Coach parties welcome

FIR TREE   NZ13

Duke of York Country Inn

Crook DL15 8DG
☎ 01388 762848 ▤ 01388 767055
✉ suggett@firtree-crook.fsnet.co.uk

Dir: on A68 towards Scotland, 12m W
of Durham

*A former drovers' and coaching inn on the old
York to Edinburgh coach route, this 18th-
century white-painted inn is noted for its
furniture which contains the famous carved
mouse trademark of Robert Thompson, a
renowned Yorkshire woodcarver. There's also
a collection of flint arrowheads, axes and
Africana. Typical fare includes home-made
steak and kidney pie, pork Zaccharoff, fresh
cod in Black Sheep beer batter, and soups
that are so popular, people often ask for the
recipe. Large landscaped beer garden.*

Open: 11-2.30 6.30-10.30
Bar Meals: L served all week 12-2 D served
all week 6.30-9 Av main course £7.50
Restaurant: L served all week 12-2 D served
all week 6.30-9 Av 3 course · à la carte £20
Brewery/Company: FREE HOUSE
◧: Black Sheep, Worthington, Stones, Carling
Children's Facilities: Licence Play area
Portions/Menu High Chairs Food Warming
Nearby: Hamsterley Forest, Beamish Museum
Notes: No Dogs (except Assist Dogs) Water
Garden Food Served Outside Garden at rear
of pub, patio area Parking 65 Coach parties
welcome

MIDDLESTONE NZ23

Ship Inn

Low Road Bishop Auckland DL14 8AB
☎ 01388 810904
✉ graham@snaithg.freeserve.co.uk

Dir: On B6287 Kirk Merrington to Coundon road

Beer drinkers will appreciate the string of CAMRA accolades received by this family-run pub on the village green. In the last three years regulars could have sampled well over 500 different beers. Ask about the pub's challenge for regulars to visit as many pubs as possible with 'ship' in their name. Home-cooked food in the bar and restaurant. The rooftop patio has spectacular views over the Tees Valley and Cleveland Hills.

Open: 4-11 (Thur-Sat 12-11 Sun 12-10)
Bar Meals: L served Fri-Sun 12-2.30 D served Mon, Wed-Sat 5-9 (Sun 12-2)
Restaurant: L served Fri-Sun 12-2.30 D served Mon, Wed-Sat 5-9 (Sun 12-2)
🍺:Timothy Taylor Landlord & 5 Guest Ales
Children's Facilities: Fam room Play area (Swings on village green) Games High Chairs Food Warming
Notes: Dogs Allowed Village green Parking 6 Coach parties welcome No credit cards

TRIMDON NZ33

The Bird in Hand

Salters Lane TS29 6JQ
☎ 01429 880391

Village pub nine miles west of Hartlepool with fine views over surrounding countryside from an elevated position. There's a cosy bar and games room, stocking a good choice of cask ales and guest beers, a spacious lounge and large conservatory restaurant. Traditional Sunday lunch goes down well, as does breaded plaice and other favourites. In summer you can sit outside in the garden, which has a roofed over area for climbing plants.

Open: 12-3 7-11 (Fri-Sat 12-11, Sun 12-10.30)
Bar Meals: L served Tues-Sun 12-3 D served Tues-Sun 7-9 Av main course £3.50
Children's Facilities: Fam room Portions/Menu Cutlery Games High Chairs Food Warming
Notes: Dogs Allowed Garden Food Served Outside Enclosed area with gazebo type roof Parking 30 Coach parties welcome

BLACKMORE END   TL73

The Bull Inn 🕙 ♀

Nr Braintree CM7 4DD
☎ 01371 851037 📠 01371 851037

*Off the beaten track in the heart of tranquil
north Essex, not far from the showpiece village
of Finchingfield this traditional village pub,
created from two 17th-century cottages and an
adjoining barn, is full of original beams and
open hearths. Herbs used in the kitchen are
grown in the attractive garden. The no-nonsense
menu caters for most tastes with a good choice
of starters such as broccoli and Stilton soup,
deep-fried whitebait and nachos, or crispy
mushrooms, backed up with main courses
including steaks, rack of ribs, seafood, spaghetti
arrabbiata and Thai chicken curry and rice. On
Sundays there's a set-price lunch, with
traditional roasts and a good selection of
sweets.*

Open: 12-3 6-11 **Closed:** Mon lunch
Bar Meals: L served all week 12-3 D served all
week 7-9 (Sun 12-3, 6-9) Av main course £6.95
Restaurant: L served Tue-Sun 12-2.30 D
served Mon-Sun 6-9 Av 3 course · à la carte £12
Brewery/Company: FREE HOUSE
🍺: Greene King IPA, Abbot Ale,
Adnams Best, London Pride
Children's Facilities: Fam room Play area
(Toys, books) Portions/Menu Cutlery Games
High Chairs Food Warming
Notes: No Dogs (except Assist Dogs) Water
bowl Food Served Outside Beer garden,
outdoor eating, BBQ Parking 36 Coach parties
welcome

CASTLE HEDINGHAM   TL73

The Bell Inn ♀

St James Street Halstead CO9 3EJ
☎ 01787 460350
✉ bell-inn@ic24.net

Dir: On A1124 N of Halstead, R to
Castle Hedingham

*The Bell dates from the 15th century and was
the principle coaching inn on the Bury St
Edmunds to London route. The pub has been
in the same family since 1967 and still has
beams, wooden floors, open fires and gravity-
fed real ale straight from the barrel. Other
features are the barrel-vaulted function room,
walled garden and vine-covered patio.
Monday is fish night (try it barbecued), while
other favourites are smoked prawns,
shepherds pie and treacle tart.*

Open: 11.30-3 6-11 (Sun 12-3, 7-10.30, Fri
11.30-11) **Closed:** 25 Dec (eve)
Bar Meals: L served all week 12-2 D served
all week 7-9.30 Av main course £7.50
Brewery/Company: GRAYS 🍺: Mild
Adnams Broadside, Greene King IPA , Adnams
Bitter
Children's Facilities: Fam room Play area
(Swings) Games High Chairs Food Warming
Changing
Nearby: Steam Trains, Castle
Notes: Dogs Allowed by arrangement only
Garden Food Served Outside Large walled
orchard garden Parking 15

CLAVERING TL43

The Cricketers 🐕 ♀

Saffron Walden CB11 4QT
☎ 01799 550442 📠 01799 550882
📧 cricketers@lineone.net

Dir: From M11 J10 take A505 E. Then
A1301, B1383. At Newport take B1038

*Owned and run by the parents of celebrity chef
Jamie Oliver–who grew up and worked in the
kitchen here–this popular 16th-century inn is at
the heart of an unspoilt village. It stands near
the cricket pitch, and cricketing memorabilia dot
the bars and restaurant. The choice of food is
extensive and varied with interesting light
snacks and starters available in the bar and
fixed-price menus. Fish and seafood are well
represented and the 'specials' are changed daily.
The dessert menu is equally mouth-watering.*

Open: 10.30-11 Closed: 25-26 Dec
Bar Meals: L served all week 12-2 D served
all week 7-10
Restaurant: L served 12-2 D served all week
7-10 Av 3 course · à la carte £26 Av 3 course
fixed price £26
Brewery/Company: FREE HOUSE
🍺: Adnams Bitter, Tetley Bitter
Rooms: 14 en suite s£70 d£100 (◆◆◆◆)
Children's Facilities: Fam room Play area
(Fenced patio) Portions/Menu High Chairs
Food Warming
Nearby: Audley End Model Railway, Stansted
Castle, Audley End House
Notes: No Dogs Garden Food Served Outside
patio Parking 100 Coach parties welcome

ELSENHAM TL52

The Crown 🐕

The Cross High Street nr Bishop's Stortford
CM22 6DG
☎ 01279 812827

Dir: M11 J8 towards Takeley,
L at traffic lights

*A pub for 300 years, with oak beams, open
fireplaces and Essex pargetting at the front.
The menu, which has a large selection of fresh
fish, might offer cottage pie with cheese
topping, gammon steak, three cheese pasta
bake, steak and kidney pie, baked trout with
almonds and honey, steak and mushroom pie,
home-made burgers, and steaks cooked to
order.*

Open: 11-3 6-11 (Sun 12-4, 7-10.30)
Bar Meals: L served all week 12-2 D served
Tue-Sat 7-9 Av main course £8.50
Restaurant: L served all week 12-2 D served
Tue-Sat 7-9 Av 3 course · à la carte £16
Brewery/Company: PUNCH RETAIL
🍺: Youngs PA, Adnams Broadside,
Spitfire & Guest Beers
Children's Facilities: Play area High Chairs
Food Warming
Nearby: Mole Hill Wildlife Park, Toy Museum,
Castle
Notes: Dogs Allowed Water Garden Food
Served Outside enclosed grassed area, tables
patio garden Parking 28 Coach parties
welcome

GREAT YELDHAM   TL73

The White Hart ❀ ♀

Poole Street Halstead CO9 4HJ
☎ 01787 237250 📠 01787 238044
✉ reservations@whitehartyeldham.co.uk

Dir: On A1017 between Haverhill & Halstead

A picturesque timber-framed house and former coaching inn now celebrating its 500th birthday. The interior is full of character, with low beamed ceilings, period furniture and, in winter, a roaring log fire. Whether your choice is a quick snack or a romantic candle-lit dinner, the award-winning food offers a wide range of options from light dishes to more sophisticated choices in the restaurant.

Open: 11-3 6-11 (Sun 12-3, 7-10.30)
Bar Meals: L served all week 12-2 D served all week 6.30-9.30 (Sun 7-9.30)
Restaurant: L served all week 12-2 D served all week 6.30-9.30 Sun evening from 7 Av 3 course · à la carte £27.50 Av 2 course fixed price £10.50
Brewery/Company: FREE HOUSE
🍺: Guest ales (local & nationwide)
Children's Facilities: Licence Play area (Toy box) Portions/Menu Cutlery Games High Chairs Food Warming
Nearby: Hedingham Castle, Colne Valley Steam Railway
Notes: No Dogs (except Assist Dogs) Garden Food Served Outside large garden small river Parking 40 Coach parties welcome

LITTLE CANFIELD   TL52

The Lion & Lamb 🐕 ♀

Dunmow CM6 1SR
☎ 01279 870257 📠 01279 870423
✉ info@lionandlamb.co.uk

Dir: M11 J8 B1256 towards Takeley

There's a friendly welcome at this traditional country pub restaurant, with its soft red bricks, oak beams and winter log fires. Handy for Stansted Airport and the M11, the pub's charm and individuality make it a favourite for business or leisure. Choices from the bar menu include steak and ale pie, while the restaurant offers, perhaps, braised lamb shanks with a ragout of white beans, or wild mushroom risotto. There is a separate fresh fish board.

Open: 11-11 (Sun 12-10.30)
Bar Meals: L served all week 11-10 D served all week 11-10 (Sun 12-10) Av main course £12.50
Restaurant: L served all week 11-10 D served all week 11-10 (Sun 12-10) Av 3 course · à la carte £22.50 Av 3 course fixed price £16
Brewery/Company: RIDLEY & SONS LTD
🍺: Ridleys IPA, Old Bob, Prospect & Seasonal Beers.
Children's Facilities: Play area (Garden, Wendy house) Portions/Menu Cutlery Games High Chairs Food Warming Changing
Nearby: Hatfield Forest
Notes: No Dogs (except Assist Dogs) Water Garden Food Served Outside Lrg enclosed garden over-looking farmland Parking 50 Coach parties welcome

MANNINGTREE TM13

The Mistley Thorn Hotel 🐾 ♈

High Street Mistley CO11 1HE
☎ 01206 392821 📠 01206 392133
✉ sherrisingleton@aol.com

Historic pub in the centre of Mistley, which stands on the estuary of the River Stour near Colchester and is the only surviving Georgian port in England today. It is now the first completely non-smoking pub in Essex. An accomplished menu is offered with emphasis on locally sourced produce with a leaning towards fresh seafood. Imaginative menu ideas include flattened organic chicken with Tuscan bread salad; seared cod fillet with spiced lentils; whole wild sea bass with balsamic potatoes and thyme; chargrilled pork and leek sausages with onion mash and Bramley apple confit; crab cake with Chipolte mayonnaise.

Open: 12-11
Bar Meals: L served all week 12-2.30 D served all week 7-10 Av main course £9.50
Restaurant: L served all week 12-2.30 D served Mon-Sat 7-9.30
Brewery/Company: FREE HOUSE
🍺 Greene King IPA, Adnams, St. Peters
Children's Facilities: Portions/Menu Cutlery Games High Chairs Food Warming Changing
Notes: Dogs Allowed Parking 6 Non-smoking establishment

NORTH FAMBRIDGE TQ89

The Ferry Boat Inn 🐾

Ferry Lane Chelmsford CM3 6LR
☎ 01621 740208
✉ sylviaferryboat@aol.com

> **Dir:** From Chelmsford take A130 S then A132 to South Woodham Ferrers, then B1012. R to village

The 500-year-old inn is located on the River Crouch, close to the well-known yachting centre and the Essex Wildlife Trust's 600-acre sanctuary, with wonderful walks. Low beams and log fires characterise the interior, and there is reputed to be a poltergeist in residence. Typical pub fare includes steak and kidney pie, smoked haddock, grilled salmon, and ham, egg and chips.

Open: 11.30-3 7-11 (Sun 12-4 7-10.30)
Bar Meals: L served all week 12-2 D served all week 7-9.30 (Sun 12-2.45, 7-9) Av main course £7
Restaurant: L served all week 12-1.30 D served all week 7-9 Av 3 course · à la carte £15
Brewery/Company: FREE HOUSE
🍺 Shepherd Neame Bishops Finger, Spitfire
Rooms: 6 en suite 3 family room s£30 d£40 (♦♦♦)
Children's Facilities: Fam room Play area (Swings) High Chairs Food Warming
Nearby: Marsh Farm Country Park, Butterfly Farm, Museum of Power
Notes: Dogs Allowed Garden Food Served Outside Acre, grassed, benches Parking 30 Coach parties welcome

ALMONDSBURY ST68

The Bowl ★★ ☺ ♀

16 Church Road BS32 4DT
☎ 01454 612757 📠 01454 619910
✉ reception@thebowlinn.co.uk

Dating back to 1550, this picturesque whitewashed pub on the edge of the Severn Vale was originally a terrace of three cottages. The inn gets its name from its interesting geographical location in the escarpment of the south-western vale of the Severn. Bar menu with pies and casserole, pasta, freshly baked baguettes, and fish. In Lilies Restaurant try duck leg confit, pan-fried lemon sole, fillets of lamb, or roasted monkfish.

Open: 11-3 5-11 (Sun 12-10.30) RS: 25 Dec closed eve
Bar Meals: L served all week 12-2.30 D served all week 6-10 (Sun 12-8) Av main course £8
Restaurant: L served all week 12-2.30 D served all week 7-10 Av 3 course · à la carte £27

Brewery/Company: FREE HOUSE
🍺: Scottish Courage Courage Best, Smiles Best, Wickwar BOB, Moles Best, Interbrew Bass, guest ales
Rooms: 13 en suite s£44.50 d£71
Children's Facilities: Portions/Menu Cutlery Games High Chairs Food Warming
Notes: Dogs Allowed Garden Food Served Outside Patio area at rear. Seating on frontage Parking 50 Coach parties welcome

ANDOVERSFORD SP01

The Royal Oak Inn ☺ ♀

Old Gloucester Road Cheltenham GL54 4HR
☎ 01242 820335
✉ bleninns@clara.net

Dir: 200mtrs from A40, 4m E of Cheltenham

The Royal Oak stands on the banks of the River Coln, one of a small chain of popular food-oriented pubs in the area. Originally a coaching inn, its main dining room, galleried on two levels, occupies the converted former stables. Lunchtime bar fare of various sandwiches, lasagne and ham, egg and chips (for example), extends in the evening to Chinese crispy duck with lime and soy noodles or roast pork fillet with rosti potato and creamy cider sauce.

Open: 11-2.30 5.30-11
Bar Meals: L served all week 12-2.30 D served all week 7-9.30 Av main course £6.50
Restaurant: L served all week 12-2.30 D served all week 7-9.30 Av 3 course · à la carte £15
Brewery/Company: FREE HOUSE 🍺: Hook Norton Best, Tetleys Bitter, Draught Bass
Children's Facilities: Portions/Menu High Chairs Food Warming
Nearby: Cotswold Wild Life Park & Folly Farm
Notes: Dogs Allowed Water Garden Food Served Outside Patio area with tables on banks of the river Parking 44 Coach parties welcome

BERKELEY ST69

The Malt House ★★ 🕭

Marybrook St GL13 9BA
☎ 01453 511177 📠 01453 810257
✉ the-malthouse@btconnect.com

Dir: From A38 towards Bristol from exit 13 or 14 of M5, approx 8m Berkeley signed, the Malt House is on the main road towards Sharpness

Close by the Severn Way is this century-old former slaughterhouse which has developed over the years into a comfortable and welcoming inn with a range of menus to suit all tastes and pockets. There is a good choice of starters, perhaps followed by fillet steak forestière, Grimsby haddock and chips with mushy peas, hot 'n' spicy creel prawns, or Mediterranean vegetable lasagne. At lunchtime, snacks are available and there is a special menu with good choices at a give-away price for mature students (60 years plus!). Sunday carvery; skittle alley available.

Open: 12-11 (Sun 12-4, Mon 4-11)
Bar Meals: L served Tues-Sat 11-2 D served Mon-Sat 6-9 (Sun 12-2)
Restaurant: L served Tues-Sat 12-2 D served Mon-Sat 6-9 Sun 12-2 Av 3 course · à la carte £15 **Brewery/Company:** FREE HOUSE 🍺: Pedigree, Theakstons **Children's Facilities:** Portions/Menu Cutlery High Chairs Food Warming **Notes:** No Dogs (except Assist Dogs) Garden Small garden; Food served outside in summer Parking 40 Coach parties welcome

BIRDLIP SO91

The Golden Heart 🍷

Nettleton Bottom GL4 8LA
☎ 01242 870261 📠 01242 870599

Dir: on A417 Gloucester to Cirencester

Glorious country views are afforded from the terraced gardens of this Cotswold stone inn, while inside you will find real fires, real ales and a wide selection of wines. The regular menu is supplemented by a daily blackboard choice, and dishes range from the traditional-bubble and squeak with lamb and mint sausages, to more exotic options like ostrich, bacon and mushroom pudding. A meeting room and private dining areas can be arranged.

Open: 11-3 5.30-11 (Fri-Sat 11-11, Sun 12-10.30)
Bar Meals: L served all week 12-3 D served all week 6-10 (Sun 12-10) Av main course £10
Restaurant: L served all week 12-3 D served all week 6-10 Sun 12-10
Brewery/Company: FREE HOUSE 🍺: Interbrew Bass, Timothy Taylor Landlord & Golden Best, Archers Bitter, Young's Special
Children's Facilities: Fam room Play area (Garden) Portions/Menu Games High Chairs Food Warming
Notes: Dogs Allowed water Garden Food Served Outside Terrace, 3 levels, large patio area, seating Parking 60 Coach parties welcome

BISLEY
SO90

The Bear Inn

George Street GL6 7BD
☎ 01452 770265

Dir: E of Stroud off B4070

Constructed as a courthouse with meeting rooms for the village in the 16th century, The Bear became an inn around 1766 and has continued as such ever since. Its outstanding features include a huge inglenook fireplace, a bread oven and an old priest hole; though the rock-hewn cellars, including a 60ft well, are more likely to be Tudor. Menu items include bear burgers, bear necessities (sauté potatoes with various ingredients mixed in) and bear essentials such as steak, kidney and Guinness pie.

Open: 11.30-3 6-11 (Sun 12-3, 7-10.30)
Closed: 25-26 Dec
Bar Meals: L served all week 12-2 D served Mon-Sat 7-9 (No food Sun pm) Av main course £9.45
Brewery/Company: PUBMASTER
🍺: Tetley, Flowers IPA, Charles Wells Bombardier, Marstons
Children's Facilities: Fam room Portions/Menu Food Warming
Notes: Dogs Allowed Garden Food Served Outside Food served outside Parking 20

CHIPPING CAMPDEN
SP13

The Eight Bells Inn ♀

Church Street GL55 6JG
☎ 01386 840371 📄 01386 841669
✆ neil.hargreaves@bellinn.fsnet.co.uk

The inn was originally in the 14th century to house the stonemasons and store the bells during construction of the nearby church. This tiny, stone-built free house has two atmospheric bars where the original oak beams, open fireplaces and even a priest's hole still survive. In these delightful surroundings, local food is offered from a seasonal menu that reflects a serious approach to food.

Open: 11-3 5.30-11 (all day Jul-Aug)
Closed: 25 Dec
Bar Meals: L served all week 12-2.30 D served all week 6.30-9.30 Av main course £9.50
Restaurant: L served all week 12-2.30 D served all week 6.30-9.30 Av 3 course · à la carte £20
Brewery/Company: FREE HOUSE
🍺: Hook Norton Best, Goff's Jouster
Rooms: 4 en suite 1 family s£50 d£85 (◆◆◆)
Children's Facilities: Fam room Play area Portions/Menu Cutlery Games High Chairs Food Warming
Nearby: Warwick Castle, Shakespeare's Birthplace, Cotswold Water Park
Notes: Dogs Allowed Water Garden Food Served Outside Terrace, courtyard, great views Coach parties welcome

CHIPPING CAMPDEN SP13

The Bakers Arms

Broad Campden GL55 6UR
☎ 01386 840515

Small Cotswold inn with a great atmosphere-visitors are welcomed and regulars are involved with the quiz, darts and crib teams. The traditional look of the place is reflected in its time-honoured values, with good meals at reasonable prices and a choice of four or five real ales. Typical main courses are chicken curry, mariner's pie, cottage pie, and liver and bacon; these are backed by specials such as breaded salmon fishcakes and pork chops cooked in cider.

Open: 11.30-2.30 4.45-11 (Fri-Sat 11.30-11, Sun 12-10.30, Summer 11.30-11) Closed: 25 Dec RS: 26 Dec closed evening
Bar Meals: L served all week 12-2 D served all week 6-9 (Apr-Oct 12-9)
Restaurant: L served all week 12-2 D served all week 6-9
Brewery/Company: FREE HOUSE
🍺: Hook Norton, Stanway Bitter, Bombardier, Timothy Taylor Landlord
Children's Facilities: Play area (Swings) Portions/Menu Cutlery High Chairs Food Warming
Notes: Dogs Allowed Garden only. Water provided Garden Food Served Outside Large grassed area Parking 30 Coach parties welcome No credit cards

CIRENCESTER SP00

Bathurst Arms

North Cerney GL7 7BZ
☎ 01285 831281 📠 01285 831155

Dir: The Bathurst Arms is setback from Cheltenham road (A435)

Former coaching inn with bags of period charm - antique settles on flagstone floors, stone fireplaces, beams and panelled walls. The pretty garden stretches down to the River Churn, and a large barbecue is in use most summer weekends. Local delicacies include grilled Cerney goats' cheese with mixed leaves and walnuts, and trio of organic sausages with garlic mash and red onion gravy.

Open: 11-3 6-11 (Sun 12-3, 7-10.30)
Bar Meals: L served all week 12-2 D served all week 7-9 Av main course £10
Restaurant: L served all week 12-2 D served all week 7-9.30 Av 3 course · à la carte £20
Brewery/Company: FREE HOUSE
🍺: Hook Norton, Cotswold Way, rotation of guest beers
Children's Facilities: Portions/Menu Cutlery High Chairs Food Warming Changing
Notes: Dogs Allowed Dog bowl Garden Food Served Outside Riverside with boules pitch Parking 40 Coach parties welcome

CLEARWELL   SO50

Wyndham Arms ★★★ ⊗ ♀

Nr Coleford GL16 8JT
☎ 01594 833666 📠 01594 836450
✉ nigel@thewyndhamhotel.co.uk

Dir: In village centre on B4231

The quintessentially English village of
Clearwell in the Royal Forest of Dean takes its
name from the Dunraven Well on the hotel
boundary. The building itself dates back to the
14th century and over the centuries since then
it has evolved into a highly civilised small
hotel, run with great style and enthusiasm.
In either the bustling bar or the quieter
restaurant, a three-course meal might
comprise wild mushroom and onion tartlet as
a starter, calf's liver, and Madeira sauce, or
baked mullet stuffed with sun-dried tomato,
olives and tarragon as a main course, and
bread and butter pudding for dessert.

Open: 11-11 (Sun 12-10.30)
Bar Meals: L served all week 12-2 D served
all week 6.45-9 Av main course £9.95
Restaurant: L served all week 12-2 D served
all week 6.45-9.30 Av 3 course · à la carte
£17.50 **Brewery/Company:** FREE HOUSE
🍺: Speculation Bitter, Freeminer Bitter
Rooms: 18 en suite 2 family s£45 d£65
Children's Facilities: Portions/Menu Cutlery
Games High Chairs Food Warming Changing
Nearby: Puzzlewood, Clearwell Caves
Notes: Dogs Allowed Field for exercise
Garden Parking 50

EBRINGTON   SP14

Ebrington Arms

Ebrington GL55 6NH
☎ 01386 593223 📠 01386 593763

A charmingly down-to-earth Cotswold village
pub dating from the mid-18th century. Stone
flagfloors, large open fires and beautiful
surrounding countryside give it plenty of
character. Walkers frequent the pub for its
locally-brewed ales and good home-cooked
food, including butterflied breast of chicken
with chilli butter and Mediterranean
vegetables and cod with deep-fried leeks.

Open: 11-2.30 6-11 (open all day from Etr)
Days closed: Mon Lunch
Bar Meals: L served Tue-Sun 12-2 D served
Tue-Sat 6-9 Av main course £8
Restaurant: L served Tue-Sun 12-2 D served
Tue-Sat 6-9
Brewery/Company: FREE HOUSE 🍺: Hook
Norton Best, Fullers London Pride &
Bombadier
Children's Facilities: Licence Fam room
Portions/Menu Cutlery Games High Chairs
Food Warming
Notes: Dogs Allowed Water Garden Food
Served Outside Lawn and patio area Parking
12 Coach parties welcome

EWEN   SU09

The Wild Duck ★★ ⊛ ⓒ ♀

Drakes Island Cirencester GL7 6BY
☎ 01285 770310 📠 01285 770924
✉ wduckinn@aol.com

Dir: From Cirencester take A429, at Kemble take L turn to Ewen, pub in village centre

An Elizabethan inn of mellow Cotswold stone, the Wild Duck has evolved over the years from a collection of buildings. It has beams, oak panelling, open fires, and ancestral portraits adorning the walls. The country-style dining room offers food that is traditionally British with a hint of European and Oriental influence. Vegetarian choices are always available.

Open: 8-11 (Sun 12-10.30) RS: 25 Dec closed eve
Bar Meals: L served all week 12-2 D served all week 7-10 Av main course £9.95
Restaurant: L served all week 12-2 D served all week 7-10 Av 3 course · à la carte £25
Brewery/Company: FREE HOUSE 🍺:
Scottish Courage Theakston Old Peculier, Wells Bombardier, Greene King Old Speckled Hen
Rooms: 11 en suite s£60 d£80
Children's Facilities: Portions/Menu Cutlery Games High Chairs Food Warming Changing
Nearby: Keynes Country Park, Butts Farm Rare Breed Farm
Notes: Dogs Allowed Garden Food Served Outside Enclosed courtyard, giant chess board Parking 50 Coach parties welcome

FORD   SP02

Plough Inn ♦♦♦♦

Nr Temple Guiting GL54 5RU
☎ 01386 584215 📠 01386 584042
✉ info@theploughinnatford.co.uk

Dir: 4m from Stow-on-the-Wold on the Tewkesbury road

This 16th-century inn, steeped in history and character, continues to provide all that one associates with a traditional English pub; flagstone floors, log fires and lively conversation. Meals made from local produce are cooked to order and include half a slow roasted shoulder of lamb, luxury fish pie, braised beef; the inn is renowned for its fresh, seasonal asparagus.

Open: 11-11 (Sun 12-10.30) **Closed:** 25 Dec
Bar Meals: L served all week 12-2 D served Mon-Sun 6.30-9 (weekends food all day 12-9) Av main course £8.95
Restaurant: L served all week 11.30-2 D served all week 6.30-9
Brewery/Company: DONNINGTON
🍺: Donnington BB & SBA, Bottled Double Donnington
Rooms: 3 en suite 1 family room s£35 d£55
Children's Facilities: Play area (Play fort in garden) Portions/Menu Cutlery Games High Chairs
Nearby: Cotswold Farm Park, Model Village, Bird Land
Notes: No Dogs Water Garden Food Served Outside Lrg court, beer garden with heat lamps Parking 50 Coach parties welcome

GREET
SP03

The Harvest Home ♀

Evesham Road nr Winchcombe GL54 5BH
☎ 01242 602430
✉ sworchardbarn@aol.com

Dir: M5 J9 take A435 towards Evesham, then B4077 & B4078 towards Winchcombe. 200yds from station.

Set in the beautiful Cotswold countryside, this traditional country inn draws steam train enthusiasts aplenty, as a restored stretch of the Great Western Railway runs past the end of the garden. Built around 1905, the pub is handy for Cheltenham Racecourse and Sudeley Castle. Expect a good range of snacks and mains, including locally-reared beef and tempting seafood dishes.

Open: 12-3 6-11 (Sun 6-10.30) RS: 25 & 31 Dec closed eve
Bar Meals: L served all week 12-2 D served all week 6-9 Av main course £8
Restaurant: L served all week 12-2 D served all week 6-9 Av 3 course · à la carte £16 Av 2 course fixed price £5.95
Brewery/Company: ENTERPRISE INNS ◖: Old Speckled Hen, Goffs Jouster, Deuchars IPA
Children's Facilities: Licence Play area (Large garden) Portions/Menu Cutlery High Chairs Food Warming
Nearby: GWR Steam Railway, Sudeley Castle
Notes: Dogs Allowed Water Garden Food Served Outside Grass area, picnic tables, countryside views Parking 30 Coach parties welcome

GUITING POWER
SP02

The Hollow Bottom ♦♦♦♦ ☺ ♀

Cheltenham GL54 5UX
☎ 01451 850392 📠 01451 850945
✉ hello@hollowbottom

An 18th-century Cotswold stone pub with a horse-racing theme, frequented by the racing fraternity associated with Cheltenham. Its nooks and crannies lend themselves to an intimate drink or meal, and there's a separate dining room plus tables outside for fine weather. Freshly made dishes include calves' liver, grilled seabass, marlin, and fillet steak, as well as exotic treats such as kangaroo and crocodile tail.

Open: 11-11
Bar Meals: L served all week 12-D served all week-9.30 Av main course £9.50
Restaurant: L served all week 12-D served all week-9.30 Av 3 course · à la carte £19.50
Brewery/Company: FREE HOUSE
◖: Hook Norton Bitter, Goff's Jouster, Timothy Taylor Landlord, Fullers London Pride, Caledonian IPA
Rooms: 4 bedrooms 3 en suite s£45 d£65
Children's Facilities: Licence Portions/Menu Cutlery Games High Chairs Food Warming Changing
Nearby: Cotswold Farm Park, Sudeley Castle, Cotswold Water Park
Notes: Dogs Allowed Garden Food Served Outside Bench, table, patio heaters Parking 15 Coach parties welcome

LECHLADE

SU29

The Trout Inn ♀

St Johns Bridge GL7 3HA
☎ 01367 252313 ▤ 01367 252313
✉ chefpjw@aol.com

Dir: From A40 take A361 then A417. From M4 to Lechlade then A417 to the Trout Inn

Dating from around 1220, a former almshouse with a large garden on the banks of the Thames. Things are generally humming here, with tractor and steam events, and jazz and folk festivals. The interior is all flagstone floors and beams in a bar that overflows into the old boat-house. The extensive menus offer choices ranging from appetising small snacks to pork fillet in a creamy whole-grain mustard sauce; fish pie with haddock and prawns; or sweetcorn, red pepper and spinach puff pastry parcel.

Open: 10-3 6-11 (open all day in Summer) Closed: 25 Dec
Bar Meals: L served all week 12-2 D served all week 7-10 (Sun 7-9.30)
Restaurant: L served all week 12-2 D served all week-Av 3 course · à la carte £16
Brewery/Company: UNIQUE ◖: Courage Best, John Smiths, Bass, Smiles, Bombadier & Guest
Children's Facilities: Fam room Play area Portions/Menu Cutlery Games High Chairs Food Warming
Notes: Dogs Allowed Water Garden Food Served Outside, overlooking Weir Pool Parking 30 Coach parties welcome

LITTLE WASHBOURNE

SO93

Hobnails Inn ♀

Tewkesbury GL20 8NQ
☎ 01242 620237 ▤ 01242 620458
✉ info@hobnailsinn.com

Dir: From J9 of the M5 take A46 towards Evesham then B4077 to Stow-on-the-Wold. Hobnails is 1.5 m on the L

15th-century exposed beams, a log fire and various other character features complement this charming old inn which, until recently, had been owned by the same family for about 250 years. The menu offers the likes of Hobnails' lamb - a half-shoulder slowly roasted until tender and laced with a minted port and red wine sauce; chicken cous-cous; and house risotto with sun-dried tomatoes, onions, peppers, mushrooms and basil. Lighter bites include filled baps and burger with salad and chips.

Open: 12-3 6-11 (Easter-Sept 11-11)
Bar Meals: L served all week 12-2 D served closed Monday (Easter-Sep) 6.30-9.30 (Sun 12-9) Av main course £6.25
Restaurant: D served all week 6.30-9.30 Av 3 course · à la carte £18
Brewery/Company: ENTERPRISE INNS ◖: London Pride, Flowers IPA, Bass, 6X
Children's Facilities: Licence Portions/Menu Cutlery Games High Chairs Food Warming
Nearby: Toddington Steam Railway, Sudley Castle, Ragley Hall
Notes: Dogs Allowed Garden Food Served Outside Large patio area with tables Parking 80 Coach parties welcome

MARSHFIELD

ST77

The Lord Nelson Inn ♀

1 & 2 High Street Chippenham SN14 8LP
☎ 01225 891820 & 891981
✉ clair.vezey@btopenworld.com

Family-run 17th-century coaching inn located in the Cotswolds, in a village on the outskirts of Bath. A friendly atmosphere, various real ales and cosy open fires add to the appeal and character of the place. The Cotswolds is also a haven for hikers and countryside lovers. Appetising menu features the likes of monkfish, fresh salmon, Thai King prawns, and prime fillet of beef garnished with Mont D'or potatoes and a rich Madeira reduction.

Open: 12-2.30 5.30-11 (Winter: Sun 12-3, 6.30-10.30, Summer Sun 12-3, 7-10.30)
Bar Meals: L served all week 12-2 D served all week 6-9 (Sun 12-3, 6-9) Av main course £9.75
Restaurant: L served all week 12-2 D served all week 6-9 Sun 12-3, 6-9 Av 3 course · à la carte £22.50
🍺:Courage Best, Butcombe
Children's Facilities: Portions/Menu Cutlery Games High Chairs Food Warming
Nearby: Bowood House, Bristol Zoo, Bath Park
Notes: Dogs Allowed Garden Food Served Outside small patio area with seating Coach parties welcome

MISERDEN

SO90

The Carpenters Arms 🛏 ♀

Nr Stroud GL6 7JA
☎ 01285 821283
✉ bleninns@clara.net

Dir: Leave A417 at Birdlip, take B4010 toward Stroud, after 3m Miserden signed

Named after the carpenter's workshop on the Miserden Park Estate, this old inn retains its inglenook fireplaces and original stone floors. Worn benches still carry the nameplates used by the locals a century ago to reserve their seats at the bar. Supplemented with daily specials, the main menu includes beer battered cod, chicken breast in honey mustard sauce, and salmon with parsley sauce. Good range of vegetarian dishes. The unspoilt village is very popular with film crews.

Open: 11.30-2.30 6.30-11 (Sun 12-3, 7-10.30)
Bar Meals: L served all week 12-2.30 D served all week 7-9.30 Av main course £5.50 **Restaurant:** L served all week 12-2.30 D served all week 7-9.30
Av 3 course · à la carte £13
Brewery/Company: FREE HOUSE
🍺: Greene King IPA, Wadworths, Guest Beer
Children's Facilities: Licence Portions/Menu High Chairs Food Warming
Nearby: Chickley Hill, Misedan Park, Painswick
Notes: Dogs Allowed Water Garden Food Served Outside garden with patio Parking 22 Coach parties welcome

NEWLAND
SO50

The Ostrich Inn

nr Coleford GL16 8NP
☎ 01594 833260 📠 01594 833260
✉ kathryn@theostrichinn.com

Dir: Follow Monmouth signs from Chepstow (A466), Newland is signed from Redbrook

An early 13th-century inn with a huge open fireplace, old furniture, and friendly pub dog. In the bar expect the likes of olde English sausages, steak and ale pie and three cheese tart. The restaurant offers butterflied boneless trout with a chive butter sauce, tarte tatin of caramelized red onions, goat's cheese and coriander, or rack of lamb. Specials board changes weekly. Eight constantly changing ales always available.

Open: 12-3 6.30-11 (Sat/BHs 6-11)
Bar Meals: L served all week 12-2.30 D served all week 6.30-9.30 Av main course £9.50
Restaurant: L served all week 12-2.30 D served all week 6.30-9.30 (Sat 6-9.30) Av 3 course · à la carte £22
Brewery/Company: FREE HOUSE
🍺: Timothy Taylor Landlord, Pitchfork, Butty Bach, Old Speckled Hen, Abbot Ale, Pigs Ear
Children's Facilities: Portions/Menu Cutlery Games Food Warming
Nearby: Forest of Dean, Clearwell Caves & Puzzle Wood
Notes: Dogs Allowed Water Garden Food Served Outside. Lawn & patio areas Coach parties welcome

PAINSWICK
SO80

The Falcon Inn 🐕 ♀

New Street GL6 6UN
☎ 01452 814222 📠 01452 813377
✉ bleninns@clara.net

Dir: On A46 in centre of Painswick

Boasting the world's oldest known bowling green in its grounds, the Falcon dates from 1554 and stands at the heart of a conservation village. For three centuries it was a courthouse, but today its comfy accommodation and friendly service extends to a drying room for walkers' gear. The seasonal menu might offer game terrine or Greek salad to start, then venison en croute, chicken korma or Irish stew to follow.

Open: 11-4 5.30-11 (Sun 12-4, 6-10.30)
Bar Meals: L served all week 12-2.30 D served all week 7-9.30 Av main course £6.50
Restaurant: L served all week 12-2.30 D served all week 7-9.30 Av 3 course · à la carte £16
Brewery/Company: FREE HOUSE
🍺: Hook Norton Best, Old Hooky, Wadworth 6X, Greene King IPA
Rooms: 12 en suite 4 family s£42 d£68
Children's Facilities: Licence Portions/Menu High Chairs Food Warming
Nearby: Painswick Rococo Gardens, Cotswold Wild Life Park
Notes: Dogs Allowed Water Garden Food Served Outside Courtyard and large bowling green to rear Parking 35 Coach parties welcome

PAINSWICK SO80

The Royal Oak Inn 🐾 ♈

St Mary's Street GL6 6QG
☎ 01452 813129
✉ bleninns@clara.net

Dir: In the centre of Painswick on the A46 between Stroud & Cheltenham

Tucked away behind the church of this conservation village, the Royal Oak features very low ceilings, old paintings and artefacts, and a huge, open fire. In summer, a sun-trap rear courtyard contributes to its atmosphere. Food takes a solidly 'Olde English' approach using fresh produce delivered daily. Starters might include prawns with brown bread and Marie Rose sauce; move on to a variety of grills, sausage and mash or something more elaborate-duck breast with mango and brandy sauce, for example. Good range of snacks too.

Open: 11-2.30 5.30-11
Bar Meals: L served all week 12-2.30 D served all week 7-9.30 Av main course £5.50
Restaurant: L served all week 12-2.30 D served all week 7-9.30 Av 3 course · à la carte £12.50
Brewery/Company: FREE HOUSE
🍺: Hook Norton Best, Wadworth 6X, Black Sheep Bitter plus Guest Ales
Children's Facilities: Portions/Menu High Chairs Food Warming
Nearby: Rococo Gardens, Pomswill Beacon Park
Notes: Dogs Allowed Water Garden Food Served Outside Patio and courtyard

PAXFORD SP13

The Churchill Arms ◉ ♈

Nr Chipping Camden GL55 6XH
☎ 01386 594000 📄 01386 594005
✉ info@thechurchillarms.com

Dir: 2m E of Chipping Campden

In the heart of a picturesque village, the Churchill Arms enjoys glorious views over rolling countryside and is popular with walkers and lovers of outdoor pursuits. Menus change daily: starters might include cod fishcake with pickled cucumber and avocado; game terrine with green tomato chutney; or vanilla risotto with gruyere, smoked haddock and pancetta. For mains, try grilled flounder, sherry, rosemary and tomato; monkfish with sweet and sour sauce and okra; or one of several vegetarian options.

Open: 11-3 6-11
Bar Meals: L served all week 12-2 D served all week 7-9 Av main course £11
Restaurant: L served all week 12-2 D served all week 7-9 Av 3 course · à la carte £22
Brewery/Company: FREE HOUSE
🍺: Hook Norton Bitter, Arkells, Moonlight
Children's Facilities: Portions/Menu High Chairs Food Warming
Nearby: Cotswold Farm Park
Notes: No Dogs (except Assist Dogs) Garden Food Served Coach parties welcome

STROUD   SO80

The Ram Inn

South Woodchester GL5 5EL
☎ 01453 873329 📠 01453 873329
✉ drink@raminn.com

Dir: A46 from Stroud to Nailsworth, R after 2m into S.Woodchester (brown tourist signs)

From the terrace of the 400-year-old Cotswold-stone Ram Inn there are splendid views over five valleys, although proximity to the huge fireplace may prove more appealing in winter. Rib-eye steak, at least two fish dishes, home-made lasagne and Sunday roasts can be expected, washed down by regularly changing real ales. The Stroud Morris Men regularly perform.

Open: 11-11 (Sun 12-10.30)
Bar Meals: L served all week 12-2.30 D served all week 6-9.30 (Sun 12-2.30, 6-8.30) Av main course £7
Restaurant: L served all week 12-2.30 D served all week 6-9.30 Sun 12-2.30, 6-8.30 Av 3 course · à la carte £11 Av 2 course fixed price £9.95
Brewery/Company: FREE HOUSE
🍺: Scottish Courage, John Smiths, Uley Old Spot, Wickwar BOB, Wychwood Hobgoblin, Archers Golden **Children's Facilities:** Portions/Menu Cutlery High Chairs Food Warming Changing **Nearby:** Westonbirt Aboretum, Slimbridge Bird Sanctuary, Owlfen Manor **Notes:** Dogs Allowed Water Garden Food Served Outside 2 large Patio areas, Parking 60 Coach parties welcome

TETBURY   ST89

Gumstool Inn ♀

Calcot Manor GL8 8YJ
☎ 01666 890391 📠 01666 890394
✉ reception@calcotmanor.co.uk

Dir: In Calcot (on jct of A4135 & A46, 3m W of Tetbury)

The Gumstool is the pub at Calcot Manor Hotel, a charmingly converted English farmhouse set around a flower-filled courtyard of ancient barns and stables. Built in the 14th century by Cistercian monks, the inn provides a cosy contrast to the manor, with a real English pub atmosphere. An eclectic menu offers a wide choice of interesting dishes to suit all tastes and appetites; most portions can be either `ample' or `generous', like Portabello mushroom topped with grilled goats cheese and Thai spiced crab cakes with chilli jam.

Open: 11.30-2.30 5.30-11 (Sat 11.30-11, Sun 12-10.30)
Bar Meals: L served all week 12-2 D served all week 7-9.30 Av main course £9.50
Restaurant: L served all week 12-2 D served all week 7-9.30 Av 3 course · à la carte £20
Brewery/Company: FREE HOUSE
🍺: Scottish Courage Courage Directors, Best & Theakston XB, Greene King Spitfire, Wickwar BOB
Children's Facilities: Fam room Play area (OFSTED registered playzone) Cutlery Games High Chairs Food Warming
Notes: No Dogs Garden Food Served Outside Parking 100 Coach parties welcome

ALRESFORD   SU53

The Globe on the Lake ⌕ ⚲

The Soke Broad Street SO24 9DB
☎ 01962 732294 ▤ 01962 736211
✉ duveen-conway@supanet.com

On the banks of a reed-fringed lake and wildfowl sanctuary, The Globe is in a glorious setting. Inside the bar, a log fire blazes on cooler days, while a smart dining room and unusual garden room share the stunning outlook over the water. In summer freshly prepared food can be enjoyed in the garden and on the heated rear terrace. The blackboard features several fish dishes, like tiger prawns cooked with fresh lime and chilli.

Open: 11-3 6-11 (Winter Sun 12-8, Summer wknd 11-11) Closed: 25-26 Dec
Bar Meals: L served all week 12-2 D served all week 6.30-9.30 (Winter Sun to 8) Av main course £8.25
Restaurant: L served all week 12-2 D served all week 6.30-9 (Winter Sun to 7)
Brewery/Company: UNIQUE PUB CO LTD
🍺: Wadworth 6X, Scottish Courage Directors,Henley Brakspear Bitter
Children's Facilities: Fam room Play area (Play house) Portions/Menu Cutlery High Chairs Changing
Nearby: Watercress Line Steam Railway
Notes: No Dogs (except Assist Dogs) Water Large lakeside garden Coach parties welcome

BASINGSTOKE   SU65

Hoddington Arms ⌕ ⚲

Upton Grey RG25 2RL
☎ 01256 862371 ▤ 01256 862371
✉ monca777@aol.com

Log fires and 18th-century beams contribute to the relaxing atmosphere at this traditional pub, which is located near the duck pond at Upton Grey, Hampshire's best kept village for several years. In addition to a choice of bar snacks and a set price menu of the day, blackboard specials include the likes of cod and pancetta fish cake, minted lamb casserole, and home-cooked Hoddington pies. There's also a peaceful rear terrace and garden.

Open: 12-3 6-11
Bar Meals: L served Mon-Sun 12-2 D served Mon-Sat 7-9.30 Av main course £8
Restaurant: L served Mon-Sun 12-2 D served Mon-Sun 7-9.30 Av 3 course · à la carte £19 Av 2 course fixed price £10
Brewery/Company: GREENE KING
🍺: Greene King IPA, Old Speckled Hen, Ruddles Best, Fosters
Children's Facilities: Fam room Play area (Outside play area) Portions/Menu Games High Chairs Food Warming
Notes: Dogs Allowed Water Garden Large patio with play area Parking 30 Coach parties welcome

HAMPSHIRE

BENTWORTH   SU64

The Sun Inn ♀

Sun Hill Alton GU34 5JT
☎ 01420 562338

This delightful flower-decked pub is located down a narrow lane on the edge of Bentworth village; it's the first building in or the last one out, depending on which way you are travelling, and always seems to come as a surprise. The two original cottages have been opened up to make three interconnecting rooms, each with its own log fire. Lots of pews, settles and scrubbed pine tables add to the relaxed atmosphere, and the place is especially inviting in the evening when the table candles are lit. Food is hearty and traditional, with the likes of sausages; liver and bacon with creamy mash; cheesy haddock bake; giant filled Yorkshire puddings; Mediterranean lamb; and venison in Guiness and pickled walnuts. Everything, ranging from the 14 varieties of soup to dessert is home made.

Open: 12-3 6-11 (Sun 12-10.30)
Bar Meals: L served all week 12-2 D served all week 7-9.30
Brewery/Company: FREE HOUSE
◀: Cheriton Pots Ale, Ringwood Best & Old Thumper, Brakspear Bitter, Fuller's London Pride
Children's Facilities: Fam room Cutlery High Chairs Food Warming
Notes: Dogs Allowed Water Garden Food Served Outside Parking

BROCKENHURST   SU30

The Filly Inn 🍲

Lymington Road Setley SO42 7UF
☎ 01590 623449 📠 01590 623449
🌐 pub@fillyinn.co.uk

One of the most picturesque, cosy traditional pubs in the heart of the New Forest. Locals attest to frequent sightings of George, the resident ghost, thought to be a long-dead, repentant highwayman. The far from spooky menu offers a wide range of bar snacks of baguettes, filled jacket potatoes and home-baked pies of the day. Daily specials could include braised pheasant, roast ribs in a barbecue sauce, or Filly haddock in a creamy wine sauce of prawns. There is also a Hindi vegetarian menu.

Open: 10-11
Bar Meals: L served all week (Summer-Food served all day) 10-2.15 D served all week (Summer-Food served all day) 6.30-10
Restaurant: L served all week (Summer-Food served all day) 10-2.15 D served all week (Summer-Food served all day) 6.30-10 Av 3 course · à la carte £19.50
Brewery/Company: FREE HOUSE
◀: Ringwood Best, Old Thumper, Badger Tanglefoot
Rooms: 6 bedrooms 5 en suite s£55 d£65
(♦♦♦) Children's Facilities: Play area (Garden) Portions/Menu Games High Chairs Food Warming **Nearby:** Beaulieu
Notes: Dogs Allowed Water Garden Food Served Outside 0.75 acre lawn Parking 90 Coach parties welcome

BROOK SU21

The Bell Inn ★★★ @ ☜

nr Lyndhurst SO43 7HE
☎ 023 80812214 📠 023 80813958
✉ bell@bramshaw.co.uk

Dir: From M27 J1 (Cadnam) take B3078 signed Brook, 0.5m on R

Dating from 1782, this handsome listed inn is part of Bramshaw Golf Club and has remained in the same family for its entire history. The inn, retains many period features, particularly the imposing inglenook fireplace. The quality of cuisine is a source of pride, reflected in a bar menu that changes daily and a good wine list. There is something for every taste, with fresh locally-caught fish and game in season. Starters include duck leg confit with Caesar-style salad. Continue with honey and mustard chicken supreme with couscous.

Open: 11-11 (Sun 12-10.30)
Bar Meals: L served all week 12-2.30 D served all week 6.30-9.30 Av main course £8.95
Restaurant: L served all week 12-2 D served all week 6.30-9.30 Av 3 course fixed price £14.95
Brewery/Company: FREE HOUSE
🍺: Ringwood Best, Scottish Courage Courage Best, John Smiths, Worthington, 6X
Rooms: 25 en suite s£65 d£90
Children's Facilities: Fam room Play area (Play area in garden) Portions/Menu Cutlery Games High Chairs Food Warming Changing
Notes: No Dogs (except Assist Dogs) Garden Food Served Outside Parking 60 Coach parties welcome

CHALTON SU71

The Red Lion ☜ ♀

Nr Horndean PO8 0BG
☎ 023 92592246 📠 023 92596915
✉ redlionchalton@aol.com

Dir: Just off A3 between Horndean & Petersfield. Take exit near Queen Elizabeth Country Park

Thatched and immaculately maintained, Hampshire's oldest pub dates back to 1147, and was originally a workshop for craftsmen building the Norman church opposite. Imaginative dishes from the daily menu include guinea fowl in Calvados, teriyaki beef and fresh Mahi Mahi fish in coconut, as well as the usual pub snacks. Large garden has spectacular views of the South Downs.

Open: 11-3 6-11 RS: 25-26 Dec closed evening
Bar Meals: L served all week 12-2 D served Mon-Sat 6.30-9.30 Av main course £8.75
Restaurant: L served all week 12-2 D served Mon-Sat 6.30-9.30
Brewery/Company: GEORGE GALE & CO
🍺: Gales Butser, Winter Brew, GB & HSB
Children's Facilities: Fam room Portions/Menu Cutlery Games High Chairs Food Warming
Nearby: Roman Villa, Buster Ancient Farm, Country Park
Notes: Dogs Allowed Dogs welcome in public bar Garden Food Served Outside Parking 80 Coach parties welcome

DAMERHAM — SU11

The Compasses Inn ◆◆◆◆ 🛏 ♀

Nr Fordingbridge SP6 3HQ
☎ 01725 518231 📠 01725 518880
✉ info@compassesinn.net

Dir: From Fordingbridge (A338) follow signs for Sandleheath/Damerham.

Located in the village centre overlooking the cricket pitch, this 300-year-old coaching inn was once almost self-sufficient, with its own brew tower, dairy, butchery and well. Atmosphere a-plenty in both of the bars, and in the cottagey bedrooms. Real ales, including their own brew and regular guests, and a fine collection of over 100 malt whiskies. Locally produced fresh food, with plenty of fish on offer.

Open: 11-3 6-11 (all day Sat, Sun 12-4, 7-10.30)
Bar Meals: L served all week 12-2.30 D served all week 7-9.30 (Sun 7-9) Av main course £7.95 **Restaurant:** L served all week 12-2.30 D served all week 7-9.30 Sun 7-9 Av 3 course à la carte £17 **Brewery/Company:** FREE HOUSE ◀: Ringwood Best, Hop Back Summer Lightning **Rooms:** 6 en suite 1 family room s£39.50 d£69 **Children's Facilities:** Licence Play area (Outside swings & see saw) Portions/Menu Cutlery High Chairs Food Warming Changing
Nearby: Paulton's Park, Moors Valley Country Park, New Forest
Notes: Dogs Allowed By arrangement Garden Food Served Outside Large garden, Parking 30 Coach parties welcome

EAST TYTHERLEY — SU22

Star Inn ◆◆◆◆ ◎◎ 🛏 ♀

Nr Romsey SO51 0LW
☎ 01794 340225 📠 01794 340225
✉ info@starinn-uk.com

Dir: 5m N of Romsey off A3057. Take L turn Dunbridge B3084. Left for Awbridge & Lockerley. Through Lockerley then 1m

A 16th-century country inn, on the village cricket ground, with award-winning food. Dine where you like, in the bar, in the main dining room, or outside on the patio. There are two menus, the carte and the classical. The former offers the more sophisticated dishes and there are vegetarian options too.

Open: 11-2.30 6-11 **Closed:** 26 Dec
Days closed: Mon **Bar Meals:** L served Tue-Sun 12-2 D served Tue-Sun 7-9 Av main course £8.50
Restaurant: L served Tue-Sun 12-2 D served Tue-Sun 7-9 Av 3 course · à la carte £20 Av 3 course fixed price £20
Brewery/Company: FREE HOUSE ◀: Ringwood Best plus guest beers **Rooms:** 3 en suite 2 family room s£50 d£70 **Children's Facilities:** Play area Portions/Menu Cutlery Games High Chairs Food Warming
Notes: Dogs Allowed Water bowl Garden Food Served Outside Patio area, country garden with furniture. Parking 60 Coach parties welcome

FORDINGBRIDGE   SU11

The Augustus John ☜ ♀

116 Station Road SP6 1DG
☎ 01425 652098
✉ peter@augustusjohn.com

Named after the renowned British painter who lived in the village (the pub was also his local), this unassuming brick building has developed a reputation as a smart dining venue. The daily changing menu is based on seasonally available produce. Liver and bacon with mash, steak and Guinness casserole, and rack of lamb are favourite dishes along with daily fresh fish and vegetarian specialities such as baked avocado with fresh tomato and basil concasse.

Open: 11.30-3.30 6-12
Bar Meals: L served all week 11.30-2 D served all week 6.30-9 Av main course £10
Restaurant: L served all week 11.30-2 D served all week 6.30-9 Av 3 course · à la carte £18
Brewery/Company: ELDRIDGE POPE
🍺: Bass, Tetley, Flowers IPA
Children's Facilities: Play area Portions/Menu Cutlery High Chairs Food Warming
Nearby: New Forest
Notes: Dogs Allowed Garden Food Served Outside Parking 40 Coach parties welcome

LYMINGTON   SZ39

Mayflower Inn ♀

Kings Saltern Road SO41 3QD
☎ 01590 672160 📠 01590 679180
✉ info@themayflower.uk.com

Dir: A337 towards New Milton, L at rdbt by White Hart, L to Rookes Ln, R at mini-rdbt, pub 0.75m

Solidly built mock-Tudor inn by the water's edge with views over the Solent and Lymington River. It's a favourite with yachtsmen and walkers with dogs, and welcomes families with its purpose-built play area for children and on-going summer barbecue, weather permitting. The bar menu offers sandwiches, light meals, main meals and puds. For dinner in the non-smoking restaurant, expect mains like lamb en croûte or roasted duck sizzler.

Open: 11-11 (Sun 12-10.30)
Bar Meals: L served all week 12-9.30 D served all week 6.30-9.30 Av main course £7
Restaurant: L served all week 12-9.30 D served all week 6.30-9.30 Av 3 course · à la carte £20
Brewery/Company: ENTERPRISE INNS
🍺: Ringwood Best, Fuller's London Pride, Greene King Abbot Ale & Old Speckled Hen
Rooms: 6 en suite 2 family room s£45 d£65
Children's Facilities: Play area (Large garden with play area) Portions/Menu High Chairs Food Warming
Nearby: Sailing on river, New Forest
Notes: Dogs Allowed Water, baskets Garden Food Served Outside Large lawns Parking 30

LYNDHURST SU30

The Trusty Servant 🔊

Minstead SO43 7FY
☎ 02380 812137

Popular New Forest pub overlooking the village green, retaining many original Victorian features. The famous sign is taken from a 16th-century Winchester scholar's painting portraying the qualities of an ideal college servant. Menu choices include seafood chowder, smoked salmon and cream cheese roulade, sea bass, red snapper, skate wing, tenderloin of pork with wild mushrooms and Marsala sauce, and venison with blueberry and port sauce. Children will love the large garden.

Open: 11-11 (Sun 12-10.30)
Bar Meals: L served all week 12-2.30 D served all week 7-10
Restaurant: L served all week 12-2.30 D served all week 7-10
Brewery/Company: ENTERPRISE INNS
🍺: Ringwood Best, Fuller's London Pride, Wadworth 6X, Gale's HSB
Children's Facilities: Fam room Portions/Menu High Chairs Food Warming
Nearby: Paultons Park, Longdown Dairy Farm, Owl & Otter Centre
Notes: Dogs Allowed Water Garden Food Served Outside Heated barn area seats 30, picnic benches Parking 16 Coach parties welcome

NORTH WALTHAM SU54

The Fox ♀

Basingstoke RG25 2BE
☎ 01256 397288 📠 01256 398564
❸ info@thefox.org

Dir: From M3 J7 take A30 towards Winchester. Village signposted on R. Take 2nd signed rd.

Built as three farm cottages in 1624, this peaceful village pub is situated down a quiet country lane enjoying splendid views across fields and farmland. Its three large flat gardens also have attractive flower beds. The menu changes monthly to reflect the seasonal produce available, but expect dishes such as chicken breast stuffed with parma ham, baby spinach and brie; Hampshire venison on a potato rösti and a trio of award-winning sausages with mash and onion gravy.

Open: 11-12 (all day wknd)
Bar Meals: L served all week 12.30-2.30 D served all week 6.30-10 Av main course £8
Restaurant: L served all week 12.30-2.30 D served all week 6.30-10 Av 3 course · à la carte £19.50
Brewery/Company: INNSPIRED
🍺: Scottish Courage Courage Best, Gales HSB, Oakleaf Farmhouse, Bombardier
Children's Facilities: Licence Play area (Activity area) Portions/Menu High Chairs Food Warming
Notes: Dogs Allowed Water Garden Food Served Outside Large, flat grass area Parking 40 Coach parties welcome

PORTSMOUTH & SOUTHSEA SZ69

The Still & West ☺ ♀

2 Bath Square Old Portsmouth PO1 2JL
☎ 023 92821567 📠 02302 826560
Dir: Bath Square, top of Broad Street

Nautically themed pub close to HMS Victory and enjoying excellent views of Portsmouth Harbour and the Isle of Wight. Built in 1504, the main bar ceilings are hand-painted with pictures relating to local shipping history. Plenty of fish on the menu including trout, black beam, seafood paella, and the famous Still & West fish grill of fresh fish and mussels.

Open: Mon-Sat 10-11,
Sun 11-10.30 Closed: 25 Dec
Bar Meals: L served all week 12-3 (Sun L 12-4) Av main course £5.95
Restaurant: L served all week 12-2.30 D served all week 6-9 Av 3 course · à la carte £17 **Brewery/Company:** GALES ◀: HSB, GB, Butsers,Stella, Fosters
Children's Facilities: Portions/Menu High Chairs Food Warming Changing
Nearby: Historic docklands, 10 hole pitch and putt **Notes:** No Dogs (except Assist Dogs) In the garden only Garden Food Served Outside Overlooks harbour Coach parties welcome

ROMSEY SU32

The Mill Arms ♦♦♦♦ ☺ ♀

Barley Hill Dunbridge SO51 0LF
☎ 01794 340401 📠 01794 340401
✉ millarms@aol.co.uk

This 18th-century coaching inn is set in a picturesque Test Valley village. The inn is surrounded by colourful gardens and offers a warm welcome inside, with its flagstone floors, oak beams and open fires; there's even a skittle alley with its own private bar to hire! The fun continues with the selection of real ales: Test Tickler is specially brewed for the pub, or how about a pint of Mottisfont Meddler? The wide selection of food includes traditional pub favourites, as well as a range of steaks and salads. Starters include crab cakes on a sweet chilli sauce, followed by home-made steak and ale pie; or pan-fried duck breast with apricot and thyme gravy.

Open: 12-3 6-11 (open all day Fri-Sun)
Bar Meals: L served all week 12-2.30 D served all week 6-9.30
Restaurant: L&D served all week
Brewery/Company: FREE HOUSE
◀: Dunbridge Test Tickler, Mottisfont Meddler
Rooms: 6 en suite s£50 d£50
Children's Facilities: Play area (Wendy house & bouncy castle) Portions/Menu Cutlery High Chairs Food Warming
Nearby: Paultons Park, Marwell Zoo
Notes: Dogs Allowed Water Garden Food Served Outside Large garden, patio area Parking 90 Coach parties welcome

ROWLAND'S CASTLE   SU71

The Fountain Inn ◆◆◆◆

34 The Green PO9 6AB
☎ 023 9241 2291 ▤ 02392 412 291
✉ fountaininn@amserve.com

*Once a coach house, and now a lovingly
refurbished Georgian building on a village
green. Owned by one-time Van Morrison band
member Herbie Armstrong, who holds
frequent live music gigs here. New menus
from a Savoy-trained chef offer 'real' corned
beef, parsnip and carrot hash; and potted
Selsey crab and prawns at both lunchtime and
dinner. Some dishes, like beetroot risotto,
broad beans and Parmesan, for instance,
appear for dinner only.*

Open: 12-2.30 5-11 (Fri-Sun 12-11)
Bar Meals: L served Tue-Sun 12-3 D served
Tue-Sat 6-10.30
Restaurant: L served Tue-Sun 12-3 D served
Tue-Sat 6-10.30
🍺: Ruddles IPA, Abbot, Ruddles Cask,
Kronenberg 1994
Rooms: 4 en suite 1 family room s£25 d£50
Children's Facilities: Play area (Slides swings
& climbing frame) Portions/Menu High Chairs
Nearby: Staunton Park, Hayling Island,
Stansted House
Notes: Dogs Allowed Garden Food Served
Outside Enclosed back garden, eight tables
Parking 20 Coach parties welcome

SOUTHAMPTON   SU41

The White Star Tavern & Dining Rooms ♀

28 Oxford Street SO14 3DJ
☎ 020 8082 1990 ▤ 023 8090 4982
✉ manager@whitestartavern.co.uk

*Located in the historic and sensitively restored
part of the city close to Ocean Village and the
marina, what was formerly a seafarers' hotel is
a blend of old and new; a cosy bar area with
original flagstone floors and fireplaces, and a
stylish panelled dining room with huge
windows. The tavern prides itself on a
frequently changing modern British menu
using fresh and locally sourced ingredients.
Quality dishes include terrine of Dorset ham
and parsley, crab and cucumber risotto, and
confit lamb shoulder. On sunny days patrons
can enjoy a cocktail and watch the world go
by while dining al fresco on pavement seating.*

Open: 12-11 Closed: 25-26 Dec, 1 Jan
Bar Meals: L served all week 12-3 Av main
course £13
Restaurant: L served all week 12-3 D served
all week 6.30-10.30 Sun 12-9
Av 3 course · à la carte £20
🍺:London Pride, Bass
Children's Facilities: Portions/Menu High
Chairs Food Warming
Nearby: New Forest, Poultons Park
Notes: No Dogs (except Assist Dogs)

WARSASH   SU40

The Jolly Farmer Country Inn 🐾 ♀

29 Fleet End Road Southampton SO31 9JH
☎ 01489 572500 📄 01489 885847
✉ mail@thejollyfarmeruk.com

Dir: Exit M27 Jct 9, towards A27 Fareham,
turn R onto Warsash Rd Follow for 2m then
L onto Fleet End Rd

*Not far from the Hamble River, this pub has
an Irish landlord with a famous sense of
humour-you won't miss the multi-coloured
classic car parked outside. The pub also has
its own golf society and cricket team. The bars
are furnished in rustic style with farming
equipment on walls and ceilings, there's a
patio for al fresco eating. The menu offers
local fish, salads and grills, as well as
specialities like medallions of beef fillet with
brandy and peppercorn sauce.*

Open: 11-11
Bar Meals: L served all week 12-2.30
D served all week 6-10 Av main course £6.95
Restaurant: L served all week 12-2.30
D served all week 6-10
Av 3 course · à la carte £15
Brewery/Company: WHITBREAD
🍺: Gale's HSB, Fuller's London Pride,
Interbrew Flowers IPA
Children's Facilities: Fam room Play area
(Swings, See-saw, Wendy house, castle)
Portions/Menu Cutlery Games High Chairs
Food Warming **Notes:** Dogs Allowed Water
Garden Food Served Outside Large play area
Parking 50 Coach parties welcome

DORMINGTON   SO54

Yew Tree Inn 🐾

Len Gee's Restaurant Priors Frome HR1 4EH
☎ 01432 850467 📄 01432 850467
✉ len@lengees.info

Dir: A438 Hereford to Ledbury, turn at
Dormington towards Mordiford, 0.5m on L.

*This former hop pickers' pub has fantastic
panoramic views over Hereford towards the
Black Mountains of Wales. With many country
walks in the surrounding area, it is the ideal
place to take a relaxing stroll before enjoying
a home-cooked meal in Len Gee's restaurant.
The menu features classic European dishes, as
well as a splendid carvery, with four joints of
meat and a wide selection of vegetables. For
something a little different, try the tempting
fish specials, including baked red snapper
with lime butter and chargrilled shark with
chilli oil and peppers.*

Open: 12-2 7-11 (Closed Tue Jan-Mar)
Bar Meals: L served all week 12-2 D served
all week 7-9 Av main course £8.95
Restaurant: L served all week 12-2 D served
all week 7-9 Av 3 course · à la carte £18 Av 3
course fixed price £14.95
Brewery/Company: FREE HOUSE 🍺:
Carlsberg-Tetley Tetley, Wye Valley, Greene
King Old Speckled Hen
Children's Facilities: Portions/Menu High
Chairs Food Warming
Notes: Dogs Allowed Waterbowls Garden
Food Served Outside Terraced Garden with
views Parking 40 Coach parties welcome

DORSTONE SO34

The Pandy Inn ♀

Golden Valley HR3 6AN
☎ 01981 550273 ▤ 01981 550277

Dir: Off B4348 W of Hereford

Oliver Cromwell was a frequent visitor to the Pandy, the oldest inn in Herefordshire, built in 1185 to house workers building Dorstone Church. Alongside the usual pub favourites, the South African owners offer traditional dishes from back home (bobotie and bredie) along with duck stirfry, courgette bake with goats' cheese, pork fillet with apricots, and lamb's liver with mash and onions, plus various hot and cold desserts.

Open: 12-3 6-11 (Sat 12-11, Sun 12-10.30, Mon 6-11 only)
Bar Meals: L served Tue-Sun 12-2.30
D served all week 7-9.30 Av main course
£9.50 **Restaurant:** L served Tue-Sun 12-2.30
D served all week 7-9.30
Brewery/Company: FREE HOUSE
◀: Wye Valley Butty Bach & Dorothy
Goodbody **Children's Facilities:** Licence
Play area (Swings) Portions/Menu Cutlery
Games Food Warming Changing
Notes: Dogs Allowed Garden Food Served
Outside Large garden, lots of benches and
tables Parking 50 Coach parties welcome

HAMPTON BISHOP SO53

The Bunch of Carrots ♀

Hereford HR1 4JR
☎ 01432 870237 ▤ 01432 870237
● bunchofcarrotts@buccaneer.co.uk

Dir: From Hereford take A4103, A438,
then B4224

Friendly pub with real fires, old beams and flagstones. Its name comes from a rock formation in the River Wye which runs alongside the pub. There is an extensive menu plus a daily specials board, a carvery, salad buffet and simple bar snacks.

Open: 11-3 6-11
Bar Meals: L served all week 12-2.30
D served all week 6-10 (Sun 9)
Restaurant: L served all week 12-2
D served all week 6-10
Brewery/Company: FREE HOUSE
◀: Bass, Hook Norton, Directors, Theakstons
Children's Facilities: Play area Cutlery
High Chairs
Nearby: Cathedral, Brecon Mountains
Notes: Dogs Allowed Garden Food Served
Outside Parking 100 Coach parties welcome

LEDBURY   SO73

The Feathers Hotel ★★★ @ ⊚ ⏟

High Street HR8 1DS
☎ 01531 635266 📠 01531 638955
📧 mary@feathers-ledbury.co.uk

Dir: S from Worcester A449, E from Hereford A438, N from Gloucester A417.

The Feathers is a distinctive building with its striking black and white timbered frontage. Travellers have been coming here since Elizabethan times, and the fine old inn retains it oak beams, panelled walls and open log fires. Meals are served in Quills Restaurant, Fuggles Brasserie and the Top Bar. Locally sourced meats are a feature, including Herefordshire beef, lamb, duck and pheasant.

Open: 11-11 (Sun 12-10.30)
Bar Meals: L served all week 12-2 D served all week 7-9.30 Av main course £14
Restaurant: L served all week 12-2 D served all week 7-9.30 Av 3 course · à la carte £25
Brewery/Company: FREE HOUSE
🍺: Coors Worthington's Bitter, Interbrew Bass, Fuller's London Pride,
Rooms: 19 en suite 3 family room s£79.50 d£99.50
Children's Facilities: Fam room Games High Chairs
Nearby: Eastnor Castle, Queens Wood
Notes: No Dogs (except Assist Dogs) Garden Food Served Outside Courtyard garden Parking 30 Coach parties welcome

ORLETON   SO46

The Boot Inn

SY8 4HN
☎ 01568 780228 📠 01568 780228
📧 thebootorleton@hotmail.com

Dir: Follow the A49 S from London (approx 7 miles) to the B4362 (Woofferton), 1.5 miles off B4362 turn L. The Boot Inn is in the centre of the village

Relaxed and welcoming, this black and white timbered inn dates from the 16th century, and its peaceful atmosphere is undisturbed by music or games. In winter a blazing fire in the inglenook warms the bar, where an appetising selection of snacks and sandwiches extends the menu along with a list of specials: fish mixed grill, rack of lamb, local game in season, and cheese and lentil loaf; real ales and cider are on tap. Behind the pub is a one-up, one-down timbered house, believed to be the smallest in Herefordshire.

Open: 12-3 6-11 (Sun 12-3, 6-10.30)
Bar Meals: L served Tue-Sun 12-2 D served all week 7-9 Av main course £5
Restaurant: D served all week 7-9 Av 3 course · à la carte £13
Brewery/Company: FREE HOUSE
🍺: Hobsons Best, Local Real Ales
Children's Facilities: Licence Play area Portions/Menu Games High Chairs Food Warming
Notes: Dogs Allowed Water Garden Food Served Outside Lawn, BBQ area Parking 20 Coach parties welcome

HEREFORDSHIRE

PEMBRIDGE SO35

New Inn 🐾

Market Square Leominster HR6 9DZ
☎ 01544 388427 🖷 01544 388427

Dir: From M5 J7 take A44 W through
Leominster towards Llandrindod Wells

*A black and white timbered inn at the centre
of a picture-postcard village full of quaint
cottages. It dates from the early 14th century,
and is one of the oldest pubs in England, once
used as the local courthouse and reputedly
haunted. Full of old beams, wonky walls and
worn flagstones. The menu lists home-cooked
dishes such as creamed kidneys on toast, duck
breast in port and cranberry sauce, port cider
casserole with sage dumplings, fish and chips,
seafood stew, and T-bone steak in Stilton
sauce.*

Open: 11-2.30 6-11
Bar Meals: L served all week 12-2 D served
all week 7-9.30
Restaurant: L served 12-2 D served 7-9.30
Brewery/Company: FREE HOUSE
🍺: Fuller's London Pride, Kingdom Bitter,
Wood Shropshire Lad, Black Sheep Best,
Timothy Taylor
Children's Facilities: Fam room
Portions/Menu High Chairs Food Warming
Nearby: Small Breeds Farm Kington, Judges
Lodge Prestiegne, Ludlow Castle
Notes: No Dogs (except Assist Dogs) Garden
Food Served Outside Patio, seating under the
Market Sq Parking 25

PEMBRIDGE SO35

The Cider House Restaurant

Dunkerton's Cider Mill Luntley nr Leominster
HR6 9ED
☎ 01544 388161 🖷 01544 388654

Dir: W on A44 from Leominster, L in
Pembridge centre by New Inn, 1m on L

*A converted, half-timbered 16th-century barn
with natural oak beams, and beautiful view
over rolling countryside. Susie and Ivor
Dunkerton started the restaurant after years
of cider-making on the farm, and are
dedicated to fresh local produce and home
cooking. Expect carrot and apple soup with
sesame bread; leek and almond tartlet with
sorrel sauce; or organic Hereford beef, cider
and parsley pie with red onion relish. Breads,
cakes and desserts all made on the premises.*

Open: 10-5 (Please telephone)
Closed: 1 Oct-Easter; Sun, Mon & Tues except
hols **Bar Meals:** L served Wed-Sat 12-2.30
Av main course £10
Restaurant: L served Wed-Sat 12-2.30
Av 3 course · à la carte £18.50
Brewery/Company: FREE HOUSE
🍺: Caledonian Golden Promise
Children's Facilities: Portions/Menu Cutlery
High Chairs Food Warming
Nearby: Small Breeds Centre, Croft Ambrey,
Teddy Bear Centre
Notes: No Dogs (except Assist Dogs) Terrace
overlooking fields Parking 30 Coach parties
welcome

ROSS-ON-WYE   SO52

The Moody Cow 🐨 ♀

Upton Bishop HR9 7TT
☎ 01989 780470

The Moody Cow is an old stone-built inn with a patio area out front offering plenty of seating in summer. Inside, you can eat in the Fresco or the restaurant. One extensive menu serves all, supplemented by daily blackboard specials. Options include chef's bouillabaisse, Moody's Caesar salad, BLT sandwich, tempura battered king prawns, and pasta carbonara. Main dishes are divided between unchanging staples-freshly battered cod and chips, chicken or king prawn jalfrezi, and Moody Cow Pie, plus more elaborate dishes. Everything is home made and freshly cooked to order.

Open: 12-2.30 6.30-11 (Sun 12-3)
Days closed: Sun eve, Mon
Bar Meals: L served Tues-Sun 12-2 D served Tues-Sat 6.30-9.30 Av main course £10.95
Restaurant: L served Tues-Sun 12-2 D served Tues-Sat 6.30-9.30 Av 3 course · à la carte £18.95 **Brewery/Company:** FREE HOUSE
🍺: Cats Whiskers, Hook Norton Best, Wye Valley Best **Children's Facilities:** Portions/Menu Games High Chairs Food Warming **Nearby:** Butterfly Maze, Symonds Yat, Forest of Dean
Notes: Dogs Allowed Water provided Garden Food Served Outside Patio area Parking 40 Coach parties welcome

TILLINGTON   SO44

The Bell

HR4 8LE
☎ 01432 760395 📠 01432 760580
📧 beltill@aol.com

Popular family-run pub in an area renowned for its apple orchards and fruit farms-a good base for exploring the scenic countryside of the Welsh Borders. Plenty of character features inside, including a new English oak floor in the lounge bar. Good and appetising menu features fresh cod in batter, pork fillet medallions, Mrs Jessop's lamb cutlets, pheasant supreme, and mussels steamed with fresh herbs and Indian spices. Various grills and a choice of 'winter warmer' dishes such as flamed rib-eye steak and beef, and Wye Valley ale and mushroom pie.

Open: 11-3 6-11 (Sat all day, Sun to 5)
Bar Meals: L served all week 12-2.15
D served Mon-Sat 6-9.15 (Sun 12-2.30)
Av main course £7.50
Restaurant: L served all week 12-2.15
D served Mon-Sat 6-9.15
Av 3 course · à la carte £20
🍺: London Pride, Hereford Bitter, local ales
Children's Facilities: Play area (Tree-house, tunnell, swings, slide) Portions/Menu Cutlery Games High Chairs Food Warming
Nearby: Mountain boarding
Notes: Dogs Allowed In public bar Garden Food Served Outside Small paved area & large lawn with tables Parking 60

HEREFORDSHIRE

ULLINGSWICK SO54

Three Crowns Inn @@ ♉

Hereford HR1 3JQ
☎ 01432 820279 📠 01432 820279
✉ info@threecrownsinn.com

Dir: From Burley Gate rdbt take A465 toward Bromyard, after 2m L to Ullingswick, L after 0.5m, pub 0.5m on R

An unspoilt country pub in deepest rural Herefordshire, where food sources are so local their distance away is referred to in fields, rather than miles. New parterres in the garden give additional space for growing varieties of herbs, fruit and vegetables. The menus change daily, but there is always fish, such as line-caught poached monkfish. Soufflés often appear too. Meat dishes have included braised belly of Berkshire pork, and confit of Gressingham duck. Tuesday tasting evenings feature a set four-course dinner.

Open: 12-2.30 7-11 (May-Aug 12-3, 6-11)
Closed: 2wks from Dec 25 **Days closed:** Mon
Bar Meals: L served all week 12-3 D served all week 7-10.30
Restaurant: L served all week 12-2 D served all week 7-9.30
Brewery/Company: FREE HOUSE
🍺: Hobsons Best, Wye Valley Butty Bach & Dorothy Goodbody's
Children's Facilities: Portions/Menu Cutlery Games High Chairs Food Warming Changing
Notes: No Dogs (except Assist Dogs) except when food is being served in bar, Garden Food Served Outside Formal garden Parking 20

WELLINGTON SO44

The Wellington

HR4 8AT
☎ 01432 830367
✉ thewellington@hotmail.com

Dir: Take Wellington turning between Hereford & Leominster on the A49

A Victorian country pub, with original open fireplaces, antique furniture, and a good selection of real ales and local ciders. A meal from the changing restaurant menu might be locally smoked salmon with beetroot and lime relish; Herefordshire rib-eye steak with Roquefort butter; and treacle tart with clotted cream. Local sausages are a speciality. A bar menu offers an enticing range of lighter meals, and a good value children's section.

Open: 12-3 6-11 (Sun 12-3, 7-10.30) **Days closed:** Mon lunch
Bar Meals: L served Tue-Sun 12-2 D served Mon-Sat 7-10 Av main course £11.50
Restaurant: L served Tue-Sun 12-2 D served Mon-Sat 7-10 Av 3 course · à la carte £20 Av 2 course fixed price £6.95
🍺:Hobsons, Wye Valley Butty Bach, Coors Hancocks HB, Guest Real Ales
Children's Facilities: Play area (Small play area in garden) Portions/Menu Cutlery Games High Chairs Food Warming
Nearby: Hampton Court, Queenswood Country Park
Notes: Dogs Allowed Water Garden Food Served Outside Beer garden, ample seating Parking 20 Coach parties welcome

WHITNEY-ON-WYE SO24

Rhydspence Inn ★★ ⌂

HR3 6EU
☎ 01497 831262 📠 01497 831751
✉ info@rhydspence-inn.co.uk

Dir: N of A438 1m W of Whitney-on-Wye

In the 14th-century it was a manorial hall house, but by Tudor times it had become an inn used by Welsh and Irish drovers taking the Black Ox Trail to markets as far away as London. Different menus apply in each area, the elegant dining room, brasserie or bar, all overlooking the Wye Valley. Fillet of Hereford steak, Welsh lamb, peppered venison, and grilled Dover sole are near certainties, along with grills, hot and spicy curry, and vegetarian options. Ask for the interesting explanation of the pub's name.

Open: 11-2.30 7-11 Closed: 2 wks in Jan
Bar Meals: L served all week 11-2 D served all week 7-9.30 Av main course £8.50
Restaurant: L served all week 11-2 D served all week 7-9.30 Av 3 course · à la carte £23
Brewery/Company: FREE HOUSE
🍺: Robinsons Best, Interbrew Bass
Rooms: 7 en suite s£37.50 d£75
Children's Facilities: Fam room Play area (Large grass area) Cutlery High Chairs Changing
Notes: No Dogs (except Assist Dogs) Garden Food Served Outside 2/3 acres, mostly lawn Parking 30

ASHWELL TL23

The Three Tuns ⌂ ♀

High Street SG7 5NL
☎ 01462 742107 📠 01462 743662
✉ claire@tuns.co.uk

There are many original features in this 19th-century inn, providing an old-world atmosphere in the heart of Ashwell village. The hotel was completely refurbished in 1998, and the chefs have established an excellent local reputation for home-cooked food, and the menus are changed daily. Typical choices include cubed pork in paprika sauce; Scotch salmon fillet with hollandaise sauce; or cheese and mushroom omelette.

Open: 11-11 (Sun 12-10.30)
Bar Meals: L served all week 12-2.30 D served all week 6.30-9.30 Av main course £10
Restaurant: L served all week 12-2.30 D served all week 6.30-9.30 Av 3 course · à la carte £18
Brewery/Company: GREENE KING
🍺: Greene King IPA, Ruddles, Abbot
Children's Facilities: Fam room Play area Portions/Menu Games High Chairs Food Warming
Notes: Dogs Allowed Garden Food Served Outside Large, terrace at top, seats around 100 Parking 20 Coach parties welcome

BARLEY — TL43

The Fox & Hounds ♀

High Street SG8 8HU
☎ 01763 848459 🖷 01763 849274
✉ thefoxbarley@aol.com

Dir: A505 onto B1368 at Flint Cross, pub 4m

Set in a pretty village, this former 17th-century hunting lodge is notable for its pub sign which extends across the lane. It has real fires, a warm welcome and an attractive garden. The menu offers a good range of standards such as Cumberland sausage, sirloin steak, gammon, scampi and chilli, while for something lighter there are sandwiches, baguettes, home-made burgers, garlic bread with cheese, and potato boats with chilli and sour cream.

Open: 12-11 (Sun 12-10.30)
Bar Meals: L served all week 12-3 D served all week 6-9 (Sun 12-5) Av main course £5
Restaurant: L served 12-3 D served 6-9
Brewery/Company: PUNCH TAVERNS
🍺: IPA, 6X
Children's Facilities: Play area Portions/Menu Games Food Warming
Notes: Dogs Allowed Garden Food Served Outside L-shaped garden with tables and chairs Parking 25 Coach parties welcome

BUNTINGFORD — TL32

The Sword in Hand 🐾 ♀

Westmill SG9 9LQ
☎ 01763 271356
✉ heather@swordinhand.ndo.co.uk

Dir: Off A10 1.5m S of Buntingford

Early 15th-century inn, once the home of the Scottish noble family, Gregs. The pub's name is taken from a motif within their family crest. The dining room looks out over open countryside, and offers a regularly changing menu. This may include Barbary duck Wellington with red wine and cranberry sauce, roasted garlic and herb rack of lamb, fillet steak topped with melted Stilton, breast of pheasant wrapped in bacon on honey-soused winter vegetables, or salmon fillet wrapped in Parma ham with tomato and basil sauce.

Open: 12-3 5.30-11 (Open Mon L in Summer) Days closed: Mon
Bar Meals: L served Tue-Sun 12-2.30 D served Tue-Sun 6.30-9.30 Av main course £10
Restaurant: L served Tue-Sun 12-2.30 D served Tue-Sun 6.30-9.30 Av 3 course · à la carte £20
Brewery/Company: FREE HOUSE
🍺: Greene King IPA, Young's Bitter, Shephard & Neame Spitfire, Batemans & Guest Ales
Children's Facilities: Play area (Large garden for ball games, play area) Portions/Menu High Chairs Food Warming
Notes: Dogs Allowed Garden Food Served Outside Large, beautiful view, patio area, pergola Parking 25 Coach parties welcome

FLAUNDEN   TL00

The Bricklayers Arms 🐾 ♀

Hogpits Bottom Nr Hemel Hempstead
HP3 0PH
☎ 01442 833322 📠 01442 834841
📧 goodfood@bricklayersarms.co.uk

Dir: M1 J8 through H Hempstead to
Bovington then follow Flaunden sign. M25
J18 through Chorleywood to
Chenies/Latimer then Flaunden

*This traditional country pub with its low
beams, exposed brickwork and open fires has
been extensively renovated and refurbished by
the owners, who have many years of
experience in the trade. It is popular with
walkers and locals, as well as those who
enjoy relaxing in the delightful garden in the
summer months. The menu offers, say,
monkfish tail with lime butter; breast of duck
served with a gooseberry vinegar jus; or quail
stuffed with mushrooms and served with a
balsamic sauce.*

Open: 11.30-11.30
Bar Meals: L served all week 12-2 D served
all week 6-9.30 Av main course £13
Restaurant: L served all week 12-3 D served
all week 6-9.30 Av 3 course · à la carte £23
Brewery/Company: FREE HOUSE 🍺: Old
Speckled Hen, Brakspear Bitter, Ringwood Old
Thumper, Marston's Pedigree
Children's Facilities: Portions/Menu High
Chairs Food Warming
Notes: Dogs Allowed Water Garden Food
Served Outside Sunny & Secluded Parking 40

HEXTON   TL13

The Raven 🐾 ♀

Hitchin SG5 3JB
☎ 01582 881209 📠 01582 881610
📧 jack@ravenathexton-f9.co.uk

*Named after Ravensburgh Castle up in the
neighbouring hills, this neat 1920's pub has
comfortable bars and a large garden with
terrace and play area. The traditional pub
food menu is more comprehensive than many,
with baguettes, filled jackets, pork ribs, steaks
from the Duke of Buccleuch's Scottish estate,
surf and turf, ribs, hot chicken and bacon
salad, Mediterranean pasta bake and a whole
lot more. Daily specials are on the blackboard.*

Open: 11-3 6-11 (Sun 12-10.30)
Bar Meals: L served all week 12-2 D served
all week 6-10 Av main course £7.50
Restaurant: L served all week 12-2 D served
all week 6-10
Brewery/Company: ENTERPRISE INNS
🍺: Greene King Old Speckled Hen, Fullers
London Pride, Greene King IPA
Children's Facilities: Cutlery Games High
Chairs Food Warming Changing
Nearby: Woburn
Notes: Dogs in garden only. Water provided
Garden Food Served Outside Table & chair
seating for 50, benches & tables Parking 40
Coach parties welcome

HERTFORDSHIRE

OLD KNEBWORTH   TL22

The Lytton Arms 🏠 ♇

Park Lane SG3 6QB
☎ 01438 812312 📠 01438 817298
✉ thelyttonarms@btinternet.com

Dir: From A1(M) take A602. At Knebworth turn R at rail station. Follow signs 'Codicote'. Pub 1.5m on R

Popular with ramblers, horse-riders and cyclists in picturesque north Hertfordshire countryside, this 1877 Lutyens-designed inn claims to have served over 4,000 real ales in 14 years. Now refurbished, inside and out, the Lytton offers ten cask-conditioned real ales changing daily, a selection of light bites and a daily specials board. Food options may include home-made pies, sausages, liver and bacon, curries, seafood pasta, and battered fish and chips.

Open: 11-11 (Sun 12-10.30)
Bar Meals: L served Mon-Sun 12-2.30 D served Mon-Sat 7-9.30 (Sun 12-5) Av main course £7.50
Restaurant: L served Mon-Sun 12-2.30 D served Mon-Sat 6.30-9.30 Sun 12-5
Brewery/Company: FREE HOUSE
🍺: Fuller's London Pride, Adnams Best Bitter, Broadside, Wherry
Children's Facilities: Licence Portions/Menu High Chairs Food Warming Changing
Nearby: Knebworth Park, Hatfield House, Stevenage Leisure Centre
Notes: Dogs Allowed Water Garden Food Served Outside Large umbrella protected decking Parking 40 Coach parties welcome

WELLPOND GREEN   TL42

Nag's Head ♦♦♦♦ 🏠

Standon SG11 1NL
☎ 01920 821424

The Nag's Head is a family-run free house in a sleepy hamlet in pretty rolling countryside, half a mile off the A120. The menu offers a variety of seafood and fish main courses, including skate wing, mussels, and lemon sole. Other popular dishes are calves' liver with sautéed onions and bacon; breast of duck with an orange and brandy sauce; vegetarian stirfry flavoured with ginger and served with pilau rice; and grilled lamb cutlets. Comfortable accommodation in attractive en suite bedrooms.

Open: 12-2.30 6-11 Days closed: Mon L and Sun Eve
Bar Meals: L served Tue-Sun 12-2 D served Mon-Sat 6.30-9.30 Av main course £6.95
Restaurant: L served Tue-Sun 12-2 D served Mon-Sat 6.30-9.30 Av 3 course · à la carte £18
Brewery/Company: FREE HOUSE
🍺: Greene King IPA & Ruddles County
Rooms: 5 en suite 1 family room s£50 d£70
Children's Facilities: Play area (Swings) Portions/Menu High Chairs Food Warming
Notes: No Dogs (except Assist Dogs) Garden Food Served Outside Lawn, full size boules pitch, Patio Parking 28 Coach parties welcome

BOSSINGHAM TR14

The Hop Pocket

The Street Canterbury CT4 6DY
☎ 01227 709866 📠 01227 709866
✉ forgan50@aol.com

Birds of prey and an animal corner for children are among the more unusual attractions at this family pub in the heart of Kent. Canterbury is only five miles away and the county's delightfully scenic coast and countryside are within easy reach. All meals are cooked to order, using fresh produce. Expect supreme of chicken, spicy salmon, Cajun beef, chilli nachos and mushroom Stroganoff. Extensive range of sandwiches and omelettes.

Open: 11-3 6.30-11
Bar Meals: L served Tue-Sun 12-2.30 D served Mon-Sun 7-9.15 (Sunday 12-4 & 6.30-9) Av main course £9.25
Restaurant: L served Tue-Sun 12-2.30 D served Mon-Sun 7-9.15 Av 3 course · à la carte £17.50 Av 3 course fixed price £16
🍺:London Pride, Shepherd Neame Admiral
Children's Facilities: Portions/Menu Cutlery High Chairs Food Warming
Nearby: Howletts Zoo, Dymchurch Railway, Canterbury Cathedral
Notes: Dogs Allowed Garden Food Served Outside Parking 30 No credit cards

BOYDEN GATE TR26

Gate Inn ♀

North Stream Canterbury CT3 4EB
☎ 01227 860498

Dir: From Canterbury on A28 turn L at Upstreet

This rural retreat is surrounded by marshland and pasture, with a beautiful garden overlooking a stream populated by ducks and geese. On display is the Chislet Prize, which the locals will explain better than this guide! Inside, quarry-tiled floors and pine furniture feature in the family-friendly interconnecting bars. It might be a challenge to decide on what to eat, since the huge menu offers a wide range. There are 17 sandwich fillings; 9 different 'ploughpersons'; jacket potatoes with 16 different fillings; and 'Gateburgers' filled with various delights. A similarly tempting range of side orders includes garlic bread, sausages on sticks and nachos.

Open: 11-2.30 6-11 (Sun 12-4, 7-10.30)
Bar Meals: L served all week 12-2 D served all week 6-9 Av main course £5.95
Brewery/Company: SHEPHERD NEAME 🍺: Shepherd Neame Master Brew, Spitfire & Bishops Finger, Seasonal Beers
Children's Facilities: Fam room Portions/Menu Cutlery Games High Chairs Food Warming Changing
Notes: Dogs Allowed Water & dog biscuits Garden Food Served Outside Parking 14 Coach parties welcome No credit cards

BROOKLAND TQ92

Woolpack Inn

Romney Marsh TN29 9TJ
☎ 01797 344321

Partly built from old ship timbers and set in Kentish marshland, this 15th-century cottage inn was originally a beacon-keeper's house, and is particularly popular with birdwatchers. One of the long Victorian tables has penny games carved into the top. Home-made wholesome pub food includes steak pie, chicken Kiev, pork chops, lasagne, grilled trout, a variety of steaks, and the usual sandwiches, jackets and ploughmans. Also see the blackboard for specials.

Open: 11-3 6-11 (Open all day Sat & Sun)
Bar Meals: L served all week 12-2 D served all week 6-9
Brewery/Company: SHEPHERD NEAME ◀:
Shepherd Neame Spitfire Premium Ale, Master Brew Bitter
Children's Facilities: Fam room Play area (animals) Portions/Menu High Chairs Food Warming Changing
Nearby: Camber Sands, Lydd Raceway, Wind Surfing
Notes: Dogs Allowed Water Garden Food Served Outside Large beer garden with 2 tables Parking 30 Coach parties welcome

CHIDDINGSTONE TQ54

Castle Inn

TN8 7AH
☎ 01892 870247 🖺 01892 870808
✉ info@castleinn.co.uk

Dir: S of B2027 between Tonbridge & Edenbridge

The Castle's picturesque mellow brick exterior has served many times as a film set. The building dates back to 1420 and was first licensed to sell ale in about 1730. Today it is still full of nooks and crannies and curios. There's a bar menu but chips are definitely not served. The Fireside Menu provides informal dinners in the saloon bar and at the top end of the dining range, a small, very individual restaurant with waiter service caters for those special occasions.

Open: 11-11
Bar Meals: L served all week 11-9.30 D served all week (Sun 12-6) Av main course £6.40
Restaurant: L served Wed-Mon 12-2 D served Wed-Mon 7.30-9.30 Av 3 course · à la carte £22 Av 3 course fixed price £22
Brewery/Company: FREE HOUSE
◀: Larkins Traditional, Harveys Sussex
Children's Facilities: Licence Portions/Menu Cutlery Games High Chairs Food Warming Changing
Notes: Dogs Allowed Water Garden Food Served Outside Patio, lawn, sheltered, bar Coach parties welcome

DOVER TR34

The Clyffe Hotel ⌂

High Street St Margaret's at Cliffe CT15 6AT
☎ 01304 852400 🖷 01304 851880
📧 stay@theclyffehotel.com

Dir: 3m NE of Dover

Kentish clapboard building dating from 1584, which has at times been a shoemaker's and an academy for young gentlemen. It is located opposite the parish church, just half a mile from the white cliffs of Dover, and the main bar and neatly furnished lounge lead out into the delightful walled rose garden. Seafood is a speciality of the house, including lobster, bass and mussels as popular options alongside New Romney rack of lamb.

Open: 11-3 5-11 (Sun 12-10.30)
Bar Meals: L served all week 11-2 D served all week 6-9.30 Av main course £6.95
Restaurant: L served all week 12-2 D served all week 6.30-9.30
Brewery/Company: FREE HOUSE
🍺: Shepherd Neame Spitfire, Masterbrew, Fullers London Pride
Children's Facilities: Licence Play area (Large garden, playhouse, toys) Portions/Menu Games High Chairs Food Warming
Nearby: Wingham Wild Life Park, Howletts Zoo, Kids Safari
Notes: No Dogs (except Assist Dogs) Garden Food Served Outside Traditional English walled garden Parking 20

FOLKESTONE TR23

The Lighthouse

Old Dover Road Capel le Ferne CT18 7HT
☎ 01303 223300 🖷 01303 256501

Breathtaking panoramic sea views and spectacular countryside distinguish this former wine and ale house. The food is good too, and children have their own Jolly Little Sailor menu. Eight comfortable bedrooms.

Bar Meals: L served all week 12-2.15 D served all week 5.30-9 (Sunday 12-8.30) Av main course £7
Restaurant: L served all week 12-2.15 D served all week 5.30-9 Sunday 12-8.30 Av 3 course · à la carte £17
🍺:Abbot Ale, Greene King IPA, Guest Ales, Ramsgate No5
Rooms: 8 en suite 2 family room s£40 d£50 (◆◆◆◆)
Children's Facilities: Fam room Play area (Garden area/equipment) Portions/Menu Cutlery Games High Chairs Food Warming Changing
Notes: No Dogs (except Assist Dogs) Garden Food Served Outside lawn, large patio Parking 80

KENT

LITTLEBOURNE   TR25

King William IV ◆◆◆ ⓥ

4 High Street Canterbury CT3 1UN
☎ 01227 721244 ▤ 01227 721244
✉ paulharvey@kingwilliam04.fsbusiness.co.uk

Dir: From A2 follow signs to Howletts Zoo. After zoo & at end of road, pub ahead

Located just outside the city of Canterbury, the King William IV overlooks the village green and is well placed for Sandwich and Herne Bay. With open log fires and exposed oak beams, this friendly inn offers a good choice of wholesome food. Seafood choices include salmon and Mediterranean vegetables, seabass on minted ratatouille, and paupiette of plaice and leek with thermidor sauce, while non-fishy dishes include confit of duck with mustard mash, pot roast pheasant, and chicken stuffed with Stilton.

Open: 11-3 6-11 (Sat 11-11)
Bar Meals: L served all week 12-2.30 D served Mon-Sat 7-9.30 Av main course £12.50
Restaurant: L served all week 12-2.30 D served all week 7-9.30 Av 3 course · à la carte £20
Brewery/Company: FREE HOUSE
◖: Shepherd Neame Master Brew Bitter, Scottish Courage John Smith's, Adnams Bitter
Rooms: 7 en suite s£35 d£50
Children's Facilities: Portions/Menu Games High Chairs Food Warming Changing
Nearby: Howletts Zoo, Wingham Bird Park
Notes: No Dogs (except Assist Dogs) Garden Food Served Outside Patio to rear, Parking 15 Coach parties welcome

MAIDSTONE   TQ75

The Ringlestone Inn ◆◆◆◆◆ ⓨ

Ringlestone Nr Harrietsham ME17 1NX
☎ 01622 859900 ▤ 01622 859966
✉ bookings@ringlestone.com

Dir: A20 E from Maidstone, at rdbt L to Hollingbourne. Through village, R at x-rds

Built in 1533, the Ringlestone was a hospice for monks and then became an ale house in the 1600s. Today, the weekday lunchtime menu offers a good range of panninis, bagels and hot dishes. In the evening, the choice broadens and includes speciality pies. Desserts are both traditional English and European classic, they are all home made and all the same price.

Open: 12-3 6-11 (Sat-Sun 12-11)
Closed: 25 Dec
Bar Meals: L served all week 12-2 D served all week 7-9.30
Restaurant: L served all week 12-2 D served all week 7-9.30 Av 3 course · à la carte £24.50
◖:Shepherd Neame Bishops Finger & Spitfire, Greene King Abbot Ale, Theakston Old Peculier
Rooms: 3 en suite s£89 d£99
Children's Facilities: Licence Play area Portions/Menu Cutlery Games High Chairs Food Warming
Nearby: Cobtree Museum, Leeds Castle
Notes: No Dogs (except Assist Dogs) manager's discretion Garden Food Served Outside gardens, seating Parking 50 Coach parties welcome

BILSBORROW   SD53

Owd Nell's Tavern 🛏 ♇

Guy's Thatched Hamlet Canal Side
Nr Garstang PR3 0RS
☎ 01995 640010 📠 01995 640141
✉ info@guysthatchedhamlet.com

Owd Nell's is part of Guy's thatched hamlet, which also includes Guy's Eating Establishment, Guy's Lodge, a cricket ground and Boddington's Pavilion. The tavern, a 16th-century former farmhouse, offers a wide selection of guest ales, 50 malt whiskies and 40 wines by the glass. Favourite dishes are stuffed mushrooms, Aberdeen Angus steaks, oysters, lobster, pasta and pizza.

Open: 11-11 **Closed:** 25 Dec
Bar Meals: L served all week 11-10.30 D served all week 11-10.30 Av main course £5
Restaurant: L served all week 12-2.30 D served all week 5.30-10.30 Sun 12-10.30 Av 3 course · à la carte £15 Av 2 course fixed price £6 **Brewery/Company:** FREE HOUSE
🍺: Interbrew Boddingtons Bitter & Flowers, Jennings Bitter, Castle Eden Ale
Rooms: 65 en suite 6 family room s£46 d£46 (♦♦♦♦)
Children's Facilities: Fam room Play area (Tunnels, swings, see-saw) Portions/Menu Games High Chairs Food Warming Changing
Notes: Dogs Allowed Water Garden Food Served Outside Patio areas by Canal, 200 seats Parking 300 Coach parties welcome

CARNFORTH   SD47

Dutton Arms

Station Lane Burton LA6 1HR
☎ 01524 781225 📠 01524 782662

Dir: from M6 take A6 signed Milnthorpe (Kendal), 3m before Milnthorpe turn R signed Burton/Holme

Close to a host of tourist attractions, including Morecambe Bay, the Lancashire Canal and the Northern Yorkshire Dales, the Dutton Arms was originally the Station Hotel serving the nearby mainline station, and was built in 1860.

Open: 10-3.30 6-11
Bar Meals: L served all week 11-2.30 D served all week 6-9.30 Av main course £11
Restaurant: L served all week 12-2 D served all week 6-9 Av 3 course · à la carte £11
Brewery/Company: FREE HOUSE
🍺: Interbrew Boddingtons, Black Sheep & Guest Beer
Children's Facilities: Fam room Play area (Play area inside and out) Portions/Menu High Chairs Food Warming Changing
Nearby: South Lakes Wildlife Oasis, Brewery Art Centre
Notes: No Dogs (except Assist Dogs) Water Garden Food Served Outside Lawned area with adventure playground Parking 30 Coach parties welcome

CHIPPING SD64

Dog & Partridge

Hesketh Lane Preston PR3 2TH
☎ 01995 61201 ▤ 01995 61446

Dating back to 1515, this comfortably modernised rural free house in the Ribble Valley enjoys wonderful views of the surrounding fells. The barn has been converted into an additional dining area, and the emphasis is on home-made food using local produce. Diners can choose from bar snacks, or a carte menu in the restaurant. The latter includes roast local duckling, home-made steak and kidney pie, and jumbo scampi in batter. Vegetarians are well catered for.

Open: 11.45-3 6.45-11 (Sun 11.45-10.30)
Bar Meals: L served all week 12-1.45
Restaurant: L served all week 12-1.30
D served all week 7-9, Sun L 12-3,
à la carte 3.30-8.30
Brewery/Company: FREE HOUSE
🍺: Carlsberg-Tetley
Children's Facilities: Portions/Menu High Chairs Food Warming
Nearby: Bowland Wild Boar Park
Notes: No Dogs (except Assist Dogs) Parking 30 Coach parties welcome

HASLINGDEN SD72

Farmers Glory ☺

Roundhill Road Rossendale BB4 5TU
☎ 01706 215748 ▤ 01706 215748

Dir: 7 miles equidistant from Blackburn, Burnley and Bury, 1.5m from M66

Stone-built, 350-year-old pub situated high above Haslingden on the edge of the Pennines. Formerly a coaching inn on the ancient route to Whalley Abbey, it now offers locals and modern A667 travellers a wide-ranging traditional pub menu of steaks, roasts, seafood, pizzas, pasta, curries and sandwiches. Live folk music every Wednesday and a large beer garden with ornamental fishpond.

Open: 12-3 7-11.30
Bar Meals: L served all week 12-2.30 D served all week 7-9.30 Av main course £6.50
Restaurant: L served all week 12-2.30 D served all week 7-9.30 Av 3 course · à la carte £12
Brewery/Company: PUBMASTER
🍺: Carlsberg-Tetley Tetley Bitter, Marston's Pedigree, Greene King IPA, Jennings
Children's Facilities: Portions/Menu Cutlery Games High Chairs Food Warming Changing
Nearby: Camelot, Winfields, Rossendale Ski Slope
Notes: No Dogs (except Assist Dogs) Garden Food Served Outside 0.5 acre, fixed seating, ornamental fish pond Parking 60 Coach parties welcome

MERECLOUGH   SD83

Kettledrum Inn ♀

302 Red Lees Road Cliviger BB10 4RG
☎ 01282 424591 🗋 01282 424591

> **Dir:** from Burnley town centre, past Burnley
> FC, 2.5m, 1st pub on L

*The Kettledrum is an inviting and well-kept
country inn with superb views of the famous
Pendle Hill, below which lived Mother
Demdike and Mother Chattox, accused in
1652 of witchcraft and taken to Lancaster to
be hanged. In addition to traditional pub food
there are dishes like venison sausage,
Gressingham duck breast, seafood tagliatelle,
braised knuckle of lamb, steaks, wild
mushroom risotto, and gnocchi. A separate
fish section on the menu lists fillet of Scotch
salmon, baked mackerel fillet, and Thai green
tiger prawn curry.*

Open: 12-3 6-11 (Sun open all day)
Bar Meals: L served all week 12-2.30
D served all week 6-9 Av main course £7
Restaurant: L served all week 12-2.30
D served all week 6-9 Av 3 course ·
à la carte £12
Brewery/Company: PUBMASTER
🍺: Black Sheep, John Smiths
Children's Facilities: Fam room
Portions/Menu Cutlery High Chairs Food
Warming
Nearby: Cawthorpe Hall, Towneley Park
Notes: No Dogs (except Assist Dogs) Food
Served Outside Seating Area Parking 30 Coach
parties welcome

PARBOLD   SD41

The Eagle & Child ☜ ♀

Maltkiln Lane Nr Ormskirk L40 3SG
☎ 01257 462297 🗋 01257 464718

> **Dir:** From M6 J27 to Parbold. At bottom of
> Parbold Hill turn R on B5246 to Hilldale.
> Then 4th L to Bispham Green

*The emphasis at this dining pub is firmly placed
on good ales, cider, and varied freshly cooked
food. The pub's unusual name is an allusion
to the story of Lord Derby's bastard child.
Nowadays, flagged floors and oak settles grace
the interior. The pub also hosts an annual beer
festival each May. The interesting range of light
meals includes sandwiches with side salad and
chips, whilst other menu options range from
sausage and mash to grilled mullet, chick peas,
shrimps and capers.*

Open: 12-3 5.3-11 (Sun 12-10.30) RS: 25
Dec closed eve
Bar Meals: L served all week 12-2 D served
all week 6-8.30 (Sun 12-8.30) Av main course
£9.50
Restaurant: L served all week 12-2 D served
all week 6-8.30 Fri & Sat 6-9, Sun 12-8.30 Av
3 course · à la carte £20
Brewery/Company: FREE HOUSE
🍺: Moorhouses Black Cat, Thwaites Bitter,
5 changing guest beers
Children's Facilities: Fam room
Portions/Menu High Chairs Food Warming
Notes: Dogs Allowed Garden Food Served
Outside Large patio, wooden benches, bowling
green Parking 50 Coach parties welcome

PRESTON SD52

Cartford Country Inn & Hotel ☜ ♀

Little Eccleston PR3 0YP
☎ 01995 670166 ▤ 01995 671785

This old, pleasantly rambling three-storey inn guards a historic toll bridge over the tidal River Wyre. Inside, an open log fire may be blazing. A good range of food on the bar menu includes sandwiches, pizzas (evenings only), jacket potatoes, salads, chicken and bacon pasta, lamb Henry and seafood platter. Various specials might include curries, and lemon sole with crabmeat. The choice for vegetarians has been extended. Meals can also be taken outside overlooking the river, along part of which runs a four-mile walk that conveniently starts and finishes at the pub.

Open: 12-3 6.30-11 (Open 6.30 in summer, Sun 12-10.30)
Bar Meals: L served all week 12-2 D served all week 6.30-9.30 Av main course £5
Brewery/Company: FREE HOUSE
🍺: Hart Beers, Fullers London Pride, Moorhouse, Guest ales
Children's Facilities: Fam room Play area (Climbing frame and slide) High Chairs Food Warming
Notes: Dogs Allowed Parking 60 Coach parties welcome

WRIGHTINGTON SD51

The Mulberry Tree ⊛⊛ ☜ ♀

WN6 9SE
☎ 01257 451400 ▤ 01257 451400

Dir: M6 J27 into Mossy Lea Road 2m on right

Former Roux brothers' head chef Mark Prescott has been ranked in Great Britain's top ten of contemporary chefs, so it's no surprise that The Mulberry Tree is a sought-after venue for discerning diners. Customers from near and far feel at home in its clean, airy ambience whilst choosing from a veritable feast of options. The bar menu has speciality sandwiches (lunchtime only); starters which may include deep-fried crottin with spiced pear, rocket and Parmesan; and main courses like honey-glazed crown of woodpigeon with celeriac purée, wild mushrooms and pancetta. The dinner menu continues with similarly accomplished dishes, or you can keep it simple with Russian Sevruga caviar followed by fresh lobster.

Open: 12-3 6-11 Closed: 26 Dec, 1 Jan
Bar Meals: L served Mon-Sun 12-2 D served Mon-Sun 6-9.30 (All day Sun, Fri-Sat 6-10) Av main course £12.95
Restaurant: L served all week 12-2 D served all week 6-10 Sun 12-3 Av 3 course · à la carte £25.95 Av 3 course fixed price £17.95
Brewery/Company: FREE HOUSE
🍺: Interbrew Flowers IPA,
Children's Facilities: Portions/Menu Cutlery High Chairs
Notes: No Dogs Parking 100

FLECKNEY   SP69

The Old Crown ♀

High Street LE8 8AJ

☎ 0116 2402223

✉ old-crown-inn@fleckney7.freeserve.co.uk

Close to the Grand Union Canal and Saddington Tunnel, a traditional village pub that is especially welcoming to hiking groups and families. Noted for good real ales and generous opening times offering a wide choice of popular food. Choose from a variety of platters, grills, baguettes, burgers, jacket potatoes and more. Chef's Specials include lamb in a red wine and plum sauce, poached salmon, lamb and mint pudding, and pork in a mushroom and brandy sauce. Garden has lovely views of fields and the canal, as well as a pétanque court.

Open: 11-11 (Sun 12-10.30)
Bar Meals: L served all week 12-2 D served Tue-Sat 5-9 Av main course £8
Restaurant: L served all week 12-2 D served Tue-Sat 8-9
Brewery/Company: EVERARDS BREWERY
🍺: Everards Tiger & Beacon, Scottish Courage Courage Directors, Adnams Bitter, Greene King Abbot Ale, Marston's Pedigree
Children's Facilities: Fam room Play area (Bouncy castle, playhouse) Portions/Menu Cutlery Games High Chairs Food Warming Changing
Notes: Dogs Allowed Water Garden Food Served Outside Very large, wonderful views Parking 60 Coach parties welcome No credit cards

MARKET HARBOROUGH   SP78

The Queens Head Inn 🐾 ♀

Main Street Sutton Bassett LE16 8HP

☎ 01858 463530

✉ queens.head@freeuk.com

Dir: Towards Colby L into Uppingham Rd

This community-owned traditional English pub, overlooking the beautiful Welland Valley, offers real ales, bar meals, a separate restaurant and an enclosed garden which has been extensively improved by the owners. More than 30 main courses include a good choice of fish dishes such as red snapper, fresh tuna, haddock and cod. Well-kept real ales are like Timothy Taylor's and Adnams are always available.

Open: 12-2.30 5-11 (Sat 12-11.30, Sun 12-10.30)
Bar Meals: L served all week 12-2.30 D served all week 5-9.30 Av main course £10.75
Restaurant: L served all week 12-2.30 D served all week 7-11 (All day Sat & Sun) Av 3 course · à la carte £17
Brewery/Company: FREE HOUSE
🍺: Adnams, Timothy Taylor Landlord & Green King IPA
Children's Facilities: Portions/Menu High Chairs Food Warming Changing
Notes: No Dogs (except Assist Dogs) garden only Garden patio, BBQ, food served outside Parking 20 Coach parties welcome

SOMERBY SK71

Stilton Cheese Inn 🐾 ♀

High Street LE14 2QB
☎ 01664 454394

*At the heart of a working village in beautiful
countryside, this sandstone building dates
from the 16th century. The same menus
service both bar and restaurant areas, with
good selections to be found on the specials
boards. Try smoked cod with parsley sauce;
trout with a honey and almond glaze; wild
boar and apple sausages with cider sauce; or
medallions of pork fillet with Marsala and
apple sauce. Interesting selection of vegetarian
specials and a good range of real ales.*

Open: 12-3 6-11
Bar Meals: L served all week 12-2 D served
all week 6-9 (Sun 7-9) Av main course £6.75
Restaurant: L served all week 12-2 D served
all week 6-9 Av 3 course £13.50
Brewery/Company: FREE HOUSE
🍺: Grainstore Ten Fifty, Brewster's Hophead,
Belvoir Star, Carlsberg-Tetley Tetley's Cask,
Marston's Pedigree
Children's Facilities: Fam room
Portions/Menu Cutlery High Chairs Food
Warming
Nearby: Twin Lakes, Borough Hill Iron Age
Hillfort, Melton Country Park
Notes: No Dogs (except Assist Dogs) Garden
Food Served Outside Small patio, seats around
20 Parking 14 Coach parties welcome

STATHERN SK73

Red Lion Inn ◉ 🐾 ♀

Red Lion Street LE14 4HS
☎ 01949 860868 📠 01949 861579
✉ info@theredlioninn.co.uk

Dir: From A1, A52 Nottingham turn L signed
Belvoir Castle, Redmile. Stathern on L

*The young team here is passionate about
traditional pub values, aiming to serve
excellent food, beer and wine in a friendly and
enjoyable atmosphere. Seasonal highlights
include mulled wine and roast chestnuts by the
open fire in winter, and home-made lemonade
or Pimms cocktails at summer barbecues.
Produce from the best local suppliers is used
to create a daily-changing menu.*

Open: 12-3 6-11 (Sat 12-11, Sun 12-5.30)
Closed: 26 Dec, 1 Jan; Sun eve
Bar Meals: L served all week 12-2 D served
Mon-Sat 7-9.30 (Sun 12-3) Av main course
£10.95
Restaurant: L served all week 12-2 D served
Mon-Sat 7-9.30 Sun 12-3 Av 3 course · à la
carte £21 Av 3 course fixed price £11.50
Brewery/Company: RUTLAND INN
COMPANY LTD 🍺: Grainstore Olive Oil,
Brewster's VPA, Exmoor Gold. London Pride
Children's Facilities: Play area (Toys)
Portions/Menu Cutlery Games High Chairs
Food Warming
Nearby: Belvoir Castle & Maze, Langar
Karting, Tumbledown Park
Notes: Dogs Allowed Water Garden Food
Served Outside Enclosed, decking area, tables,
heaters Parking 25

The Wishing Well Inn 🐾

Main Street Dyke PE10 0AF
☎ 01778 422970 📠 01778 394508

Dir: Inn 1.5m from A15, 12m from A1, Colsterworth rdbt

Village inn dating back 300 years, with old oak beams and two inglenook fireplaces in the bar and restaurant areas. The place is named after the wishing well in the smaller of the two restaurants. Outside is an attractive beer garden and children's play area, plus a paddock where an annual family fun day is held. Favourite dishes are village grills, jumbo cod, steak and ale pie, and minted lamb chops.

Open: 11-3 6-11
Bar Meals: L served all week 12-2 D served all week 6.30-9 Av main course £8
Brewery/Company: FREE HOUSE
🍺: Greene King Abbot Ale, Everards Tiger Bitter, 3 Guest beers
Children's Facilities: Licence Play area Portions/Menu Games High Chairs Food Warming
Nearby: Grimsthorpe Castle, Rutland Water, Nene Valley Railway
Notes: No Dogs Garden Food Served Outside Parking 100 Coach parties welcome

The Jolly Miller

Brigg Road Wrawby DN20 8RH
☎ 01652 655658 📠 01652 657506

Dir: 1.5m E of Brigg on the A18, on L

Popular country inn situated a few miles south of the Humber estuary. Pleasant bar and dining area fitted out in traditional pub style. Saturday night entertainment and facilities for christenings, weddings and other functions. Children are particularly welcome, with a swing, slide, roundabout and climbing frame in the garden, as well as a children's menu. Straightforward dishes offer the likes of chilli, curry and Sunday lunches.

Open: 3-11 (Thu-Sun 12-11)
Bar Meals: L served all week from 12 D served all week from 8 Av main course £5
Brewery/Company: FREE HOUSE
🍺: Two changing guest ales
Children's Facilities: Play area (Swing, slide round about & climbing frame) Portions/Menu Cutlery Games High Chairs Food Warming Changing
Nearby: Elsham Hall with Zoo
Notes: No Dogs Garden Food Served Outside outdoor eating, patio Parking 40 Coach parties welcome

LINCOLNSHIRE

CONINGSBY — TF25

The Lea Gate Inn ♀

Leagate Road LN4 4RS
☎ 01526 342370
✉ theleagateinn@hotmail.com

Dir: Off B1192 just outside Coningsby

The oldest licensed premises in the county, dating from 1542, this was the last of the Fen Guide Houses that provided shelter before the treacherous marshes were drained. The oak-beamed pub has a priest's hole and a very old Inglenook fireplace among its features. The gardens have a koi carp pond and play area. Typical bar menus list pork cooked with Stilton, and confit of duck.

Open: 11.30-2.30 6.30-11 (Sun 12-2.30, 6.30-10.30) Closed: Oct 19-26
Bar Meals: L served 12-2 D served 6.30-9.30
Restaurant: L served all week-D served all week 6.30-9.15
Brewery/Company: FREE HOUSE
🍺: Scottish Courage Theakston XB, Marston's Pedigree
Rooms: 8 en suite 1 family room s£50 d£65 (♦♦♦♦)
Children's Facilities: Play area (Wooden play area, bouncy castle in summer) Portions/Menu
Notes: No Dogs (except Assist Dogs) Garden Food Served Outside Large with play area Parking 60

EWERBY — TF14

The Finch Hatton Arms ☜

43 Main Street Sleaford NG34 9PH
☎ 01529 460363 📠 01529 461703
✉ bookings@finchhatton.fsnet.co.uk

Dir: from A17 to Kirkby-la-Thorne, then 2m NE. Also 2m E of A153 between Sleaford & Anwick

Originally known as the Angel Inn, this 19th-century pub was given the family name of Lord Winchelsea who bought it in 1875. After a chequered history and a short period of closure, it reopened as a new-style pub/restaurant in the 1980s. The extensive, varied menu offers such dishes as salmon, sweet and sour chicken, steak and kidney pie, and sea bass. Real ales include Major Bitter from the Riverside micro-brewery in Wainfleet All Saints.

Open: 11.30-2.30 6.30-11 Closed: 25-26 Dec
Bar Meals: L served all week 11.30-2.30 D served all week 6.30-11
Restaurant: L served all week 11.30-2.30 D served all week 6.30-11
Brewery/Company: FREE HOUSE
🍺: Everards Tiger Best, Dixons Major
Rooms: 8 en suite s£44 d£66 (★★)
Children's Facilities: Portions/Menu Cutlery Games High Chairs Food Warming Changing
Notes: No Dogs (except Assist Dogs) Garden Food Served Outside Parking 60 Coach parties welcome

LINCOLN　　　　　　　　SK97

Wig & Mitre ⊛ ♀

30/32 Steep Hill LN2 1TL
☎ 01522 535190 📠 01522 532402
✉ email@wigandmitre.com

Dir: Town centre adjacent to cathedral

Located in the upper part of medieval Lincoln, this is a reassuringly civilised pub-restaurant. A haven of peace, free of music and amusement machines, it offers continuous service from 8am to around midnight every day, all year round. It is justifiably popular for its food and extensive wine selection, many available by the glass. Food choices range from sandwiches to set three course meals, with a wide variety of individual dishes in between. Among the starters expect cherry tomato and baby spinach soufflé, while main courses might include Thai crab cakes with a lemon grass and coriander butter sauce.

Open: 8-midnight
Bar Meals: L&D served all week 8-11
Av main course £13.95
Restaurant: L&D served all week 8-11 D
served all week 8-11 Av 3 course · à la carte
£26 Av 3 course fixed price £13.95
Brewery/Company: FREE HOUSE
🍺: Greene King, Marstons Pedigree
& Ruddles Best
Children's Facilities: Portions/Menu Games
High Chairs Food Warming
Nearby: Lincoln Castle, Cathedral, Museum
of Licolnshire Life
Notes: Dogs Allowed

LOUTH　　　　　　　　TF38

Masons Arms 🐕 ♀

Cornmarket LN11 9PY
☎ 01507 609525 📠 0870 7066450
✉ ron@themasons.co.uk

Situated in the Cornmarket, this former posting inn dates from 1725 and some relics of its past association with the Masons can be found on doors and windows. Today it still provides a 'downstairs' for informal eating and an 'upstairs' where the carte features steaks, sautéed duck breast, and fresh Bateman's beer-battered Grimsby haddock. Well-kept real ales complement the mainly traditional fare.

Open: 10-11 12-10.30 (Sun 12-10.30)
Bar Meals: L served all week 12-2 D served
Mon-Sat 6-9 Av main course £7.95
Restaurant: L served Sun 12-2 D served Fri-
Sat 7-9.30 Av 3 course · à la carte £10
Brewery/Company: FREE HOUSE 🍺:
Timothy Taylor Landlord, Marston's Pedigree,
Samuel Smiths, Batemans XB Bitter, XXXB
Rooms: 10 bedrooms 5 en suite s£25 d£38
Children's Facilities: Licence Portions/Menu
High Chairs Food Warming
Nearby: Fantasy Island, Pleasure Beach
Notes: No Dogs Parking 7 Coach parties
welcome

STAMFORD TF00

The George of Stamford
★★★ ◎ ☜ ♀

71 St Martins PE9 2LB
☎ 01780 750750 📠 01780 750701
✉ reservations@georgehotelofstamford.com

Dir: A1 N from Peterborough. At rdbt signed B1081 Stamford, to lights. Hotel on L

The George we see today is essentially 16th century, but its crypt underneath the cocktail bar suggests its origins are certainly medieval. Informal meals are served in the Garden Lounge, the York Bar, or outside in the ivy-clad courtyard. In the magnificent antique oak-panelled restaurant, a three-course meal is offered.

Open: 11-2.30 6-11
(Sat-Sun open all day from 11)
Bar Meals: L served all week 7-11 Av main course £8.95
Restaurant: L served all week 12.30-2.30 D served all week 7.30-10.30 Av 3 course · à la carte £33 Av 2 course fixed price £17.50
Brewery/Company: FREE HOUSE
🍺: Adnams Broadside, Fuller's London Pride, Greene King Ruddles Bitter
Rooms: 47 en suite 20 family rms s£78 £110
Children's Facilities: Portions/Menu Cutlery High Chairs Food Warming Changing
Nearby: Nene Valley Railways, Rutland Water, Burghley Park & Stately Home
Notes: Dogs Allowed dog pack, Garden, Parking 120

WOODHALL SPA TF16

Village Limits Motel

Stixwould Road LN10 6UJ
☎ 01526 353312 📠 01526 353312
✉ enquiries@villagelimits.com

Dir: At rdbt in main street follow signs for Petwood Hotel. 500yds

Traditional pub food in the motel's restaurant and bar includes steaks, grilled gammon, chargrilled chicken, wholetail scampi, grilled rainbow trout, battered and smoked haddock, and salads. In World War II, the famous Dambusters requisitioned nearby Petwood House for their Officers' Mess.

Open: 12-2.30 6-11
Bar Meals: L served all week 12-2 D served all week 6-9
Restaurant: L served all week 12-2 D served all week 6.30-9
Brewery/Company: FREE HOUSE
🍺: Bateman XB, Black Sheep Best, Barnsley Bitter, Carlsberg-Tetley Tetley's Smooth Flow, Highwood Tom Wood's Best
Children's Facilities: Portions/Menu Food Warming
Nearby: Jubilee Park, Kinema in the Woods
Notes: No Dogs (except Assist Dogs) Garden Food Served Outside Enclosed garden with superb views Parking 30 Coach parties welcome

E3

The Crown ♀

223 Grove Road E3 5SN
☎ 020 8981 9998 📠 020 8980 2336
✉ crown@singhboulton.co.uk

Dir: Nearest tube: Mile End Central Line & District line. Buses 277 to Victoria Park

A beautifully-restored, listed building spread over two floors. The open-plan bar is equally suited to lively conversation or some peaceful newspaper reading on quiet afternoons. The European cuisine is presented on seasonal, twice-daily changing menus. Brunch is served at weekends and on bank holidays, the menu offering grilled kippers, scrambled eggs and roast tomatoes; Spanish white bean and pepper stew with baked egg; muffins with rare breed ham, poached egg and hollandaise; and liver and bacon with polenta.

Open: 12-11 (Mon 5-11, Wknd phone for details) Closed: 25 Dec
Bar Meals: L served Tue-Sun 12.30-3.30 D served Mon-Sun 6.30-10.30 Av main course £10.50
Restaurant: L served Tue-Sun 12.30-3.30 D served Mon-Sun 6.30-10.30
Brewery/Company: FREE HOUSE
🍺: St Peter's Organic Ale & Best Bitter, Pitfield Eco Warrior & East Kent Goldings
Children's Facilities: Licence Portions/Menu High Chairs Food Warming Changing
Notes: Dogs Allowed Garden Food Served Outside Paved area at front of pub Coach parties welcome

EC1

The Eagle 🛏 ♀

159 Farringdon Road EC1R 3AL
☎ 020 7837 1353

Dir: Angel/Farringdon Stn

In 1990, The Eagle became the first of the genre of smart eating and drinking establishments we know as the gastropub. The Eagle has remained one of the neighbourhood's top establishments-no mean feat, given the competition today. The airy interior has a wooden-floored bar and dining area, a random assortment of furniture, and an open-to-view kitchen which produces a modern, creative daily-changing menu with a pretty constant Southern European/South American/Pacific Rim theme. Seen frequently are gazpacho Andaluz; bruschetta with spiced aubergines, roast cherry tomatoes and Mozzarella, and cuttlefish stew.

Open: 12-11 Closed: 1Wk Xmas, BHs Sun eve
Bar Meals: L served all week 12.30-3 D served Mon-Sat 6.30-10.30 (Sun 12.30-3.30) Av main course £9
Restaurant: L served all week-D served Mon-Sat
Brewery/Company: FREE HOUSE
🍺: Wells Eagle IPA & Bombardier
Children's Facilities: Portions/Menu Food Warming
Nearby: Guardian Archive, Sadlers Well Theatre, Karl Marx House
Notes: Dogs Allowed

N1

The Compton Arms ♀

4 Compton Avenue Off Canonbury Road
N1 2XD
☎ 020 7359 6883
✉ 4334@greeneking.co.uk

The best kept secret in N1. A late 17th-century country pub in the middle of town with a peaceful, rural feel. Frequented by a mix of locals, actors and musicians. Real ales from the hand pump, and good value steaks, mixed grill, big breakfast and Sunday roast. Expect a busy bar when Arsenal are at home. No under 4s.

Open: 12-6 6-11 **Closed:** 25 Dec (afternoon)
Bar Meals: L served all week 12-2.30 D served all week 6-9 Av main course £5.95
Brewery/Company: GREENE KING
◖: Greene King IPA, Abbot Ale, Ruddles County, plus guest ale
Children's Facilities: Fam room Portions/Menu Games
Nearby: Highbury Fields, London Museum
Notes: No Dogs Garden Food Served Outside Courtyard Coach parties welcome

N6

The Flask ⌂ ♀

Highgate West Hill N6 6BU
☎ 020 8348 7346
✉ info@theflaskhighgate.co.uk

A 17th-century former school in one of London's loveliest villages. Dick Turpin hid from his pursuers in the cellars, and TS Elliot and Sir John Betjeman enjoyed a glass or two here. The interior is listed and includes the original bar with sash windows which lift at opening time. Enjoy a glass of good real ale, a speciality bottled beer (choice of 15), or a hot toddy while you peruse the menu, which changes twice a day. Choices range through sandwiches and platters to char-grills and home-made puddings.

Open: 11-11 (Nov-Mar open 12 noon)
RS: 31 Dec closed eve
Bar Meals: L served all week 12-3 D served all week 6-10 (Sun 12-4, 6-9.30) Av main course £8
Brewery/Company: SIX CONTINENTS RETAIL ◖: Adnams, Tim Taylor Landlord, Caledonian IPA, Harveys Sussex, Oakham JHB
Children's Facilities: Portions/Menu High Chairs Food Warming
Nearby: Hampstead Heath, Kenwood House, Highgate Cemetary
Notes: Dogs Allowed Water, Doggie Snacks Garden Food Served Outside large terrace

NW1

The Chapel ♀

48 Chapel Street NW1 5DP
☎ 020 7402 9220 📠 020 7723 2337
✉ thechapel@btconnect.com

Dir: By A40 Marylebone Rd & Old Marylebone Rd junction

There's a relaxed, informal atmosphere at this bright and airy gastropub. The daily chalkboard menus give the place a trendy Anglo-Mediterranean feel. Food is served throughout the building and the attractive tree-shaded garden. On any given day expect starters such as courgette, lemon and mint soup or focaccia with roasted vegetables and St Albray cheese. Follow with pan-fried guinea fowl or stuffed globe artichoke with risotto, smoked Cheddar and tomato coulis.

Open: 12-11 (Sun 12-10.30)
Closed: Dec 24-Jan 2
Bar Meals: L served all week 12-2.30
D served all week 7-10 (Sun 12.30-3, 7-10)
Av main course £11.75
Restaurant: L served all week 12-2.30
D served all week 7-10 (Sun 12.30-3, 7-10)
Av 3 course · à la carte £20
Brewery/Company: PUNCH TAVERNS
🍺: Greene King IPA, Adnams
Children's Facilities: Portions/Menu Cutlery Food Warming
Nearby: Madame Tussauds, Hyde Park,
Notes: Dogs Allowed Garden Food Served Outside Paved area, shaded tables
Coach parties welcome

SE1

The Fire Station ◉ ♀

150 Waterloo Road SE1 8SB
☎ 020 7620 2226 📠 020 7633 9161
✉ firestation@wizardinns.co.uk

Close to Waterloo Station, and handy for the Old Vic Theatre and the Imperial War Museum, this remarkable conversion of a genuine early-Edwardian fire station has kept many of its former trappings intact. An interesting menu includes dishes such as Fire Station avocado Caesar salad, baked cod with cheese polenta and pimento and pesto dressing, roast spiced pork belly with sticky rice and pak choi. Alternatively try Tandoori seared yellowfin tuna loin, calves' liver with bacon or mustard mash or lemon sole with Jerusalem artichokes.

Open: 11-11 (Sun 12-10.30)
Closed: 25/26 Dec
Bar Meals: L served all week 12-5.30 D served N all 5.30-10.30 Av main course £5.95
Restaurant: L served all week 12-2.45 D served all week 5-11 (Sat 12-11, Sun 12-9.30) Av 3 course · à la carte £20 Av 3 course fixed price £13.50
Brewery/Company: WIZARD INNS
🍺: Adnams Best Bitter & Broadside, Fuller's London Pride, Young's Bitters
Children's Facilities: Portions/Menu High Chairs Food Warming
Nearby: Aquarium, London Eye
Notes: No Dogs (except Assist Dogs) Coach parties welcome

SE1

The Bridge House Bar & Dining Room ☺ ⛄

218 Tower Bridge Road SE1 2UP
☎ 020 7407 5818 📠 020 7407 5828

Dir: 5 min walk from London Bridge/Tower Hill tube stations

The nearest bar to Tower Bridge, on the south side, The Bridge House has great views of the river and city. It comprises a bar, dining room and new café, plus facilities for private functions. Dishes range through home-ground beef burger with fat chips and chilli relish; slow roasted Norfolk duck with braised red cabbage, basil mash and red wine gravy; and field mushroom, plum tomato and artichoke tart with mixed leaves and lentil dressing.

Open: 11.30-11 (Sun 12-10.30) Closed: 25-26 Dec, 1 Jan
Bar Meals: L served all week 11.30-10 D served all week 5-10 (Sun 12-9.30)
Restaurant: L served 12-4 D served 6-10
🍺:Adnams Best Bitter, Adnams Broadside
Children's Facilities: Fam room Portions/Menu Food Warming
Nearby: London Dungeon, The Tower of London, Shakespear's Globe
Notes: No Dogs (except Assist Dogs)

SE16

The Mayflower Inn ☺ ⛄

117 Rotherhithe Street Rotherhithe SE16 4NF
☎ 020 7237 4088 📠 020 7064 4710

Dir: Exit A2 at Surrey Keys roundabout onto Brunel Rd, 3rd L onto Swan Rd, at T jct L, 200m to pub on R

From the patio of the Mayflower Inn you can still see the renovated jetty from which the eponymous 'Mayflower' embarked on her historic voyage to the New World. The pub has maintained its links with the famous ship through a range of memorabilia, as well as its unusual licence to sell both British and American postage stamps. Pub fare includes stuffed pork loin; Cajun chicken supreme; and fresh pasta with smoked bacon, spinach and mushrooms. Children are only allowed in the restaurant.

Open: 11-3 6-11 (Sun 12-10.30)
Bar Meals: L served all week 12-2.30 D served all week 6.30-9.30 (Sun 12-4) Av main course £5.50
Restaurant: L served Mon-Sun 12-2.30 D served Mon-Sat 6.30-9 (Sun 12-4)
Brewery/Company: GREENE KING **🍺:** Greene King Abbot Ale, IPA, Old Speckled Hen
Children's Facilities: Portions/Menu High Chairs Food Warming Changing
Nearby: Brunel Museum, Film Studios
Notes: Dogs Allowed Jetty over river, Food served outside Coach parties welcome

SE5

The Sun and Doves ♀

61-63 Coldharbour Lane Camberwell SE5 9NS
☎ 020 7924 9950 🖷 020 7924 9330
✉ mail@sunanddoves.co.uk

Attractive Camberwell venue known for good food, drink and art - all with a contemporary flavour. For a London pub it also has a decent sized garden, great for the summer months. The menu is stylishly simple, with a daily soup and stew, and snacks like marinated olives and nachos. Otherwise there's a choice of starters/light meals including hot sandwiches, eggs Benedict, and cured meats and pickles. Grills and mains take in speciality skewers-marinaded ingredients (chicken, swordfish, halloumi) grilled on a beech skewer-alongside Cumberland sausage and mash, and fish in beer batter.

Open: 11-11 Closed: 25/26 Dec
Bar Meals: L served all week 12-10.30 D served all week 12-10.30 (Sun 12-9) Av main course £8
Restaurant: L&D served 11-11 Av 3 course · à la carte £18
Brewery/Company: SCOTTISH & NEWCASTLE ◀: Greene King Old Speckled Hen, Scottish Courage John Smith's Smooth
Children's Facilities: Portions/Menu Games High Chairs Food Warming
Nearby: Brockwell Park, Ruskin Park
Notes: Dogs Allowed Water Garden Food Served Outside Secluded, Coach parties welcome

SW11

Duke of Cambridge ♀

228 Battersea Bridge Road SW11 3AA
☎ 020 7223 5662 🖷 020 7801 9684
✉ info@geronimo-inns.co.uk

An award-winning community pub with an eclectic mix of locals and just a stone's throw from Battersea Park and two of London's most famous Thames crossings - Battersea Bridge and Albert Bridge. Popular Saturday brunch menu and traditional Sunday roasts. The interesting range of dishes includes bacon wrapped venison steaks, sea bass fillet with pesto and tomato roulade and chicken breast stuffed with mushrooms. The Duke of Cambridge makes a donation to the Haven Trust breast cancer support centres every time one of its designated dishes, which are healthy and carcinogen free, is sold.

Open: 11-11
Bar Meals: L served all week 12-2.30 D served all week 7-9.45 (Sun 12-4) Av main course £9.50
Restaurant: L served all week 12-3 D served all week 7-9.45 Sun 6-9.30 Av 3 course · à la carte £16
Brewery/Company: YOUNG & CO BREWERY PLC ◀: Youngs Bitter & Special,Stella, Fosters, Guiness
Children's Facilities: Portions/Menu
Nearby: Battersea Park
Notes: Dogs Allowed Garden Beer garden, patio, food served outdoors, BBQ Coach parties welcome

SW4

The Windmill on the Common
★★★ ♀

Clapham Common South Side SW4 9DE
☎ 020 8673 4578 📠 020 8675 1486
✉ windmillhotel@youngs.co.uk

Dir: Nearest tube: Clapham Common or Clapham South

The windmill on this site in 1655 is long gone, but in more recent times the building has been a popular watering hole for crowds returning from the Epsom races. There are two spacious bars and a conservatory. Food ranges from filled baguettes and burgers to crab fishcakes, curries and steak and ale pie. There is separate oak-panelled restaurant.

Open: 11-11 (Sun 12-10.30)
Bar Meals: L served all week 12-2.30 D served all week 6-10 Av main course £7
Restaurant: L served all week 12-2.30 D served all week 7-10 Sun 12-9 Av 3 course · à la carte £15
Brewery/Company: YOUNG & CO BREWERY PLC 🍺: Youngs Bitter, Special, Winter Warmer, Waggledance
Rooms: 29 en suite s£99 d£115
Children's Facilities: Licence Fam room Portions/Menu High Chairs Food Warming
Nearby: Clapham Common
Notes: Dogs Allowed Water bowl Garden Food Served Outside Benches, seats approx 50, garden bar Parking 16 Coach parties welcome

W10

Paradise by Way of Kensal Green ♀

19 Kilburn Lane Kensal Rise W10 4AE
☎ 020 8969 0098 📠 020 8960 9968
✉ paradise.bywayof@virgin.net

A truly eclectic pub atmosphere with bare boards, bric-á-brac, oriental tapestries and wrought iron chandeliers creating a Bohemian setting for working artists, musicians and actors. The unusual name derives from the last line of G K Chesterton's poem 'The Rolling English Road', and there are plenty of original Victorian features in keeping with its late 19th-century origins. The food at this lively venue stands up well to the demands placed on it by weekly live jazz and special events like weddings, but don't expect bar snacks or too much flexibility. The self-styled gastro-pub serves classy food from the carte.

Open: 12-11 (Sun 12-10.30) **Closed:** 25 Dec & Jan 1
Bar Meals: L served all week 12-4 D served all week 7.30-11 Av main course £12
Restaurant: L served all week 12.30-4 D served all week 7.30-11 (Sun 12.30-9) Av 3 course · à la carte £20 Av 2 course fixed price £18
Brewery/Company: FREE HOUSE 🍺: Shepherds Neame Spitfire, Hoegarden
Children's Facilities: Licence Portions/Menu Games High Chairs Changing
Nearby: Queens Park City Farm, Mini Golf,
Notes: Dogs Allowed Water provided Garden Food Served Outside Courtyard Coach parties welcome

White Horse Hotel ☜ ⅄

4 High Street NR25 7AL
☎ 01263 740574 📠 01263 741303
📧 enquiries@blakeneywhitehorse.co.uk

Dir: From A148 (Cromer to King's Lynn rd) turn onto A149 signed to Blakeney.

Blakeney is a delightful fishing village of narrow streets lined with flint-built cottages, and Blakeney's first pub, a 17th-century coaching inn, is located just 100 yards from the tidal quay affording fine views across the harbour. Not surprisingly, given its proximity to the sea, seafood is a speciality of the house. Bar meal options range from filled ciabattas and granary sandwiches to pork and leek sausages with mash and onion gravy. The restaurant, overlooking a courtyard is served by a separate kitchen.

Open: 11-3 6-11 (Sun 12-3, 7-10.30)
Closed: 7-21 Jan **Bar Meals:** L served all week 12-2 D served all week 6-9 Av main course £9 **Restaurant:** D served Tue-Sun 7-9 Av 3 course · à la carte £26
Brewery/Company: FREE HOUSE
🍺: Adnams Bitter, Adnams Broadside, Woodfordes Wherry, Woodfordes Nelson
Children's Facilities: Fam room Portions/Menu Cutlery High Chairs Food Warming Changing **Nearby:** Crabbing on Blakeney Key, seal trips **Notes:** No Dogs (except Assist Dogs) Garden Food Served Outside Courtyard, picnic tables and umbrellas Parking 14

The Kings Arms ☜ ⅄

Westgate Street Holt NR25 7NQ
☎ 01263 740341 📠 01263 740391
📧 kingsarms.blakeney@btopenworld.com

A choice of real ales, Guinness and cider awaits you inside this Grade II listed free house on the north Norfolk coast. The Kings Arms is an ideal centre for walking, or perhaps a ferry trip to the nearby seal colony and world-famous bird sanctuaries. Locally-caught fish and seasonal seafood feature on the menu, together with local game, home-made pies and pastas.

Open: 11-11
Bar Meals: L served all week 12-9.30 D served all week 12-9.30 (Sun 12-9) Av main course £7
Brewery/Company: FREE HOUSE
🍺: Greene King Old Speckled Hen, Woodfordes Wherry Best Bitter, Marston's Pedigree, Adnams Best Bitter
Children's Facilities: Fam room Play area (Swings) Portions/Menu Games High Chairs Food Warming Changing
Nearby: Dinosaur Park, Beaches
Notes: Dogs Allowed Water Garden Food Served Outside Very safe large patio and grass area Parking 10 Coach parties welcome

BRANCASTER STAITHE   TF74

The White Horse ★★ ◎ ☜ ♈

Main Road King's Lynn PE31 8BY
☎ 01485 210262 📠 01485 210930
✉ reception@whitehorsebrancaster.co.uk

Dir: On the A149 coastal road

Expect a friendly welcome at this stylish dining pub, which enjoys a wonderful situation in an unspoilt part of North Norfolk. The pub's enviable reputation is based on its renowned seafood which can be enjoyed in the airy conservatory restaurant, the bar, or on the sun deck; this is a popular spot in summer. According to season freshly-harvested local mussels, oysters and samphire often appear on the menu. At midday, a light lunch menu offers the fresh shellfish already mentioned, supplemented by fish of the day with green pease pudding and tartar. There are meat dishes too.

Open: 11-11 (Sun 12-10.30)
Bar Meals: L served all week 11.30-3 Av main course £8.50
Restaurant: L all week 12-3 D all week 6-10 Av 3 course · à la carte £27
Brewery/Company: FREE HOUSE ◗:
Adnams Best Bitter, Adnams Regatta, Fullers London Pride, Woodfordes Nelsons Revenge
Rooms: 15 en suite 3 family room s£72 d£104
Children's Facilities: Portions/Menu Cutlery Games High Chairs Food Warming Changing
Nearby: Sea Life Centre, Fun Fair, Beaches
Notes: Dogs Allowed Garden Food Served Outside Sun deck terrace Parking 80

BURNHAM THORPE   TF84

The Lord Nelson ☜ ♈

Walsingham Road King's Lynn PE31 8HL
☎ 01328 738241 📠 01328 738241
✉ david@nelsonslocal.co.uk

Built around 1637, this unspoilt gem was named after England's most famous seafarer. Inside, you'll find a timeless atmosphere of huge high-backed settles and open fires. Nelson himself drank here, and you can sample a dram of 'Nelson's Blood'- a secret, rum-based recipe made and sold on the premises. Lunchtime brings salads and light meals, as well as bacon or red Leicester granary doorsteps. Dinner might feature Shooter's game pie; salmon pieces in wine and pepper cream; or asparagus ravioli with Pomodora sauce and molten cheese. Families are warmly welcomed.

Open: 11-3 6-11 (Sun 12-3 6.30-10.30)
Days closed: Mon in winter
Bar Meals: L served all week 12-2 D served Mon-Sat 7-9
Restaurant: L all week 12-2 D served Mon-Sat 7-9 Av 3 course · à la carte £20
Brewery/Company: GREENE KING ◗:
Greene King Abbot Ale & IPA, Woodforde's Wherry, Nelsons Revenge, Old Speckled Hen (summer only)
Children's Facilities: Play area (Large wooded play area & equipment; toys inside) Portions/Menu Games High Chairs Food Warming Changing
Nearby: Sealife Sanctuary, Wildlife Park,
Notes: Dogs Allowed Water Garden Food served outside Very large garden; seating; Parking 30 Coach parties welcome

FAKENHAM TF92

The White Horse Inn ♦♦♦♦ 🛏

Fakenham Road East Barsham NR21 0LH
☎ 01328 820645 📠 01328 820645
📧 rsteele@btinternet.com

Ideally located for birdwatching, walking, cycling, fishing, golf and sandy beaches, this refurbished 17th-century inn offers en suite rooms and a characterful bar with log-burning inglenook. Good range of beers and malt whiskies. Fresh ingredients are assured in daily specials, with fish especially well represented: cod, plaice, scampi, haddock, bream and a seafood platter usually appear on the menu. Enclosed courtyard at rear.

Open: 11-3 6-11
Bar Meals: L served all week 12-2 D served all week 7-9.30
Restaurant: L served all week 12-2 D served all week 7-9.30
Brewery/Company: OAK TAVERNS
🍺: Adnams Best, Adnams Broadside, Tetley, Wells Eagle IPA
Rooms: 3 en suite 2 family s£35 d£50
Children's Facilities: Portions/Menu Games High Chairs Food Warming
Nearby: Sandringham, Dinosaur Park
Notes: No Dogs (except Assist Dogs) Garden Food Served Outside Patio area & enclosed courtyard Parking 50 Coach parties welcome

HORSTEAD TG21

Recruiting Sergeant 🛏 ♀

Norwich Road Norwich NR12 7EE
☎ 01603 737077 📠 01603 738827

Dir: on the B1150 between Norwich & North Walsham

The name of this inviting country pub comes from the tradition of recruiting servicemen by giving them the King or Queen's shilling in a pint of beer. It offers good food, ales and wines in homely surroundings with a patio and lawned garden for alfresco dining. The menu is ever changing, with inventive dishes such as fresh oysters with a tabasco, lime and red onion dressing, duck breast on an apple and potato rosti and chicken breast stuffed with mozzarella and chorizo. There is also a vast daily specials menu, including fish and vegetarian dishes.

Open: 11-11
Bar Meals: L served all week 12-2 D served all week 6.30-9.30 Av main course £7.95
Restaurant: L served all week 12-2 D served all week 6.30-9.30 Av 3 course · à la carte £16
Brewery/Company: FREE HOUSE
🍺: Adnams, Woodefordes, Greene King Abbot Ale, Scottish Courage
Children's Facilities: Portions/Menu High Chairs Food Warming Changing
Nearby: Wroxham Barns, Yale Valley Railway
Notes: Dogs Allowed Water Garden Food Served Outside Large patio, seats approx 40, enclosed lawn Parking 50 Coach parties welcome

REEDHAM   TG40

Railway Tavern ♀

17 The Havaker nr Beccles NR13 3HG
☎ 01493 700340
✉ railwaytavern@tiscali.co.uk

A classic Victorian station pub in the middle of the Norfolk Broads, with as many summer visitors arriving by boat as by car. Good home-cooked meals are served in the restaurant, bar or beer garden, from a varied and innovative menu. Starters may include orange and Cointreau pâté; and red Thai salmon fishcakes with coriander and lemongrass mayonnaise. Main courses include home-made fish and beef and ale pies; fillet of beef Wellington; and haloumi salad with chargrilled vegetables. Weekly fish specials could be mixed seafood tagliatelle; skate wing; or salmon en croûte.

Open: 11-3 6-11 (Fri-Sun 11-11)
Bar Meals: L served all week 11.30-3 D served all week 6-9 Av main course £8.50
Restaurant: L served all week 11.30-3 D served all week 6-9.30 (Fri-Sun all day) Av 3 course · à la carte £15
Brewery/Company: FREE HOUSE
🍺: Adnams, plus guest ales
Children's Facilities: Licence Fam room Play area (Sand pit, Wendy house) Portions/Menu Games High Chairs Food Warming
Nearby: Animal Adventure Park
Notes: Dogs Allowed Water provided Garden Food Served Outside converted stable block Parking 20 Coach parties welcome

SNETTISHAM   TF63

The Rose & Crown ★★ ⊛ ☺ ♀

Old Church Road Kings Lynn PE31 7LX
☎ 01485 541382 🖷 01485 543172
✉ info@roseandcrownsnettisham.co.uk

Dir: N from Kings Lynn on A149 signed Hunstanton. Inn in centre

Long, low and covered in roses, the family-run Rose and Crown is all a village pub should be. The menu offers fresh fish and chips or chargrilled steak, plus exotic choices like grilled polenta, squid and chorizo salad and roast cod and pumpkin hash with parsley velouté. At dinner you'll find main courses might be crisp confit duck leg, hash browns and pomegranate molasses and risotto Nero with crispy shallots. Puddings are equally desirable.

Open: 11-11 (Sun 12-10.30)
Bar Meals: L served all week 12-2 D served all week 9.30-9 (Sat-Sun 12-2.30, Fri & Sat 9.30) Av main course £9
Restaurant: L served all week 12-2 D served all week 6-9 (Sat-Sun 12-2.30, Fri & Sat 9.30) Av 3 course · à la carte £18
Brewery/Company: FREE HOUSE 🍺:
Adnams Bitter & Broadside, Interbrew Bass, Fuller's London Pride, Greene King IPA
Rooms: 11 en suite 4 family s£50 d£70
Children's Facilities: Fam room Play area (Large play fort) Portions/Menu Cutlery Games High Chairs Food Warming Changing
Nearby: Park Farm, Sandringham & Beaches
Notes: Dogs Allowed Water Garden Food Served Outside Lrg walled garden Parking 70

THOMPSON TL99

Chequers Inn ♦♦♦♦ ⓢ

Griston Road Thetford IP24 1PX
☎ 01953 483360 📠 01953 488092
✉ themcdowalls@barbox.net

Historic 16th-century pub which over the years has been a manor court, doctor's surgery and meeting room. Many original features remain. With a growing reputation for exciting, imaginative and good quality food and a regularly-changing menu encompassing both traditional pub favourites and more exotic dishes, it's hardly surprising that large numbers of drinkers and diners are drawn here.

Open: 11.30-2.30 6.30-11 (Sun 12-3, 6.30-10.30)
Bar Meals: L served all week 12-2 D served all week 6.30-9.30 Av main course £7.50
Restaurant: L served all week 12-2 D served all week 6.30-9.30 Av 3 course · à la carte £23

Brewery/Company: FREE HOUSE
🍺: Fuller's London Pride, Adnams Best, Wolf Best, Greene King IPA, Woodforde's Wherry Best **Rooms:** 3 en suite 1 family room s£40 d£60 **Children's Facilities:** Play area Portions/Menu High Chairs Food Warming Changing **Nearby:** Melsop Farm Park, Thetford Forse **Notes:** Dogs Allowed Water, Garden Food Served Outside lawned area Parking 35 Coach parties welcome

TITCHWELL TF74

Titchwell Manor Hotel ★★⑧⑧ ⓢ

Brancaster PE31 8BB
☎ 01485 210221 📠 01485 210104
✉ margaret@titchwellmanor.com

Dir: A149 (coast rd)

Built at the tail-end of the 19th century as a farmhouse, this family-run hotel is in the centre of a small coastal hamlet. The sea, of course, is a major influence on lunch menus, so fish and seafood lovers will be in their element, choosing between grilled sardines, Norfolk smoked eel, seared swordfish loin, Brancaster oysters and mussels and Cromer crab. But it's not all fish, at least not in the evenings, when delicious alternatives include chargrilled fillet of beef and pan-roasted corn-fed chicken breasts rubbed with fenugreek and peanut butter.

Open: 11-11
Bar Meals: L served all week 12-2 D served all week 6.30-9.30 Av main course £10
Restaurant: L served all week 12-2 D served all week 6.30-9.30 Av 3 course · à la carte £20
Brewery/Company: FREE HOUSE
🍺: Greene King IPA & Abbot Ale
Rooms: 16 en suite 6 family rooms
Children's Facilities: Play area (Books, games, TV, VCR) Portions/Menu Cutlery Games High Chairs Food Warming Changing **Nearby:** Hunstanton Sealife Centre, Bircham Windmill, RSPB Bird Reserve Activity Centre **Notes:** Dogs Allowed Water, kennel Garden Food Served Outside Large walled garden, Parking 50 Coach parties welcome

UPPER SHERINGHAM   TG14

The Red Lion Inn 🐾

The Street NR26 8AD
☎ 01263 825408

Dir: A140 (Norwich to Cromer) then A148 to Sheringham/Upper Sheringham

About 400 years old, flint-built, with original floors, natural pine furniture, a large wood-burning stove, and a Snug Bar haunted by a female ghost. Local produce is used extensively, with fish, including plaice, haddock, halibut, cod and crab, featuring in a big way. Other options are liver and bacon in port and orange gravy, steak and ale pie; Thai red chicken curry; a half pheasant in cranberry sauce; and chicken stuffed with prawns on a crab sauce.

Open: 11.30-3 6.30-11 Open all day Sun in Summer holidays
Bar Meals: L served all week 12-2 D served all week 6.30-9 Av main course £7.50
Restaurant: L served all week 12-2 D served all week 6.30-9 Av 3 course · à la carte £15
Brewery/Company: FREE HOUSE
🍺: Woodforde's Wherry, Greene King IPA
Children's Facilities: Fam room Portions/Menu Games Food Warming Changing
Nearby: North Norfolk Railway, Splash Leisure Pool
Notes: Dogs Allowed Water Garden Food Served Outside Large lawned area with fruit trees Parking 16 Coach parties welcome No credit cards

WINTERTON-ON-SEA   TG41

Fishermans Return 🐾 ♀

The Lane Great Yarmouth NR29 4BN
☎ 01493 393305 📠 01493 393951
✉ fishermans_return@btopenworld.com

Dir: 8m N of Gt Yarmouth on B1159

This 300-year-old brick and flint pub is within walking distance of long beaches (sensible shoes essential for clambering over dunes!), and National Trust land, where you can enjoy a spot of bird or seal watching. Dogs are also welcome. There is a vast choice of malts and ciders, and a good, traditional menu. Dishes might include a seafood platter, fish pie, and various omelettes and burgers, as well as a changing specials board.

Open: 11-2.30 6.30-11 (Sat 11-11, Sun 12-10.30)
Bar Meals: L served all week 11.30-2 D served all week 6.30-9 Av main course £8.75
Brewery/Company: FREE HOUSE 🍺:
Woodforde's Wherry & Norfolk Nog, Adnams Best Bitter & Broadside and Greene King IPA
Children's Facilities: Fam room Play area (Slide, climbing frame, swing) Portions/Menu High Chairs
Nearby: Sandy Beach, Broadland Boats
Notes: Dogs Allowed Water & chews Garden Food Served Outside Large enclosed, with tables, play equipment Parking 50 Coach parties welcome

ASHBY ST LEDGERS   SP56

The Olde Coach House Inn ♀

Rugby CV23 8UN
☎ 01788 890349 📠 01788 891922
✉ oldcoachhouse@traditionalfreehouses.com

Dir: M1 J18 follow signs A361/Daventry.
Village on L

*A late 19th-century farmhouse, skilfully
converted into a pub with dining areas and
accommodation, set in a village that dates
back to the Domesday Book. The village was
home to Robert Catesby, one of the
Gunpowder plotters. Beer is taken seriously
here with up to eight regularly changing real
ales and legendary beer festivals. The pub
also serves fresh, high quality food, featuring
game casserole, seafood linguine, massive
mixed grills and summer barbecues.*

Open: 12-11 (Sun 12-10.30)
Bar Meals: L served all week 12-2.30 D
served all week 6-9.30
Restaurant: L served all week 12-2 D served
all week 6-9.30
Brewery/Company: FREE HOUSE
🍺: Everards Original, Everards Tiger, Fuller's
London Pride, Hook Norton Best
Rooms: 6 en suite 1 family room s£51 d£65
Children's Facilities: Fam room Play area
(Large wooden adventure playground)
Portions/Menu Games High Chairs Food
Warming Changing
Notes: No Dogs (except Assist Dogs) Water
Garden Food Served Outside Landscaped
garden Parking 50 Coach parties welcome

CLIPSTON   SP78

The Bulls Head 🛏

Harborough Road Nr Market Harborough
LE16 9RT
☎ 01858 525268

Dir: On B4036 S of Market Harborough

*American airmen once pushed coins between
the beams as a good luck charm before
bombing raids, and the trend continues with
foreign paper money pinned all over the inn.
In addition to its good choice of real ales, the
pub has an amazing collection of over 500
whiskies. The menu now offered includes
shark steaks, whole sea bass, hot toddy duck,
and steak pie.*

Open: 11.30-3 5.30-11 (Open Sat & Sun all
day in summer) RS: Mon closed Lunch
Bar Meals: L served all week 12-2 D served
all week 6.30-9 (Sat 6.30-9.30) Av main
course £7.95
Restaurant: L served all week 11.30-2 D
served all week 6.30-9.30 Av 3 course · à la
carte £17.50
Brewery/Company: FREE HOUSE
🍺: Tiger, Becon, Guest Beers & Seasonal
Children's Facilities: Licence Portions/Menu
High Chairs Food Warming Changing
Nearby: Foxton Locks
Notes: Dogs Allowed Garden Food Served
Outside Patio & Lawned Area Parking 40
Coach parties welcome

FARTHINGSTONE   SP65

The Kings Arms

Main Street nr Towcester NN12 8EZ
☎ 01327 361604 📠 01327 361604
✉ paul@kingsarms.fsbusiness.co.uk

Dir: from M1 take A45 W, at Weedon join A5 then R on road signed Farthingstone

This cosy 18th-century, Grade II listed inn is tucked away in unspoilt countryside near Canons Ashby (NT), adorned with a collection of stone gargoyles. Excellent real ales are served here. The menu is short and consists of things like British cheese platters, sausage and mash, or Yorkshire pudding filled with steak and kidney or beef in Guinness. The landlord also sells cheeses and a variety of speciality regional foods.

Open: 12-3 7-11 (Lunchtime wknds only)
Days closed: Mon & Wed RS: Mon-Fri open evenings only
Bar Meals: L served Sat-Sun 12-2 Av main course £6.50
Brewery/Company: FREE HOUSE
🍺: Hook Norton, Timothy Taylor Landlord, Shepherd Neame Spitfire Premium Ale, Jennings Bitter, Adnams
Children's Facilities: Fam room Play area (Books, Puzzles, Available, Room) Portions/Menu Games Food Warming
Nearby: Sulgrave Manor, Milton Keynes Snowdome
Notes: Dogs Allowed Water Garden Food Served Outside Many plants, herb garden, innovative design Parking 20 No credit cards

FOTHERINGHAY   TL09

The Falcon Inn ◎ ♀

Nr Oundle PE8 5HZ
☎ 01832 226254 📠 01832 226046

Dir: N of A605 between Peterborough & Oundle

Overlooks Fotheringhay church and is close to the site of Fotheringhay Castle, where Mary, Queen of Scots was beheaded and Richard III was born. This attractive 18th-century stone-built inn is set in a garden redesigned by landscape architect Bunny Guinness. Eat what you like where you like, and accompany your meal with excellent wines or a pint of good ale. Settle in the locals' tap bar, the smart rear dining room or the conservatory extension and choose from the blackboard snack selection or the seasonal carte.

Open: 11.30-3 6-11 (Sun 12-3,7-10.30)
Bar Meals: L served all week 12-2.15 D served all week 7-9.30 Av main course £9.50
Restaurant: L served all week 12-2.15 D served all week 6.30-9.30 Av 3 course · à la carte £24 Av 2 course fixed price £11.75
Brewery/Company: FREE HOUSE
🍺: Adnams Bitter, Greene King IPA, Scottish Courage John Smith's, Nethergate
Children's Facilities: Play area (Toys, highchairs) Portions/Menu High Chairs Food Warming
Nearby: Castle ruin & good walks
Notes: No Dogs (except Assist Dogs) Garden Food Served Outside Parking 30

GREAT OXENDON   SP78

The George Inn 🐾 ⏹

LE16 8NA
☎ 01858 465205 📠 01858 465205

A dining pub up on a bank by the side of the road. Good quality, reasonably priced food served in the bar includes snacks, light bites and the more substantial sirloin steak au poivre, loin of lamb Florentine, and roast fillet of cod with crispy bacon. Dinner options include roast fillet of salmon on chive mash, baked breadcrumbed escalope of chicken Savoyarde, and pan-fried duck breast. Vegetarians should ask for a list of what's available.

Open: 11.30-3 6-11 RS: Sun closed eve
Bar Meals: L served all week 12-2.30 D served Mon-Sat 7-10 (Closed Sun pm) Av main course £8.95
Restaurant: L served Tues-Sun 12-2.30 D served Mon-Sat 7-10 Av 3 course · à la carte £25 Av 3 course fixed price £14.95
Brewery/Company: FREE HOUSE
◀: Interbrew Bass, Adnams Bitter
Children's Facilities: Portions/Menu Games High Chairs Food Warming
Nearby: Swimming Pool, Desboro
Notes: Dogs Allowed Water Garden Food Served Outside Large formal, large patio for dining Parking 34 Coach parties welcome

MARSTON TRUSSELL   SP68

The Sun Inn ★★ ⏣ 🐾 ⏹

Main Street Market Harborough LE16 9TY
☎ 01858 465531 📠 01858 433155
✉ manager@suninn.com

Dir: S of A4304 between Market Harborough & Lutterworth

At this late 17th-century dining pub you'll find roaring winter fires, a friendly welcome, well-kept ales and a carefully chosen wine list. In the non-smoking restaurant, expect traditional and exotic cuisine to suit all tastes. Start, perhaps, with chargrilled aubergine, red onion and goats' cheese tartlet; or pan-fried Cornish scallops with pea and bacon purée. Main course choices include herb-crusted rack of lamb; pan-fried pheasant; grilled Dover sole. In summer, al fresco meals are also served on the paved front patio.

Open: 12-2 6-11 Closed: Dec 26, Jan 2
Bar Meals: L served Mon-Sun 12-1.45 D served all week 7-9.30 (Sun 12-2) Av main course £16.50
Restaurant: L served Mon-Sun 12-1.45 D served all week 7-9.30 Av 3 course · à la carte £26.50 Av 3 course fixed price £27.50
Brewery/Company: FREE HOUSE
◀: Bass, Hook Norton Best, Marstons Pedigree, Charles wells Bombardier, Ruddles
Rooms: 20 en suite 2 family s£59 d£69
Children's Facilities: Portions/Menu Cutlery Games High Chairs Changing
Nearby: Twycross Zoo, Rutland Water,
Notes: No Dogs (except Assist Dogs) Front patio, Parking 60 Coach parties welcome

NORTHAMPTON SP76

The Fox & Hounds ♀

Main Street Great Brington NN7 4JA
☎ 01604 770651 📠 01604 770164
📧 althorpcoachinn@aol.com

Located just a mile from Althorp House, ancestral home of the Spencer family, the Fox and Hounds is a much photographed stone and thatch coaching inn dating from the 16th century. Its many charms include a pretty courtyard and garden, real fires, numerous guest ales and a reputation for quality food. Expect plenty of game in season, Sunday roasts and main courses ranging from Drambuie fillet or stuffed chicken breast to international favourites such as mahi mahi fillet or Moroccan lamb. Vegetarian dishes and salad selections also available.

Open: 11-11 (Sun 12-10.30)
Bar Meals: L served all week 12-2.30 D served all week 6.30-9.30 Av main course £5.85
Restaurant: L served all week 12-2.30 D served all week 6.30-9.30 Av 3 course · à la carte £19.95
🍺:Green King IPA, Speckled Hen, Fullers London Pride, Abbot Ale, 6 Guest Ales
Children's Facilities: Play area (Books, crayons) Portions/Menu Games High Chairs Food Warming
Nearby: Falconry Centre, Activity Centres & Karting
Notes: Dogs Allowed Water bowls, toys, dog chews Garden Food Served Outside Secluded wall area, lots of trees Parking 50 Coach parties welcome

WADENHOE TL08

The King's Head

Church Street Nr Oundle PE8 5ST
☎ 01832 720024
📧 lou@kingzed.co.uk

A peaceful 16th-century stone free house, quietly located beside the River Nene. Diners will appreciate the relaxed atmosphere of the lounge bar or cottage room, whilst in summer you might be tempted to enjoy al fresco dining against a background of boats drifting past on the river. Bar meals range from soup with farmhouse bread to large filled rolls and jacket potatoes. In the evening, the cooking shifts up a notch, and typical main dishes include roast Gressingham duck; chicken breast with Stilton and New Zealand green-lipped mussels; and roast trout with Brazil nuts and Pernod jus.

Open: 12-3 7-11 (Wed-Sat 12-3, 6.30-11, Sun 12-4) **Days closed:** Tue
Bar Meals: L served all week 12-2 D served N Wed-Sat 7-9 (Sun 12-2) Av main course £6.50
Restaurant: D served Wed-Sat 7-9
Brewery/Company: FREE HOUSE
🍺: Adnams, Timothy Taylor Landlord, Oakham JHB, Adnams Broadside, Black Sheep
Children's Facilities: Play area (Large paddock, children must be supervised) Portions/Menu Cutlery Games High Chairs Food Warming Changing **Nearby:** Nene Valley Railway, Ferry Meadows Country Park
Notes: Dogs Allowed Water Garden Food Served Outside Large paddock, courtyard, patio, Parking 20 Coach parties welcome

ALNWICK NU11

Masons Arms ♀

Stamford Nr Rennington NE66 3RX
☎ 01665 577275 🖷 01665 577894
🕲 bookings@masonsarms.net

Dir: 3.5m from A1 on B1340

*Known by the local community as the
Stamford Cott, this 200-year-old coaching
inn has been tastefully modernised and is a
useful staging post for visitors to Hadrian's Wall,
Lindisfarne and the large number of nearby
golf courses. The same substantial home-
cooked food is available in the bar and
restaurant, using the best of local produce.
Expect Orkney herrings with oatcakes, game
casserole, seafood lasagne and chicken with
orange and lemon sauce.*

Open: 12-2 6.30-11 (Sun 12-2 7-10.30)
Bar Meals: L served all week 12-2 D served
all week 6.30-9 Av main course £6.50
Restaurant: L served all week 12-2 D served
all week 7-9 Av 3 course · à la carte £7
Brewery/Company: FREE HOUSE
🍺: Scottish Courage John Smith's, Theakston
Best, Secret Kingdom, Gladiator
Rooms: 12 en suite 3 family s£40 d£54
(♦♦♦♦)
Children's Facilities: Licence Fam room
Portions/Menu Cutlery High Chairs Food
Warming
Nearby: Alnwick Gardens, Bamburgh Castle
Notes: No Dogs (except Assist Dogs) Garden
Food Served Outside Parking 50 Coach parties
welcome

BELFORD NU13

Blue Bell Hotel ☜

Market Place NE70 7NE
☎ 01668 213543 🖷 01668 213787
🕲 bluebell@globalnet.co.uk

*A long-established and creeper-clad coaching
inn. Just off the A1 it makes a convenient
base for exploring Northumberland's
magnificent coastline and the Cheviot Hills.
The inn offers a friendly, relaxed atmosphere,
and a good range of real ales. Choices from
the menu in the elegant restaurant may
include tournedos of Aberdeen Angus steak
with wild mushroom sauce, and roasted
monkfish, while lamb balti, chicken fajitas,
and steak and kidney pie with Newcastle
brown are typical of the bar and buttery.*

Open: 11-2.30 6.30-11
Bar Meals: L served all week 11-2 D served
all week 6.30-9 Av main course £9.50
Restaurant: L served Sun 12-2 D served all
week 7-8.45 Av 3 course · à la carte £27 Av 5
course fixed price £25
Brewery/Company: FREE HOUSE 🍺:
Interbrew Boddingtons Bitter, Northumbrian
Smoothe, Calders, Tetleys Smooth
Rooms: 17 en suite s£36 d£82 (★★★)
Children's Facilities: Fam room
Portions/Menu Cutlery Games High Chairs
Food Warming
Notes: No Dogs (except Assist Dogs) Garden
Food Served Outside 3 acres Parking 17 Coach
parties welcome

CARTERWAY HEADS NZ05

The Manor House Inn ⚲ ♈

Shotley Bridge DH8 9LX
☎ 01207 255268

Dir: A69 W from Newcastle, L onto A68 then S for 8m. Inn on R

This small family-run free house enjoys spectacular views across open moorland and the Derwent Reservoir. The cosy stone-walled bar, with its log fires and low-beamed ceiling, offers a good range of well-kept real ales and around 70 malt whiskies. While the menu is not overwhelmingly large, only the best quality ingredients, locally sourced where possible, are used. Home-made puddings are a feature, as is the choice of up to 16 local cheeses.

Open: 11-11 RS: 25 Dec closed evening
Bar Meals: L served all week 12-9.30 D served all week-Av main course £11
Restaurant: L served all week 12-2.30 D served all week 7-9.30 (Sun 9) Av 3 course · à la carte £19
Brewery/Company: FREE HOUSE
⚑: Theakstons Best, Mordue Workie Ticket, Greene King Ruddles County, Scottish Courage Courage Directors, Bombardier
Rooms: 4 en suite s£38 d£60 (◆◆◆◆)
Children's Facilities: Licence Portions/Menu High Chairs Food Warming
Nearby: Beamish Open Air Museum
Notes: Dogs Allowed (in bedroom by arrangement) Garden Food Served Outside Small picnic area Parking 60 Coach parties welcome

CHATTON NU02

The Percy Arms Hotel ⚲ ♈

Main Road Alnwick NE66 5PS
☎ 01668 215244 ▤ 01668 215277

Dir: From Alnwick take A1 N, then B6348 to Chatton

Traditional 19th-century forming coaching inn, situated in the heart of rural Northumberland. Expect a warm, traditional pub welcome, as well as a selection of fine beers, wines and tempting food. Bar menu includes Aberdeen Angus steaks, deep-fried haddock, steak and kidney pie and a wide selection of fish and seafood dishes.

Open: 11-11 (Sun 12-10.30)
Bar Meals: L served all week 12-2.30 D served all week 6.30-9.30 Av main course £7
Restaurant: L served all week 12-2.30 D served all week 6.30-9.30
Brewery/Company: FREE HOUSE
⚑: Jenkins Beers
Children's Facilities: Licence Portions/Menu Cutlery Games High Chairs Food Warming Changing
Nearby: Pot a Doodle Do, Chillingham Castle, Baniburgh Castle & Beach
Notes: No Dogs Garden Food Served Outside patio/terrace, front beer garden Parking 30 Coach parties welcome

EGLINGHAM NU11

Tankerville Arms 🐾

Alnwick NE66 2TX
☎ 01665 578444 📠 01665 578444

Dir: B6346 from Alnwick

Picturesquely located in the foothills of the Cheviots, this traditional stone-built pub has a good reputation for its real ales and food. The local castles (including Alnwick, featured in the Harry Potter movies), countryside and beaches make it a favourite with walkers and cyclists alike. From the menu, expect duck, orange and apricot sausage with Savoy cabbage and thyme sauce; cannon of venison on a red onion tart with a rich port sauce; or ProvenÁal bean cassoulet. There is also a very good range of soups, salads and sandwiches.

Open: 12-2 7-11 (Times may vary)
closed: 25 Dec, Mon & Tues (Jan/Feb)
Bar Meals: L served all week 12-2
D served all week 6-9
Restaurant: L served all week 12-2
D all week 6-9 Av 3 course · à la carte £20
Brewery/Company: FREE HOUSE
🍺: Greene King Ruddles Best, Scottish Courage Courage Directors, Black Sheep Best, Mordue Workie Ticket, Timothy Taylor Landlord
Children's Facilities: Portions/Menu Cutlery High Chairs Food Warming Changing
Nearby: Alnwick Castle, Alnwick Tree House
Notes: No Dogs (except Assist Dogs) Garden Food Served Outside Country garden, good views Parking 15 Coach parties welcome

FALSTONE NY78

The Pheasant Inn ♦♦♦♦ 🐾

Stannersburn NE48 1DD
☎ 01434 240382 📠 01434 240382
📧 enquiries@thepheasantinn.com

Dir: From A68 onto B6320, or from A69, B6079, B6320, follow signs 'Kielder Water'

This 17th-century free house is close to Kielder Water, the largest artificial lake in Europe, and some of Northumberland's most unspoilt countryside. The snug interior includes a wealth of beams, exposed stone walls and open fires. The restaurant is a relaxing environment in which to enjoy a good selection of traditional home-cooked food.

Open: 11-3 6-11 (times vary) Closed: Dec 25-26 Mon-Tue (Nov-Mar)
Bar Meals: L served all week 12-2.30
D served all week 7-9
Restaurant: L served all week 12-2.30
D served all week 7-9 Sun 12-2, from 8
Brewery/Company: FREE HOUSE
🍺: Theakston Best, Marstons Pedigree, Timothy Taylor Landlord
Rooms: 8 en suite 1 family s£35 d£65
Children's Facilities: Fam room Play area (Open garden, small stream with bridge) Portions/Menu Cutlery Games High Chairs Food Warming Changing
Nearby: Kielder Water Leisure Park, Hadrians Wall, Newcastle Centre for Life
Notes: Dogs by arrangement only Garden Food Served Outside Grassed courtyard, stream Parking 30

FALSTONE — NY78

The Blackcock Inn ◆◆◆ ♀

nr Kielder NE48 1AA
☎ 01434 240200
📧 blackcock@falstone.fsbusiness.co.uk

Dir: Off unclassified rd from Bellingham (accessed from A68 or B6320)

A traditional 18th-century stone-built inn, close to Kielder Reservoir and Forest, with some lovely walks accessible from the village. The pub is also handy for the Rievers Cycle Route. Old beams and open log fires make for a cosy atmosphere, and food is served in the bar, lounge and dining area alongside a good choice of beers. Dishes are based on the best local produce, ranging from snacks to steaks, with fish and vegetarian options. Try one of the Yorkshire puddings with a variety of fillings.

Open: 11-3 6-11 (Winter 7-11)
Bar Meals: L served all week 11-2 D served all week 7-9 Av main course £6.95
Restaurant: L served N all-D served Fri-Sun 7-9 Av 3 course · à la carte £16
Brewery/Company: FREE HOUSE 🍺: Blackcock Ale, Wylam Bitter, Theakston Cool Cask, Magnet Ale, Marston's Pedigree
Rooms: 5 en suite 1 family s£35 d£55
Children's Facilities: Fam room Play area (Swings, climbing frame) Portions/Menu High Chairs Food Warming
Notes: Dogs Allowed Garden Food Served Outside lawn, flower beds, picnic benches Parking 20 Coach parties welcome

HALTWHISTLE — NY76

Milecastle Inn ☜

Military Road Cawfields NE49 9NN
☎ 01434 321372
📧 clarehind@aol.co.uk

Dir: Leave A69 at Haltwhistle, pub about 2 miles from Haltwhistle at junction with B6318

Spectacular views from the gardens towards Hadrian's Wall are a treat for tourists arriving at this stone-built rural inn. Even scenery-hardened locals are probably deep-down aware of how lucky they are to have such a backdrop to their eating and drinking. The beamed bar has open fires and even a resident ghost. The owners have developed a menu strong on the likes of game pie, venison, pheasant, steaks, gammon, Whitby scampi, seafood medley and other fish, as well as vegetarian dishes.

Open: 12-2.30 6.30-11 Mar-Nov 12-11
Bar Meals: L served all week 12-3 D served all week 6-9
Restaurant: L served N Sun 12-2.30 D served Sun-Sat 7-9
Brewery/Company: FREE HOUSE 🍺: Northumberland Castle, Carlsberg-Tetley Tetley Bitter, Marsdens Pedigree, Old Speckled Hen
Children's Facilities: Portions/Menu Food Warming
Nearby: Hadrians Wall, Roman Army Museums, outdoor swimming pool
Notes: No Dogs (except Assist Dogs) Garden Food Served Outside Walled with benches, seats 25 Parking 30

HAYDON BRIDGE   NY86

The General Havelock Inn

Ratcliffe Road Hexham NE47 6ER
☎ 01434 684376 📠 01434 684283
✉ GeneralHavelock@aol.com

Dir: On A69, 7m west of Hexham

Not far from Hadrian's Wall, this 19th-century roadside inn takes its name from a British Army officer. The pub was built as a private house in 1840 but has been licensed since 1890. The restaurant, in a converted barn at the back, overlooks the River Tyne. Ingredients are sourced locally for the no-nonsense pub food. Typical main courses are pan-fried calves' liver with onion gravy; chicken, leek and cheddar pie; and moules marinières. Round off with glazed bread and butter pudding with apricot compôte.

Open: 12-2.30 7-11 **Days closed:** Mon, some Tues in Jan
Bar Meals: L served Tue-Sun 12-2 D served Tue-Sat 7-9 Av main course £8
Restaurant: L served Tue-Sun 12-2 D served Tue-Sat 7-9 Av 3 course · à la carte £23 Av 3 course fixed price £14.25
Brewery/Company: FREE HOUSE 🍺: Hesket Newmarket, Courage Directors, Wylam Magic, Helvellyn Gold, Mordue Al Wheat Pet
Children's Facilities: Portions/Menu Games High Chairs Food Warming
Notes: Dogs Allowed Garden Food Served Outside Patio area on river bank, lots of plants Coach parties welcome

HEDLEY ON THE HILL   NZ05

The Feathers Inn

Stocksfield NE43 7SW
☎ 01661 843607 📠 01661 843607

From its hilltop position, this small stone-built free house overlooks the Cheviots. The three-roomed pub is well patronised by the local community, but strangers, too, are frequently charmed by its friendly and relaxed atmosphere. Families are welcome, and a small side room can be booked in advance if required. Old oak beams, coal fires and rustic settles set the scene. Although the pub has no garden, food and drinks can be served at tables on the green in good weather. The menus change regularly, and the imaginative home cooking includes an extensive choice of vegetarian meals.

Open: 12-3 6-11 (Sun 12-3, 7-10.30) **Closed:** 25 Dec
Bar Meals: L served Sat-Sun 12-2.30 D served Tue-Sun 7-9 Av main course £8.10
Brewery/Company: FREE HOUSE
🍺: Mordue Workie Ticket, Big Lamp Bitter, Fuller's London Pride, Yates Bitter, Northumberland County
Children's Facilities: Licence Fam room Portions/Menu Food Warming
Nearby: Beamish Museum, Hadrians Wall, Waterworld
Notes: No Dogs (except Assist Dogs) Water Food Served Outside Tables outside at the front Parking 12 Coach parties by arrangement.

HEXHAM NY96

Dipton Mill Inn ♀

Dipton Mill Road NE46 1YA
☎ 01434 606577
🌐 glb@hexhamshire.co.uk

Dir: 2m S of Hexham on HGV route to Blanchland (B6306) (Dipton Mill Rd)

This quintessential country pub with a millstream running through its garden and real fires warming the bar in winter, is in serious walking country near Hadrian's Wall and other Roman sites. The low-ceilinged, panelled bar has a quiet, friendly atmosphere. All food is freshly prepared, whether it's the Ploughman's with a variety of local cheeses, chicken breast in sherry sauce, steak and kidney pie, or the cheese and broccoli flan. Puddings include chocolate cake, Pavlova roulade or syrup sponge with custard.

Open: 12-2.30 6-11 (Sun 12-4, 7-10.30)
Closed: 25 Dec
Bar Meals: L served all week 12-2.15 D served all week 6.30-8.30 (Sun 12-2.15, 7.30-8.30) Av main course £6
Brewery/Company: FREE HOUSE
🍺: Hexhamshire Shire Bitter, Old Humbug, Devil's Water, Devil's Elbow & Whapweasel
Children's Facilities: Licence Food Warming
Nearby: Riding stables
Notes: No Dogs (except Assist Dogs) Garden Food Served Outside Grassed and terraced area, small aviary Coach parties welcome No credit cards

HEXHAM NY96

Miners Arms Inn

Main Street Acomb NE46 4PW
☎ 01434 603909

Dir: 17m W of Newcastle on A69, 2m W of Hexham.

Close to Hadrian's Wall in a peaceful village, this charming 18th-century pub has stone walls, beamed ceilings and open fires. Real ales are a speciality, as is good home-cooked food. There is no jukebox or pool table, so visitors will have to entertain themselves with conversation, and some choices from a menu that includes lasagne, curry, Italian chicken, steak and kidney pie, chilli, and a special trifle. Good setting for cyclists and walkers, and the garden has an aviary.

Open: 5-11 (Sat 12-11, Sun 12-10.30)
Bar Meals: L served all week 12-9 D served all week 5-9 (Sun 12-5.30) Av main course £5.35
Restaurant: L served all week 12-9 D served all week 5-9 Sunday 12-5.30
Brewery/Company: FREE HOUSE
🍺: Jennings Best, Yates, Northumberland Smooth, Durham White Velvet, Boddingtons
Children's Facilities: Fam room Portions/Menu Cutlery Games High Chairs Food Warming
Nearby: Hadrians Wall, Sele Park
Notes: Dogs Allowed Water Garden Food Served Outside Secluded sun trap beer garden, seating, BBQ Coach parties welcome No credit cards

LONGFRAMLINGTON NU10

The Anglers Arms

Weldon Bridge Morpeth NE65 8AX
☎ 01665 520271 570655 ▤ 01665 570041
✉ johnyoung@anglersarms.fsnet.co.uk

A traditional old coaching inn dating from the 1760s, standing by picturesque Weldon Bridge over the River Coquet. Assiduous attention by management and staff apart, what helps to give it a warm and friendly atmosphere are the little touches found at every turn-antiques, bric-a-brac, hand-painted wall tiles and, not unexpectedly, fishing memorabilia. Typical dishes at the bar, or in the decidedly sophisticated old Pullman railway carriage restaurant, are home-made steak and ale pie, Northumbrian sausage Lyonnaise, mixed grill, steaks, chicken in bacon, grilled rainbow trout, and balti curry. Overnight guests can expect a hearty Northumbrian breakfast.

Open: 11-3 6-11
Bar Meals: L served all week 12-2 D served all week 6-9.30 Av main course £8
Restaurant: L served all week 12-2 D served all week 6-9.30
🍺:Worthington, Carling, Boddingtons & 3 Guest Ales
Rooms: 5 en suite 1 family room (◆◆◆◆)
Children's Facilities: Licence Fam room Play area (Play area in garden, climbing frame) Portions/Menu High Chairs Food Warming
Notes: Dogs Allowed Garden Food Served Outside 0.5 acre garden Parking 30 Coach parties welcome

LONGHORSLEY NZ19

Linden Tree ♀

Linden Hall Morpeth NE65 8XF
☎ 01670 500033 ▤ 01670 500001
✉ stay@lindenhall.co.uk

Dir: Off the A1 on the A697 1m N of Longhorsley

Originally two large cattle byres, this popular bar takes its name from the linden trees in the grounds of Linden Hall Hotel, an impressive Georgian mansion. Straightforward meals range from aubergine and broccoli bake, braised lamb shank, or medallions of pork, to grilled salmon, or poached smoked cod fillets.

Open: 11-11 (Sun 12-10.30) Closed: 1 Jan
Bar Meals: L served all week 12-2 D served all week 6-9.30 Av main course £18.95
Restaurant: L served all week 12-2 D served all week 6-9.30
Brewery/Company: FREE HOUSE
🍺: Worthingtons, Worthington 1744, Pedigree
Children's Facilities: Portions/Menu Games High Chairs Food Warming Changing
Notes: Dogs Allowed Garden Food Served Outside Large open court yard Parking 200 Coach parties welcome

NEWTON ON THE MOOR   NU10

Cook and Barker Inn ♀

Felton NE65 9JY
☎ 01665 575234 📠 01665 575234

Dir: 0.5m from A1 S of Alnwick

Traditional Northumbrian inn located in a picturesque village with outstanding views over the coast. Good quality fare, including some exotic specialities, make this inn a popular dining destination. In the evening, a carte menu offers appetisers like fresh crab salad with lemon and chive mayonnaise; forest and field main courses like pot roast lamb shank on a basil and rosemary mash; and fish like seared west coast scallops with ginger.

Open: 12-3 6-11
Bar Meals: L served all week 12-2 D served all week 6-9 Av main course £6.95
Restaurant: L served all week 12-2 D served all week 7-9 Av 3 course · à la carte £25 Av 3 course fixed price £19.50
Brewery/Company: FREE HOUSE
🍺: Timothy Taylor Landlord, Theakstons Best Bitter, Fuller's London Pride, Batemans XXXB, Scottish Courage Courage Directors
Children's Facilities: Fam room Portions/Menu Cutlery High Chairs Food Warming
Nearby: Alnwick Gardens, Alnwick Castle, Druridge Bay
Notes: No Dogs (except Assist Dogs) Garden Food Served Outside Pretty area with lots of space for children Parking 60 Coach parties welcome

WARDEN   NY96

The Boatside Inn 🐕

Hexham NE46 4SQ
☎ 01434 602233 601061

Dir: Just off A69 west of Hexham, follow signs to Warden Newborough & Fourstones

This attractive stone pub nestles beneath Warden Hill Iron Age fort and sits next to where the North and South Tyne rivers meet. The name comes from the rowing boat that ferried people across the river before the bridge was built. A popular destination for walkers, that promises real ale and good food cooked from local produce. Expect dishes such as fish pie, mussels, liver and bacon casserole and chicken curry. The garden has a lawn area and a barbeque.

Open: 11-3 6-11
Bar Meals: L served all week 12-2 D served all week 6.30-9.30 Av main course £7
Restaurant: L served all week 12-2 D served all week 6.30-9.30
Brewery/Company: FREE HOUSE
🍺: Jennings, Cumberland, Cumberland Cream, Jennings Bitter, Old Smoothy
Children's Facilities: Portions/Menu High Chairs Food Warming
Notes: Dogs Allowed Water Garden Food Served Outside Paved patio with lawn area, hanging baskets Parking 70 Coach parties welcome

CAUNTON

Caunton Beck ♀

Newark NG23 6AB
☎ 01636 636793 ▤ 01636 636828
✉ cautonbeck@aol.com

Dir: 5m NW of Newark on A616

*It's somewhat out of the ordinary to find a
country pub that opens for breakfast at 8am
and offers a continuous service right through
until around midnight, every day of the year.
But then this civilised pub-restaurant is no
ordinary establishment. The business is
constructed around a 16th-century cottage, set
amid herb gardens and a dazzling rose arbour.
Greene King, Ruddles and John Smith's beers
complement the extensive international wine
list and regularly changing blackboard menus.
A full English breakfast is amongst the options
to start your day, which might progress
through the traditional sandwich menu to one
of the freshly cooked main course dishes.*

Open: 8am-midnight
Bar Meals: L&D served all week 8am-11pm
Av main course £13.50
Restaurant: L&D served all week 8am-11pm
Av 3 course - à la carte £24 Av 3 course fixed
price £13.95
Brewery/Company: FREE HOUSE
🍺: Greene King Ruddles Best, Scottish
Courage John Smith's, Springhead Best Bitter
Children's Facilities: Licence Portions/Menu
Games High Chairs Food Warming
Nearby: Newark Castle, Southwell Races
Notes: Dogs Allowed Garden Food Served
Outside Terrace & lawns Parking 30

COLSTON BASSETT

The Martins Arms Inn 🛏 ♀

School Lane NG12 3FD
☎ 01949 81361 ▤ 01949 81039

Dir: From M1 J22 take A50 then A46 N
towards Newark. Colston Bassett is E of
Cotgrave or M1 J21A then A46 to Newark

*This inn was converted from a 17th-century
farmhouse to an inn in the mid 19th century by
local Squire Martin, hence its name. Today, this
listed building has a country house feel to it,
with period furnishings, and seasonal fires in
the Jacobean fireplace. Regional ingredients
are a feature of the menu, with maybe roasted
turbot with truffled stew of haricot beans,
spinach, garlic, rosemary and caper butter
or, perhaps, ballotine of turkey with potato
fondant, caramelised onions and white onion
sauce on the menu. Over 14s only in the bar.*

Open: 12-3 6-11 RS: 25 Dec Closed eve
Bar Meals: L served all week 12-2 D served
6-10 Av main course £11.50
Restaurant: L served all week 12-2 D served
Mon-Sat 6-9.30 Sun 12-1.30
Brewery/Company: FREE HOUSE
🍺: Marston's Pedigree, Interbrew Bass,
Greene King Abbot Ale, Timothy Taylor Landlord
Children's Facilities: Fam room
Portions/Menu Food Warming
Nearby: Belvoir Castle, Butterfly Farm
Notes: Dogs Allowed Only in garden; water
available Garden Food Served Outside Acre of
landscaped garden with 80 covers Parking 35
Coach parties welcome

KIMBERLEY SK44

The Nelson & Railway Inn

12 Station Road Eastwood NG16 2NR
☎ 0115 938 2177

Dir: 1m N of M1 J26

The landlord of 34 years gives this 17th-century pub its distinctive personality. Next door is the Hardy & Hanson brewery that supplies many of the beers, but the two nearby railway stations that once made it a railway inn are now sadly derelict. A hearty menu includes monster mixed grill, a feast of sausage, and chicken curry, plus a choice of rolls and sandwiches.

Open: 11-11 (Sun 12-10.30)
Bar Meals: L served all week 12-2.30 D served all week 5.30-9 (Sun 12-6)
Restaurant: L served all week 12-2.30 D served all week 5.30-9 (Sun 12-6)
Brewery/Company: HARDY & HANSONS PLC 🍺: Hardys, Hansons Best Bitter, Classic, Cool & Dark, Olde Trip
Children's Facilities: Licence Fam room High Chairs Food Warming
Notes: Dogs Allowed water provided Garden Food Served Outside Food served outdoors, patio/terrace Parking 50 Coach parties welcome

LAXTON SK76

The Dovecote Inn 🐾 ♀

Moorhouse Road NG22 0NU
☎ 01777 871586 📠 01777 871586
📧 dovecoteinn@yahoo.co.uk

Set in the only village that still uses the 'three field system', (pop into the local Visitor Centre to find out what that is), this 18th-century pub is an ideal stopping point for walkers. Dishes on offer include chicken stuffed with asparagus in a smokey bacon and cream sauce; roast rack of lamb in a rosemary, mint, onion and mushroom gravy; and mushroom Stroganoff and seafood platter. There is also a range of light bites-baguettes, sandwiches and jacket potatoes.

Open: 11.30-3 6.30-11.30 (Fri-Sat 6-11.30)
Bar Meals: L served all week 12-2 D served all week 6.30-9.30 Av main course £9
Restaurant: L served all week 12-2 D served all week 6.30-9.30
Brewery/Company: FREE HOUSE
🍺: Mansfield Smooth, Banks Smooth, Marston's Pedigree
Rooms: 2 en suite s£35 d£50 (◆◆◆◆)
Children's Facilities: Portions/Menu Cutlery High Chairs Food Warming
Nearby: Medieval Farming Visitor Centre, Sherwood Forest, Rufford Country Park
Notes: Dogs Allowed Garden Food Served Outside Table & chairs in front garden Parking 45 Coach parties welcome

Lincolnshire Poacher ♀

161-163 Mansfield Road NG1 3FR
☎ 0115 941 1584

Dir: M1 J26. Town centre

Traditional wooden-floored town pub with settles and sturdy wooden tables. Bustles with real ale fans in search of the 12 real ales on tap-regular brewery evenings and wine tastings. Also, good cider and 70 malt whiskies-a great drinkers pub. Large summer terrace.

Open: 11-11 (Sun 12-10.30) Closed: 1 Jan
Bar Meals: L served all week 12-8 D served Mon-Fri-(Mon 12-3, Fri 12-3 & 5-7, Sun 12-4) Av main course £5.50
Brewery/Company: TYNEMILL LTD
🍺: Bateman XB, XXXB, Castle Rock, JHB, Poachers Gold
Children's Facilities: Fam room
Notes: Dogs Allowed Garden beer garden, food served in garden Coach parties welcome

Ye Olde Trip to Jerusalem ♀

1 Brewhouse Yard Castle Road NG1 6AD
☎ 0115 9473171
🌐 yeoldtrip@hardysandhansons.plc.uk

Allegedly Britain's oldest pub, and also one of the most unusual, with parts of it penetrating deep into the sandstone of Castle Rock. In Middle English, a 'tryppe' was a resting place, as Richard the Lionheart's Crusaders would have known, since they 'trypped' here in 1189. The caves were once used for brewing, with malting taking place in the Rock Lounge which, like the Museum Room, has a sixty-foot chimney piercing the rock above. Most gustatory wishes are met by a menu which runs from sandwiches, jackets, burgers and salads, to main courses typified by giant meat- or vegetable-filled Yorkshire puddings, chicken tikka masala, salmon Florentine, steak and Kimberley ale pie, and red pepper and mushroom lasagne (one of several vegetarian options).

Open: 11-11 (Sun 12-10.30)
Bar Meals: L served all week 11-6 (Sun 12-6) Av main course £6.50
Brewery/Company: HARDYS & HANSONS
🍺: Hardys & Hansons Kimberley Best Bitter, Best Mild, Ye Olde Trip Ale, Guest Beers
Children's Facilities: Licence Fam room Portions/Menu
Nearby: Nottingham Castle, Caves of Nottingham, Brewhouse Yard
Notes: No Dogs (except Assist Dogs) Garden Food Served Outside Seating in front & rear courtyard Coach parties welcome

NOTTINGHAMSHIRE

SOUTHWELL　　　　SK65

French Horn 🐕 ♟

Main Street Upton NG23 5ST
☎ 01636 812394 📠 01636 815497
✉ duckstock@hotmail.com

An 18th-century former farmhouse handy for visiting the racecourse and nearby Southwell Minster. It offers real ales, 24 wines by the glass and good food. Seafood is a speciality and popular seafood evenings are held on a Thursday. Typical dishes are grilled red mullet with lobster and mango curry, and wild sea bass with green bean salad and saffron vinaigrette. Children are welcome and there is a large enclosed garden to the rear.

Open: 11.30-3 5.30-11 **Days closed:** Tues
Bar Meals: L served all week 12-2.15 D served all week 6-9.30 Sun 12-4 Av main course £10.50
Restaurant: L served Sun-Mon, Wed-Sat 12-2.30 D served Tue-Sat 7-9.30 Sun 12-4 A 3 course · à la carte £21.50 Av 3 course fixed price £12
🍺: Directors, Adnams
Children's Facilities: Licence Portions/Menu Games High Chairs Food Warming
Nearby: Southwell Minster, Wonderland, White Post Farm
Notes: Dogs Allowed Water Garden Food Served Outside Large enclosed garden Parking 100 Coach parties welcome

THURGARTON　　　SK64

The Red Lion 🐕

Southwell Road NG14 7GP
☎ 01636 830351

> **Dir:** On A612 between Nottingham & Southwell

This 16th-century inn was once a monks' alehouse. The extensive bar menu offers beef and Guinness casserole, chicken tikka masala, grilled salmon, vegetable lasagne and a good choice of salads. Specials might include lobster thermidor, or venison, black cherry and port casserole. Look for the 1936 Nottingham Guardian cutting on the wall that reports the murder of a previous landlady by her niece.

Open: 11.30-2.30 6.30-11 (Open all day Sat-Sun & BHs)
Bar Meals: L served all week 12-2 D served all week 7-10 Sat & Sun 12-9.30 Av main course £6.95
Restaurant: L served all week 12-2 D served all week 7-10
Brewery/Company: FREE HOUSE 🍺:
Greene King Abbot Ale, Jenning Cumberland, Carlsberg-Tetley, Black Sheep, Mansfield Cask
Children's Facilities: Portions/Menu Cutlery High Chairs Food Warming
Nearby: White Post Farm, Newark Castle, Nottingham City
Notes: No Dogs (except Assist Dogs) Garden Food Served Outside Large spacious, well kept Parking 40 Coach parties welcome

ARDINGTON
SU48

The Boars Head ♀

Church Street Wantage OX12 8QA
☎ 01235 833254 📄 01235 833254
✉ info@boarsheadardington.co.uk

Dir: Off A417 E of Wantage

Tucked away beside the church, the pretty, 400-year-old Boars Head is situated within the beautifully maintained Lockinge Estate, laid out in the 19th century by Lord Wantage. Although dining is important, it's still very much the village local. Log fires blaze when they should, candles are lit in the evenings, and there are always fresh flowers. Fish dishes are a house speciality, with supplies from Cornwall arriving daily. The words 'fresh', 'locally grown', and 'seasonal' underpin the innovative, refreshingly unwordy menus, and from bread to ice creams, pasta to pastries, everything is home made.

Open: 12-3 6.30-11
Bar Meals: L served all week 12-2.30 D served all week 7-10 Av main course £9.50
Restaurant: L served all week 12-2.30 D served all week 7-10 Av 3 course · à la carte £25
Brewery/Company: FREE HOUSE
🍺: Hook Norton Old Hooky, West Berkshire Berwery Dr. Hexter's, Warsteiner, Butts Brewery, Barbus Barbus
Children's Facilities: Portions/Menu Games High Chairs Food Warming Changing
Nearby: White Horse at Uttington, Didcot Steam Railway Centre
Notes: No Dogs (except Assist Dogs) Garden Food Served Outside Patio area, three tables Parking 10 Coach parties welcome

BAMPTON
SP30

The Romany

Bridge Street nr Witney OX18 2HA
☎ 01993 850237 📄 01993 852133
✉ romany@barbox.net

A shop until 20 years ago, The Romany is housed in an 18th-century building of Cotswold stone with a beamed bar, log fires and intimate dining room. The choice of food ranges from bar snacks and bar meals to a full carte restaurant menu, with home-made specials like hotpot, Somerset pork, or steak and ale pie. There is a good range of vegetarian choices. Regional singers provide live entertainment a couple of times a month.

Open: 11-11
Bar Meals: L served all week 12-2 D served all week 6.30-9 Av main course £6
Restaurant: L served all week 12-2 D served all week 6.30-9
Brewery/Company: FREE HOUSE
🍺: Archers Village, plus guests
Children's Facilities: Play area Portions/Menu Games High Chairs Food Warming
Notes: Dogs Allowed Water Garden Food Served Outside Food served outside Parking 8 Coach parties welcome

BURFORD — SP21

The Inn for All Seasons ★★ ♀

The Barringtons OX18 4TN
☎ 01451 844324 ▧ 01451 844375
✉ sharp@innforallseasons.com

Dir: 3m W of Burford on A40

This 16th-century Grade II listed Cotswold coaching inn has a mix of ancient oak beams, original fireplaces and complementary period furniture. Menus plough an 'all-seasons' furrow, taking in everything from noisette of Cotswold lamb to pan-fried chop of old spot Gloucester pork. Vegetarians are imaginatively catered for but pride of place undoubtedly goes to the selection of fish, fresh from Brixham.

Open: 11-2.30 6-11 (Sun 12-3, 7-10.30)
Bar Meals: L served all week 11.30-2.2 D served all week 6.30-9.30 Av main course £8
Restaurant: L served all week 11.30-2.30 D served all week 6.30-9.30 Av 3 course · à la carte £16.75
Brewery/Company: FREE HOUSE
◀: Wadworth 6X, Interbrew Bass, Wychwood, Badger, Sharps, Doom Bar
Rooms: 10 en suite 2 family s£54 d£90
Children's Facilities: Play area (Garden) Portions/Menu Cutlery Games High Chairs Food Warming Changing
Nearby: Cotswold Wildlife Park, Birdland Bourton on Water, Model Village
Notes: Dogs Allowed Garden Food Served Outside Small grass area, tables, good views Parking 80 Coach parties welcome

The Lamb Inn ★★★ ◉◉ ☜ ♀

Sheep Street OX18 4LR
☎ 01993 823155 ▧ 01993 822228
✉ info@lambinn-burford.co.uk

Dir: From M40 J8 follow signs for A40 & Burford. Off High Street

If your idea of a traditional English inn includes stone flagged floors, real ale and log fires, you'll not be disappointed at the 500-year-old Lamb. But there's nothing old-world about the menus, which present a delicious blend of modern and traditional English cooking. The chef uses locally produced meat, cheese and vegetables whenever possible, as well as organic meat and fish when available. Menus are changed regularly, and include contemporary dishes such as chargrilled squid with chorizo and pesto salad; or classic Caesar salad with prawns.

Open: 11-2.30 6-11 (Sun 12-4, 7-10.30)
Bar Meals: L Mon-Sat 12-2.30 D Mon-Sun 7-9.30 Sat no bar menu in evening Av main course £12 **Restaurant:** L Mon-Sun 12.30-2.30 D Mon-Sun 7-9.30 Av 3 course fixed price £32 **Brewery/Company:** FREE HOUSE
◀: Wadworth 6X, Hook Norton Best
Rooms: 15 en suite s£80 d£130
Children's Facilities: Fam room Portions/Menu Games High Chairs Food Warming Changing **Nearby:** Cotswold Wildlife Park **Notes:** Dogs Allowed Water Garden Food Served Outside walled cottage garden

CHALGROVE   SU69

The Red Lion Inn 🐾 �glass

The High Street OX44 7SS
☎ 01865 890625 📠 01865 890795

Dir: B480 from Oxford Ring rd, through
Stadhampton, L then R at mini-rdbt,
at Chalgrove Airfield R fork into village

*A pub owned by the village church? The Red
Lion is, and has been since 1637, when it
provided free dining and carousing for the
'naughty' church wardens. Expect a warm
welcome, a good pint of real ale, and both
traditional and imaginative eating. A bar
menu offers the simple favourites of beer-
battered fish and chips with mushy peas and
traditional cottage pie with vegetables. Dinner
menu choices are varied and there are
specials too, usually three starters and four
mains. Vegetarians are well catered for.*

Open: 12-3 6-11 (Winter 12-2.30, 5.30-11,
Sun 7-10.30) **Closed:** 1 Jan
Bar Meals: L served all week 12-2 D served
Mon-Sat 6-9 Av main course £6.50
Restaurant: L served all week 12-2 D served
Mon-Sat 7-9 Av 3 course · à la carte £18.50
Brewery/Company: FREE HOUSE
🍺: Fuller's London Pride, Adnams Best,
Wadworth 6X
Children's Facilities: Portions/Menu Cutlery
Food Warming
Notes: Dogs Allowed Water Garden Food
Served Outside Large, with seating Parking 20
Coach parties welcome

DEDDINGTON   SP43

Deddington Arms ★★★ ⊛ 🐾 ♩

Horsefair OX15 0SH
☎ 01869 338364 📠 01869 337010
✉ deddarms@aol.com

Dir: A43 to Northampton, B4100 to Aynho,
B4031 to Deddington. M40 J11 to Banbury.
Follow signs for hospital, then towards
Adderbury & Deddington, on A4260.

*From its timbered bars, with open fires
blazing away when you need them, this inn
has offered a warm welcome to travellers and
locals for 400 years. A bar meal could be a
sandwich or something hot and more
substantial main courses in the smart air-
conditioned restaurant might be pheasant
breast with bubble and squeak, smoked bacon
and thyme mousse, and Madeira jus; fillet of
beef, garlic mash, carrot broth and seared foie
gras; and sun-dried tomato and basil risotto
with chive beurre blanc.*

Open: 11-11
Bar Meals: L served all week 12-2 D served
all week 6.30-9 Av main course £9.50
Restaurant: L served all week 12-2 D served
all week 6.30-10 Sun 7-9 Av 3 course · à la
carte £27
Brewery/Company: FREE HOUSE 🍺:
Carlsberg-Tetleys Tetleys Bitter, Green King IPA
Rooms: 27 en suite 3 family s£75 d£85
Children's Facilities: Portions/Menu
High Chairs
Nearby: Blenheim Palace, Warwick Castle
Notes: No Dogs (ex Assist Dogs) Parking 36

OXFORDSHIRE

FIFIELD   SP21

Merrymouth Inn 🛏 ♀

Stow Road OX7 6HR
☎ 01993 831652 🖷 01993 830840
✉ tim@merrymouthinn.fsnet.co.uk

Dir: Situated on the A424 between Burford (3m) and Stow-on-the-Wold (4m)

The Merrymouth takes its name from the Murimouth family who were feudal lords of Fifield. The inn dates back to the 13th century and has a wonderful vaulted cellar, and rumour has it that there was once a secret passage to Bruern Abbey. A blackboard of fresh fish and vegetarian dishes supplements the Merrymouth menu, options from which might include gilt head sea bream, and breast of chicken with Gruyère and mushrooms.

Open: 12-2.30 6-10.30 (Closed Sun eve in winter)
Bar Meals: L served all week 12-2 D served all week 6.30-9 Sun 7-8.30 Av main course £9.95
Restaurant: L served all week 12-2 D served all week 6.30-9 Av 3 course · à la carte £18.50
Brewery/Company: FREE HOUSE 🍺: Hook Norton Best Bitter, Adnams Broadside
Children's Facilities: Portions/Menu Games High Chairs Food Warming
Nearby: Cotswold Wildlife Park, Birdland, Cotswold Farm Park
Notes: Dogs Allowed Garden Food Served Outside Small patio & enclosed garden at pubs front Parking 70

GORING   SU68

Miller of Mansfield ♀

High Street nr Reading RG8 9AW
☎ 01491 872829 🖷 01491 874200

Dir: From Pangbourne A329 to Streatley, then R on B4009, 0.5m to Goring

An 18th century, ivy-clad former coaching inn in the Goring Gap, the point where the River Thames flows between the Chilterns and the Berkshire Downs. In addition to the oak-beamed bar, where you can have full meals and snacks, there is a separate restaurant with a substantial menu, on which typical dishes are grilled duck breast with orange sauce; pork tenderloin with Calvados, apple and cream; and pan-fried sea bass with butter sauce. English roasts are available for Sunday lunch.

Open: 11-11 (Sun 12-10.30)
Bar Meals: L served all week 12-2 D served all week 6.30-10 (Sun 12-4, 6.30-9.30) Av main course £9.50
Restaurant: L served all week 12-2 D served all week 7-10 Av 3 course · à la carte £17.50
Brewery/Company: FREE HOUSE
🍺: Greene King Old Speckled Hen, Brakspear Bitter, Adnams Best
Rooms: 10 en suite s£45 d£65 (♦♦♦)
Children's Facilities: Portions/Menu Cutlery Games High Chairs Food Warming Changing
Notes: Dogs Allowed Water Parking 8 Coach parties welcome

HENLEY-ON-THAMES   SU78

The Golden Ball

Lower Assendon RG9 6AH
☎ 01491 574157 ▤ 01491 576653
✉ Golden.Ball@theseed.net

Dir: A4130, R onto B480, pub 300yds on L

Dick Turpin hid in the priest hole at this 400-year-old building tucked away in the Stonor Valley close to Henley. It has a traditional pub atmosphere with well-used furnishings, open fire, exposed timbers, brasses and a collection of old bottled ales. Well-kept beer and home-cooked food are served, and there's a south-facing garden with plenty of garden furniture and undercover accommodation. Favourite fare includes sausage and mash, fish pie and lasagne.

Open: 11-3 6-11
Bar Meals: L served all week 12-2 D served all week 7-9 Av main course £8.95
Brewery/Company: BRAKSPEAR
🍺: Brakspear Bitter & Special, 2 monthly seasonal beers
Children's Facilities: Fam room Play area (Climbing frame, slide) Portions/Menu Games High Chairs Food Warming Changing
Notes: Dogs Allowed water outside, hitching rail Garden Food Served Outside Large south facing garden Parking 50 Coach parties welcome

HENLEY-ON-THAMES   SU78

The White Hart Hotel ★ ◉◉ ⌂ ♀

High Street Nettlebed RG9 5DD
☎ 01491 642145 ▤ 01491 649018
✉ Info@whitehartnettlebed.com

Dir: On A4130

This beautifully restored brick and flint building dating from the 17th century was used as a billeting house for loyalist troops during the English Civil War. Chris Barber, former private chef to the Prince of Wales, serves up delicious food in two chic dining venues. Bistro dishes might include mushroom risotto; rib-eye of local Charolais beef with dauphinoise potatoes; or White Hart bouillabaisse with garlic rouille. The restaurant offers Chris's favourite dishes: diver caught scallops with squid ink risotto; Jerusalem artichoke soup with truffle oil; and pan-fried sea bass with ratatouille and pepper nage.

Open: 11-11 **Bar Meals:** L served all week 12-2.3 D served all week 6-10 Av main course £11 **Restaurant:** L served Tue-Sat-D served Thu-Sat 7-9 Av 3 course · à la carte £45
🍺: Brakspear, Guinness **Rooms:** 12 en suite 3 family d£105 **Children's Facilities:** Licence Fam room Play area Portions/Menu Cutlery Games High Chairs Food Warming Changing
Nearby: River Rides, Rowing Museum
Notes: No Dogs (except Assist Dogs) Garden Food Served Outside Large lawned area with seating Parking 50

OXFORDSHIRE

KINGSTON LISLE   SU38

The Blowing Stone Inn ♀

Wantage OX12 9QL
☎ 01367 820288 📠 01367 821102
✉ luke@theblowingstoneinn.com

Dir: B4507 from Wantage toward
Ashbury/Swindon, after 6m R
to Kingston Lisle

Combining modern times with old-fashioned
warmth and hospitality, this attractive country
pub derives its name from the Blowing Stone,
located on the outskirts of the village. Popular
with walkers and horse racing fans, it is run
by Radio Five Live racing presenter Luke
Harvey and his sister. Menu choices include
pork loin steak with honey and mustard glaze
and butterflied chicken with a garlic and
mushroom sauce.

Open: 12-2.30 6-11 (open all day Fri-Sun)
Bar Meals: L served Tue-Sun 12-3 D served
all week 7-9.30 Av main course £10.50
Restaurant: L served all week 12-2.30 D
served all week 7-9.30
Brewery/Company: FREE HOUSE
🍺: Courage Best, Fuller's London Pride
& Guest Beers
Children's Facilities: Portions/Menu Cutlery
Games High Chairs Food Warming Changing
Nearby: The Blowing Stone, The Ancient
Ridgeway, White Horse Hill
Notes: Dogs Allowed Water Garden Food
Served Outside Large with pond and fountain
Parking 30 Coach parties welcome

LOWER SHIPLAKE   SU77

The Baskerville Arms 🐾 ♀

Station Road Henley-on-Thames RG9 3NY
☎ 0118 940 3332 📠 0118 940 7235
✉ enquiries@thebaskerville.com

Set on the popular Thames Path, not far from
picturesque Henley, the attractive brick-built
Baskerville Arms is handy for both the river
and the railway station. A good restaurant
and a lovely garden add to the appeal.
Starters might include tiger prawns tossed in
chilli, Stilton soup, Thai crab cakes and old-
fashioned prawn cocktail, while typical main
courses range from grilled fillet steak set on a
potato and parsnip rosti, vegetable crumble,
blackened fillet of Cajun-style salmon, and
roast breast of corn-fed chicken wrapped in
pancetta and stuffed with herbed cheese.

Open: 11.30-2.30 6-11 (Fri 11.30-2.30,
5.30-11.30, Sun 11.30-2.30, 5.30-11)
Bar Meals: L served all week 12-2 D served
Mon-Sat 7-9.30 Av main course £9
Restaurant: L served Mon-Sun 12-2 D served
Mon-Sat-Av 3 course · à la carte £20 Av 3
course fixed price £9.95
🍺: London Pride, Brakspear, Stella Artois,
Castlemaine & Hoppit
Children's Facilities: Play area
Portions/Menu High Chairs Food Warming
Notes: Dogs Allowed Garden Food Served
Outside Spacious garden with play area &
BBQ Parking 12 Coach parties welcome

SHIPTON-UNDER-WYCHWOOD SP21

The Shaven Crown Hotel ♀

High Street OX7 6BA
☎ 01993 830330 ▤ 01993 832136
✉ reservations@shavencrown.co.uk

Dir: On A361, halfway between Burford and Chipping Norton opposite village green and church

Built of honey-coloured Cotswold stone around a medieval courtyard, the Shaven Crown is up to 700 years old in parts. The bar is small and cosy with a log fire and a convivial atmosphere. Imaginative bar food includes Cotswold lamb cutlets, chicken curry, risotto stuffed peppers with spinach sauce, and grilled sea bass with sweet potato mash. Pre-dinner drinks can be taken in the impressive Great Hall, and there's a fixed-price menu in the intimate candlelit dining room.

Open: 12-2.30 5-11
Bar Meals: L served all week 12-2 D served all week 5.30-9.30 Av main course £10
Restaurant: L served Sun 12-2 D served all week 7-9 Av 3 course - à la carte £20.50
Brewery/Company: FREE HOUSE
🍺: Hook Norton Best, Old Hooky, Speckled Hen & Archers Wychwood
Children's Facilities: Portions/Menu Games High Chairs Food Warming
Nearby: Cotswold Wildlife Park
Notes: Dogs Allowed Water Garden Food Served Outside Enclosed courtyard, lawned with trees Parking 15 Coach parties welcome

STANTON ST JOHN SP50

Star Inn ☺ ♀

Middle Road OX33 1EX
☎ 01865 351277 ▤ 01865 351006
✉ stantonstar@supanet.com

Dir: At A40/Oxford ring road rdbt take Stanton exit, follow rd to T junct, R to Stanton, 3rd L, pub on L 50yds

Although the Star is only a short drive from the centre of Oxford, this popular pub still retains a definite 'village' feel. The oldest part of the pub dates from the early 17th century, and in the past, the building has been used as a butcher's shop and an abattoir. The garden is peaceful and secluded. A varied menu features steak and Guinness pie, lamb in redcurrant and rosemary, deep-fried whitebait, Thai curry, lasagna, and moussaka.

Open: 11-2.30 6.30-11
Bar Meals: L served all week 12-2 D served all week but Sun eve 6.30-9.30 Av main course £7.95

Brewery/Company: WADWORTH
🍺: Wadworth 6X, Henrys IPA & JCB, Stella
Children's Facilities: Fam room Play area (Large secure garden, play area)
Portions/Menu Cutlery Games High Chairs Food Warming
Notes: Dogs Allowed Water bowls Garden Food Served Outside Large secure garden Parking 50 Coach parties welcome

WHEATLEY SP50

Bat & Ball Inn ◆◆◆ ☺ ♀

28 High Street OX44 9HJ
☎ 01865 874379 📠 01865 873363
✉ bb@traditionalvillageinns.co.uk

Dir: Through Wheatley towards Garsington, take L signed Cuddesdon

Do not be surprised to discover that the bar of this former coaching inn is packed to the gunnels with cricketing memorabilia. The comprehensive menu, supplemented by daily specials, is likely to feature steaks, fresh-baked pie of the day, herb-battered fresh cod, and maybe chargrilled Toulouse sausages. Lighter meals include homemade lasagne, lamb Peshwari, and warm spinach and pancetta salad.

Open: 11-11
Bar Meals: L served all week 12-2.45 D served all week 6.30-9.45 (Sun 12-9.45) Av main course £9.50
Restaurant: L served all week 12-2.45 D served all week 6.30-9.45 (Sun 12-9.45)
Brewery/Company: MARSTONS
🍺: Marston's Pedigree & Original, LBW
Rooms: 7 en suite 1 family room s£50 d£65
Children's Facilities: Portions/Menu Games High Chairs Food Warming
Nearby: Go Kart Racing, Bowling Alley, Multiplex Cinema
Notes: Dogs Allowed Water Bowl Garden Food Served Outside Patio with good views Parking 15 Coach parties welcome

WITNEY SP31

The Bell Inn ♀

Standlake Road Ducklington OX29 7UP
☎ 01993 702514 📠 01993 706822

Dir: One mile south of Witney in Ducklington village off A415 Abingdon road.

Nearly 700 years have passed since the men building the adjacent church also erected their own living accommodation. Their hostel eventually became the Bell. Today it is a popular, traditional village local, with many original features-and a collection of some 500 bells. Home-made pies, stews and burgers are a speciality, and there's a pig roast on Boxing Day.

Open: 12-3 5-11 (Fri-Sun 12-11) RS: 25, 26 Dec & 1 Jan closed eve
Bar Meals: L served all week 12-2 D served Mon-Sat 6-9 Av main course £8.50
Restaurant: L served all week 12-2 D served Mon-Sat 6-9 Av 3 course · à la carte £15
🍺: Greene King, IPA & Old Speckled Hen, Morland Original
Rooms: 7 en suite 2 family s£35 d£55
Children's Facilities: Play area (Climbing frame, swings) Portions/Menu Cutlery Games High Chairs Food Warming
Nearby: Burford Wildlife Park, Cogges Farm Museum
Notes: No Dogs Garden Food Served Outside Terrace at front and rear Parking 12 Coach parties welcome

EXTON   SK91

Fox & Hounds ♀

nr Oakham LE15 8AP
☎ 01572 812403 📠 01572 812403

*This late 17th-century, former coaching inn
stands on Exton's village green. There's a
large walled garden for al fresco summer
dining, and the pub is just a short drive from
Rutland Water. Jacket potatoes and filled
ciabattas feature on the casual lunch menu,
beside an extensive choice of traditional
Italian pizzas. Other dishes include pan-fried
calves' liver and bacon; chicken with roasted
peppers and linguine; and grilled halibut with
Mediterranean vegetables.*

Open: 11-3 6-11
Bar Meals: L served all week 12-2 D served
all week 6.30-9 No food Sun eve Av main
course £9
Restaurant: L served all week 12-2 D served
all week 6.30-9 Av 3 course · à la carte £18
Brewery/Company: FREE HOUSE
🍺: Greene King IPA, Grainstore Real Ales,
John Smiths Smooth
Children's Facilities: Play area (Large
garden) Portions/Menu Games High Chairs
Food Warming
Nearby: Rutland Water, Butterfly Farm, Burley
Falconry Centre
Notes: Dogs Allowed Water Garden Food
Served Outside Large walled garden & patio
area Parking 20 Coach parties welcome

LYDDINGTON   SP89

Old White Hart ♀

51 Main St LE15 9LR
☎ 01572 821703 📠 01572 821965

Dir: On A6003 between Uppingham
and Corby, take B672

*A honey-coloured 17th-century stone pub,
close to good walks and Rutland Water.
Freshly prepared food is served in the cosy
main bar, with its heavy beams and splendid
log fire, and in the adjoining dining areas. The
blackboard menu may offer deep-fried
Grimsby haddock and chips; home-made steak
and kidney pudding; herb-crusted cod with
pesto dressing; wild mushroom and asparagus
risotto; home-made Gloucester Old Spot
sausages; or confit neck of lamb on mash.
Ambitious evening carte. There is a rear
garden with 10 pétanque pitches.*

Open: 12-3 6.30-11 Closed: 25 Dec
Bar Meals: L served all week 12-2 D served
Mon-Sat 6.30-9 Av main course £12
Restaurant: L served all week 12-2 D served
Mon-Sat 6.30-9 Av 3 course · à la carte £20
Av 3 course fixed price £12.95
Brewery/Company: FREE HOUSE
🍺: Greene King IPA & Abbot Ale, Timothy
Taylor Landlord
Children's Facilities: Portions/Menu Games
High Chairs Food Warming
Nearby: Park in village, Rutland Water
Notes: No Dogs (except Assist Dogs) Water
Garden Food Served Outside Beer garden,
heated patio Parking 50 Coach parties
welcome

RUTLAND

OAKHAM · SK80

Barnsdale Lodge Hotel ★★★ ⏺ ♀

The Avenue Rutland Water, North Shore
LE15 8AH
☎ 01572 724678 📠 01572 724961
✉ enquiries@barnsdalelodge.co.uk

An Edwardian-style hotel overlooking Rutland Water in the heart of this picturesque little county. Its rural connections go back to its 17th-century origins as a farmhouse, but nowadays the Barnsdale Lodge offers modern comforts and hospitality. Real ales including local brews are served in the bar, with dishes such as escalope of springbok, and tagliatelle of monkfish from the gourmet menu, or typically posh fish and chips, or steak and kidney pie amongst house specialities.

Open: 7-11
Bar Meals: L served all week 12.15-2.15 D served all week 7-9.45 Av main course £10
Restaurant: L served all week 12.15-2.15 D served all week 7-9.45 Av 3 course · à la carte £35
Brewery/Company: FREE HOUSE
🍺: Rutland Grainstore, Marstons Pedigree, Scottish Courage Courage Directors
Rooms: 46 en suite 4 family s£75 d£99.50
Children's Facilities: Play area (Swings, slide, croquet, crazy golf) High Chairs Food Warming Changing
Notes: Dogs Allowed Water Garden Food Served Outside Courtyard, established garden with lawns Parking 280 Coach parties welcome

STRETTON · SK91

Ram Jam Inn ★★ ⏺ 🐕 ♀

The Great North Road Oakham LE15 7QX
☎ 01780 410776 📠 01780 410361
✉ rji@rutnet.co.uk

Dir: On A1 N-bound past B1668, through service station into car park

The inn is believed to have acquired its name in the 18th century when the landlord's sign advertised 'Fine Ram Jam'. The comprehensive all-day menu offers everything from sandwiches and clotted cream teas through to appealing three-course meals-all home made. Examples from the range are smoked beef salad with horseradish dressing, roast breast of pheasant with creamy wild mushroom risotto, and pasta piperade with roast Mediterranean vegetables and daily changing fish dishes are offered from the specials board.

Open: 7am-11pm Closed: 25 Dec
Bar Meals: L served all week 12-9.30 D served all week-Av main course £8.95
Restaurant: L served all week 12-9.30 D served all week 3 course · à la carte £18
Brewery/Company: FREE HOUSE
🍺: Fuller's London Pride, Scottish Courage John Smith's Cask and Smooth
Rooms: 7 en suite 1 family s£47 d£57
Children's Facilities: Play area (Large outside area) Portions/Menu Cutlery Games High Chairs Food Warming Changing
Nearby: Rutland Water, Burghley House,
Notes: Dogs Allowed Garden Food Served Outside Patio Parking 64 Coach parties welcome

BISHOP'S CASTLE   SO38

Boars Head ♦♦♦ ♀

Church Street SY9 5AE
☎ 01588 638521 ▤ 01588 630126
✉ sales@boarsheadhotel.co.uk

One of Bishop's Castle's oldest buildings, this former coaching inn received its first full licence in 1642. Legend tells that it escaped burning during the Civil War because half the King's men were drinking here, while the rest were out vandalising the town. The exposed beams are genuine, and a chimney contains a priest hole. The inn is celebrated for its lunchtime steak, chicken and sausage sizzlers, while scrumpy pork, lamb shank, salmon béarnaise, and paella appear on the carte.

Open: 11.30-11 (Sun 12-10.30)
Bar Meals: L served all week 12-2 D served all week 6.30-9.30 (Sun 12-9.30) Av main course £7
Restaurant: L served all week 12-2 D served all week 6.30-9.30 Av 3 course · à la carte £12.50
Brewery/Company: FREE HOUSE
🍺: Scottish Courage Courage Best & Courage Directors & regular guests
Rooms: 4 en suite 1 family s£38 d£60
Children's Facilities: Licence Portions/Menu Games High Chairs Food Warming
Nearby: Hoo Farm, Wonderland, Secret Hills
Notes: No Dogs (except Assist Dogs) Parking 20 Coach parties welcome

BRIDGNORTH   SO79

The Bear ♀

Northgate WV16 4ET
☎ 01746 763250
✉ thebearinn@aol.com

Dir: From High Street (Bridgnorth) through Northgate (sandstone archway) and the pub is on the L

Traditional Grade II listed hostelry in one of the loveliest of the Severn-side towns. The way it clings to the top of a high sandstone cliff gives it an almost continental flavour. A former coaching inn, the award-winning Bear boasts two carpeted bars which are characterised by whisky-water jugs, gas-type wall lamps and wheelback chairs. Good quality, appetising menu offers the likes of ham, egg and chips, braised lamb shank, wild mushroom and spinach risotto, and salmon and herb fishcakes. Daily-changing real ales and a choice of seven malts.

Open: 11-3 5-11 (Sun 7-10.30)
Bar Meals: L served all week 12-2 Av main course £5.50
Brewery/Company: ENTERPRISE INNS
🍺: guest ales
Children's Facilities:
Notes: Dogs Allowed Garden Food served outside Parking 18

CRESSAGE SJ50

The Riverside Inn ♀

Cound nr Shrewsbury SY5 6AF
☎ 01952 510900 📠 01952 510980

Dir: On A458 Shrewsbury-Bridgnorth rd

In three acres of garden alongside the River Severn, this extensively refurbished coaching inn offers river-view dining both outdoors and in a modern conservatory. The single menu serves both dining areas and spacious bar, furnished and decorated in haphazard country style. Traditional pub dishes include hot crab pâté and mushrooms with Shropshire blue cheese, followed by local lamb noisettes with parsnip chips, and salmon fishcakes with hollandaise. Exotic alternatives follow the lines of Peking duck pancakes with hoisin sauce, Pee-kai chicken breasts with satay sauce, and spinach, sorrel and Mozzarella parcels.

Open: 12-3 6-11
Bar Meals: L served all week 12-2.30 D served all week 6.30-9.30 Av main course £7.50
Restaurant: L served all week 12-2.30 D served all week 7-9.30 Av 3 course · à la carte £22

Brewery/Company: FREE HOUSE
🍺: Various cask ales & regular guest beers
Children's Facilities: Fam room Play area
Notes: Dogs Allowed Garden beer garden, patio, outdoor eating Parking 100

IRONBRIDGE SJ60

The Malthouse ◆◆◆◆ ♀

The Wharfage TF8 7NH
☎ 01952 433712 📠 01952 433298
✉ enquiries@malthousepubs.co.uk

The pub, a converted malthouse located only 250 yards from the bridge's main visitor centre, has been an inn since the turn of the 20th century. It has been extensively refurbished, and now offers six rooms above a popular jazz bar where live music can be heard from Wednesday to Saturday. On one side there is a bar with its own menu and kitchen, and on the other a full-service restaurant serving modern British food. Fish is well represented with tempura-battered monkfish with curried chickpeas, spinach and coriander dressing; red mullet and sole are also served. A sister pub with additional accommodation has been opened 50 metres away.

Open: 11-11 (Sun 12-3 6-10.30)
Closed: 25-26 Dec
Bar Meals: L served all week 12-2.30 D served all week 6-9.30 Av main course £8
Restaurant: L served all week 12-2 D served all week 6.30-9.45
Av 3 course · à la carte £21.20
Brewery/Company: INN PARTNERSHIP
🍺: Flowers Original, Boddingtons, Tetley
Rooms: 6 en suite 2 family s£55 d£60
Children's Facilities: Portions/Menu Cutlery Games High Chairs Food Warming Changing
Notes: No Dogs Garden Food Served Outside Parking 15

IRONBRIDGE SJ60

The Grove Inn/Fat Frog ♦♦♦

10 Wellington Road Coalbrookdale TF8 7DX
☎ 01952 433269 📠 01952 433269
✉ frog@fat-frog.co.uk

Dir: M54 J6, follow signs for Ironbridge.

Tucked away in a basement of The Grove Inn, the Fat Frog Restaurant brings a Provençale flavour to the Ironbridge Gorge. With its red check tablecloths, the restaurant is filled with French murals, mannequins and skeletons-not to mention the resident ghost! Owner/chef Johnny Coleau serves a varied selection of English, continental and vegetarian dishes that include fillet au poivre; supreme de saumon citron; and entrecôte Forestière.

Open: 12-2.30 5.30-11 (Sun 12-5.30)
Bar Meals: L served all week 12.30-2 D served Mon-Sat 6.30-8.30 (Sun 12-3) Av main course £8.95
Restaurant: L served all week 12.30-2 D served Mon-Sat 7-9.30 (Sun 12-3) Av 3 course fixed price £21.50
Brewery/Company: FREE HOUSE
🍺: Banks Original, Traditional, Harp Irish
Rooms: 5 en suite 2 family s£30 d£45
Children's Facilities: Portions/Menu Cutlery High Chairs Food Warming Changing
Nearby: Enginuity, Blists Hill
Notes: Dogs Allowed Water, food if required Garden Food Served Outside Large lawned flowered garden Parking 12 Coach parties welcome

MADELEY SJ60

The New Inn

Blists Hill Victorian Town Legges Way Telford TF7 5DU
☎ 01952 588892 📠 01952 243447
✉ rhamundy@btinternet.com

Dir: Between Telford & Broseley

Here's something different-a Victorian pub that was moved brick by brick from the Black Country and re-erected at the Ironbridge Gorge Open Air Museum. The building remains basically as it was in 1890, and customers can buy traditionally brewed beer at five-pence farthing per pint-roughly £2.10 in today's terms-using pre-decimal currency bought from the bank. The mainly traditional menu includes home-made soup, steak and kidney pudding, and ham and leek pie.

Open: 11-4 **Closed:** Dec 24-25
Bar Meals: L served all week 12-2.30 Av main course £5
Restaurant: L served all week 12-2.30 Av 3 course fixed price £10
Brewery/Company: IRONBRIDGE GORGE MUSEUMS 🍺: Banks Bitter, Banks Original, Pedigree
Children's Facilities: Fam room Play area Portions/Menu High Chairs Food Warming
Nearby: Wonderland, Enginuity
Notes: No Dogs (except Assist Dogs) Garden Food Served Outside Food served outside Parking 300 Coach parties welcome

SHROPSHIRE

MORVILLE   SO69

The Acton Arms 👻

nr Bridgnorth WV16 4RJ
☎ 01746 714209 📠 01746 714102
✉ acton-arms@madfish.com

Dir: On A458, 3m W of Bridgnorth

Successive landlords have all frequently seen the apparition making this one of Britain's most haunted pubs. Described as 'like a sheet flicking from one door to another', the spectre may be a former abbot of Shrewsbury who lived in the village in the 16th century. There's nothing spectral about the food, though, with completely worldly dishes such as salmon, halibut or plaice fillets; lamb shanks; venison pie; or lamb in honey and ginger.

Open: 11.30-2.30 6-11 (all day during Summer and Sat, Sun)
Bar Meals: L served all week 12-2 D served all week 6-9 (All day Sat/Sun)
Restaurant: L served all week 12-2.30 D served all week 7-9.30 All day Sat/Sun
Brewery/Company: WOLVERHAMPTON & DUDLEY 🍺: Bank's Hanson's Mild & Banks Bitter
Children's Facilities: Play area (Toys, Bouncy Castle (weather permitting)) Portions/Menu High Chairs Food Warming
Notes: Dogs Allowed Water Garden Food Served Outside Large area with benches & seats Parking 40 Coach parties welcome

MUCH WENLOCK   SO69

The George & Dragon

2 High Street TF13 6AA
☎ 01952 727312

Dir: On A458 halfway between Shrewsbury & Bridgnorth

There's a remarkable collection of brewery memorabilia, including over 500 water jugs hanging from the ceiling, in this historic Grade II listed building. Adjacent to the market square, Guildhall and ruined priory, the inn's cosy and inviting atmosphere makes this an obvious choice for locals and visitors alike. Expect a good range of popular dishes, with snacks (sandwiches, baguettes, Ploughman's etc) available at lunch time then dinner, which offers Thai chicken curry; chicken breast in apricot, mead and cream; or salmon poached in dill and white wine.

Open: 12-3 6-11 (Fri-Sun 12-11, 12-10.30, Wknds & summer Jun-Sep all day)
Bar Meals: L served Mon-Sun 12-2 D served Mon-Tue, Thur-Sat 6-9 Av main course £7.95
Restaurant: L served Mon-Sun 12-2 D served Mon-Tue, Thur-Sat 6.30-9 Av 3 course · à la carte £16.95
Brewery/Company: PUNCH RETAIL 🍺: Greene King Abbot Ale, Old Speckled Hen & IPA, Adnams Broadside, Hobsons Town Crier, Timothy Taylors Landlord
Children's Facilities: Menu
Notes: No Dogs (except Assist Dogs) Parking Coach parties welcome

MUCH WENLOCK · SO69

Longville Arms

Longville in the Dale TF13 6DT
☎ 01694 771206 🖹 01694 771742

Dir: From Shrewsbury take A49 to Church Stretton, then B4371 to Longville

Prettily situated in a scenic corner of Shropshire, ideally placed for walking and touring, this welcoming country inn has been carefully restored and now includes a 70-seat dining room. Solid elm or cast-iron-framed tables, oak panelling and wood-burning stoves are among the features which help to generate a warm, friendly ambience inside. Favourite main courses include steak and ale pie, chicken wrapped in bacon and stuffed with pâté, or a range of steaks.

Open: 12-3 7-11 (Sat-Sun all day)
Bar Meals: L served all week 12-2.30 D served all week 7-9.30 Av main course £
Restaurant: L served all week 12-2.30 D served all week 7-9.30
Brewery/Company: FREE HOUSE
🍺: Scottish Courage Directors, John Smiths & Best, Wells Bombardier
Children's Facilities: Play area (Swings, slides, playhouse, trampoline) Portions/Menu Cutlery High Chairs Food Warming
Nearby: Wenlock Edge, Secret Hills, Acton Scott Farm
Notes: Dogs Allowed Garden Food Served Outside Patio area Parking 40

NESSCLIFFE · SJ31

The Old Three Pigeons Inn 🐾 ♀

nr Shrewsbury SY4 1DB
☎ 01743 741279 🖹 01743 741259

Dir: On A5, 8m W of Shrewsbury

A 600-year-old inn built of ship's timbers, sandstone, and wattle and daub, set in two acres of land looking towards Snowdonia and the Bretton Hills. There is a strong emphasis on fish, with a choice of many seasonal dishes, and it is a venue for gourmet club and lobster evenings. Characteristic dishes include seafood platter, duck and cranberry, braised oxtails, liver and bacon, chicken Merango, and oak-smoked haddock.

Open: 12-3 6-11
Bar Meals: L served all week 12-2.30 D served N all 6.30-9.30 Av main course £7
Restaurant: L served all week 12-2.30 D served all week 6.30-9.30 Av 3 course · à la carte £18
Brewery/Company: FREE HOUSE
🍺: Shropshire Gold, Archers & guest ale
Children's Facilities: Menu
Notes: Dogs Allowed Garden Food Served Outside Lawn, lake, excellent views Parking 50 Coach parties welcome

SHROPSHIRE

UPPER AFFCOT   SO48

The Travellers Rest Inn ♀

SY6 6RL
☎ 01694 781275 📠 01694 781555
📧 reception@travellersrestinn.co.uk

Dir: On A49

Traditional south Shropshire inn located between Church Stretton and Craven Arms. Customers come some distance to enjoy the friendly atmosphere, great range of real ales and good pub meals, which are served right through from lunch till 9pm. Food options include freshly made sandwiches, jacket potatoes, dragon's fire curry, mixed grill, and vegetable lasagne. Finish with an old-fashioned pudding like treacle sponge or apple pie with custard.

Open: 11-11 (Sun 12-10.30)
Bar Meals: L served all week 11.30-D served all week-8.30 Av main course £7
🍺:Wood Shropshire Lad, Hobsons Best Bitter, Bass, Guiness, Boddingtons
Rooms: 12 en suite 4 family s£35 d£55
Children's Facilities: Licence Portions/Menu High Chairs Changing
Nearby: Shropshire Hills Discovery Centre, Ludlow Castle
Notes: Dogs Allowed Garden Food Served Outside Parking 50

WENTNOR   SO39

The Crown Inn

Bishops Castle SY9 5EE
☎ 01588 650613 📠 01588 650436
📧 crowninn@wentnor.com

Dir: From Shrewsbury A49 to Church Stretton, follow signs over Long Mynd to Asterton, R to Wentnor

Standing in the shadow of the famous Long Mynd, in an area with vast potential for walking and other outdoor pursuits, the Crown is a traditional, unspoilt 17th-century coaching inn with log fires, beams and horse brasses. Sophisticated meals are served in the bar and non-smoking Restaurant: pork tenderloin filled with marinated fruits, pan-fried breast of duck with a burnt orange sauce, and grilled sea bass with couscous are typical of the choices.

Open: 12-3 7-11 (Sat 12-3 6-11, Sun 10.30, Summer wknds all day) Closed: 25 Dec
Bar Meals: L served all week 12-2 D served all week 7-9
Restaurant: L served all week 12-2 D served all week 7-9
Brewery/Company: FREE HOUSE
🍺: Hobsons, Greene King Old Speckled Hen, Salopian Shropshire Gold
Children's Facilities: Play area
Notes: No Dogs Garden Food Served Outside Parking 20 Coach parties welcome

ASHCOTT ST43

The Ashcott Inn ♀

50 Bath Road TA7 9QQ
☎ 01458 210282 ▤ 01458 210282

Dir: M5 J23 follow signs for A39
to Glastonbury

Dating back to the 16th century, this former coaching inn has an attractive bar with beams and stripped stone walls, as well as quaint old seats and an assortment of oak and elm tables. Outside is a popular terrace and a delightful walled garden. A straightforward menu offers 'Home Favourites' such as Cumberland sausages, pasta carbonara, Spanish omelette and steak baguette, while poultry and seafood choices include chicken provençal, tuna steak with salad, or chicken tikka masala. Vegetarians may enjoy mushroom Stroganoff with gherkins and capers, or Stilton and walnut salad.

Open: 11-11
Bar Meals: L&D served all week- Av main course £7
Restaurant: L served all week 12-2.45 D served all week 5.30-9.30 Av 3 course · à la carte £17
Brewery/Company: HEAVITREE ◖: Otter
Children's Facilities: Play area (Play equipment)
Notes: No Dogs (except Assist Dogs) Garden Food Served Outside Large seclude area, shaded with large trees Parking 50

ASHILL ST31

Square & Compass

Windmill Hill Nr Ilminster TA19 9NX
☎ 01823 480467

Dir: Turn off A358 at Stewley Cross service station (Ashill) 1m along Wood Road, behind service station

Beautifully located overlooking the Blackdown Hills in the heart of rural Somerset, a traditional country pub with a warm, friendly atmosphere. Lovely gardens make the most of the views, and the refurbished bar area features hand-made settles and tables. Good choice of food includes pasta, steaks, fish such as breaded plaice, battered cod, and seafood crêpes, and specials like tenderloin of pork with an apple and cider sauce, or cauliflower cheese topped with mushrooms or bacon.

Open: 12-2.30 6.30-11 (Sun 7-11) RS: Tue-Thu closed lunch
Bar Meals: L served all week 12-2.30 D served all week 7-10
Brewery/Company: FREE HOUSE
◖: Exmoor Ale & Gold Moor Withy Cutter, Wadworth 6X, Branscombe Bitter, Exmoor Ale, WHB, HSD
Children's Facilities: Play area (Swings, slides, climbing frame)
Notes: Dogs Allowed Garden Food Served Outside Very large garden, patio area, amazing views Parking 30

SOMERSET

COMBE HAY   ST75

The Wheatsheaf Inn

Bath BA2 7EG
☎ 01225 833504 📠 01225 833504
✉ jakica@btclick.com

Dir: Take A369 from Bath to Odd Down, L at park towards Combe Hay. Approx 2m to thatched cottage & turn L

Nestling on a hillside overlooking a peaceful valley, the 17th-century Wheatsheaf is a pretty, black and white timbered pub, an ideal spot for summer imbibing. The unspoilt character of the rambling bar has been maintained, with massive solid wooden tables and open log fire. Food on the varied carte features home-cooked dishes, notably local game in season and fresh fish. Typical choices may include ploughman's lunches, terrines, and locally caught trout, in addition to roast rack of lamb.

Open: 11-3 6-11 (Sat 11-11, Sun 12-10.30) Closed: 25-26 Dec, Jan 1
Bar Meals: L served all week 12-2.30 D served all week 6.30-9.30 Av main course £7
Restaurant: L served all week 12-2 D served all week 6.30-9.30 Av 3 course · à la carte £18
Brewery/Company: FREE HOUSE
🍺: John Smith, Guest Ales
Children's Facilities: Play area (Large area in pub field)
Notes: Dogs Allowed on leads Garden Parking 100 Coach parties welcome

CROWCOMBE   ST13

Carew Arms ♀

Taunton TA4 4AD
☎ 01984 618631
✉ info@thecarewarms.co.uk

Dir: Village is 10 miles from both Taunton and Minehead, off A358

Set in glorious Somerset countryside this friendly pub offers local beers, including Exmoor and Otter Ales, which accompany hearty meals such as tender belly pork with mashed potatoes, pan-fried lambs' liver and kidneys with grilled bacon, ruby red fillet mignon, and chicken Dolcelatte. Fresh fish choices usually include mussels, king scallops and sea bass. Eat inside or enjoy the views from the garden in summer.

Open: 11-3 6-11
Restaurant: L served all week 12-2.30 D served Mon-Sat 7-10 Av 3 course · à la carte £22
Brewery/Company: FREE HOUSE
🍺: Exmoor Ale, Otter Ale, Cotleigh Ales
Children's Facilities: High Chairs
Notes: Dogs Allowed Garden Food Served Outside Beautiful garden with countryside views Parking 40

EAST COKER ST51

The Helyar Arms ◆◆◆◆ ☺ ♀

Moor Lane BA22 9JR
☎ 01935 862332 🗎 01935 864129
✆ info@helyar-arms.co.uk

Dir: from Yeovil, take A30 or A37, follow signs for East Coker

This Grade II listed country inn dates back in part to 1468. Log fires warm the old world bar, while the separate restaurant was restored from an original apple loft. Superior cooking and wine list here. Expect dishes such as bresaola (with air-cured Somerset beef); honey-glazed home-baked ham; and roast fillet of Dartmoor venison. These are backed by steaks, pork and sausages from the grill, and specials on the blackboard.

Open: 11-3 6-11 (Sun 12-3, 6-10.30)
Bar Meals: L served all week 12-2.30 D served all week 6.30-9.30 (Sun 12-4.30 Jan-Apr) Av main course £11
Restaurant: L served all week 12-2.30 D served all week 6.30-9.30 Sun 12-4.30 Jan-Apr Av 3 course · à la carte £20 Av 3 course fixed price £16.95
Brewery/Company: PUBMASTER 🍺: Bass, Flowers Original, Fullers London Pride
Rooms: 6 en suite 3 family s£59 d£70
Children's Facilities: Fam room Play area (Basket of toys/books) Cutlery Games High Chairs Food Warming **Nearby:** Cricket St Thomas, Fleet Air Museum, Haynes Motor Museum **Notes:** Dogs Allowed Garden Food Served Outside Grassed area seats 40, BBQ in summer Parking 40

EXFORD SS83

The Crown Hotel ★★★ ☺☺ ♀

Exmoor National Park TA24 7PP
☎ 01643 831554 🗎 01643 831665
✆ info@crownhotelexmoor.co.uk

Dir: From M5 J25 follow signs for Taunton. Take A358 then B3224 via Wheddon Cross to Exford

A warm welcome awaits customers at Exmoor's oldest coaching inn. The 17th-century building is set in three acres of water gardens and woodland. The cosy bar and smart non-smoking dining-room are both served by a single menu that makes imaginative use of good quality local produce. Lentil and bacon soup or garlic king prawns might precede honey-baked loin of pork; roast rack of lamb with fondant potato, creamed cabbage and rosemary jus; or monkfish with crushed garlic potatoes and fennel.

Open: 11-3 6-11
Bar Meals: L served all week 12-2 D served all week 6.30-9.30 Av main course £8.95
Restaurant: L served Sun 12-2 D served all week 7-9 Av 3 course · à la carte £32.50 Av 4 course fixed price £27.50
Brewery/Company: FREE HOUSE
🍺: Exmoor Ale, Gold & Stag, Cotleigh Tawny,
Rooms: 17 en suite 1 family s£55 d£95
Children's Facilities: Portions/Menu High Chairs Food Warming
Notes: Dogs Allowed Water Garden Food Served Outside Water garden, next to stream Parking 20 Coach parties welcome

SOMERSET

FROME ST74

The Talbot 15th-Century Coaching Inn ◆◆◆◆

Selwood Street Mells BA11 3PN
☎ 01373 812254 📠 01373 813599
✉ roger@talbotinn.com

Dir: From A36(T), R onto A361 to Frome, then A362 towards Radstock, 0.5m then L to Mells 2.5m

Rambling 15th-century, stone coaching inn. Inside there are lots of little terracotta-painted, stone-floored bars and eating areas. Examples of main courses include confit leg of Barbary duck with braised red cabbage and peppercorn sauce; grilled bratwurst with garlic mash and coarse grain mustard sauce; steamed steak and kidney pudding; and wild mushroom and asparagus tagliatelle in a herb cream sauce.

Open: 12-2.30 6.30-11 (Sun 12-3 7-10.30)
Closed: 25-26 Dec
Bar Meals: L served all week 12-2 D served all week 7-9 Av main course £7.50
Restaurant: L served all week 12-2 D served all week 7-9 Av 3 course · à la carte £21
Brewery/Company: FREE HOUSE
🍺: Butcombe Bitter & guest ales
Rooms: 8 en suite 2 family s£75 d£95
Children's Facilities: Play area (Cottage Garden)
Notes: Dogs Allowed Water Garden Food Served Outside Cottage garden Parking 10 Coach parties welcome

ILMINSTER ST31

New Inn

Dowlish Wake TA19 0NZ
☎ 01460 52413

Dir: From Ilminster follow signs for Kingstone then Dowlish Wake

A 350-year-old stone-built pub tucked away in a quiet village close to Perry's thatched cider mill. There are two bars with woodburning stoves, bar billiards and a skittle alley. The menu features local produce and West Country specialities, including fish, steaks and home-made pies.

Open: 11-3 6-11 (Sun 12-3, 7-10.30)
RS: 25 Dec closed eve
Bar Meals: L served all week 12-2.30 D served Mon-Sat 7-9.30 Av main course £6.50
Brewery/Company: FREE HOUSE
🍺: Butcombe Bitter, guest beers
Children's Facilities: Fam room Play area (Slide and climbing frame)
Notes: Dogs Allowed Garden Beer garden, Food served outdoors Parking 50

KINGSDON   ST52

Kingsdon Inn ♀

nr Somerton TA11 7LG
☎ 01935 840543

Dir: From A303 take A372 towards Langport then B3151 toward Street, 1st R and R again

Plenty of wooden seating makes the front garden a lovely spot in summer from which to absorb the peaceful Somerset scene, while the rambling bars are an all-year-round delight. The warmly decorated original front rooms have low beamed ceilings, stripped and scrubbed pine furniture. Good value lunch dishes include poached salmon in parsley sauce; lamb's liver, bacon and onions; braised oxtail in Guinness; and grilled goat's cheese salad on ciabatta bread. In the evening you might start with crab and prawn mornay, or wild boar pâté, then follow with half a roast duck in scrumpy cider sauce or trio of cod, salmon and sole in a prawn sauce.

Open: 11-3 6-11
Bar Meals: L served all week 12-2 D served all week 7-10 (Sun 7-9) Av main course £9.20
Brewery/Company: FREE HOUSE
🍺: Cotleigh Barn Owl, Otter Bitter, Cottage Golden Arrow, Butcombe Best
Children's Facilities: Portions/Menu High Chairs Food Warming
Notes: No Dogs (except Assist Dogs) Garden Food Served Outside Lawn at front, picnic benches etc Parking 18 Coach parties welcome

LANGPORT   ST42

The Old Pound Inn ♦♦♦

Aller TA10 0RA
☎ 01458 250469 🖹 01458 250469

Built as a cider house, the Old Pound Inn dates from 1571 and retains plenty of historic character with oak beams, open fires and a garden that used to be the village pound. It's a friendly pub with a good reputation for its real ale and home-cooked food, but also provides function facilities for 200 with its own bar. Whimsically named dishes include portly venison, horsy wild boar, and fruit 'n' nut trout.

Open: 11-11
Bar Meals: L served all week 12-2.45 D served all week 6-9.45 Av main course £5.50
Restaurant: L served all week 12-2.45 D served all week 6-9.45 Av 3 course · à la carte £20
🍺: Butcombe, Butcombe Gold, Yorkshire Bitter, Courage Best
Rooms: 6 en suite s£35 d£55
Children's Facilities: Portions/Menu Cutlery High Chairs Food Warming Changing
Nearby: Fleet Air Museum
Notes: Dogs Allowed Garden Food Served Outside Parking 30

LITTON   ST55

The Kings Arms

BA3 4PW
☎ 01761 241301

Full of nooks and crannies, this 15th-century local at the heart of the Mendips has a large garden with a stream running through it, and boasts a separate children's play area and outdoor eating. Menus offer smoked haddock fish pie, homemade chilli, and steak, mushroom and Guinness pie. Kings Arms Platters include Pigman's Platter-jumbo pork Lincolnshire sausage with eggs and chips.

Open: 11-2.30 6-11 (Sun 12-3 7-10.30)
Bar Meals: L served all week 12-2.30
D served all week 6.30-10 Av main course £8
Brewery/Company: FREE HOUSE
🍺: Bass, Butcombe, Wadworth 6X, Flowers
Children's Facilities: Fam room Play area
Notes: Dogs Allowed (In garden only.
On lead at all times.) Garden Parking 50

MARSTON MAGNA   ST52

The Marston Inn

Yeovil BA22 8BX
☎ 01935 850365 📠 01935 850397

Grade II listed building close to Yeovilton Air Museum, and handy for the link road to the West Country. The oldest parts of the inn are reputed to be haunted, and there's a skittle alley for the energetic. The menu offers rump steak with Stilton sauce, chicken breast grilled with mushrooms, seafood fettuccine, and ham and eggs, washed down with seasonal guest ales.

Open: 12-2.30 6-11 (Open all day Sat,
Sun 12-10.30)
Bar Meals: L served all week 12-2 D served
Mon-Sat 6-9.30 Av main course £5.95
Restaurant: L served all week 12-2
D served Mon-Sat 6-9.30 Av 3 course ·
à la carte £15
Brewery/Company: INNSPIRED 🍺: Banks
Bitter, Worthington Cream Flow, Stella Artois,
Seasonal Guest Ale
Children's Facilities: Fam room Play area
(Skittle alley)
Notes: Dogs Allowed Water & Toys Garden
Food Served Outside Walled patio area, secure
play area Parking 16 Coach parties welcome

MONKSILVER　　　　　ST03

The Notley Arms ♀

Taunton TA4 4JB

☎ 01984 656217 📠 01984 656576

An English country dining pub on the edge of Exmoor with some interesting African influences. Building on a reputation for good home cooking, the owners, from Zimbabwe, have made this a dining destination and have a policy of local sourcing for their ingredients. They are introducing some Zimbabwean and South African dishes such as ostrich fillet, and biltong, (air-dried beef). All meals are freshly prepared on the premises, and nothing is fried, which means no chips! Children will be happily occupied in the garden in summer and in the children's room with books and games in the winter.

Open: 11.30-2.30 6.30-11
Bar Meals: L served all week 12-2 D served all week 7-9.30 (Weekdays in winter 7-9) Av main course £7.25
Brewery/Company: UNIQUE PUB CO LTD
🍺: Exmoor Ale, Wadworth 6X, Smiles Best
Children's Facilities: Fam room Play area (Children's room with books & games) Portions/Menu Games High Chairs Food Warming
Nearby: Dunster Castle, Combe Sydenham Country Park
Notes: Dogs Allowed On lead, water provided Garden Food Served Outside garden by stream Parking 26

MONTACUTE　　　　　ST41

Kings Arms Inn 🛏 ♀

TA15 6UU

☎ 01935 822513 📠 01935 826549

✉ Kingsarmsinn@realemail.co.uk

Dir: Turn off A303 at A3088 roundabout signed Montacute. Hotel in village centre

At the foot of a steep hill, or the Mons Acutus that gave the village its name, the 17th-century, ham stone-built King's Arms offers a relaxed, country house atmosphere. Daily changing menus can be perused in either of two restaurants, or the bar. Often available will be tender lamb shank, baked breast of duck, steak and kidney pie, soft filled pancakes, liver and bacon, honey roast ham and Stilton salad, and crab and prawn risotto.

Open: 11-11 (Sun 12-10.30)
Bar Meals: L served all week 12-2.30 D served all week 7-9 Av main course £10.95
Restaurant: L served all week 12-2.30 D served all week 7-9 Av 3 course · à la carte £23.90 Av 3 course fixed price £21.95
🍺:Greene KIng Abbot & IPA, Old Speckled Hen, Ruddles County
Children's Facilities: High Chairs Food Warming
Notes: Dogs Allowed Water Garden Food Served Outside Large lawn, orchard Parking 12 Coach parties welcome

SOMERSET

NORTH CURRY ST32

The Bird in Hand

1 Queen Square Taunton TA3 6LT
☎ 01823 490248

A friendly 300-year-old village inn with large stone inglenook fireplaces, flagstone floors, exposed beams and studwork. Cheerful staff make you feel at home. Blackboard specials concentrate on local produce.

Open: 12-3 7-11 RS: 25 Dec closed eve
Bar Meals: L served Mon-Sun 12-2 D served Mon-Sun 7-9.30 Av main course £5
Restaurant: L served Mon-Sun 12-2 D served Mon-Sun 7-9.30 Av 3 course · à la carte £20
Brewery/Company: FREE HOUSE
◖: Badger Tanglefoot, Exmoor Gold, Otter Ale, Cotleigh Barn Owl, Hop Back Thunderstorm, Butcombe Gold, Teignwothy Old Moggie
Children's Facilities: Menu
Notes: Dogs Allowed Parking 20

PITNEY ST42

The Halfway House

Langport TA10 9AB
☎ 01458 252513

Dir: on B3153 between Langport and Somerton

This is a pub largely dedicated to the promotion of real ale as produced by the many excellent micro-breweries in Somerset, Devon and Wiltshire. There are always six to ten of these available in tip-top condition. There is also an excellent choice of bottled Continental beers. This delightfully old-fashioned rural pub draws customers from a huge area. Three homely rooms boast open fires, books and games, but no music or electronic games. Home-cooked meals (except Sundays when it is too busy with drinkers) include soups, local sausages, sandwiches and a good selection of curries and casseroles in the evening.

Open: 11.30-3 5.30-11 (Sun 12-3, 7-10.30) Closed: 25 Dec
Bar Meals: L served Mon-Sat 12-2 D served Mon-Sat 7-9.30
Brewery/Company: FREE HOUSE
◖: Butcombe Bitter, Teignworthy, Otter Ale, Cotleigh Tawny Ale, Hop back Summer Lightning
Children's Facilities: Play area Portions/Menu Games Food Warming
Notes: Dogs Allowed Water Garden Food Served Outside Parking 30

PRIDDY   ST55

New Inn ♀

Priddy Green nr Wells BA5 3BB
☎ 01749 676465

Dir: From M4 J18 take A39 R to Priddy 3m before Wells. From J19 through Bristol onto A39. From M5 J21 take A371 to Cheddar, then B3371

Overlooking the village green high up in the Mendip Hills, this old, former farmhouse is popular with walkers, riders and cavers, and once served beer to the local lead miners. A typical dinner menu features liver and bacon, chargrilled steaks, Brixham plaice, and fillet of pork with braised red cabbage. Plus New Inn pies, including a vegetarian version, various jacket potatoes, omelettes and toasties. Skittle alley. Priddy hosts the 'friendliest folk festival in England' every July.

Open: 11.30-2.30 7-11 (Sun & Mon 12-2.30)
Bar Meals: L served all week 12-2 D served all week 7-9.30 Av main course £5.25
Restaurant: L served all week 12-2 D served all week 7-9.30 Av 3 course · à la carte £15
Brewery/Company: FREE HOUSE
🍺: Interbrew Bass, Fuller's London Pride, Wadworth 6X, New Inn Priddy
Children's Facilities: Fam room Play area (Slide, see-saw, play equipment)
Notes: Dogs Allowed Water Garden Food Served Outside Large garden Parking 30 Coach parties welcome

SHEPTON MALLET   ST64

The Three Horseshoes ♀

Batcombe BA4 6HE
☎ 01749 850359 📠 01749 850615

Dir: Take A359 from Frome to Bruton. Batcombe signed on R

Built of honey-coloured stone, this 16th-century coaching inn is tucked away in a pretty village. Exposed stripped beams and a fine stone inglenook with log fire are to be found in the main bar, where good real ales make a suitable accompaniment to the food. Grilled venison on sautéed potatoes with lemon, gin and juniper berry sauce; and pot-roasted half duck in garlic and herbs with apricot and walnut stuffing, are two of the interesting main courses. Steaks and pies are also on offer.

Open: 12-3 6.30-11 Closed: 25-26 Dec
Bar Meals: L served all week 12-2 D served all week 7-9.30 Av main course £9
Restaurant: L served all week 12-2 D served all week 6.30-9.30 Av 3 course · à la carte £16
Brewery/Company: FREE HOUSE
🍺: Butcombe Bitter, Wadworth 6X, Adnams Bitter
Children's Facilities: Play area (Adventure playground)
Notes: Dogs Allowed Water Garden Food served outside Parking 25

SOMERSET

SPARKFORD ST62

The Sparkford Inn

High Street Yeovil BA22 7JH
☎ 01963 440218 📄 01963 440358
📧 sparkfordinn@sparkford.fsbusiness.co.uk

Dir: just off A303, 400yds from rdbt at Sparkford

A picturesque 15th-century former coaching inn characterised by its popular garden, beamed bars and fascinating old prints and photographs. Nearby are the Haynes Motor Museum and the Yeovilton Fleet Air Arm Museum. A varied menu offers a selection of traditional meals and home-cooked favourites, including salmon and spinach pie, deep-fried breaded plaice, jumbo sausages, spinach and ricotta cannelloni, cottage pie with cheese topping, and a good lunchtime carvery.

Open: 11-11
Bar Meals: L served all week 12-2 D served all week 7-9.30
Restaurant: L served all week 12-2 D served all week 7-9.30
Brewery/Company: FREE HOUSE
🍺: Interbrew Bass, Otter Ale, Butcombe Bitter, Greene King Abbot, Courage Directors
Children's Facilities: Play area Portions/Menu High Chairs Food Warming Changing
Nearby: Haynes Motor Museum
Notes: Dogs Allowed Garden Food Served Outside Parking 50 Coach parties welcome

STANTON WICK ST66

The Carpenters Arms ☜ ♀

Nr Pensford BS39 4BX
☎ 01761 490202 📄 01761 490763
📧 carpenters@buccaneer.co.uk

Dir: A37 onto A368 towards Weston-S-Mare, 1st R

In its tranquil hamlet, this charming free house was formerly a row of miners' cottages. Behind the pretty façade, you'll find a comfortable bar with low beams and a chatty, music-free atmosphere. There are warming winter fires and, in summer, guests can enjoy al fresco meals on the spacious patio. The Cooper's Parlour, with an extensive daily chalkboard, is the focus of imaginative snacks and bar food.

Open: 11-11 (Sun 12-10.30) **Closed:** 25/26 Dec
Bar Meals: L served all week 12-2 D served all week 7-10 (Sun 7-9) Av main course £11
Restaurant: L served all week 12-2 D served all week 7-10 Sun 7-9 Av 3 course · à la carte £22 **Brewery/Company:** BUCCANEER HOLDINGS 🍺: Interbrew Bass, Butcombe Bitter, Scottish Courage Courage Best, **Rooms:** 12 en suite 1 family s£64.50 d£89.50 (◆◆◆◆)
Children's Facilities: Portions/Menu High Chairs
Nearby: Chew Valley Lake, Bristol Zoo
Notes: No Dogs (except Assist Dogs) Water Garden Food Served Outside Landscaped. Patio area, pond, heaters Parking 200 Coach parties welcome

The City Arms ♀

69 High Street BA5 2AG
☎ 01749 673916 📠 01749 672901
📧 query@thecityarmsatwells.co.uk

At the heart of the historic cathedral city, in Tudor times this used to be the old jail. Today, as a free house, it provides a warm welcome, offering a range of fine ales, and a menu featuring freshly cooked, often seasonal, local produce. Favourite dishes include salmon and spinach fishcakes; calves' liver with fried onions and smoked bacon; and organic pork chops on mash with a local cider and apple sauce. City Arms burger, and sausage and mash are popular bar snacks.

Open: 9-11
Bar Meals: L&D served all week
Restaurant: L served all week from 12-D served all week 6-9 Av 3 course · à la carte £15 Av 3 course fixed price £17.50
🍺: Butcombe, Greene King, Sharps
Children's Facilities: Licence Fam room Portions/Menu Games Food Warming
Nearby: Wookey Hole Caves, Longleat, Cheddar Gorge
Notes: Dogs Allowed Garden Food Served Outside Coach parties welcome

Crossways Inn ☜ ♀

Withy Rd Highbridge TA9 3RA
☎ 01278 783756 📠 01278 781899
📧 crossways.inn@virgin.net

Dir: On A38 3.5m from M5 J22/23

A 17th-century coaching inn, in the same family for over 30 years, provides a roomy yet intimate space to enjoy home-made food and a good range of ales without the distraction of piped music, pool or darts. The menu offers a choice of traditional steak and kidney, and beef and Guinness pies and beer battered cod alongside more exotic dishes. There is a family room and safe rear garden.

Open: 12-3 5.30-11 (Sun 12-4.30, 7-10.30)
Closed: 25 Dec
Bar Meals: L served all week 12-2 D served all week 6.30-9 (Sun; roast served 12-2.30, full menu 12-2, 7-9) Av main course £5.80
Restaurant: L served all week 12-2 D served all week 6.30-9 Av 3 course · à la carte £10.50
Brewery/Company: FREE HOUSE
🍺: Interbrew Bass, Flowers IPA, Fuller's London Pride, Greene King Abbot Ale, Exmoor Stag
Rooms: 3 en suite 2 family s£24 d£34
Children's Facilities: Fam room Play area (Indoor games, skittles) Portions/Menu High Chairs Food Warming Changing
Nearby: Secret World, Burnham-on-Sea,
Notes: Dogs Allowed water Garden Food Served Outside Seating, food served outside Parking 60 Coach parties welcome

SOMERSET

WHEDDON CROSS   SS93

The Rest and Be Thankful Inn
◆◆◆◆ ☺ ♀

Exmoor TA24 7DR
☎ 01643 841222 📠 01643 841813
✉ enquiries@restandbethankful.co.uk

Dir: 5m S of Dunster

Wonderful views of the moors can be enjoyed from this old coaching inn, located in the highest village on Exmoor. Old world charm blends with friendly hospitality in the cosy bar and spacious restaurant, where both traditional and contemporary food is served. Bar snacks from ploughman's to pies join vegetable lasagne, macaroni cheese, duckling à l'orange, scampi and rump steak, with perhaps profiteroles or apple and blackberry pie to round off.

Open: 9.30-3 6.30-11 Winter (7pm Opening)
Bar Meals: L served all week 12-2 D served all week 7-9.30
Restaurant: L served all week 12-2 D served all week 7-10
Brewery/Company: FREE HOUSE
🍺: Tawny, Otter Ale, Worthington Bitter, Abbott Ale
Rooms: 5 en suite s£30 d£60
Children's Facilities: Fam room Play area High Chairs Food Warming
Notes: No Dogs Garden Food Served Outside Paved Patio Parking 50 Coach parties welcome

WOOKEY   ST54

The Burcott Inn ♀

Wells Road Wells BA5 1NJ
☎ 01749 673874

A convenient stop for visitors to Wells or the Mendip Hills, this stone-built roadside inn sits opposite a working water mill, and is characterised by beams, open fires, pine tables and settles. Freshly prepared food is available in the bars, restaurant or large garden. The menu includes such dishes as salmon and prawns in garlic butter; grilled lamb cutlets with honey, mint and berry sauce; mixed fish grills, and various home-made pasta dishes. French sticks, sandwiches and salads are also available. Try your hand at the traditional pub games.

Open: 11.30-2.30 6-11 Closed: 25/26 Dec, 1 Jan
Bar Meals: L served all week 12-2.30 D served Tue-Sat 6.30-9.30 Av main course £8.45
Restaurant: L served all week 12-2.30 D served Tue-Sat 6.30-9.30 Av 3 course · à la carte £16
Brewery/Company: FREE HOUSE
🍺: Teignworthy Old Moggie, Cotleigh Barn Owl Bitter, RCH Pitchfork, Branscombe BVB, Sharps Doom Bar
Children's Facilities: Fam room Food Warming
Notes: No Dogs (except Assist Dogs) Garden Food Served Outside Large garden, beautiful views Parking 30 Coach parties welcome

BUTTERTON SK05

The Black Lion Inn 🛏 ♀

Nr Leek ST13 7SP
☎ 01538 304232

Dir: From A52 (between Leek & Ashbourne)
take B5053

*This charming, 18th-century village inn lies on
the edge of the Manifold Valley, in the heart
of the Peak District's walking and cycling
country. Winter fires add to the pleasure of a
well-kept pint. The popular bar menu includes
pies and steaks, as well as lamb casserole,
spinach and ricotta cannelloni, and plenty of
interesting fish dishes. A comfortable base
from which to explore the National Park.*

Open: 12-3 7-11 RS: Mon closed lunch
Bar Meals: L served Tues-Sun 12-2 D served
all week 7-9
Restaurant: L served Tue-Sun 12-2 D served
all week 7-9.30
Brewery/Company: FREE HOUSE
🍺: Scottish Courage Theakston Best, Interbrew
Bass, Everards Tiger Best, Timothy Taylor
Children's Facilities: Fam room
Notes: No Dogs (except Assist Dogs) Garden
Food Served Outside Parking 30

CHEADLE SK04

The Queens At Freehay

Counslow Road Freehay ST10 1RF
☎ 01538 722383 📠 01538 722383

Dir: Two miles from Alton Towers

*Located just a couple of miles from Alton
Towers, The Queens was transformed a few
years ago from a run-down pub into a popular
eating house. The freshly cooked meals
include fish and game in season-usually found
on the specials board-along with a range of
choices from the grill with classic sauces
(chasseur, Diane) as optional extras. Home-
made beef and Guinness pie or Moroccan
lamb tagine are representative of the dishes
elsewhere on the menu.*

Open: 12-2.30 6-11 **Closed:** 25-26 Dec, 31
Dec (eve), 1 Jan (eve)
Bar Meals: L served all week 12-2 D served
all week 6-9.30 (Sun 12-2.30, 6.30-9.30) Av
main course £9.95
Restaurant: L served all week 12-2 D served
all week 6-9.30 Av 3 course · à la carte £18
Av 3 course fixed price £9.95
Brewery/Company: FREE HOUSE
🍺: Draught Bass, Draught Worthington Bitter
Children's Facilities: Portions/Menu
Food Warming
Nearby: Alton Towers
Notes: No Dogs Garden Food Served Outside
Small garden with four benches Parking 30

STAFFORDSHIRE

ECCLESHALL SJ82

The George ♀

Castle Street ST21 6DF
☎ 01785 850300 ▤ 01785 851452
✉ information@thegeorgeinn.freeserve.co.uk

A family-run, 16th-century former coaching inn with its own micro-brewery, where the owners' son produces award-winning Slater's ales. Occasional beer festivals are held, and the menu features a good, wide variety of dishes, including lamb steak in a gin and redcurrant sauce, half chicken with barbecue sauce and steak and kidney pie cooked in the inn's prize ale. A selection of salads, jackets and sandwiches is also available.

Open: 11-11 (12-10.30 Sun)
Closed: 25 Dec
Bar Meals: L served all week 12-9.30 D served all week 6-9.45
Restaurant: L served all week 12-2.30 D served all week 6-9.45
Brewery/Company: FREE HOUSE
🍺: Slaters Ales
Children's Facilities: High Chairs Food Warming
Notes: Dogs Allowed Parking 30 Coach parties welcome

HIMLEY SO89

Crooked House ☜

Coppice Mill DY3 4DA
☎ 01384 238583 ▤ 01384 214911
Dir: 1.5m E on B4176 off A449

One of Britain's most aptly-named pubs, this really is a crooked house. It was built as a farmhouse in 1765, but when mineshafts beneath collapsed in the mid-19th century, it was condemned, but finally saved by Banks's Brewery. Kids in particular love the wonky grandfather's clock, and ball-bearings that appear to roll uphill, while adults find them quite unsettling after a few pints! The perfectly upright menu lists grills, salads, rotisserie chicken, and giant battered cod.

Open: 11.30-2.30 5-11 (Open all day Mar-Oct)
Bar Meals: L served Mon-Sun 12-2 D served Mon-Sun 6-9 Av main course £7.50
Restaurant: L served Mon-Sun 12-2 D served Mon-Sun 6-9
Brewery/Company: WOLVERHAMPTON & DUDLEY BREWERIES PLC 🍺: Bank's
Children's Facilities: Licence Play area (Play area) Cutlery Games High Chairs Food Warming
Nearby: Black Country Museum, Dudley Castle & Zoo, Himley Hall
Notes: Dogs Allowed Water Garden Food Served Outside Patio area with tables Parking 40 Coach parties welcome

LEEK SJ95

Abbey Inn ♀

Abbey Green Road ST13 8SA
☎ 01538 382865 📠 01538 398604
✉ martin@abbeyinn.co.uk

Set in beautiful countryside on the Staffordshire moorlands, this 17th-century inn is on the outskirts of Leek, and handy for the potteries of Stoke-on-Trent. It is also conveniently close to Alton Towers and Tittesworth Reservoir, and with its spacious bars and restaurant, and large terrace, it is an ideal destination for a meal or a drink.

Open: 11-2.30 6.30-11 (Sun 12-3 7-10.30)
Bar Meals: L served all week 11-2 D served all week 6.30-9 Av main course £4
Brewery/Company: FREE HOUSE
🍺: Interbrew Bass
Children's Facilities: Licence Play area
Notes: No Dogs (except Assist Dogs) Garden Parking 30

LEEK SJ95

Three Horseshoes Inn ★★ ⊛ ♀

Buxton Road Blackshaw Moor ST13 8TW
☎ 01538 300296 📠 01538 300320

Dir: Telephone for directions

A sprawling creeper-covered inn geared to catering for visitors and locals in three smart eating outlets. Choose from the traditional décor and food of the bar carvery, the relaxed atmosphere of the brasserie, and the more formal restaurant. The award-winning menu offers dishes ranging from traditional (tournedos Rossini; bangers and mash) to steamed monkfish in banana leaf or Thai duck curry.

Open: 12-3 6-11
Bar Meals: L served all week 12-2 D served all week 6.30-9 Av main course £7.25
Restaurant: L served Sun 12.30-1.30 D served Sun-Fri 6.30-9
Brewery/Company: FREE HOUSE
Rooms: 7 en suite
Children's Facilities: Play area
Notes: No Dogs (except Assist Dogs) Garden Parking 100

STAFFORDSHIRE

NEWCASTLE-UNDER-LYME SJ84

Mainwaring Arms ♀

Whitmore ST5 5HR
☎ 01782 680851 📠 01782 680224
✉ info@mannersrestaurant.co.uk

A welcoming old creeper-clad inn on the Mainwaring family estate. Crackling log fires set the scene at this very traditional country retreat, where daily blackboard specials support the popular bar menu. Expect freshly-made sandwiches, home-made steak and kidney pie, pork and leek sausages with chive mash, grilled plaice with mustard sauce, or battered cod with chips and mushy peas.

Open: 12-11 (Sun 12-10.30)
Bar Meals: L served all week 12-2.30 D served all week 6-8.30 Av main course £5
Brewery/Company: FREE HOUSE
🍺: Boddingtons, Marstons Pedigree, Bass plus guest ales
Children's Facilities: Menu
Notes: Dogs Allowed only when food service is over Garden Patio seats 25-30, food served outside Parking 60

ONNELEY SJ74

The Wheatsheaf Inn ♦♦♦♦ ♀

Barhill Road nr Crewe CW3 9QF
☎ 01782 751581 📠 01782 751499
✉ thewheatsheaf.inn@virgin.net

Dir: On the A525 between Madeley & Woore, 6.5m W of Newcastle-under-Lyme

Overlooking the local golf course and village cricket ground, this renovated wayside inn has been a hostelry since 1769. Solid oak beams, roaring log fires and distinctive furnishings are a fine setting for some fine dining. Specials include Chateaubriand roast, steamed halibut steak on buttered spinach, pan-fried kangaroo, and chicken breast in smoked bacon with creamy grape and cheese sauce. Bar meals also available.

Open: 12-2.30 6-11
Bar Meals: L served all week 12-2.30 D served all week 6-9.30 Av main course £6
Restaurant: D served all week 6.30-9.30 Av 3 course · à la carte £15
Brewery/Company: FREE HOUSE
🍺: Bass, Worthington, Guest Ales
Rooms: 6 en suite s£65 d£69
Children's Facilities:
Notes: No Dogs In the garden only Garden Food served outside Parking 60 Coach parties welcome

STAFFORD   SJ92

The Hollybush Inn ♀

Salt ST18 0BX
☎ 01889 508234 📠 01889 508058
✉ geoff@hollybushinn.co.uk

Reputedly the second oldest licensed inn in the country, the heavy beams and straw-thatched roof of the Hollybush Inn make this easy to believe. Traditional dishes are at the heart of the operation, with specials like braised ham hock with horseradish sauce; venison braised with shallots, root vegetables and Bass beer with spiced dumpling; and slow-roast lamb shank with redcurrant gravy. Seafood dishes include monkfish tails pan fried with fresh fennel, shallots and morels finished with crème fraîche. Lunchtime offerings include triple-decker sandwiches, jacket potatoes and toasties. The pub regularly wins awards for its summer flower displays, and in summer the beer garden plays host to jazz concerts and hog roasts.

Open: 12-2.30 6-11 (open all day Sat-Sun)
Bar Meals: L served all week 12-2 D served all week 6-9.30
Brewery/Company: FREE HOUSE
🍺: Boddingtons, Pedigree & Guest Ales
Children's Facilities: Portions/Menu Food Warming
Notes: Dogs Allowed Water provided Garden Food Served Outside Large lawned garden with seatings Parking 25

TATENHILL   SK22

Horseshoe Inn ♀

Main Street Burton-on-Trent DE13 9SD
☎ 01283 564913 📠 01283 511314

Dir: From A38 at Branston follow signs for Tatenhill

Probably five to six hundred years old, this historic pub retains much original character, including evidence of a priest's hiding hole. In winter, log fires warm the bar and family area. In addition to home-made snacks like chilli con carne, and Horseshoe brunch, there are sizzling rumps and sirloins, chicken curry, moussaka, battered cod with chips and mushy peas, and a pasta dish of the week. And specials too - beef bourguignon, or steak and kidney pudding, for instance.

Open: 11-11
Bar Meals: L served all week 2-9.30 D served all week 12-9.30 Av main course £6.50
Restaurant: L served all week 12-9.30 D served all week 12-9.30
Brewery/Company: WOLVERHAMPTON & DUDLEY 🍺: Marstons Pedigree, Banks Original, Stella Artois, Fosters
Children's Facilities: Fam room Play area (Play area, pets corner)
Notes: Dogs Allowed Water Garden Food Served Outside Small enclosed garden with fish pond Parking 70 Coach parties welcome

WATERHOUSES SK05

Ye Olde Crown ♦♦

Leek Road Stoke on Trent ST10 3HL
☎ 01538 308204

A traditional village local, Ye Olde Crown dates from around 1648 when it was built as a coaching inn. Sitting on the bank of the River Hamps, it's also on the edge of the Peak District National Park and the Staffordshire moorlands. Inside are original stonework and interior beams, and open fires are lit in cooler weather. Sample menu includes roast beef, steak and kidney pie, chicken tikka masala, battered cod, and tuna pasta bake. Homely accommodation includes an adjacent cottage.

Open: 11.30-3 6.30-11 (Sun 12-3, 6.30-11)
Closed: 25 Dec RS: Sun eve closed in Jan-Feb
Bar Meals: L served all week 12-2 D served all week 7-9 Av main course £7
Brewery/Company: FREE HOUSE
🍺: Carlsberg-Tetley Tetley Bitter, Burton Ale
Rooms: 7 bedrooms 6 en suite s£32.50 d£65
Children's Facilities: Menu
Notes: No Dogs (except Assist Dogs) (overnight by arrangement) Parking 30 Coach parties welcome

YOXALL SK11

The Crown

Main Street DE13 8NQ
☎ 01543 472551

Dir: On A515 N of Lichfield

In a picturesque village, this pub is reputedly over 250 years old - its name possibly deriving from its former use as the local courthouse. Within easy reach of Uttoxeter racecourse and Alton Towers it's a great spot to enjoy locally sourced, home-cooked food prepared by the landlord. Expect on the regularly changing menu such lunchtime bites as a breakfast brunch and hot filled baguettes whilst evening options such as steak and Guinness pie are supplemented by offerings posted on the chalkboard.

Open: 11.30-3 5.30-11 (Sat-Sun & BHs open all day)
Bar Meals: L served all week 12-2 D served Mon-Sat 6.30-9 Av main course £6.50
Brewery/Company: MARSTONS
🍺: Marston's Pedigree, Stella Artois
Children's Facilities: Menu
Notes: Dogs Allowed Garden Food Served Outside Parking 20 Coach parties welcome No credit cards

BILDESTON   TL94

The Crown Hotel ☜

104 High Street IP7 7EB
☎ 01449 740510 🖷 01449 741583
✉ hayley@thecrown.plus.com

Dir: On B1115 between Hadleigh & Stowmarket

A beautiful 15th-century half-timbered former coaching inn with oak-beamed bars and lounge, maintaining its original charming character. Originally a wool merchants, it claims to being one of the most-haunted pubs in Britain. The menu uses the best local produce available. Confit rabbit terrine, cockle and parsley risotto and warm chocolate fondant are mixed with classic dishes such as steak and kidney pudding or fish and chips.

Open: 10-3 6-11 (Sat 10am-11pm)
Bar Meals: L served all week 12-3 D served all week 7-10 (Sun 7-9.30) Av main course £10
Restaurant: L served all week 12-3 D served all week 7-10 Sun 7-9.30 Av 3 course · à la carte £23
Brewery/Company: FREE HOUSE
🍺: Adnams, Broadside, Moletrap
Children's Facilities: Portions/Menu Games High Chairs Food Warming
Nearby: Gnome World, Hollow Trees Farm, Colchester Zoo
Notes: Dogs Allowed Garden Food Served Outside Quiet grassed flat garden at rear of hotel Parking 30

BROCKLEY GREEN   TL74

The Plough Inn ♀

Hundon CO10 8DT
☎ 01440 786789 🖷 01440 786710
✉ ploughdave@aol.com

Dir: Take B1061 from A143, approx 1.5m beyond Kedington

Quality and service are the hallmark of this delightfully situated free house, which has been run by the same family since 1957. The traditional interior retains its oak beams and soft red brickwork, whilst major extensions have added a restaurant. The distinctive bar menu includes steak and kidney pudding, T-bone steak and daily specials such as Mexican chilli beef, whilst restaurant diners could expect duck terrine with caramelised red onion chutney followed by white swordfish loin steak with tomato coulis. Separate seafood specials are available. No under 3s.

Open: 12-2.30 5-11
Bar Meals: L served all week 12-2 D served all week 7-9.30 Av main course £9
Restaurant: L served all week 12-2 D served all week 7-9.30
Brewery/Company: FREE HOUSE
🍺: Greene King IPA, Adnams Best, Fuller's London Pride, Woodforde's Wherry Best Bitter, Shepherd Neame Spitfire
Children's Facilities: Portions/Menu Games High Chairs Food Warming
Notes: Dogs Allowed Water bowls Garden Food Served Outside A Large lawn bordered by shrubs Parking 50 Coach parties welcome

SUFFOLK

BROME TM17

Cornwallis Country Hotel ♀

Eye IP23 8AJ
☎ 01379 870326 📠 01379 870051
✉ info@thecornwallis.com

Dir: Just off A140 at Brome, follow B1077 to Eye. Pub is 30 metres on the left

New owners have arrived at this handsome looking building, dating from 1561. Within its 21 peaceful acres are an avenue of limes and yew topiary, while inside many of the original beams, panels and oak and mahogany settles remain from earliest times. In the log-fired Tudor Bar look into the murky depths of a 60-foot well. Virtually everything emanating from the kitchen uses fresh, mostly locally supplied ingredients, whether it's roasted cod with chorizo mash, wilted spinach and cockles; winter warmer sausages with braised vegetables; or cannelloni of butternut squash and Amaretto with ginger and onion marmalade, salsify and crispy leeks.

Open: 11-11
Bar Meals: L served all week 12-2.30 D served all week 6-9.45 Av main course £9.50
Restaurant: L served all week 12-2.30 D served all week 6.30-9.45 Av 3 course fixed price £24
Brewery/Company: FREE HOUSE
🍺: Adnams, Greene King IPA, St Peters Best
Children's Facilities: High Chairs
Notes: No Dogs (except Assist Dogs) Water Garden Food Served Outside Gardens, pond Parking 400 Coach parties welcome

BURY ST EDMUNDS TL86

The Three Kings ♦♦♦♦ 🛏

Hengrave Road Fornham All Saints IP28 6LA
☎ 01284 766979 📠 01284 723308
✉ enquiries@the-three-kings.com

Plenty of exposed wood and interesting artefacts create a traditional atmosphere at this pretty pub. Bedroom accommodation is also provided in converted Grade II listed outbuildings. Food is served in the bar, conservatory, restaurant and courtyard. There are at least four fresh grilled fish dishes every day, a choice of steaks, and old favourites like steak and ale pie or liver and bacon.

Open: 11-11 (Sun 12-10.30)
Bar Meals: L served all week 11.30-2 D served all week 5.30-9.30 (Sun 12-2.30, 6-8.30) Av main course £5.95
Restaurant: L served Tue-Sun 12-2 D served Tue-Sat 7-8.30 Sun 12-2.30
Brewery/Company: GREENE KING
🍺: Greene King IPA & Abbot
Rooms: 9 en suite 2 family s£55 d£75
Children's Facilities: Licence Portions/Menu Cutlery High Chairs Food Warming
Nearby: West Stow Country Park, Abbey Gardens, Ickworth Park
Notes: No Dogs (except Assist Dogs) Water offered Garden Food Served Outside Patio area, benches Parking 28 Coach parties welcome

CAVENDISH   TL84

Bull Inn ♀

High Street CO10 8AX
☎ 01787 280245

Dir: A134 Bury St Edmunds to Long
Melford, then R at green, pub 5m on R

A Victorian pub set in one of Suffolk's most
beautiful villages, with an unassuming façade
hiding a splendid 15th-century beamed
interior. Expect a good atmosphere and
decent food, with the daily-changing
blackboard menu listing perhaps curries,
shank of lamb, fresh fish and shellfish, and a
roast on Sundays. Outside there's a pleasant
terraced garden.

Open: 11-3 6-11 (Sun 12-10.30)
Bar Meals: L served Tue-Sun 12-2 D served
Tue-Sun 6.30-9 Av main course £7.95
Restaurant: L served Tue-Sun 12-2
D served Tue-Sun 6.30-9 Av 3 course ·
à la carte £18
Brewery/Company: ADNAMS
🍺: Adnams Bitter & Broadside
Children's Facilities: Portions/Menu High
Chairs Food Warming
Notes: Dogs Allowed Garden Food Served
Outside Terraced Garden Parking 30 Coach
parties welcome

CHELMONDISTON   TM23

Butt & Oyster ♀

Pin Mill Lane Ipswich IP9 1JW
☎ 01473 780764 📠 01473 780764

The role of this 16th-century pub on the eerie
Suffolk coast has always been to provide
sustenance for the local bargees and rivermen
whose thirst for beer is near legendary. Today,
with its character still thankfully intact, the
Butt & Oyster is a favourite haunt of locals,
tourists and yachtsmen. A mixture of seafood
and traditional dishes characterises the menu,
including toad in the hole, steak and kidney
pie and scampi and chips.

Open: 11-11 (Sun 12-10.30) RS: Dec 25-26
Dec 31 closed eve
Bar Meals: L&D served all week (Food served
all day, Sun 12-9.30) Av main course £8
Brewery/Company: PUBMASTER
🍺: IPA, Adnams, Flowers Original, Broadside,
Greene King
Children's Facilities: Fam room
Notes: Dogs Allowed Garden only, Water
Garden outdoor eating, riverside Parking 40
Coach parties welcome

DUNWICH TM47

The Ship Inn 🛏

St James Street nr Saxmundham IP17 3DT
☎ 01728 648219 🖨 01728 648675
📧 shipinn@tiscali.co.uk

Dir: N on A12 from Ipswich through Yoxford, R signed Dunwich

Dunwich, a famous seaport before the sea swept it away in the Middle Ages, is now merely an attractive seaside village. All that is left of its former glory are the friary ruins, and of course the Ship Inn. This old smugglers' haunt exudes great warmth and character, and is noted for traditional food and local ales. As one would expect, fresh local fish features prominently on the menu, including cod, mackerel, prawns, scampi, and fishcakes. The specials board may supplement these with sole, haddock, sardines and crab according to availability. Non-fish dishes include, bacon and walnut salad; black pudding with apple cider and wholegrain mustard sauce; steak and ale casserole; pork in peach and Madeira sauce; and several salads.

Open: 11-11 Sun 12-10.30
Bar Meals: L served all week 12-3 D served all week 6-9 Av main course £6.85
Restaurant: L served all week 12-3 D served all week 7-9
Brewery/Company: FREE HOUSE 🍺:
Adnams, Mauldons
Children's Facilities: Portions/Menu High Chairs Food Warming
Notes: Dogs Allowed Garden Food Served Outside Large terraced area Parking 10

ERWARTON TM23

The Queens Head 🛏

The Street Ipswich IP9 1LN
☎ 01473 787550

Dir: From Ipswich take B1456 to Shotley

Views of the coast and countryside can be enjoyed from this handsome 16th-century building in traditional Suffolk style. Low oak-beamed ceilings make this an atmospheric stop for a beer. Alternatively, choose from traditional pub favourites in the conservatory restaurant overlooking the River Stowe - prawn cocktail or breaded mushrooms to start; then steak and kidney pudding or gammon steak with egg or pineapple; and finishing with chocolate 'lumpy bumpy' or Belgian apple pie.

Open: 11-3 6.30-11 (Sun 12-3, 7-10.30)
Closed: 25 Dec
Bar Meals: L served all week 12-2.45 D served all week 7-9.30
Restaurant: L served all week 12-2.45 D served all week 7-9.30
Brewery/Company: FREE HOUSE 🍺:
Adnams Bitter & Broadside, Greene King IPA
Children's Facilities: Portions/Menu High Chairs Food Warming
Notes: No Dogs (except Assist Dogs) Garden Food Served Outside Parking 30 Coach parties welcome

FRAMLINGHAM TM26

The Station Hotel ♀

Station Road nr Woodbridge IP13 9EE
☎ 01728 723455

Dir: Bypass Ipswich towards Lowestoft on A12

Since trains stopped coming to Framlingham in 1962 the buildings of the former station hotel have been put to good use. One is a vintage motorcycle repair shop, while another is an antique bed showroom. The hotel has established itself as a popular destination, with a good reputation for seafood and locally brewed beers. Check out the menu for rollmop herrings, seafood platter, Loch Fyne oysters, smoked trout salad, greenlip mussels and corn beef hash with a cheese topping.

Open: 12-2.30 5-11
Bar Meals: L served all week 12-2 D served all week 7-9.30 Av main course £6.95
Restaurant: L served all week 12-2 D served all week 7-9.30 Av 3 course · à la carte £11
Brewery/Company: FREE HOUSE
🍺: Earl Soham Victoria, Albert & Mild
Children's Facilities: Fam room
Notes: Dogs Allowed Water, Biscuits Garden Pond, patio, food served outdoors Parking 20 Coach parties welcome

HADLEIGH TM04

The Marquis of Cornwallis ♀

Upper Street Layham Ipswich IP7 5JZ
☎ 01473 822051 📠 01473 822051
✉ marquislayham@aol.com

Dir: On the A12 between Colchester and Ipswich, take B1070 to Hadleigh. Upper Layham 1m before Hadleigh.

Known locally as the 'Noodle', this late 16th-century inn stands in two acres of gardens overlooking the Brett Valley, and is named after a British military commander defeated in the American War of Independence. Traditional bar snacks and home-made pies are supplemented by dishes which are cooked to order from local Suffolk produce and served in the candlelit restaurant. These include cidered chicken casserole, spare ribs of pork, and lamb and coconut curry.

Open: 12-3 6-11 (Sun 12-10.30)
Bar Meals: L served all week 12-2.30 D served all week 7-9.30 Av main course £7.25
Restaurant: L served all week 12-2.30 D served all week 7-9.30 Av 3 course · à la carte £14.65
Brewery/Company: FREE HOUSE
🍺: Adnams & Broadside, Greene King IPA & Abbot Ale
Children's Facilities: Portions/Menu Cutlery High Chairs Food Warming
Notes: Dogs Allowed Water Garden Food Served Outside 2 acres, overlooking River Brett & Valley Parking 30 Coach parties welcome

SUFFOLK

HOLBROOK   TM13

The Compasses 🐾

Ipswich Road nr Ipswich IP9 2QR
☎ 01473 328332 📠 01473 327403

Dir: From A137 S of Ipswich, take B1456/B1080

Holbrook is bordered by the Rivers Orwell and Stour, and this traditional 17th-century country pub was for several decades a staging post between London and Ipswich. The menu is varied and appetising; it's also reasonably priced. Good fish options include grilled or battered cod or haddock, fish pie, and seafood lasagne. Special mains include kleftico, a large lamb joint slowly cooked in red wine and herbs, Stroganoffs, carbonades, goulashes-the list continues and not to the exclusion of favourites such as ham, egg and chips.

Open: 11-2.30 6-11 (Sun 12-3, 6-10.30)
Closed: 25-26 Dec, 1 Jan
Bar Meals: L served all week 11.30-2.15 D served all week 6-9.15 (Sun food times, 12-2.15, 6-9.15) Av main course £8
Restaurant: L served all week 11.30-2.15 D served all week 6-9.15 (Sun food times, 12-2.15, 6-9.15)
Brewery/Company: PUBMASTER
◀: Carlsberg, Greene King IPA, Adnams Bitter, Kronenbourg & Guest Ales
Children's Facilities: Play area High Chairs **Nearby:** Bourne Hill Ski Slope, Alton Water
Notes: No Dogs (except Assist Dogs) Water Bowl Garden Food Served Outside Six picnic benches, Parking 30 Coach parties welcome

HONEY TYE   TL93

The Lion 🐾 ♈

Leavenheath CO6 4NX
☎ 01206 263434 📠 01206 263434

Dir: On A134 between Colchester & Sudbury

Low-beamed ceilings and an open log fire are charming features of this traditional country dining pub on the Essex/Suffolk border. The menu is concise yet offers enticing choices - seared breast of pigeon or deep-fried sardines could lead on to baked breast of chicken filled with green pesto and Mozzarella, or duo of duck sausages with orange-scented sweet potato. Fish such as grilled darne of salmon, baked rainbow trout, or roast fillets of sea bass are also available; a couple of thoughtful vegetarian options complete the picture.

Open: 11-3 5-11 (Sun 12-10.30)
Bar Meals: L served all week 12-2 D served all week 6-9.30 (Sun 12-9.30) Av main course £8.50
Restaurant: L served all week 12-2 D served all week 6-9.30 Sun 12-9.30
Brewery/Company: FREE HOUSE
◀: Greene King IPA, Adnams Bitter, quest ale
Children's Facilities: Portions/Menu High Chairs Food Warming
Notes: Dogs Allowed Garden Food Served Outside Patio with tables and umbrellas Parking 40 Coach parties welcome

HORRINGER TL86

Beehive ♀

The Street Bury St Edmunds IP29 5SN
☎ 01284 735260 📠 01638 730416

Dir: From A14, 1st turning for Bury
St Edmunds, sign for Westley & Ickworth Park

Buzzing (what else?) with activity, the Beehive is close to the National Trust's Ickworth House. Its succession of cosy dining areas is furnished with antique pine tables and chairs. In season, visitors head for the tables on the patio and the picnic benches in the walled beer garden. The proprietors respond to changing customer appetites with seasonal produce and daily changing menus. With these factors in mind therefore they may, for instance, offer starters of salmon and crayfish tail terrine with lemon dressing, or cream of parsnip soup with a hint of curry. And for main courses there could well be seared liver with balsamic jus or home-made pork apple and leek sausages.

Open: 11.30-2.30 7-11 Closed: Dec 25-26
Bar Meals: L served all week 12-2 D served Mon-Sat 7-9.45
Restaurant: L served all week 12-2
D served all week 7-9.45 Av 3 course ·
à la carte £18
Brewery/Company: GREENE KING
🍺: Greene King IPA & Abbot Ale, Guest beers
Children's Facilities: Portions/Menu
Food Warming
Notes: No Dogs (except Assist Dogs) Garden only Garden Food Served Outside Patio, picnic benches, walled garden Parking 30

SOUTHWOLD TM57

Crown Hotel ★★ 🏵🏵 ♀

The High Street IP18 6DP
☎ 01502 722275 📠 01502 727263
📧 crown.hotel@adnams.co.uk

Dir: off A12 take A1094 to Southwold,
main road into town centre, hotel on L

A posting inn, dating from 1750, today fulfilling the purposes of pub, wine bar, restaurant and small hotel. As the flagship for Adnams brewery, excellent ales and wines can be sampled. Alternatively you can visit the cellar and kitchen store for a full selection of wines and bottled beers. Good food is served in either the bar or the restaurant; the Crown's seaside location means fish is well represented on both menus. Typical imaginative dishes in the bar might be steamed mussels with parsley and garlic, or grilled squid with risotto nero. Meat dishes could include chargrilled escalope of pork with sage mash and cider gravy, or baked Suffolk chicken breast.

Open: 11-11 6-11 (all day peak times)
Bar Meals: L served all week 12-2 D served all week 7-9.30 (all day Sun) Av main course £11
Restaurant: L served all week 12.30-1.45 D served all week 7.30-8.45
Brewery/Company: ADNAMS 🍺: Adnams
Rooms: 14 bedrooms 13 en suite s£77 d£55
Children's Facilities: Fam room
Portions/Menu High Chairs Food Warming Changing
Notes: No Dogs (Assist dogs only) Parking 18

THORNHAM MAGNA   TM17

The Four Horseshoes ♀

Wickham Road Nr Eye IP23 8HD
☎ 01379 678777 ▤ 01379 678134

Dir: From Diss on A140 turn R and follow signs for Finningham, 0.5m turn R for Thornham Magna

Thornham Magna is a delightful, unspoilt village, close to Thornham Country Park and the interesting thatched church at Thornham Parva. This fine 12th-century inn is also thatched, and has timber-framed walls and even a well in the bar. Changed management in 2004.

Open: 12-11
Bar Meals: L served all week 12-9.30 D served all week-Av main course £7.50
Restaurant: L served all week 12-9.30 D served all week
Brewery/Company: GREENE KING ◖:
Greene King IPA, Abbot & Old Speckled Hen
Children's Facilities: Fam room
Notes: Dogs Allowed Garden Food Served Outside Parking 80 Coach parties welcome

WANGFORD   TM47

The Angel Inn

High Street NR34 8RL
☎ 01502 578636 ▤ 01502 578535
✉ enquiries@angelinn.freeserve.co.uk

A traditional green-and-cream-painted inn with a handsome Georgian façade, set in the heart of the pretty village of Wangford. Dating back to the 16th century, and complete with resident ghost, its cosy bar and restaurant are characterised by exposed beams and roaring log fires in winter. Home-made dishes include fresh fish (grilled sea bass steak with citrus butter; baby crayfish tails sautéed in garlic butter), hearty favourites such as steaks, pies and sausages, and good vegetarian options.

Open: 12-3 6-11
Bar Meals: L served Tues-Sun 12-2 D served Tues-Sun 6.30-9 Av main course £8
Restaurant: L served Tues- Sun 12-2 D served Tues-Sun 6.30-9 Av 3 course · à la carte £15
Brewery/Company: FREE HOUSE
◖: Adnams Best, Spitfire, Greene King Abbot Ale, Brakspear Bitter, Bass
Children's Facilities: Fam room Play area (Slide, Swings)
Notes: Dogs Allowed Garden Food Served Outside Large walled garden with benches Parking 20 Coach parties welcome

CHIDDINGFOLD   SU93

The Swan Inn & Restaurant ⊗ ♀

Petworth Road GU8 4TY
☎ 01428 682073 📠 01428 683259

*A lovely 14th-century village pub whose
sympathetic refurbishment has included bare
floors, wooden furniture and big leather sofas.
The chef makes impressive use of seafood,
fish and local game. A typical menu starts
with white bean soup with pesto tortellini and
crepe oil, followed by char-grilled rib of beef
with garlic fondant, foie gras and shallot
confit sauce, or fillets of red mullet with fresh
pasta in a rich shellfish sauce, finishing with
terrine of summer berries in red wine jelly
with vanilla and black pepper syrup. Bar
snacks are also available.*

Open: 11-3 5.30-11 (Sat 11-11,
Sun 12-10.30)
Bar Meals: L served all week 12-2.30 D
served all week 6.30-10 (Sat & Sun 12-10)
Av main course £8
Restaurant: L served all week 12-2.30
D served all week 6.30-10 Av 3 course ·
à la carte £20
Brewery/Company: FREE HOUSE
🍺: Hogs Back TEA, Ringwood Best,
Fuller's London Pride
Children's Facilities: Portions/Menu High
Chairs Food Warming Changing
Notes: Dogs Allowed Water Garden Food
Served Outside Terraced sun trap Parking 25

EGHAM   TQ07

The Fox and Hounds ♀

Bishopgate Road Englefield Green TW20 0XU
☎ 01784 433098 📠 01784 438775
✉ thefoxandhounds@4cinns.co.uk

Dir: From village green turn L into Castle
Hill Rd, then R into Bishopsgate Rd

*The Surrey border once ran through the centre
of this good English pub, which is on the edge
of Windsor Great Park, convenient for walkers
and riders. Features include a large garden,
handsome conservatory and weekly jazz
nights. Menus offer a range of daily-changing
fish specials as well as dishes like orange and
sesame chicken fillets on coriander and lime
noodles, or roast pork with grain mustard
glaze and Parmesan crisps.*

Open: 11-11 (Sun 12-10.30)
Bar Meals: L served all week 12-2.30
D served all week 6.30-9.30 Av main
course £13.50
Restaurant: L served all week 12-2.30
D served all week 6.30-10 Av 3 course ·
à la carte £25
🍺: Fullers London Pride, IPA, Courage Best
Notes: Dogs Allowed Garden Parking 60
Coach parties welcome

GUILDFORD — SU94

Red Lion ☺ ♀

Shamley Green GU5 0UB
☎ 01483 892202 🖷 01483 894055

Attractive old village pub with large front and rear gardens, ideal for whiling away summer afternoons watching the local cricket team play on the green opposite. In the cosy bar or large comfortable restaurant, peruse no fewer than four varied menus on which everything listed is home prepared including roast half duck with black cherry sauce, vegetable tartlet with Mornay sauce, fresh fish pie, and another four or more fish/seafood dishes. Young's and Adnam's in the bar.

Open: 7.30-11.30
Bar Meals: L served all week 12-3 D served all week 7-10 Av main course £10.95
Restaurant: L served all week 12-3 D served all week 7-10 Av 3 course · à la carte £22.50
Brewery/Company: PUBMASTER
🍺: Youngs Pedigree, Adnams Broadside, Stella Artois
Children's Facilities: Licence
Notes: No Dogs (except Assist Dogs) Garden Food Served Outside Large front and rear garden Parking 20 Coach parties welcome

HINDHEAD — SU83

Devil's Punchbowl Inn ♀

London Road GU26 6AG
☎ 01428 606565 🖷 01428 605713

Dir: From M25 take A3 to Guildford, then A3 & follow Portsmouth signs

Dating from the early 19th century, this inn stands 900ft above sea level with wonderful views as far as London. The 'punchbowl' is a large natural bowl in the ground across the road. The menu, while not large, has something from everyone, with a separate snack menu for a quick meal.

Open: 7-11
Bar Meals: L served all week 12-3 D served all week 6-10 Av main course £
Restaurant: L served all week 12-3 D served all week 6-10
Brewery/Company: ELDRIDGE POPE
🍺: Bass. 6X, Tetleys, Bombadier, Stella Artois
Children's Facilities: Licence Fam room Portions/Menu Cutlery High Chairs Food Warming Changing
Notes: Dogs Allowed Garden Food Served Outside Lawn area with benches Parking 65

NEWGIDATE TQ14

The Surrey Oaks

Parkgate Road RH5 5DZ

☎ 01306 631200 📠 01306 631200

Dir: From A24 or A25 follow signs to Newdigate, Pub 1m E of Newdigate on road towards Leigh/Charwood

Parts of this country pub date from 1570, the Georgian bar has been converted into a restaurant, and there are two small, beamed bars. It is a renowned real ale pub, and a regular CAMRA award-winner. Restaurant and bar menus offer a good range of dishes plus a daily choice from the blackboard-maybe steak and kidney pudding, guinea fowl, sea bass or calves' liver. Big annual beer festival over August Bank Holiday, live music and pig roasts.

Open: 11.30-2.30 5.30-11 (Sun 12-3, 7-10.30, Sat 11.30-3, 6-11)
Bar Meals: L served all week 12-2 D served Tue-Sat 7-9 Av main course £8.50
Restaurant: L served all week 12-2 D served Tue-Sat 7-9 Av 3 course · à la carte £15
Brewery/Company: PUNCH TAVERNS
🍺: Harveys Sussex Best, Adnams, guest beers
Children's Facilities: Play area (Outdoor swings, slide, climbing frame) Portions/Menu Games High Chairs Food Warming
Nearby: Bocketts Farm
Notes: Dogs Allowed Water Garden Food Served Outside Large. Child area, pond, aviary, goat paddock Parking 75 Coach parties welcome

OCKLEY TQ14

Bryce's at The Old School House
◉ 🐾 ♀

Dorking RH5 5TH

☎ 01306 627430 📠 01306 628274

✉ bryces.fish@virgin.net

Dir: 8m S of Dorking on A29

A boys' boarding academy until Bill Bryce acquired it in 1982. Bill is into fresh fish in a big way, and given that this is rural Surrey, he manages to obtain a huge range. Non-fish eaters are not forgotten, but the choice is restricted. The restaurant, offers seven starters and seven main courses - all fish. Begin with skate knobs fried in herb crumbs or Portland crab and asparagus salad. Mains include crisp fillets of black sea bream on rocket and Parmesan salad; and rare-grilled fillet of Shetland salmon on Arbroath smokie kedgeree.

Open: 11-3 6-11 (Closed Sun pm Nov, Jan, Feb) Closed: 25 Dec, 1 Jan
Bar Meals: L served all week 12-2.30 D served Mon-Sat 6.30-9.30 Av main course £10.50
Restaurant: L served all week 12-2.30 D served Mon-Sat 7-9.30 Av 3 course · à la carte £27.50 Av 3 course fixed price £27.50
Brewery/Company: FREE HOUSE
🍺: London Pride,GB & Butser, Scottish Courage
Children's Facilities: Portions/Menu High Chairs Food Warming
Nearby: Chessington World of Adventure
Notes: Dogs Allowed Water Food Served Outside Terrace area Parking 25 Coach parties welcome

SURREY

STAINES TQ07

The Swan Hotel 🐾 ♀

The Hythe TW18 3JB
☎ 01784 452494 📠 01784 461593
📧 swan.hotel@fullers.co.uk

Dir: Just off A308, S of Staines Bridge. 5m from Heathrow

Overlooking the Thames by Staines Bridge, this 18th-century inn was frequented by river bargemen who were paid in tokens which could be exchanged at the Swan for food and drink. The menu consists of traditional English fare - everything from fish and chips to steak and ale pie. There is also an ever-changing specials menu featuring up to six choices, and other dishes include grilled wild boar; mushroom and parsley risotto; and braised shoulder of lamb.

Open: 11-11 (Sun 12-10.30)
RS: 25 Dec open 12-3
Bar Meals: L served all week 12-6 D served all week 6-9.30 (Sun 12-8) Av main course £7.50
Restaurant: L served all week 12-6 D served all week 6-9.30
Brewery/Company: FULLER SMITH TURNER PLC 🍺 Fuller's London Pride, ESB
Children's Facilities: High Chairs Food Warming
Nearby: Thorpe Park, Legoland, Chessington
Notes: Dogs Allowed Garden Food Served Outside Patio with seating. Overlooks River Thames Coach parties welcome

VIRGINIA WATER TQ06

The Wheatsheaf Hotel ★★ ♀

London Road GU25 4QF
☎ 01344 842057 📠 01344 842932
📧 sales@wheatsheafhotel.com

Dir: From M25 Jct 13, take A30 towards Bracknell

The Wheatsheaf dates back to the second half of the 18th century and is beautifully situated overlooking Virginia Water on the edge of Windsor Great Park. Chalkboard menus offer a good range of freshly prepared dishes with fresh fish as a speciality. Popular options are beer battered cod and chips, roast queen fish with pesto crust, and braised lamb shank on mustard mash.

Open: 11-11
Bar Meals: L served all week 12-10 D served all week-Av main course £8
Restaurant: L served all week 12-10 D served all week-Av 3 course · à la carte £16
Brewery/Company: CHEF & BREWER
🍺 Guest Ales
Rooms: 17 en suite s£90 d£95
Children's Facilities: Fam room
Notes: No Dogs Garden beer garden, patio, outdoor eating Parking 90 Coach parties welcome

ARLINGTON

Old Oak Inn 🐾

nr Polegate BN26 6SJ
☎ 01323 482072 📠 01323 895454

Dir: N of A27 between Polegate & Lewes

Built in 1733 as the village almshouse, this became a pub in the early 1900s. It is close to Abbots Wood and the Cuckoo Trail - both ideal for walking. The menu offers light bites such as bacon and potato salad, or roasted flat mushrooms with Brie and bacon, as well as standards such as baguettes and jacket potatoes. Hot dishes include poached salmon, home-made fishcakes of the day, and a selection of steaks.

Open: All day every day
Bar Meals: L served all week 12-2.30 D served all week 6.30-9.30 (food all day Sat-Sun) Av main course £6.95
Restaurant: L served all week 12-2.30 D served all week 9.30-9.30 (food all day Sat-Sun) Av 3 course · à la carte £16.95
Brewery/Company: FREE HOUSE
🍺: Harveys, Badger, Adnams Broadside & guest ales
Children's Facilities: Play area (Play area, wooden adventure, frame & slide) Portions/Menu Cutlery Games High Chairs Food Warming
Nearby: Knockhatch Adventure Park, Drusillas Park
Notes: Dogs Allowed Water provided. To be kept on lead Garden Food Served Outside Grassed and hedged with tables Parking 40 Coach parties welcome

EAST CHILTINGTON

The Jolly Sportsman ♀

Chapel Lane BN7 3BA
☎ 01273 890400 📠 01273 890400
✉ thejollysportsman@mistral.co.uk

Dir: A275 from Lewes, L at Offham onto B2166 towards Plumpton, take Novington Ln, 1m L into Chapel Ln

An isolated pub with a lovely garden set on a quiet no-through road looking out to the South Downs. The small atmospheric bar has been sympathetically upgraded by respected restaurateur Bruce Wass. Well-sourced food features on the daily-changing menus. A fixed-price lunch might feature free range chicken ballantine with apples and cider, finished off with rhubarb and ginger sorbet.

Open: 12-2.30 6-11 (Sun 12-4)
Closed: 25-26 Dec; Mon ex BHs
Bar Meals: L served Tue-Sun 12.30-2 D served Tue-Sat 7-9 (Sun 12.30-3, Fri & Sat eve 7-10) Av main course £12
Restaurant: L served Tue-Sun 12.30-2 D served Tue-Sat 7-9 (Sun 12.30-3, Fri & Sat eve 7-10) Av 3 course · à la carte £26 Av 3 course fixed price £13.75
Children's Facilities: Licence Play area Portions/Menu Games High Chairs Food Warming Changing
Nearby: Bluebell Railways & Drusillas Park
Notes: Dogs Allowed Water Garden Food Served Outside Parking 30

FIRLE — TQ40

The Ram Inn ♀

Nr Lewes BN8 6NS
☎ 01273 858222
✉ nikwooller@raminnfirle.net

Dir: R off A27 3m E of Lewes

The oldest part of the Ram dates from 1542, and though added to many times - it has 14 staircases - it has changed little in recent years. Situated at the foot of the South Downs, the inn is part of the Firle Estate, seat of the Gage family. Its flint-walled garden includes picnic tables and children's play equipment. Menu choices range through burgers, pastas and six varieties of ploughman's to fish and chips and rack of pork loin ribs.

Open: 11.30-11 (Sun 12-10.30) RS: 25 Dec open 12-2
Bar Meals: L served all week 12-5.30
D served all week-(Fri-Sun 12-9)
Av main course £6.50
Brewery/Company: FREE HOUSE
🍺: Harveys Best plus regular changing ales
Children's Facilities: Licence Fam room Play area (Play equipment)
Notes: Dogs Allowed Water Garden Food Served Outside Two gardens 1 with picnic benches, 1 orchard Parking 10 Coach parties welcome

ICKLESHAM — TQ81

The Queen's Head 🐾 ♀

Parsonage Lane Winchelsea TN36 4BL
☎ 01424 814552 📠 01424 814766

Dir: Between Hastings & Rye on A259

A distinctive tile-hung pub with wonderful views to Rye and beyond. The building dates from 1632 and inside you'll find high beamed ceilings and large inglenook fireplaces. There are also stories of a ghost called George and a secret passageway to the church. Hearty home-cooked food is served, including starters/snacks, salads, sandwiches and a choice of steaks and grills. Fresh fish features among the daily blackboard specials, and hot dishes include a daily curry, lamb and mint pie, and leek, Brie and bacon pasta. The pub is on the 1066 walk route.

Open: 11-11 (Sun 12-10.30) RS: 25-26 Dec closed evenings
Bar Meals: L served all week 12-2.45
D served all week 6.15-9.30 Av main course £7.50
Restaurant: L&D served all week
Brewery/Company: FREE HOUSE
🍺: Rother Valley Level Best, Greene King Abbot Ale, Ringwood Old Thumper
Children's Facilities: Play area (wendy house) Portions/Menu Games High Chairs Food Warming
Notes: No Dogs (except Assist Dogs) Garden Food Served Outside Seating for 60, boules pitch Parking 50 Coach parties welcome

LEWES
TQ41

The Snowdrop ♀

119 South Street BN7 2BU

☎ 01273 471018

In the mid-19th century this was where Britain's biggest avalanche occurred, hence the pub's rather whimsical, deceptively-gentle name. Specialising in vegetarian and vegan food, the kitchen focuses on locally sourced seasonal fare and offers constantly changing specials. Entertainment is a big feature at The Snowdrop, with such weekly fixtures as jazz and live bands.

Open: 11-11 (Sun 12-10.30)
Bar Meals: L served all week 12-3 D served all week 5-9 Av main course £6.50
Brewery/Company: FREE HOUSE
🍺: Harveys Best, plus guests
Children's Facilities: Portions/Menu Games High Chairs Food Warming
Nearby: Drusillas Park, Stamer Park, Bluebell Railway
Notes: Dogs Allowed Water & biscuits Garden Food Served Outside Beer patio & enclosed garden area Coach parties welcome

RUSHLAKE GREEN
TQ61

Horse & Groom ☺ ♀

TN21 9QE

☎ 01435 830320 ▤ 01435 830320

✉ chappellhatpeg@aol.com

Grade II listed building on the village green with pleasant views from the well-cultivated gardens. Dishes are offered from blackboard menus in the cosy bars: steak, kidney and Guinness pudding; boiled knuckle of gammon with onion stock and butter beans; and rabbit in cider are favourites, along with the excellent fresh fish choice-perhaps monkfish stuffed with chorizo on cherry tomato compÙte, or fresh tuna on courgette tagliatelle.

Open: 11.30-3 5.30-11
Bar Meals: L served all week 12-2.30 D served all week 7-9.30
Restaurant: L served all week 12-2.30 D served all week 7-9.30 Av 3 course · à la carte £20
Brewery/Company: FREE HOUSE 🍺: Harveys, Master Brew, Shepherd Neame Spitfire
Children's Facilities: Play area (gated garden)
Nearby: Battle Abbey, Herstmonceux Castle
Notes: Dogs Allowed Garden Food Served Outside Well tended, views over lake, smart furniture Parking 20 Coach parties welcome

SUSSEX, EAST

RYE   TQ92

Mermaid Inn ★★★ ⊛ ⌂ ♟

Mermaid Street TN31 7EY
☎ 01797 223065 🖹 01797 225069
❸ mermaidinnrye@btclick.com

Once frequented by smugglers, the Mermaid had been trading for 150 years by the time Elizabeth I paid Rye a visit in 1573. Numerous ghost stories add to the appeal of the place, as do beams hewn from ancient ships' timbers, secret passages and cosy log fires. Bar menu offers traditional dishes such as steak and kidney pudding, baked fish pie, and a choice of baguettes.

Open: 11-11 (Sun 12-11)
Bar Meals: L served Mon-Sat 12-2.15 D served Sun-Fri 7-9.15 Av main course £8.50
Restaurant: L served all week 12-2.15 D served all week 7-9.15 Av 3 course · à la carte £35 Av 3 course fixed price £20
Brewery/Company: FREE HOUSE
◖: Greene King Old Speckled Hen, Scottish Courage Courage Best
Rooms: 31 en suite 6 family s£80 d£160
Children's Facilities: Portions/Menu Games High Chairs Food Warming
Nearby: Camber sands, swimming pool, cycle track
Notes: No Dogs (except Assist Dogs) Water Garden Food Served Outside Paved patio Parking 26 Coach parties welcome

WINCHELSEA   TQ91

The New Inn ⌂ ♟

German Street TN36 4EN
☎ 01797 226252
❸ newinnchelsea.co.uk

This 18th-century inn is situated in the centre of the beautiful ancient town, which was once one of the seven Cinque Ports. There are no specials, but the menu features popular dishes such as home-made pies, roasts, scallops and bacon in a wine and cream sauce and various fish dishes. To the rear of the pub is a charming garden, where guests may eat or simply relax before taking a stroll in the surrounding countryside.

Open: All day every day
Bar Meals: L served all week 12-3 D served all week 6.30-9.30 (Sun 12-9) Av main course £7.95
Restaurant: L served all week 12-2.30 D served all week 6.30-9.30 (Sun 12-9) Av 3 course · à la carte £15
Brewery/Company: GREENE KING
◖: Morlands Original, Abbots Ale, Greene King Ipa, Fosters, Old Speckled Hen
Children's Facilities: Fam room Portions/Menu High Chairs Food Warming
Nearby: Beach, Museum, Windmill
Notes: Dogs allowed Garden Food Served Outside Traditional Old English Parking 20 Coach parties welcome

AMBERLEY TQ01

The Bridge Inn

Houghton Bridge BN18 9LR
☎ 01798 831619

Dir: 5m N of Arundel on B2139

The Bridge Inn dates from 1650, and has a Grade II listing. It is very popular with cyclists and walkers, and is only a two minute walk from the Amberley chalk pits and museum. Special features are the open fires and display of original oil and watercolour paintings. Campers can arrange pitches in the garden. The menu offers a comprehensive fish choice plus dishes such as braised lamb shank, rack of pork ribs, leek and Stilton crêpes, and Lincolnshire sausage.

Open: 11-11 (Sun 12-10.30)
Bar Meals: L served all week 12-3 D served all week 6-9 Av main course £9
Restaurant: L served all week 12-3 D served all week 7-9 Av 3 course · à la carte £17
Brewery/Company: FREE HOUSE
🍺: Harveys Sussex, Fullers London Pride, Youngs, Bass
Notes: Dogs Allowed Water provided Garden Food served outside. Well kept garden Parking 20 Coach parties welcome

BILLINGSHURST TQ02

Ye Olde Six Bells ♀

76 High St RH14 9QS
☎ 01403 782124 📠 01403 780520

Dir: On the A29 between London & Bognor, 17m from Bognor

This attractive timbered pub dates from 1436 and features flagstone floors and an inglenook fireplace. Legend has it that a curse will fall on anyone who moves the old fireback, made from a re-used pattern of an iron grave slab. There is also reputed to be a smugglers' tunnel leading to the nearby church. Home-cooked food is served and the pastry is a highlight. The pub has a pretty roadside garden and is part of a Badger Ale Trail.

Open: 11-11 (Sun 12-10.30) RS: 25 Dec closed eve
Bar Meals: L served all week 12-2 D served Mon-Sat 7-9 Av main course £6.50
Restaurant: L served Mon-Sat 12-2 D served 7-9
Brewery/Company: HALL & WOODHOUSE
🍺: Badger Tanglefoot, Best and Sussex Ale
Children's Facilities: Play area
Notes: Dogs Allowed on a lead Garden Food Served Outside Large garden, rose archway, lawned area Parking 15 Coach parties welcome

SUSSEX, WEST

CHILGROVE · SU81

The White Horse ♦♦♦♦ ◎◎ ♀

High Street Nr Chichester PO18 9HX
☎ 01243 535219 📠 01243 535301
✉ info@whitehorsechilgrove.co.uk

Dir: On B2141 between Chichester & Petersfield

Picturesque South Downs hostelry, dating from 1756, with a team of French chefs and an extensive and rightly celebrated wine list - in essence a gastronomic inn, offering a fusion of French cuisine and English hospitality. Bar lunches are available but it's the restaurant that earns the culinary plaudits, offering an eclectic menu with an emphasis on the traditional. Dishes might include fresh Selsey crab salad, slow roasted duck or braised oxtail.

Open: 11-3 6-11 (Closed Mon winter months only)
Bar Meals: L served all week 11-3 D served all week 6-11 Av main course £10.50
Restaurant: L 11-3 D from 6
Brewery/Company: FREE HOUSE
🍺: Ballard's
Rooms: 8 en suite 2 family s£65 d£95
Children's Facilities: Portions/Menu Food Warming
Notes: Dogs Allowed Garden Food Served Outside Downland garden with good views Parking 100 Non-smoking premises

KIRDFORD · TQ02

The Half Moon Inn

Nr Billingshurst RH14 0LT
☎ 01403 820223 📠 01403 820224
✉ halfmooninn.kirdford@virgin.net

Dir: Off A272 between Billingshurst & Petworth. At Wisborough Green follow signs 'Kirdford'

Officially one of the prettiest pubs in Southern England, this 16th-century village inn is covered in climbing roses. Although drinkers are welcome, the Half Moon is mainly a dining pub. Lunch choices from the bistro menu might include pan-fried venison with black pudding mash and pork and leek sausages with apple mash. Lunchtime snacks take the form of battered haddock with chips, Caesar salad, vegetarian pasta, and lamb curry with coriander rice.

Open: 11-3 6-11 (Closed Sun eve)
Bar Meals: L served Mon-Sun 12-2.30 D served Mon-Sat 6-9.30 Av main course £10
Restaurant: L served Tue-Sun 12-2 D served Tue-Sat 7-9 Av 3 course · à la carte £22
Brewery/Company: LAUREL PUB PARTNERSHIPS 🍺: Fuller's London Pride
Children's Facilities: Play area (Swings, slide)
Notes: No Dogs Garden Food Served Outside 3 separate gardens for families and dining Parking 12

LURGASHALL   SU92

The Noah's Ark

The Green GU28 9ET
☎ 01428 707346 📠 01428 707742
📧 bernard@noahsarkinn.co.uk

Dir: Off A283 N of Petworth

The curious name of this pub is said to have originated when there was a pond outside the door, which customers had to cross to gain entry, like animals finding shelter in the ark. At the centre of village life, Noah's Ark hosts an annual theatrical production in summer, and overlooks the village green. An extensive snack menu is backed by a good choice of more substantial fare including steak and mushroom pie, and chargrilled bison!

Open: 11-3 6-11 Closed: 25 Dec RS: Nov-Mar closed Sunday pm
Bar Meals: L served all week 12-2.30 D served Mon-Sat 7-10 Av main course £8.50
Restaurant: L served all week 12-2 D served Mon-Sat 7-10
Brewery/Company: GREENE KING
🍺: Greene King IPA, Old Speckled Hen, Abbott Ale
Children's Facilities: Fam room Play area (Large garden) Portions/Menu High Chairs Food Warming
Notes: No Dogs (except Assist Dogs) Garden Food Served Outside Seating for over 60 Parking 20

MAPLEHURST   TQ12

The White Horse

Park Lane RH13 6LL
☎ 01403 891208

Dir: 5m SE of Horsham, between A281 & A272

In the tiny Sussex hamlet of Maplehurst, this traditional pub offers a break from modern life - no music, no fruit machines, no cigarette machines... just hearty pub food and an enticing range of ales. Sip Harvey's Best, Welton's Pride and Joy or Dark Star Espresso Stout in the bar or whilst admiring the rolling countryside from the quiet, south-facing garden. Home-made chilli con carne with garlic bread is a speciality.

Open: 12-2.30 6-11 (Sun 12-3, 7-10.30)
Bar Meals: L served all week 12-2 D served all week 6-9 (Sun 12-2.30, 7-9) Av main course £5
🍺: Harvey's Best, Welton's Pride & Joy, Dark Star Expresso Stout, King's Red River, Beer Station-Pullman
Children's Facilities: Licence Fam room Play area (Swings, slide, climbing frame) Portions/Menu Games High Chairs Food Warming
Notes: Dogs Allowed dog biscuits Large garden - great views, quiet & safe Parking 20 Coach parties welcome No credit cards

MIDHURST SU82

The Angel Hotel ★★★ ⚘ 🍷

North Street GU29 9DN
☎ 01730 812421 📠 01730 815928

An imposing and well-proportioned, late-Georgian façade hides the true Tudor origins of this former coaching inn. Its frontage overlooks the town's main street, while at the rear attractive gardens give way to meadowland and the ruins of Cowdray Castle. Bright yellow paintwork on local cottages means they are Cowdray Estate-owned. Gabriel's is the main restaurant, or try The Halo Bar where dishes range from snacks and pasta to sizzlers and steaks, with additional specials.

Open: 11-11
Bar Meals: L served all week 12-2.30 D served all week 6-9.30 Av main course £10
Restaurant: L served all week 12-2.30 D served all week 6.30-9.30 Av 3 course · à la carte £23 Av 3 course fixed price £16
Brewery/Company: FREE HOUSE
🍺: Gale's HSB & Best
Rooms: 28 en suite 18 family s£80 d£110
Children's Facilities: Licence Portions/Menu Games High Chairs Food Warming
Nearby: Petworth Park, Weald & Downland Open Air Museum
Notes: Dogs Allowed Garden Food Served Outside walled garden, pond, views of Cowdray Ruins Parking 75

NUTHURST TQ12

Black Horse Inn 🍴 🍷

Nuthurst Street Horsham RH13 6LH
☎ 01403 891272 📠 01403 892656
@ cliveh@henwood.fsbusiness.co.uk

Dir: 4m S of Horsham, off A281 & A24

True to its history as a smuggler's hideout, this lovely old free house is still hidden away in a quiet backwater. Inside you'll find stone-flagged floors, an inglenook fireplace and an exposed wattle and daub wall. There are lunch and dinner menus, one for Sundays and one featuring bar snacks. The aim is to appeal to all appetites, and the menus specify which dishes are gluten free or suitable for vegetarians. Expect traditional and imaginative cooking, including Sunday roasts, seafood and fish dishes.

Open: 12-3 6-11 (Sat-Sun, BHs open all day and food served all day)
Bar Meals: L served all week 12-2.30 D served all week 6.30-9.30
Restaurant: L served all week 12-2.30 D served all week 6.30-9.30
Brewery/Company: FREE HOUSE
🍺: Harveys Sussex, W J King, Weltons, Youngs London Pride and numerous guest ales
Children's Facilities: Portions/Menu Games High Chairs Food Warming
Notes: Dogs Allowed Water & Biscuits Garden Food Served Outside patio area, stream Parking 28 Coach parties welcome

OVING   SU90

The Gribble Inn 🐾 🍷

Nr Chichester PO20 2BP
☎ 01243 786893 📠 01243 788841
📧 brianelderfield@hotmail.com

Dir: From A27 take A259. After 1m L at roundabout, 1st R to Oving, 1st L in village

Named after local schoolmistress Rose Gribble, the inn retains all of its 16th-century charm. Large open fireplaces, wood burners and low beams set the tone. There's no background music at this peaceful hideaway, which is the ideal spot to enjoy any of the half dozen real ales from the on-site micro-brewery. Liver and bacon; spinach lasagne with red peppers; and special fish dishes are all prepared and cooked on the premises.

Open: 11-3 5.30-11 (Sun 12-4, 7-10.30)
Bar Meals: L served all week 12-2.30 D served all week 6-9.30 (Sun 7-9) Av main course £7.95
Restaurant: L served all week 12-2.30 D served all week 6-9.30 Sun 7-9
Brewery/Company: WOODHOUSE INNS LTD
🍺: Gribble Ale, Reg's Tipple, Slurping Stoat, Plucking Pheasant, Fursty Ferret
Children's Facilities: Fam room Portions/Menu High Chairs Food Warming
Notes: Dogs Allowed Toys & water provided Garden Food Served Outside Large shaded garden with seating for over 100 Parking 40 Coach parties welcome

PETWORTH   SU92

Welldiggers Arms 🍷

Polborough Road GU28 0HG
☎ 01798 342287

Dir: 1m E of Petworth on the A283

Welldiggers once occupied this rustic, 300-year-old roadside pub, which boasts low-beamed bars with open log fires and huge oak tables. It is conveniently located for racing at Goodwood and Fontwell, as well as a visit to Sir Edward Elgar's cottage. Dishes on the menu may include English steaks, butchered on the premises, fresh scallops, lobster and crab and cod with home-made chips.

Open: 11-3 6.30-10 (Sun 12-10.30)
Closed: 25 Dec
Bar Meals: L served all week 12-2 D served Tues-Sat 6.30-9.30 Av main course £8.50
Restaurant: L served all week 12-2 D served Tues- Sat 6.30-9.30 Av 3 course · à la carte £13.50
Brewery/Company: FREE HOUSE
🍺: Youngs
Children's Facilities: Play area
Notes: Dogs Allowed Garden Large lawn & patio, food served outside Parking 35

SUTTON SU91

White Horse Inn

The Street Pulborough RH20 1PS
☎ 01798 869221 📄 01798 869291

Dir: Turn off A29 at foot of Bury Hill.
After 2m pass Roman Villa on R. 1m
to Sutton

Pretty Georgian inn tucked away in a sleepy village at the base of the South Downs. In the neat bars and dining room expect imaginative food, the daily-changing choice featuring perhaps Stilton and broccoli soup, baked sea bass with lemon basil and tomato, confit of duck, lamb shank with tomatoes and red wine, and French lemon tart.

Open: 11-3 5.30-11 (Sun 12-3 7-10.30, summer wknd all day)
Bar Meals: L served all week 12-2 D served all week 7-9 Av main course £6.50
Restaurant: L served all week 12-2 D served all week 7-9 Av 3 course · à la carte £30
Brewery/Company: FREE HOUSE
🍺: Youngs Special, Courage Best, plus guests
Notes: Dogs Allowed Garden Parking 10

WALDERTON SU71

The Barley Mow 🐾

Nr Chichester PO18 9ED
☎ 023 9263 1321 📄 023 9263 1403
✉ mowbarley@aol.co.uk

Dir: From Chichester B2146 towards Petersfield. Turn R signed Walderton, pub 100yds on L. (From Havant take B2147)

Ivy-clad with hanging baskets, this pretty pub is comfortably set beside the rolling Sussex Downs, and is a magnet for walkers, cyclists and riders with a special tethering pole for horses. Famous locally for its skittle alley, it also has a reputation for good home-made pub food -: steak and ale pie, battered fresh cod, lasagne, broccoli and cheese bake, chestnut and parsnip bake, roast partridge, and a Sunday roast.

Open: 11-3 6-11.30 (Summer, all day Sun)
Bar Meals: L served all week 12-2.15 D served all week 6-9.30 Av main course £4.99
Restaurant: L served all week 12-2.15 D served all week 6-9.30
Brewery/Company: FREE HOUSE
🍺: Ringwood Old Thumper & Fortyniner, Fuller's London Pride, Itchen Valley Godfathers, Scottish Courage John Smith's
Children's Facilities: Portions/Menu High Chairs Food Warming
Notes: Dogs Allowed Garden Food Served Outside Mature garden, tables, seats, stream Parking 50 Coach parties welcome

WARNHAM   TQ13

The Greets Inn ♀

47 Friday Street RH12 3QY
☎ 01403 265047 ▤ 01403 265047

Dir: Off A24 N of Horsham

*A fine Sussex hall house dating from about
1350 and built for Elias Greet, a local
merchant. Magnificent inglenook fireplace and
head-crackingly low beams in the flagstone-
floored bar. There is a rambling series of
dining areas.*

Open: 11-2.30 6-11 (Sun 12-2, 7-10.30)
RS: 25-26 Dec 12-2 only
Bar Meals: L served all week 12-2 D served
all week 7-9 Av main course £9
Restaurant: L served all week 12-2 D served
all week 7-9 Av 3 course · à la carte £20
Brewery/Company: LAUREL PUB
PARTNERSHIPS ◀: Interbrew Flowers Original,
Fuller's London Pride, Harvey's Sussex
Notes: Dogs Allowed Water Garden Large,
food served outside Parking 30

ASTON CANTLOW   SP16

King's Head ☜ ♀

21 Bearley Road Solihull B95 6HY
☎ 01789 488242 ▤ 01789 488137

*Shakespeare's parents were married in the
ancient village of Aston Cantlow and had
their wedding breakfast at the King's Head.
It is a restored, timbered, black and white
Tudor pub flanked by a huge spreading
chestnut tree, with a large, hedged beer
garden and an attractive terrace for summer
use. The management places an emphasis on
quality food and wine with cheerful service.
Food is freshly prepared from a menu that
changes every 6-8 weeks, but the King's Head
duck supper is still a firm favourite. Fish
dishes are represented by grilled kingfish with
pineapple salsa and peppercorn butter, and
whole Dover sole.*

Open: 11-3 5.30-11 (Summer open all day)
RS: 25 Dec open 12-2 only
Bar Meals: L served all week 12-2.30 D
served all week 7-10 Av main course £11.50
Restaurant: L served all week 12-2.30 D
served all week 7-10 Av 3 course · à la carte £20
Brewery/Company: FURLONG
◀: Greene King Abbot Ale, Fuller's London
Pride, Best Bitter, Black Sheep, Mitchell &
Butler Brew XI
Children's Facilities: Portions/Menu Games
High Chairs Food Warming
Notes: Dogs Allowed Water Garden Food
Served Outside Large beer garden, food in
summer Parking 60 Coach parties welcome

BROOM   SP05

Broom Tavern ♀

High Street Alcester B50 4HL
☎ 01789 773656 ▤ 01789 772983
✉ richard@distinctivepubs.freeserve.co.uk

Dir: N of B439 W of Stratford-upon-Avon

Charming brick and timber 16th-century inn,
reputedly haunted by a cavalier killed on the
cellar steps. The same menu is offered in the
bar and restaurant. 'Tavern Favourites' include
home-made steak and kidney pie and the
Tavern crispy duck supper, while 'Your Local
Butcher' may offer fillet or sirloin steak, rack
of lamb, calves' liver, or Sunday roast. Legend
has it that William Shakespeare and friends
fell asleep under a tree outside the Broom,
after losing a drinking contest nearby.

Open: 11.30-2.30 5.30-11
Bar Meals: L served all week 12-2 D served
all week 6.30-9 Av main course £8.50
Restaurant: L served all week 12-2 D served
all week 6.30-9 Av 3 course · à la carte £15
Brewery/Company: GREENE KING
🍺: Green King IPA, Adnams Bitter, Rotation Ale
Children's Facilities: Menu
Notes: No Dogs (except Assist Dogs) Garden
Food Served Outside Front lawn with picnic
tables Parking 30 Coach parties welcome

FARNBOROUGH   SP44

The Inn at Farnborough ❀ ♀

Banbury OX17 1DZ
☎ 01295 690615 ▤ 01295 690032

Dating from around 1700, the Inn at
Farnborough is a Grade II listed free house set
in an historic and picturesque village, ideally
placed for a relaxing lunch or dinner after a
visit to the nearby National Trust property of
Farnborough Hall or the Civil War
battleground at Edge Hill. Originally the
butcher's house, the pub serves local Hook
Norton ales and menus of high-quality British
produce and meats, some of which are
organic. Dishes are prepared with refined
touches of foreign lands - roast rump of
Lighthorne lamb, for example, is served with
Moroccan spiced vegetables. Fish too is well
represented with sautéed scallops, mussels
and prawns; and roast sea bass with Japanese
lime and ginger.

Open: 12-3 6-11 (12-11 Sat/Sun)
Bar Meals: L served all week 12-3 D served
all week 6-11 (all day Sat/Sun) Av main course
£12.95
Restaurant: L served all week 12-3 D served
all week 6-11 all day Sat/Sun Av 3 course · à
la carte £22.95 Av 3 course fixed price £12.95
🍺: Abbot Ale, Spitfire, Budwar
Children's Facilities: Licence Portions/Menu
Games High Chairs Food Warming Changing
Notes: Dogs Allowed dog bowls Garden Food
Served Outside sunny, stylish, terraced garden
Parking 40 Coach parties welcome

KENILWORTH SP27

Clarendon House

High Street CV8 1LZ
☎ 01926 857668 ▤ 01926 850669
✉ info@clarendonhousehotel.com

Dir: From A452 pass castle, turn L into Castle Hill and continue into High Street

The original (1430) timber-framed Castle Tavern is incorporated into the hotel, still supported by the oak tree around which it was built. Big, comfortable sofas indoors and a heated patio outside. From the brasserie menu - Thai chicken curry and rice, salad of pigeon and pancetta, honey and lemon dressing, and kedgeree fishcakes, light curry sauce and quails' eggs. The specials board might feature pan-fried wild boar steak with crushed parsnips, roasted baby onions and cranberry and thyme jus.

Open: 11-11 (Sun 12-10.30) **Closed:** 25-26 Dec, 1 Jan
Bar Meals: L served all week 12-10 D served all week 12-10 Av main course £9.50
Restaurant: L served all week 12-10 D served all week 12-10 Av 3 course · à la carte £18
Brewery/Company: OLD ENGLISH INNS & HOTELS ◀: Greene King Abbot Ale, IPA
Children's Facilities: Menu
Notes: Dogs Allowed Garden Food Served Outside Patio garden seats about 100. Outdoor heating Parking 35 Coach parties welcome

LOWSONFORD SP16

Fleur de Lys ♀

Lapworth Street Solihull B95 5HJ
☎ 01564 782431 ▤ 01564 782431
✉ Fleurdelys.solihull@laurelpubco.com

Dir: A34 (Birmingham to Stratford)

Converted from three cottages and a mortuary and located alongside the Stratford-upon-Avon Canal, this 17th-century pub boasts a galleried dining room and atmospheric bars with low beams and real log fires. Fleur de Lys pies were originally made here. The style is casual dining with steak and Guinness pie, wild boar pie, free-range sausages with bubble and squeak and traditional fish and chips among the wholesome dishes. The large canalside garden is the ideal place to enjoy a drink or meal. Ideal for children, and there's even a safe fenced area for the under 8s.

Open: 9-11 (Sun 9-10.30)
Bar Meals: L served all week 12-10 D served all week-(Sun 12-9) Av main course £7
Brewery/Company: LAUREL PUB PARTNERSHIPS ◀: Interbrew Flowers Original & IPA, Guest Ale
Children's Facilities: Play area (Fenced area for under 8's) Portions/Menu High Chairs Food Warming
Nearby: Warwick Castle, Hatton Country World, Umberslade Children's Farm
Notes: Dogs Allowed Water Large Garden canalside Parking 150 Coach parties welcome

MONKS KIRBY SP48

The Bell Inn 🅈

Bell Lane Nr Rugby CV23 0QY
☎ 01788 832352 📠 01788 832352
📧 belindagb@aol.com

Dir: Off The Fosseway junction with B4455

The Spanish owners of this quaint, timbered inn, originally a priory gatehouse and brewhouse cottage, describe it as 'a corner of Spain in the heart of England'. Not surprisingly, there's a strong emphasis on Mediterranean cuisine and an extensive tapas menu. Choose from a wide range of steak dishes, pasta or paellas, or perhaps choose from the wide-ranging selection of seafood dishes - halibut Malagena, lobster Sarafina, deep-fried langoustines, monkfish cooked in a clay dish, or fresh poached salmon among them.

Open: 12-2.30 7-11 Closed: 26 Dec, 1 Jan; Mon **Bar Meals:** L served Tue-Sun 12-2.30 D served Tue-Sun 7-11 Av main course £12.50
Restaurant: L served Tue-Sun 12-2.30 D served all week 7-11 Av 3 course · à la carte £30 **Brewery/Company:** FREE HOUSE
🍺: Boddingtons
Children's Facilities: Portions/Menu High Chairs Food Warming
Nearby: Coombe Abbey
Notes: No Dogs Garden overlooks a stream & buttercup meadow Parking Coach parties welcome

PRINCETHORPE SP47

The Three Horseshoes 🅈

Southam Road Rugby CV23 9PR
☎ 01926 632345

Dir: On A423 at x-rds of B4455 & B4453

Traditional coaching inn, built about 1856, on the Fosse Way. It has a large garden with a range of children's play equipment overlooking open countryside. Beams, horse brasses and log fires characterise the bar, where a blackboard menu of home-cooked food is available. Why not enjoy a Sunday lunch in the inviting atmosphere?

Open: 11.30-2.30 6-11 (Sun 12-11)
Closed: 25 Dec
Bar Meals: L served all week 12-2 D served all week 6-9.30
Restaurant: L served all week 12-2 D served all week 6-11
Brewery/Company: FREE HOUSE
🍺: Ruddles Best, John Smiths, Bombadier, Pedigree
Rooms: 4 en suite s£25 d£50 (◆◆◆)
Children's Facilities: Play area (Slide, Fort, Swings) Portions/Menu High Chairs Food Warming
Notes: No Dogs (except Assist Dogs) Garden Food Served Outside Large eating area, patio Parking 50 Coach parties welcome

RATLEY SP34

The Rose and Crown ♀

nr Banbury OX15 6DS
☎ 01295 678148

Dir: Follow Edgehill signs, 7 miles N of Banbury or 13m SE of Stratford-upon-Avon on A422.

Following the Battle of Edgehill in 1642, a Roundhead was discovered in the chimney of this 11th (or 12th)-century pub and beheaded in the hearth. His ghost reputedly haunts the building. Enjoy the peaceful village location and the traditional pub food, perhaps including beef and ale pie, scampi and chips, chicken curry and the Sunday roast.

Open: 12-2.30 6.30-11 Sun (12-3.30, 7-11)
Bar Meals: L served all week 12-2 D served all week 7-9 Av main course £10.50
Restaurant: L served Tue-Sun-D served Tue-Sat 7-9.30 Av 3 course · à la carte £18
Brewery/Company: FREE HOUSE
🍺: Wells Bombardier & Eagle IPA, Greene King Old Speckled Hen & guest ale
Children's Facilities: Menu
Notes: Dogs Allowed Water, Fireplace Garden Food Served Outside Garden with wooden benches Parking 4

SHIPSTON ON STOUR SP24

The Red Lion ♦♦♦♦ ♀

Main Street Long Compton CV36 5JS
☎ 01608 684221 ▤ 01608 684221
❸ redlionhot@aol.com

Dir: On A3400 N of Chipping Norton

A Grade II listed coaching inn dating from 1748 which retains an old world charm with log fires, stone walls and oak beams yet offers the modern facilities expected today. The menu is extensive and caters for all tastes from interesting sandwiches, baguettes, and light bites to a carte candlelit dinner. From the starter menu can be found, asparagus, mushroom and tarragon risotto; Thai fish balls; and webby cheese and Parma ham flatbreads.

Open: 11-2.30 6-11 (Sun 12-3, 7-10.30)
Bar Meals: L served all week 12-2 D served all week 7-9 Av main course £8
Restaurant: L served all week 12-2 D served all week 7-9 Av 3 course · à la carte £15
Brewery/Company: FREE HOUSE
🍺: Hook Norton Best, Websters Bitter, Theakston
Rooms: 5 en suite 1 family s£40 d£60
Children's Facilities: Play area (Large garden/play equipment) Portions/Menu Cutlery Games High Chairs Food Warming
Nearby: Cotswold Wildlife Park, Blenheim Palace, Warwick Castle
Notes: Dogs Allowed Garden Food Served Outside Large garden Parking 60

WARWICKSHIRE

SHIPSTON ON STOUR   SP24

White Bear Hotel ♀

High Street CV36 4AJ
☎ 01608 661558 ▣ 01608 662612
📧 whitebearhot@hotmail.com

This former coaching inn, parts of which date from the 16th century, has a Georgian façade overlooking the market place. It is a lively pub serving good food and fine ales, and the two beamed bars are full of character. A typical menu might include Gloucester Old Spot pork chop with ginger and soy sauce; marinated sea bass with thyme, lemon and bacon; and tomato and spinach risotto. A good selection of sandwiches, baguettes and snacks is available at lunchtime.

Open: 11-11 (Sun 12-10.30)
Bar Meals: L served 12-2 D served 6.30-9.30
Restaurant: L served 12-2 D served 6.30-9.30
Brewery/Company: PUNCH TAVERNS
🍺: Marstons Pedigree, Interbrew Bass & Guest Ales
Children's Facilities: Portions/Menu High Chairs Food Warming
Notes: Dogs Allowed Water Garden Food Served Outside Patio, Parking 20

WOOTTON WAWEN   SP16

The Bulls Head

Stratford Road B95 6BD
☎ 01564 792511 ▣ 795803
📧 enquiries@thebullshead.co.uk

Dir: On A3400

This impressive 14th-century inn retains plenty of atmosphere and has quality food at sensible prices. Low beams, open fires and old pews set the scene in the bar and snug areas, and in the restaurant. The bar menu sets the pace with choices like warmed tuna pannini with roasted red onions and smoked peppers; or peanut and coriander satay chicken wrap. In the restaurant, smoked haddock brandade with Parma ham and poached egg might precede braised lamb shank; seared calves' liver with caramelised spring onions, Roquefort mash and black pudding; or baked cod supreme with fennel and olive crust.

Open: 11-11 (Sun 12-10.30)
Bar Meals: L served all week 12-2.30 D served all week 7-9.30 (Sun 12-4)
Restaurant: L served all week 12-2.30 D served Mon-Sat 7-9.30 (Sun 12-4) Av 3 course · à la carte £23
Brewery/Company: WOLVERHAMPTON & DUDLEY 🍺: Marston's Pedigree, Banks Bitter plus guest ales
Children's Facilities: Portions/Menu Games High Chairs Food Warming
Notes: No Dogs (except Assist Dogs) Water Bowls Garden Food Served Outside Lawned area patio Parking 30 Coach parties welcome

BIRMINGHAM
SP08

The Peacock

Icknield Street Forhill nr King's Norton
B38 0EH
☎ 01564 823232 ▤ 01564 829593

Despite its out-of-the-way location, at Forhill just outside Birmingham, the Peacock keeps very busy serving traditional ales and a varied menu, (booking essential). Chalkboards display the daily specials, among which you might find braised partridge on a bed of pheasant sausage and mash, whole sea bass with crab, grilled shark steak with light curry butter, pan-fried sirloin steak with mild mushroom and pepper sauce, or lamb fillet with apricot and walnut stuffing. Several friendly ghosts are in residence, and one of their tricks is to disconnect the taps from the barrels. Large gardens with two patios.

Open: 11-11 (Sun 12-10.30)
Bar Meals: L served all week 11-D served all week-10 Av main course £7.95
Restaurant: L served all week 12-10 D served all week 6.30-9.30
Brewery/Company: SPIRIT GROUP
◀: Hobsons Best Bitter, Theakstons Old Peculier, Enville Ale
Children's Facilities: High Chairs
Nearby: Cadbury World, Drayton Manor
Notes: No Dogs Water Garden Patio at front, food served outside Parking 100

SEDGLEY
SO99

Beacon Hotel & Sarah Hughes Brewery ♀

129 Bilston Street Dudley DY3 1JE
☎ 01902 883380 ▤ 01902 883381

Little has changed in 150 years at this traditional brewery tap, which still retains its Victorian atmosphere. The rare snob-screened island bar serves a taproom, snug, large smoke-room and veranda. Proprietor John Hughes reopened the adjoining Sarah Hughes Brewery in 1987, 66 years after his grandmother became the licensee. Flagship beers are Sarah Hughes Dark Ruby, Surprise and Pale Amber, with guest bitters also available. Lunchtime cheese and onion cobs are the only food.

Open: 12-2.30 5.30-10.45 (Fri 5.30-11, Sat 12-3 6-11, Sun 12-3 7-10.30)
Brewery/Company: SARAH HUGHES BREWERY ◀: Sarah Hughes Dark Ruby, Surprise & Pale Amber, Selection of Guest Beers and seasonal products
Children's Facilities: Fam room Play area (Roundabout, slide, climbing frame) Food Warming
Nearby: Black Country Museum, Dudley Zoo, Baggeridge Country Park
Notes: Dogs Allowed Water Garden Beer garden with benches, tables Parking 50 Coach parties welcome No credit cards

WEST MIDLANDS

SOLIHULL SP17

The Boat Inn 🏠 ♀

222 Hampton Lane Catherine-de-Barnes
B91 2TJ
☎ 0121 705 0474 📄 0121 704 0600
✉ steven-hickson@hotmail.com

Village pub with a small, enclosed garden located right next the canal in Solihull. Real ales are taken seriously and there are two frequently changing guest ales in addition to the regulars. There is also a choice of 14 wines available by the glass. Fresh fish is a daily option and other favourite fare includes chicken cropper, Wexford steak, and beef and ale pie.

Open: 12-11 (Sun 12-10.30)
Bar Meals: L served all week 12-9.30 D served all week 12-9.30 Av main course £7.95
🍺: Tetleys, Directors, 2 guest ales
Children's Facilities: Licence Fam room Portions/Menu Cutlery Games High Chairs Food Warming Changing
Nearby: Warwick Castle, Stratford-upon-Avon, NEC
Notes: No Dogs (except Assist Dogs) Garden Food Served Outside Small enclosed garden with tables & chairs Parking 90 Coach parties welcome

WEST BROMWICH SP09

The Vine 🏠

Roebuck Street B70 6RD
☎ 0121 5532866 📄 0121 5255450
✉ bharat@sukis.co.uk

Well-known, family-run business renowned for its good curries and cheap drinks. For over 26 years the typically Victorian alehouse has provided the setting for Suki Patel's eclectic menu. Choose from a comprehensive range of Indian dishes (chicken tikka masala, goat curry, lamb saag), a barbecue menu and Thursday spit roast, offered alongside traditional pub meals like sausage and chips, chicken and ham pie or toasted sandwiches. The Vine boasts the Midlands' only indoor barbeque.

Open: 11.30-2.30 5-11 (Fri-Sun all day)
Bar Meals: L served all week 12-2 D served all week 5-10.30 Av main course £4.25
Restaurant: D served all week 5-10.30
Brewery/Company: FREE HOUSE
🍺: Bannks, Brew XI
Children's Facilities: Fam room Play area (Children's Indoor/Outdoor play area) Portions/Menu Games Food Warming
Notes: No Dogs (except Assist Dogs) Garden Food Served Outside Large beer garden, Coach parties welcome

BEMBRIDGE

SZ68

The Crab & Lobster Inn ☜ ♀

32 Foreland Fields Road PO35 5TR
☎ 01983 872244 📠 01983 873495
📧 allancrab@aol.com

Clifftop inn with a large patio area affording superb views across the Solent and English Channel. Locals and tourists alike seek out the friendly atmosphere in the nautically-themed bars, and walkers find the cliffs and nearby stretches of the 65-mile Isle of Wight Coast Path especially good for exploring on foot. Locally caught seafood forms part of the menu throughout the year, and among the fish dishes are crab cakes and lobster. A full range of chargrilled steaks is also available.

Open: 11-3 6-11 (Wknds & summer all day)
Bar Meals: L served all week 12-2.30 D served all week 6-9.30 Av main course £10
Restaurant: L served all week 12-2.30 D served all week 7-9.30 Av 3 course · à la carte £25
Brewery/Company: ENTERPRISE INNS ☜: Interbrew Flowers Original, Goddards Fuggle-Dee-Dum, Green King IPA, John Smiths, Stella Artois
Children's Facilities: Licence Portions/Menu Cutlery Games High Chairs Food Warming Changing
Notes: Dogs Allowed Water Garden Food Served Outside Patio overlooking the beach Parking 40 Coach parties welcome

COWES

SZ49

The Folly ♀

Folly Lane PO32 6NB
☎ 01983 297171

Dir: On A3054

Reached by both land and water and very popular with the Solent's boating fraternity, the Folly is one of the island's more unusual pubs. Timber from an old sea-going French barge was used in the construction, and wood from the hull can be found in the nautical theme of the bar. Extensive specials board menu ranging from 'Crewpot' casserole - beef goulash, lamb and vegetable, or spicy sausage - to plaice, mackerel trout and salmon.

Open: 9-11 (BHs & Cowes Week late opening)
Bar Meals: L served all week 12-9.30 D served all week
Brewery/Company: LAUREL PUB PARTNERSHIPS ☜: Interbrew Flowers Original, Bass, Goddards Best Bitter
Children's Facilities: Play area Portions/Menu High Chairs Food Warming Changing
Nearby: Robin Hill Adventure Park
Notes: Dogs Allowed Water Garden Food Served Outside Parking 30 Coach parties welcome

NORTHWOOD SZ49

Travellers Joy

85 Pallance Road PO31 8LS
☎ 01983 298024

Pub deeds suggest that an alehouse first opened on this site some 300 years ago. Today's more elderly locals can remember the disturbing tale of a talking mynah bird in the bar which so upset a visiting darts team that they set it alight! Home-made steak and kidney pie, beef in black bean sauce with noodles, chicken tikka masala, mixed grill, pasta of the day, ploughman's, jacket potatoes and the curiously named chicken Cyrilburger are on the menu. Isle of Wight beers feature in the bar.

Open: 11-2 5-11 Sun Closed 3-7
Bar Meals: L served all week 12-2 D served all week 6-9 (Sun 12-2 7-9) Av main course £5.25
◗:Goddardss Special Bitter, Courage Directors, Ventnor Golden Bitter, Deuchars IPA, Hampshire King Alfred
Children's Facilities: Fam room Play area (Climbing frame) Portions/Menu Games High Chairs Food Warming
Notes: Dogs Allowed Garden Food Served Outside Large garden with patio and terrace Parking 30

ROOKLEY SZ58

The Chequers ☜

Niton Road nr Newport PO38 3NZ
☎ 01983 840314 📠 01983 840820
✉ richard@chequersinn-iow.co.uk

Horses in the neighbouring riding school keep a watchful eye on comings and goings at this 250-year-old family-friendly free house. In the centre of the island, surrounded by farms, the pub has a reputation for good food at reasonable prices. Fish, naturally, features well, with sea bass, mussels, plaice, salmon and cod usually available. Other favourites are mixed grill, pork medallions, T-bone steak, and chicken supreme with BBQ sauce and cheese.

Open: 11-11
Bar Meals: L served all week 12-10 D served all week 12-10 (Sun 12-9.30) Av main course £8
Restaurant: L served all week 12-10 D served all week-Sun 12-9.30
Brewery/Company: FREE HOUSE
◗: Gale's HSB, Greene King Old Speckled Hen,Scottish Courage John Smiths, Courage Directors, Best
Children's Facilities: Licence Fam room Play area (Play area) Portions/Menu Games High Chairs Food Warming Changing
Nearby: Robin Hill Adventure Park, Black Gang Chine
Notes: Dogs Allowed Water Garden Food Served Outside Large garden and patio with seating Parking 70

BRADFORD-ON-AVON   ST86

The Kings Arms 🐕 ♈

Monkton Farleigh BA15 2QH
☎ 01225 858705 📠 01225 858999
✉ enquiries@kingsarms-bath.co.uk

Dir: A4 to Bradford. At Bathford A363, L to Monkton Farleigh

Dating back to the 11th century and originally a monks' retreat and one of their number is said to be among several ghosts at the pub. The menu ranges the globe for titillating foreign flavours in light lunches such as nachos covered in melted cheese, salsa, sour cream and jalapeño peppers; or houmous and taramasalata dips. There's a choice of char-grilled skewers - chicken piri-piri, marinated lamb, or salmon and tiger prawns. Fish is well represented in its own right.

Open: 12-3 5.30-11 (Sat 12-1, Sun 12-10.30)
Bar Meals: L served all week 12-2.45 D served all week 6.30-9.30 (12-9.30 Sat & Sun) Av main course £7.50
Restaurant: L served all week 12-2.45 D served all week 6.30-9.30 (12-9.30 Sat & Sun) Av 3 course · à la carte £21
Brewery/Company: INNSPIRED
🍺: Greene King Old Speckled Hen, Wadworth 6X, Buttcombe Bitter, Wychwood Hobgoblin
Children's Facilities: High Chairs Changing
Notes: Dogs Allowed Food Served Outside Garden Parking 45 Coach parties welcome

BRADFORD-ON-AVON   ST86

The Cross Guns Freehouse Restaurant ♈

Avoncliff BA15 2HB
☎ 01225 862335 & 867613
✉ enquiries@crossedguns.com

A beautiful 16th-century inn nestling between the canal and the river. Exposed stone walls, low beamed ceilings and inglenook fires deliver bags of rustic charm, whilst the idyllic riverside terraces provide a perfect location to enjoy a sunny day. Don't forget to sample the acclaimed food - typical dishes include steak and ale pie, chicken stuffed with Stilton and wrapped in bacon, and salmon and monkfish lattice with white wine and cucumber sauce.

Open: 10-11
Bar Meals: L served all week 12-9 D served all week 12-9 Av main course £8
Restaurant: L served all week 12-2 D served all week 6.30-9
🍺: Millworkers, Token Ale, Worthington, Bass, Old Speckled Hen
Children's Facilities: Menu
Notes: Dogs Allowed Garden Food Served Outside Seats 300, external heaters Parking 16 Coach parties welcome

BURCOMBE   SU03

The Ship Inn 🐾 ♀

Burcombe Lane SP2 0EJ
☎ 01722 743182 📠 01722 743182
✉ neillsev@aol.com

Dir: 2m W of Milton on A30

This tranquil, cosy 17th-century pub has been given a thorough revamp by its owners, who have installed wooden and slate floors and new lighting. Visitors can relax in front of a log fire, or under willow trees in the riverside garden. Specials change twice daily, and a new menu is offered every three months to allow ingredients to reflect the seasons.

Open: 11-3 6-11
Bar Meals: L served all week 11-2.30 D served all week 6-10 Av main course £6.50
Restaurant: L served all week 11-2.30 D served all week 6-10 Av 3 course · à la carte £16
🍺:Flowers IPA, Wadworth 6X, Courage Best
Children's Facilities: Licence Portions/Menu Cutlery Games High Chairs Food Warming Changing
Nearby: Stonehenge, Farmer Giles
Notes: Dogs Allowed Garden Food Served Outside River and ducks Parking 30

DEVIZES   SU06

The Bear Hotel ★★★ ♀

The Market Place SN10 1HS
☎ 01380 722444 📠 01380 722450
✉ info@thebearhotel.net

Right in the centre of Devizes, home of Wadworth's brewery, this old coaching inn dates from at least 1559 and lists Judge Jeffreys, George III, and Harold Macmillan amongst its notable guests. You'll find old beams, log fires, fresh flowers - and a menu with starters like grilled black pudding with apple and cider vinaigrette; and main courses such as pot-roasted partridge, or broccoli and mushroom strudel. For desserts (all home made) expect elderflower and gooseberry torte, or profiteroles with chocolate sauce.

Open: 9.30-11 **Closed:** 25-26 Dec
Bar Meals: L served all week 11.30-2.30 D served all week 7-9.30 Av main course £4.50
Restaurant: L served Sun-Fri 12.15-1.45 D served Mon-Sat 7-9.30 Av 3 course · à la carte £21.95 Av 2 course fixed price £18
Brewery/Company: WADWORTH 🍺: Wadworth 6X, Wadworth IPA, Wadworth JCB, Old Timer, Malt & Hops, Summersault & Seasonal Beers
Rooms: 25 en suite 3 family s£50 d£75
Children's Facilities: Portions/Menu High Chairs Food Warming
Nearby: Stonehenge, Avebury Stone Circle, Longleat
Notes: Dogs Allowed Garden Food Served Outside Courtyard Coach parties welcome

DONHEAD ST ANDREW   ST92

The Forester Inn ♀

Lower Street SP7 9EE
☎ 01747 828038

Dir: 4.5m from Shaftsbury on A30 towards Salisbury

An attractive 14th-century thatched inn, now refurbished to add a modern feel to its rustic charm. The interior still includes an inglenook fireplace and traditional wooden furnishings, and the pub retains a good local trade. There's an increased emphasis on home-cooked food such as warm chicken, bacon and cashew nut salad; tagliatelle of oyster mushrooms, artichokes and tomatoes in a cream sauce; and crab fishcakes. Other charms include an attractive garden and lunchtime bar snacks such as ciabattas and ploughman's platters. An old well is now a central part of the terrace.

Open: 12-3 6.30-11
Bar Meals: L served all week 12-2 D served all week 7-9.30
Restaurant: L served all week 12-2 D served all week 7-9.30
🍺: 6X, Adnams, Bass, Ringwood, Butcombe
Children's Facilities: Licence Portions/Menu Games High Chairs Food Warming Changing
Nearby: Farmer Giles, Wardor Castle, The Bison Farm
Notes: Dogs Allowed Garden Food Served Outside Large patio area Parking 30

EAST KNOYLE   ST83

The Fox and Hounds

The Green Salisbury SP3 6BN
☎ 01747 830573 📄 01747 830865

Dir: Off A303 onto A350 for 200yds, then R. Pub 0.5m on L

Originally three cottages, dating from the late 15th century, this thatched pub overlooks the Blackmore Vale with fine views for up to 20 miles. East Knoyle is the birthplace of Sir Christopher Wren, and was also home to Lady Jayne Seymour.

Open: 11-2.30 6-11
Bar Meals: L served all week 12-2.30 D served all week 7-10
🍺: Fullers London Pride, Wadworth 6X, Smiles Golden, Butts Barbus Barbus, Ringwood
Children's Facilities: Fam room
Notes: Dogs Allowed Garden Parking 10

WILTSHIRE

HEYTESBURY ST94

The Angel Inn

High Street Warminster BA12 0ED
☎ 01985 840330 📠 01985 840931
✉ Angelheytesbury@aol.com

Dir: From A303 take A36 toward Bath, 8m, Heytesbury on L

With all the charm and character of a traditional coaching inn, the Angel is a dining pub in the modern idiom. The atmosphere is very relaxing and food-wise there's something for everyone. The bar menu includes a selection of pâtes with grilled country bread; potted shrimps; and lemon sole goujons. Another menu has a big variety of hand-cut, 35-day hung steaks to choose from - cooked to any degree from 'blue' to 'well done'. The Alternative Menu might have baked sea bass; roasted bream; aromatic chicken or duck confit to tempt you.

Open: 12-11 (Sun 12-10.30)
Bar Meals: L served all week 12-2.30 D served all week 7-9.30 Av main course £9.95
Restaurant: L served all week 12-2.3 D served all week 7-9.30 Av 3 course · à la carte £25
Brewery/Company: FREE HOUSE
🍺: Ringwood Best, Marstons Pedigree, Old Hooky, Ringwood Boondoogle
Children's Facilities: Licence
Notes: Dogs Allowed Water Parking 12

LOWER CHICKSGROVE ST92

Compasses Inn ◆◆◆◆ 🏠 ♀

Nr Tisbury SP3 6NB
☎ 01722 714318 📠 01722 714318
✉ thecompasses@aol.com

Dir: A30 W from Salisbury, after 10m R signed Chicksgrove

An idyllic 14th-century thatched pub deep in beautiful Wiltshire countryside, offering the very best in real ale, fine wines and freshly prepared food. Not that easy to find, but worth negotiating the narrow lanes for. Inside the latched door, there's a long, low-beamed bar with high-backed stools, stone walls, worn flagstone floors and a large inglenook fireplace with a wood-burning stove. The blackboard menu changes daily, depending on the time of year and local availability. Everything is freshly made.

Open: 12-3 6-11 Closed: 25, 26 Dec, Mon
Bar Meals: L served Tue-Sun 12-2 D served Tue-Sat 7-9 (No food Sun eve) Av main course £12
Restaurant: L served Tue-Sun 12-2 D served Tues-Sat 7-9 (No food Sun eve) Av 3 course · à la carte £20
Brewery/Company: FREE HOUSE
🍺: Interbrew Bass, Wadworth 6X, Ringwood Best, Chicksgrove Churl
Rooms: 4 en suite 3 family s£45 d£65
Children's Facilities: Play area (Swings & see-saw, rope ladder) Portions/Menu Cutlery Games High Chairs Food Warming
Nearby: Longleat, Farmer Giles Homestead
Notes: Dogs Allowed Water Garden Food Served Outside Large grass area, seats 40 Parking 30 Coach parties welcome

LOWER WOODFORD   SU13

The Wheatsheaf ♀

Salisbury SP4 6NQ
☎ 01722 782203

Dir: Take A360 N of Salisbury. Village
signposted 1st R

*Once a farm and brewhouse, now a thriving
country pub in the Avon Valley. A rustic décor
gives the interior a contemporary twist. Expect
dishes like seared tuna steak with lemon and
coriander butter, salmon and dill fishcakes,
and traditional cod and chips. Steak and
Tanglefoot ale pie, Cumberland sausage and
mash, and slow-roasted lamb shank should
also be available.*

Open: 11-11 (Sun 12.10.30)
Bar Meals: L served all week 12-9.30 D
served all week-Av main course £7.50
Restaurant: L served all week 12-2.30 D
served all week 7-9.30
Brewery/Company: HALL & WOODHOUSE
◖: Badger Dorset Best & Tanglefoot,
plus guest ales
Children's Facilities: Menu Play area
Baby changing area
Notes: Dogs Allowed In the garden only
Garden Food served outside. Enclosed garden
Parking 50 Coach parties welcome

PEWSEY   SU16

The Woodbridge Inn

North Newnton SN9 6JZ
☎ 01980 630266 📠 01980 630457
✉ woodbridgeinn@btconnect.com

Dir: 2m SW on A345

*Variously a toll house, bakery and brewhouse,
this Grade II listed, 16th-century building
stands in over four acres of beautiful grounds
by the Wiltshire/Hampshire Avon, and was
established as a coaching inn in 1850. Eating
options are described as Traditional home-
made pub food.*

Open: 12-11 (Sun 12-10.30)
Bar Meals: L served all week 12-9 D served
all week 12-9 Av main course £6.50
Restaurant: L served all week 12-9 D served
all week 12-9
Brewery/Company: WADWORTH
◖: Wadworth 6X, Henrys IPA, Summersault
& Old Timer
Children's Facilities: Play area
(Large garden with swings, slides, play area)
Portions/Menu Cutlery Games
Nearby: Stonehenge, Avebury
Notes: Dogs Allowed Water Garden Food
Served Outside Large grassed with flower
beds Parking 60 Coach parties welcome

PEWSEY SU16

The French Horn 🐾 ♀

Marlborough Road SN9 5NT
☎ 01672 562443 ▤ 01672 562785
✉ info@french-horn.co.uk

Dir: A338 through Hungerford, at Burbage take B3087 to Pewsey

Popular local pub set beside historic Pewsey Wharf on the Kennet & Avon Canal, busy with walkers and cyclists. Napoleonic prisoners of war working on the canal were summoned to the inn for meals by the sound of a French horn. Quality food is served in the restaurant-duck in cherry sauce, smoked haddock rarebit, pan-fried rib-eye steak, and the bar-vegetable quiche, beef stew and dumplings, ploughman's platter.

Open: 11.30-3 6-11 (Fri-Sat open all day, Sun 12-3 and 7-10.30) RS: 25 Dec closed evening
Bar Meals: L served all week 12-2.30 D served all week 6.30-9 (Sunday dinner 7-9) Av main course £6.80
Restaurant: L served all week 12-2.30 D served all week 6.30-9 Av 3 course - à la carte £25
Brewery/Company: WADWORTH
🍺: Wadworth 6X, Henry's Original IPA, JCB
Children's Facilities: Play area (Swings, slide, rope climbing) Portions/Menu High Chairs Food Warming Changing
Notes: Dogs Allowed Water Garden Food Served Outside Canalside beer garden Parking 20 Coach parties welcome

PITTON SU23

The Silver Plough ♀

White Hill Salisbury SP5 1DU
☎ 01722 712266 ▤ 01722 712266

Dir: From Salisbury take A30 towards Andover, Pitton signposted (approx 3m)

Surrounded by rolling countryside and with a peaceful garden, this popular pub is at the heart of a village full of thatched houses. Inside you will find beams strung with antique glass rolling pins, Toby jugs and various other artefacts. It also features a skittle alley adjacent to the snug bar. The pub offers a range of dishes both lunchtime and evening, including children's meals. House specialities include half a roast shoulder of lamb with mint and garlic gravy, and red bream fillet with caramelised onions, prosciutto and pesto sauce.

Open: 11-3 6-11 (Sun 12-3, 6-10.30) RS: 25-26 Dec, 1 Jan closed eve
Bar Meals: L served all week 12-2.30 D served all week 6-9.30 Av main course £8
Restaurant: L served all week 12-2.30 D served all week 7-9.30 Av 3 course - à la carte £18
Brewery/Company: HALL & WOODHOUSE
🍺: Badger Tanglefoot, Badger Best, IPA & King & Barnes Sussex, guest ales
Children's Facilities: Fam room Play area (Skittles alley, darts, board games)
Notes: Dogs Allowed Water, biscuits Garden Food Served Outside bench tables Parking 50 Coach parties welcome

SHERSTON ST88

The Rattlebone Inn ♀

Church Street Malmesbury SN16 0LR
☎ 01666 840871 📠 01666 840871
✉ rattleboneinn@youngs.co.uk

Dir: M4 J18 take A46 towards Stroud,then R onto B4040 through Acton Turville & onto Sherston. Or N from M4 J17 & follow signs

A 16th-century village inn standing where, according to legend, local hero John Rattlebone died of his wounds after the Battle of Sherston in 1016. The rambling series of beamed rooms have kept their existing character.

Open: 12-11
Bar Meals: L served all week 12-2.30 D served all week 6-9.30 (Sun 6-9) Av main course £7
Restaurant: L served all week 12-2.30 D served all week 6-9.30 Av 3 course - à la carte £15
Brewery/Company: YOUNG & CO BREWERY PLC 🍺: Youngs Special, Bitter, Smiles Best, Youngs Triple A , Waggledance, Smiles
Children's Facilities: Portions/Menu High Chairs Food Warming
Notes: Dogs in public bar only (except Assist Dogs) Garden Food Served Outside Food served outside Coach parties welcome

TOLLARD ROYAL ST91

King John Inn

Salisbury SP5 5PS
☎ 01725 516207

Dir: On B3081 (7m E of Shaftesbury)

Named after one of King John's hunting lodges, this Victorian building was opened in 1859. A friendly and relaxing place, it is today perhaps better known as 'Madonna's local' after she and husband Guy Richie moved in close by. Also nearby is a 13th-century church, and the area is excellent rambling country. A typical menu offers old English favourites such as bangers and apple mash; bacon, liver and kidney casserole; Dorset lamb cutlets; Wiltshire gammon with peaches; and Dover sole.

Open: 12-2.30 6.30-11 (Sun 12-10.30)
Bar Meals: L served all week 12-2 D served all week 7-9 (All day Sun summer)
Restaurant: L served all week 12-2 D served all week 7-9
Brewery/Company: FREE HOUSE 🍺: Courage Best, John Smith's, Wadworth 6X, Ringwood
Children's Facilities: Portions/Menu Cutlery High Chairs Food Warming
Notes: Dogs Allowed Water Garden Food Served Outside Terrace, Parking 18 Coach parties welcome

WILTSHIRE

WARMINSTER ST84

The Angel Inn ♀

Upton Scudamore BA12 0AG
☎ 01985 213225 📠 01985 218182
✉ theangelinn.uptonscudamore@
btopenworld.com

A relaxed and unpretentious old inn in a small village with a name Agatha Christie might have made up. Freshly prepared lunch could be Cumberland sausage with horseradish mash and blackcurrant sauce, or game casserole with juniper berries and bacon dumplings. Dinner candidates include honey-glazed breast of duck with cumin and sweet potato pancake and pineapple sauce, or bacon-wrapped gilthead fillet of sea bream with saffron mash, roasted almonds and red curry sauce. Walled terrace garden.

Open: 11-3 6-11 **Closed:** 25-26 Dec, 1 Jan
Bar Meals: L served all week 12-2 D served all week 7-9.30 Av main course £13
Restaurant: L served all week 12-2 D served all week 7-9.30 Av 3 course · à la carte £20
Brewery/Company: FREE HOUSE
🍺: Wadworth 6X, Butcombe, John Smith's Smooth, Guest Ales
Children's Facilities: Menu
Notes: Dogs Allowed Water provided Garden Food Served Outside Walled terrace Parking 30

WOOTTON RIVERS SU16

Royal Oak ♀

Marlborough SN8 4NQ
☎ 01672 810322 📠 01672 811168
✉ royaloak35@hotmail.com

Dir: 3m S from Marlborough

Set in one of Wiltshire's prettiest villages, a thatched and timbered 16th-century inn just 100 yards from the Kennet and Avon Canal, and close to Savernake Forest - a wonderful area for canal and forest walks. Menus are flexible, with light basket meals, ploughman's and sandwiches, and specials like partridge with game sauce, rich beef and Burgundy casserole, and medallions of pork and leek with a pine nut stuffing.

Open: 10.30-3.30 6-11 (Close Sun 10.30)
Bar Meals: L served all week 11.30-2.30 D served all week 6-9.30 Av main course £10
Restaurant: L served all week 11.30-2.30 D served all week 6-9.30 Av 3 course - à la carte £20 Av 3 course fixed price £12.50
Brewery/Company: FREE HOUSE
🍺: Wadworth 6X, London Pride, guest ales
Children's Facilities: Fam room
Notes: Dogs Allowed Garden Food Served Outside Large lawn area. Raised terrace with seating Parking 20 Coach parties welcome

Horse & Jockey 🐾

Far Forest DY14 9DX
☎ 01299 266239 📠 01299 266227
✉ info@horseandjockey-farforest.co.uk

Serving fresh food sourced from local farms and cooked with imagination, this peaceful country pub is a deservedly successful dining destination. The pub was first licensed to serve cider to farm workers; restoration some years ago uncovered oak beams and an inglenook fireplace. Regularly changing menus incorporate roast topside of beef with a dark shallot and chestnut sauce and slow-roasted lamb shank glazed with honey and rosemary jus. A good selection of fresh fish is delivered every Friday, so expect some adventurous as well as traditional dishes at the weekend.

Open: 12-3 6-11 open all day May-Sep
Days closed: Mon, ex BHs & summer
Bar Meals: L served Tue-Sun 12-2.30
D served Tue-Sun 6-9.30 (Sun 12-4)
Av main course £7.50
Restaurant: L served N Sun 12-2.30 D served all week 6-9.30 Sun 12-4
Av 3 course · à la carte £13.95
Brewery/Company: FREE HOUSE 🍺:
Hobsons Best, Bombadier, Boddingtons, guests
Children's Facilities: Licence Fam room Play area (Table Football, Air Hockey) Cutlery Games High Chairs Food Warming
Notes: Dogs Allowed Garden only Garden Food Served Outside Large lawn, seating, Parking 50 Coach parties welcome

The Mughouse Inn & Angry Chef Restaurant 🐾 ♀

12 Severnside North DY12 2EE
☎ 01299 402543 📠 01299 402543
✉ drew@mughousebewdley.co.uk

Historic pub located on the glorious River Severn. The inn's name dates back to the 17th century when 'mug house' was a popular term for an alehouse. Seating area at the front directly overlooks the water and is a favourite spot with customers in the summer months. Many popular walks in the nearby Wyre Forest. Lunchtime bar menu offers the likes of beer battered cod, steak and Guinness Mug Pie, and home-made faggots.

Open: 12-11 Sun 12-10.30
Bar Meals: L served all week 12-2.30 (Sun 12.30-6) Av main course £5.95
Restaurant: D served Tue-Sat 7-9
Sunday lunch Carvery 12.30-6 Av 3 course -
à la carte £23
🍺: Timothy Taylor's Landlord, Mugs Gayme plus 2 guest beers
Children's Facilities: Licence Fam room Food Warming
Notes: Dogs Allowed water Garden Food Served Outside food served at lunchtime

BREDON SO93

Fox & Hounds Inn & Restaurant ♀

Church Street Tewkesbury GL20 7LA
☎ 01684 772377 📠 01684 772377

Dir: M5 J9 into Tewkesbury take B4080
towards Pershore. Bredon 3m

Resplendent with colourful, over-flowing
hanging baskets in summer, this pretty 16th-
century thatched pub is located close to the
River Avon. Food is served in the bar areas
and dining lounge, including blackboard
specials, lunchtime bar snacks and the main
menu. Favourite dishes include chicken
Caribbean, pork tenderloin, pasta carbonara,
and the daily fresh fish selection, as well as
filled hot and cold baguettes, and various
tasty ploughman's.

Open: 11.30-3 6-10.30 (Sun 12-3, 6-10.30)
RS: 25/26 Dec closed eve
Bar Meals: L served all week 12-2 D served
all week 6.30-9.30 Av main course £7
Restaurant: L served all week 12-2 D served
all week 6.30-9.30 Av 3 course · à la carte
£20
Brewery/Company: WHITBREAD ◨: Banks,
Marstons Pedigree, Old Speckled Hen
Notes: No Dogs (except Assist Dogs) Garden
Food Served Outside Small shaded garden
with BBQ area Parking 35 Coach parties
welcome

DROITWICH SO86

The Chequers ♀

Cutnall Green WR9 0PJ
☎ 01299 851292 📠 01299 851744

This charming country pub is decorated in
traditional style, with an open fire, timbered
bar and richly-coloured furnishings. The effect
is cosy and welcoming - a good place to linger
over numerous real ales, fine wines and
perhaps a meal from the extensive menu.
Dishes range from lunch light bites through to
dinner dishes such honey-roast breast of
Gressingham duck, with confit red cabbage,
potato wedges, cinnamon sage and apple jus;
and whole grilled lemon sole, with crushed
potatoes, rocket salad, tomato, garlic and dill.

Open: 12-3 6-11 Closed: 25-26 Dec, 31
Dec, 1-2 Jan
Bar Meals: L served all week 12-2 D served
all week 6.30-9.15
Restaurant: L served all week 12-2 D served
all week 6.30-9.15
Brewery/Company: ENTERPRISE INNS
◨: Timothy Taylors, Banks Pedigree,
Banks Bitter, Banks Mild, Hook Norton
Children's Facilities: Fam room
Notes: Dogs Allowed Garden Food Served
Outside Large garden with benches, flower
borders Parking 75

KNIGHTWICK SO75

The Talbot ♀

Worcester WR6 5PH
☎ 01886 821235 📠 01886 821060
✉ admin@the-talbot.co.uk

Dir: A44 through Worcester, 8m L onto B4197

Real ales called This, That, Wot and T'other are all brewed on the premises with hops grown in the parish. In fact, everything bar the fresh fish, which comes from Wales and Cornwall, is made here from local ingredients, or from produce grown in the 'chemical free' garden. And that includes preserves, breads and black pudding. At lunchtime try fresh crab blinis and garlic mayonnaise, pheasant breast with tarragon sauce, and treacle hollygog (should ring a bell with Cambridge graduates).

Open: 11-11 (Sun 12-10.30) RS: 25 Dec closed eve
Bar Meals: L served all week 12-2 D served all week 6.30-9.30 (Sun 7-9) Av main course £13.95
Restaurant: L served all week 12-2 D served all week 6.30-9.30 (Sun 7-9) Av 3 course · à la carte £26 Av 3 course fixed price £22.95
Brewery/Company: FREE HOUSE
🍺: Teme Valley This, That , T'Other, City of Cambridge Hobsons Choice
Rooms: 11 en suite 3 family s£40 d£75 (★★)
Children's Facilities: Highchairs
Notes: Dogs Allowed Garden Food Served Outside Riverside grass area Parking 50 Coach parties welcome

OMBERSLEY SO86

The Kings Arms ♀

Main Road Droitwich WR9 0EW
☎ 01905 620142 📠 01905 620142
✉ kaombersley@btconnect.com

Dir: Just off A449

After the Battle of Worcester in 1651, the fleeing King Charles II probably needed a stiff drink, and reputedly made this his first stop. It was old even then, dating as it does from 1411. Black-and-white-timbered externally, and with an inviting, dimly lit interior with lots of nooks and crannies and blazing fires in winter. On warmer days customers spill out into the pretty walled garden to eat. A tempting selection of modern pub food is available, with the day's fresh fish listed on a blackboard. Other options are fillet of pork with bacon and rosemary and mushroom and leek shepherd's pie with goat's cheese mash.

Open: 11-3 5.30-11 (Sun all day)
Closed: 25 Dec
Bar Meals: L served all week 12-2.15 D served all week 6-10 Av main course £9
Restaurant: L served all week 12-2.15 D served all week 6-10 Av 3 course -à la carte £9
Brewery/Company: FREE HOUSE
🍺: Banks's Bitter, Marston's Pedigree, Cannon Royall Arrowhead, Morrells Varsity
Children's Facilities: Portions/Menu Food Warming Changing
Nearby: Severn Valley Railway, Safari Park
Notes: No Dogs (except Assist Dogs) Garden Food Served Outside Walled garden Parking 60 Coach parties welcome

OMBERSLEY — SO86

Crown & Sandys Arms 🐕 ♀

Main Road WR9 0EW
☎ 01905 620252 📠 01905 620769
✉ richardeverton@crownandsandys.co.uk

A classy establishment run by Richard Everton, who also has his own village deli and wine shop. Original beams and fireplaces co-exist alongside modern furniture in the trendy open-plan bar/bistro and stylish restaurant. Freshly-made sandwiches, baguettes and hot dishes are available at lunchtime. Main dishes, changed every week, always include a wide choice of fresh market fish and seafood. Other main courses are pan-fried chicken breast on a ragout of leeks, bacon and prunes; and autumn vegetable risotto with spinach, feta cheese and tomato.

Open: 11-3 5-11
Bar Meals: L served all week 11.30-2.30
D served all week 6-10 (Sun all day to 9.30)
Av main course £9.45
Restaurant: L served all week 11.30-2.30 D served all week 6-10 Av 3 course -
à la carte £15.95

Brewery/Company: FREE HOUSE
🍺: Quaff, IPA, Shropshire Lad, guest ale
Children's Facilities: Portions/Menu Games
High Chairs Food Warming Changing
Nearby: Worcester Cathedral, West Midlands
Safari Park, Worcester Rugby Club
Notes: No Dogs (except Assist Dogs) Garden
Food Served Outside Large beer garden,
Parking 100 Coach parties welcome

PENSAX — SO76

The Bell Inn ♀

Abberley WR6 6AE
☎ 01299 896677

Dir: From Kidderminster A456 to Clows Top,
B4202 towards Abberley, pub 2m on L

Friendly rural local offering five real ales by the jug at weekends to extend the choice available. There's also a beer festival held at the end of June. Home-made dishes are prepared from seasonal local produce-steaks, liver and onions, and home-cooked ham with free-range eggs. Superb views are enjoyed from the garden, and great local walks. Walkers and cyclists are welcome, and there's a registered caravan/campsite opposite. Look out for the bargain lunchtime menu.

Open: 12-2.30 5-11 (Sun 12-10.30)
RS: Mon Closed lunch except BHs
Bar Meals: L served Tues-Sun 12-2 D served all week 6-9 (Sun 12-4) Av main course £6.25
Restaurant: L served Tue-Sun 12-2
D served all week 6-9 Sun 12-4
Brewery/Company: FREE HOUSE
🍺: Timothy Taylor Best Bitter, Hobsons Best,
Hook Norton Best, Cannon Royall
Children's Facilities: Fam room Play area
Notes: Dogs Allowed Garden Food served
outside Parking 20 Coach parties welcome

STONEHALL SO84

The Fruiterer's Arms

Stonehall Common Norton WR5 3QG
☎ 01905 820462 📠 01905 820501
📧 thefruiterersarms@btopenworld.com

Dir: 2m from M5 J7. Stonehall Common is 1.5m from St Peters Garden Centre Norton

Pub on Stonehall Common, once frequented by the area's fruit pickers. Four guest ales are rotated weekly, and there's a main menu, specials menu and Sunday menu offered in the bar, restaurant, garden pavilion and garden. Favourite dishes include Swiss chicken with Alpine cheese, fillet of lamb with Madeira and rosemary, and the fresh fish of the day. The garden is large and has a purpose-built play area for children.

Open: 12-3 6-11 (all day Sat-Sun in Summer)
Bar Meals: L served all week 12-2 D served all week 6-9.15 Av main course £10
Restaurant: L served all week 12-2.30 D served all week 6-9.15 all day Sundays Av 3 course · à la carte £20 Av 2 course fixed price £10.95
🍺: Bass, Malvern Hills Black Pear, Hobsons Bitter
Children's Facilities: Licence Play area (Wood chipping base, 50mtr zip wire) Portions/Menu Cutlery Games High Chairs Food Warming Changing
Nearby: Worcester City & R. Severn Boating
Notes: Dogs Allowed watering station Garden Food Served Outside 1.7 acres, 50 seat pavillion, Parking 35 Coach parties welcome

TENBURY WELLS SO56

Peacock Inn ★ ⊛ 🐾 ♀

Worcs WR15 8LL
☎ 01584 810506 📠 01584 811236
📧 jamesvidler@btconnect.com

Dir: A456 from Worcester then A443 to Tenbury Wells. Inn is 1.25m E

A 14th-century coaching inn overlooking the River Teme, with a sympathetic extension. The relaxing bars and oak-panelled restaurant are enhanced by oak beams, dried hops and open log fires. Home-made duck liver parfait with Cumberland sauce; and Herefordshire smoked salmon with cucumber, spring onion, chilli and créme fraîche, are possible starters, with typical main courses of penne pasta with prawns, garlic and spinach in olive oil; rack of English lamb with Mediterranean vegetables and rosemary sauce; lobster with sauce Armoricaine; and venison with caramelised shallots and a port redcurrant sauce.

Open: 12.30-3 6-11
Bar Meals: L served all week 12-2.15 D served all week 6.30-9.30 Av main course £14 **Restaurant:** L served all week 12-2.15 D served all week 7-9.30 Av 3 course · à la carte £20 Av 3 course fixed price £13.45
Brewery/Company: FREE HOUSE
🍺: Hobsons Best Bitter, Adnams Bitter, Old Hooky **Rooms:** 6 en suite s£60 d£70
Children's Facilities: Portions/Menu High Chairs Food Warming
Nearby: Severn Valley Railway, West Midland Safari Park **Notes:** Dogs Allowed Garden Food Served Outside Overlooks River Parking 30

WORCESTER   SO85

The Salmon's Leap

42 Severn Street WR1 2ND
☎ 01905 726260 📠 01905 724151
📧 bernardwalker@
thesalmonsleap.freeserve.co.uk

Dir: In city centre, opposite Royal Worcester Porcelain Museum. From M5 J7 follow signs for Museum & Cathedral.

Quiet family pub, less than five minutes' walk from the cathedral, offering a regularly changing selection of cask ales from around the country and good quality pub food. Favourite dishes include smoked fish platter, home-made chicken and mushroom pie and a choice of steaks. The beer garden has a fenced off children's area with play equipment and a bouncy castle in summer. Saturday night barbecues, from 6pm, are a regular event in fine weather.

Open: 11.30-11 (Oct-Apr closed Mon lunch-open 5)
Bar Meals: L served all week 12-7.30 D served all week 12-7.30 Av main course £5.50
Restaurant: L served all week 12-7.30 D served all week 12-7.30
🍺: Timothy Taylor, 5 other guest ales
Children's Facilities: Licence Fam room Play area (Fenced area & equipment; bouncy castle-summer) Games High Chairs
Nearby: Civil War Centre, Cathedral
Notes: Dogs Allowed except in restaurant; water Garden Food Served Outside Adjacent to pub Parking 3 Coach parties welcome

WYRE PIDDLE   SO94

The Anchor Inn ♀

Main Street Nr Pershore WR10 2JB
☎ 01386 552799 📠 01386 552799
📧 ngreen32@btinternet.com

Dir: From M5 J6 take A4538 S towards Evesham

An impressive half-timbered inn on the banks of the Avon, standing in gardens that overlook the pleasure craft moored by the water's edge. Old world in style, the 400-year-old building features a cosy lounge with original low-timbered ceiling, old coaching prints around the walls and an inglenook fireplace decorated with horse brasses. The dining room enjoys a panoramic view out over the river and countryside. The asparagus supper is very popular when in season, as is local game.

Open: 12-3 6-11 (Easter & Aug BH & Sun open all day)
Bar Meals: L served all week 12-2 D served all week 7-9 Av main course £7.50
Restaurant: L served all week 12-2 D served all week 7-9 Av 3 course · à la carte £15
Brewery/Company: ENTERPRISE INNS
🍺: Banks bitter, Timothy Taylor landlord, Marston's Pedigree, Piddle Ale, Guest Ale
Children's Facilities:
Notes: No Dogs Garden Food Served Outside by River Avon, wonderful views Parking 10 Coach parties welcome

ACASTER MALBIS   SE54

The Ship Inn

Moor End YO23 2UH
☎ 01904 703888   🖷 01904 705609

Dir: From York take A1036 south, after Dringhouses take follow signs for Bishopthorpe and then Acaster Malbis

The Ship is a 17th-century coaching house in a village setting on the outskirts of York, overlooking the River Ouse. A choice of home-made dishes is served in a conservatory-style eating area, and a carte menu in the Wheel House Restaurant. Typical options include cod in beer batter, steak, gammon, pizzas, and vegetarian lasagne.

Open: 11-11 (Oct-Feb Mon-Wed closed daytime, Sun 12-10.30) RS: Oct-Feb closed Mon-Wed daytime
Bar Meals: L served all week 12-2.30 D served all week 4.30-8 Av main course £6.75
Restaurant: D served Fri-Sun 7-9.30 Av 3 course · à la carte £19 Av 3 course fixed price £15
Brewery/Company: ENTERPRISE INNS
🍺: Marston's Pedigree, Theakstons Best, John Smiths Cask, Tetley, Timothy Taylor Landlord
Children's Facilities: Fam room Play area (Wooden climbing frame, tyre swing) Portions/Menu Cutlery Games High Chairs Food Warming Changing
Nearby: Jorvik Viking Centre
Notes: Dogs Allowed Water Garden Food Served Outside Large garden with benches and tables Parking 60

APPLETREEWICK   SE06

The Craven Arms

Nr Skipton BD23 6DA
☎ 01756 720270
✉ cravenapple@aol.com

Dir: From Skipton take A59 towards Harrogate, B6160 N. Village signed on R. (Pub just outside village)

Built as a farm by Sir William Craven (a Lord Mayor of London) in the late 1500s, and later a weaving shed and courthouse, this ancient building retains its original beams, flagstone floors and magnificent Dales fireplace. The village stocks are still outside, with spectacular views of the River Wharfe and Simon's Seat. Expect home-made soup, steak pie with ale and mushrooms, cheesy cottage pie, traitor's pie (Lancashire hotpot in a giant Yorkshire pudding), local sausages, baguette sandwiches.

Open: 11.30-3 6.30-11 (Sat & BHs 11.30-11, Sun 12-10.30)
Bar Meals: L served all week 11.30-2.30 D served all week 6.30-9 (Sat 11.30-9, Sun 12-9) Av main course £5.5
Brewery/Company: FREE HOUSE
🍺: Black Sheep, Tetley, Old Bear Original
Children's Facilities: Play area Portions/Menu Cutlery High Chairs Food Warming
Nearby: Embsay & Bolton Abbey Steam Railway, Stump Cross Caverns, Bolton Abbey
Notes: Dogs Allowed Garden Food Served Outside Walled grass beer garden, hill views Parking 35 Coach parties welcome

AUSTWICK SD76

The Game Cock Inn

The Green nr Settle LA2 8BB
☎ 015242 51226 ▤ 015242 51028

In the glorious adventure playground that is the Three Peaks, this cosy village pub draws a good local crowd. Everything on the menu is home cooked and freshly prepared in-house, and among the main dishes are venison casserole, lamb shoulder, battered haddock, and pork with black pudding. Sandwiches and bar snacks are also available, and there is a large rear garden with play area, popular in summer.

Open: 11.30-3 6-11 (All day Sun)
Bar Meals: L served all week 11.30-2 D served all week 6-9 (Sun 12-9) Av main course £7.95
Restaurant: L served all week 11.30-2 D served all week 6-9 (Sun 12-9) Av 3 course - à la carte £13.50
Brewery/Company: THWAITES
🍺: Thwaites Best Bitter & Smooth
Children's Facilities: Fam room Play area (Play area and bird avairy in garden) Portions/Menu High Chairs Food Warming
Nearby: Falconry Centre, Ingleton Waterfalls, Caves at Clapham
Notes: No Dogs (except Assist Dogs) Garden Food Served Outside large beer garden Parking 6 Coach parties welcome

BROUGHTON SD95

The Bull ♀

nr Skipton BD23 3AE
☎ 01756 792065
✉ janeneil@thebullatbroughton.co.uk

Dir: On A59 3m from Skipton on A59

Like the village itself, the pub is part of the 3,000-acre Broughton Hall estate, owned by the Tempest family for 900 years. The chef-cum-manager was enticed from his much acclaimed former establishment to achieve similar if not higher standards here. His compact, thoughtful menu offers slow-roasted ham shank glazed with orange and honey, crab and lobster risotto, and chargrilled chicken breast with herby cream cheese.

Open: 12-3 5.30-11 (Sun 12-8)
Bar Meals: L served all week 12-2 D served Mon-Sat 6-9 (Sunday 12-6.30)
Restaurant: L served all week 12-2 D served Mon-Sat 6-9 Sun 12-6.30 Av 3 course · à la carte £16
Brewery/Company: FREE HOUSE
🍺: Scottish Courage, John Smith's Smooth, Bull Bitter (Local), Guest Ales, Copper Dragon
Children's Facilities: Fam room Games High Chairs Food Warming
Nearby: Embsay Steam Railway
Notes: Dogs Allowed water, dog biscuits Garden Food Served Outside Parking 60 Coach parties welcome

CROPTON SE78

The New Inn ☺ ♀

Nr. Pickering YO18 8HH
☎ 01751 417330 🖷 01751 417582
✉ info@croptonbrewery.co.uk

With the award-winning Cropton micro-brewery in its own grounds, this family-run free house on the edge of the North York Moors National Park is popular with locals and visitors alike. Meals are served in the restored village bar, and in the elegant Victorian restaurant - New Inn lamb joint, speciality sausages, steak and Scoresby Stout pie, fisherman's pie, Whitby cod, salmon, and plenty more.

Open: 11-11
Bar Meals: L served all week 12-2 D served all week 6-9 Av main course £8
Restaurant: L served all week 12-2 D served all week 6-9
Brewery/Company: FREE HOUSE
🍺 Cropton Two Pints, Monkmans Slaughter, Thwaites Best Bitter, Yorkshire Moors Bitter, Honey Gold Bitter
Rooms: 10 en suite 2 family s£39 d£54 (♦♦♦)
Children's Facilities: Fam room Play area Portions/Menu Games High Chairs Food Warming
Nearby: Flamingo Land- Zoo and Fun Park, Eden Camp, Sea Life Centre
Notes: No Dogs (except Assist Dogs) Garden Food Served Outside Beer garden Parking 50 Coach parties welcome

HARROGATE SE35

The Boars Head Hotel ★★★◎◎♀

Ripley Castle Estate HG3 3AY
☎ 01423 771888 🖷 01423 771509
✉ reservations@boarsheadripley.co.uk

Dir: On A61. Hotel in village centre

An old coaching inn situated at the heart of the Ripley Castle Estate, the Boars Head has been luxuriously furnished by Sir Thomas and Lady Ingilby to create an impressive hotel. Typical options from a winter menu are warm salad of venison sausage and wild mushrooms and beef and ale casserole served in a giant Yorkshire pudding. Daily specials are also offered.

Open: 11-11 (Sun 12-10.30, Winter Mon-Sat 11-3, 5-11, Winter Sun 12-3, 5-10.30)
Bar Meals: L served all week 12-2.30 D served all week 6.30-10 (Winter-lunch served 2pm) Av main course £9.95
Restaurant: L served all week 12-2 D served all week 7-9.30 Av 3 course fixed price £29
Brewery/Company: FREE HOUSE
🍺 Scottish Courage Theakston Best & Old Peculier, Daleside Crackshot
Rooms: 25 en suite s£99 d£120
Children's Facilities: Portions/Menu Cutlery Games High Chairs Food Warming Changing
Nearby: Ripley Castle, Fountains Abbey
Notes: Dogs (overnight in bedrooms only) (ex Assist Dogs) Garden Food Served Outside Courtyard Parking 45 Coach parties welcome

HOVINGHAM SE67

Worsley Arms Hotel ★★★ @ ⬤

Main Street YO62 4LA
☎ 01653 628234 📠 01653 628130
📧 worsleyarms@aol.com

Dir: From A1 take A64 towards Malton, L onto B1257 signed Slingsby & Hovingham.

The hotel dating from 1841, together with the separate pub, forms part of the Worsley family's Hovingham Hall estate. In the Restaurant a typical dinner might consist of chicken and duck liver pâté, followed by roast chunk of Whitby cod with plum tomato sauce, and lemon posset. The Cricketer's Bar offers a wide-ranging sandwich selection, and dishes such as glazed Swaledale goat's cheese with honey and walnut dressing; steamed mussels with shallots, garlic and cream in regular or large portions; and a rib-eye beef steak with green peppercorn sauce and chips.

Open: 12-2.30 7-11
Bar Meals: L served all week 12-2 D served all week 7-10
Restaurant: L served Sun 12-2 D served all week 7-10
Brewery/Company: FREE HOUSE
⬤: Scottish Courage John Smith's
Rooms: 20 en suite 2 family s£60 d£100
Children's Facilities: Portions/Menu Games High Chairs
Nearby: Jorvik Viking Centre
Notes: Dogs Allowed Garden Food Served Outside Formal and open gardens, mahogany furniture Parking 30 Coach parties welcome

INGLETON SD67

Marton Arms Hotel ◆◆◆◆ ⬤ ⬤

Thornton-in-Lonsdale LA6 3PB
☎ 01524 241281 📠 01524 242579
📧 mail@martonarms.co.uk

Dir: At junction A65/A687. Take road opp A687, 1st L. Pub opp church

A former coaching inn once patronised by Sir Arthur Conan Doyle, located opposite the Norman church where he was married. Real beers and over 300 Scottish malt whiskies are stocked and there's a comprehensive menu. Food options range through sandwiches, snacks, regular dishes and daily specials, such as greenlip mussels with white wine and garlic, and game pie with home-made chips.

Open: 11-11 (Sun 12-10.30)
Bar Meals: L served all week 12-2 D served all week 6-9 Av main course £3
Restaurant: L served all week 12-3 D served all week 6-9
⬤: Timothy Taylor Golden Best, Black Sheep Bitter, Theakstons, Cains, Deuchars
Rooms: 12 en suite 1 family s£42 d£64
Children's Facilities: Portions/Menu Cutlery Games High Chairs Food Warming Changing
Nearby: Ingleton Water Falls Walk, Whitescar caves/Three Peaks, cave walking
Notes: No Dogs (except Assist Dogs) Garden Food Served Outside Lawned garden with tables and shrubs Parking 40 Coach parties welcome

KIRKBYMOORSIDE SE68

George & Dragon Hotel ★★ ⚲

17 Market Place YO62 6AA
☎ 01751 433334 ▤ 01751 432933
✉ georgeatkirkby@aol.com

Dir: Just off A170 in centre of Town

A 17th-century former coaching inn offering a haven of warmth and refreshment. The pub has changed quite dramatically over the years - the restaurant used to be the brewhouse, one of the bedroom blocks the old cornmill and the garden rooms the old rectory. Sports enthusiasts will appreciate the collection of rugby and cricket memorabilia in the bar. A good variety of food is available, from snacks and blackboard specials in the bar to candlelit dinners in Knights' Restaurant or the bistro. Examples of daily specials include Mexican spiced lamb casserole with rice timbale; poached salmon fillet with a prawn and paprika cream sauce; and home-made shepherd's pie topped with mature cheddar.

Open: 10-11
Bar Meals: L served all week 12-2.15 D served all week 6.30-9.15
Restaurant: L served all week 12-2.15 D served all week 6.30-9.15 Av 3 course - à la carte £18
Brewery/Company: FREE HOUSE
🍺: Black Sheep Best, Tetley & guest beers
Rooms: 18 en suite 2 family s£49 d£79
Children's Facilities: Portions/Menu High Chairs Food Warming Changing
Nearby: Flamingon Land, Castle Howard
Notes: Dogs Allowed Garden Food Served Outside Walled garden, Parking 15

KIRKBYMOORSIDE SE68

The Lion Inn ⚲

Blakey Ridge YO62 7LQ
☎ 01751 417320 ▤ 01751 417717
✉ info@lionblakey.co.uk

Dir: From A170 follow signs 'Hutton-le-Hole/Castleton'. 6m N of Hutton-le-Hole.

The Lion stands 470mtrs above sea level, the fourth highest inn in England, with breathtaking views over the beautiful North York Moors National Park. The friendly, cosy interior with beamed ceilings, 4ft-thick stone walls and blazing fires makes up for the isolated location. Typical chef's specials are T-bone steak, steak and mushroom pie, and tournedos Rossini. Other choices on the extensive carte offer fish, vegetarian and chicken options.

Open: 10-11
Bar Meals: L served all week 12-10 D served all week 12-10 Av main course £6.95
Restaurant: L served Sun only 12-7 D served all week 7-10 Av 3 course · à la carte £18 Av 3 course fixed price £10.95
Brewery/Company: FREE HOUSE
🍺: Scottish Courage Theakston Blackbull, XB & Old Peculier, John Smith's Bitter
Rooms: 10 bedrooms 8 en suite 3 family s£18 d£50 (◆◆◆)
Children's Facilities: Portions/Menu High Chairs Food Warming Changing
Nearby: Flamingo Land, North Moors Railway
Notes: Dogs Allowed Garden Food Served Outside Large garden, picnic benches, well Parking 200 Coach parties welcome

KIRKHAM — SE76

Stone Trough Inn ⊛ ☜ ♀

Kirkham Abbey YO60 7JS
☎ 01653 618713 ◻ 01653 618819
⊕ info@stonetroughinn.co.uk

Dir: 1.5m off A64, between York & Malton

The stone 'trough' of the pub's name stands at the entrance. A cottage on the site was restored and converted to licensed premises in the early 1980s. Specials available to both bar and restaurant offer main courses like escalope of veal on buttered spring greens with a fried egg and caper butter. Dessert in the shape of 'Eton Mess' - a brandy snap basket filled with crushed meringue, strawberries and whipped cream - is pretty hard to resist.

Open: 12-2.30 6-11 (Sun 11.45-10.30)
Closed: 25 Dec **Days closed:** Mon
Bar Meals: L served Tues-Sun 12-2 D served Tues-Sun 6.30-8.30 Av main course £8.95
Restaurant: L served Sun 12-2.15 D served Tue-Sat 6.45-9.30 Av 3 course · à la carte £24
Brewery/Company: FREE HOUSE
🍺: Tetley Cask, Timothy Taylor Landlord, Black Sheep Best, Malton Brewery Golden Chance
Children's Facilities: Play area (Patio and lawn) Portions/Menu Cutlery Games High Chairs Food Warming
Nearby: Castle Howard, Eden Camp, North Yorks Moors Railway, Kirkham Priory
Notes: No Dogs (except Assist Dogs) Water Garden Food Served Outside Parking 100

KNARESBOROUGH — SE35

The General Tarleton Inn
★★★ ⊛⊛ ☜ ♀

Boroughbridge Road Ferrensby HG5 0PZ
☎ 01423 340284 ◻ 01423 340288
⊕ gti@generaltarleton.co.uk

Dir: On A6055, on crossroads in Ferrensby

The General Tarleton offers a rambling, low-beamed bar with open fires and a popular covered courtyard where you may choose to eat. The menu is impressive and wide ranging: pan roast cornfed chicken breast with asparagus, fondant potato and wild wood mushrooms; and GT's fish pie which consists of potato crust, salmon, cod, haddock, monkfish, prawns and scallops in a cheese and garden herb sauce.

Open: 12-3 6-11
Bar Meals: L served all week 12-2.15 D served all week 6-9.30 Av main course £10
Restaurant: L served Sun 12-1.45 D served Mon-Sat 6-9.30 Av 3 course fixed price £29.50
Brewery/Company: FREE HOUSE
🍺: Black Sheep Best, Timothy Taylors Landlord
Rooms: 14 en suite s£74.95 d£84.90
Children's Facilities: Portions/Menu Games High Chairs Food Warming
Nearby: Newby Hall, Fountains Abbey, Lightwater Valley
Notes: No Dogs (except Assist Dogs) Garden Food Served Outside Parking 37

LASTINGHAM   SE79

Blacksmiths Arms 🕯

YO62 6TL
☎ 01751 417247
🔵 blacksmithslastingham@hotmail.com

A 17th-century, stone-built inn in an idyllic village within the North York Moors National Park. Main courses on the menu include seafood platter; salmon and broccoli bake with sliced potato and melted cheese; roast topside of beef with Yorkshire pudding; half a crispy roast duck with orange sauce; and cottage pie with peppers. And there are daily specials.

Open: 12-3.30 6-11 (Mar-Nov open 10.30-11)
Bar Meals: L served all week 12-2.15
D served all week 7-9 (10.30-12 (snacks), 2.30-5.30 (light meals))
Restaurant: L served all week 12-2
D served all week 7-9.15
Brewery/Company: FREE HOUSE
🍺: Theakstons Best Bitter, Marston's Pedigree, Black Bull Bitter, Lastingham Best Bitter
Children's Facilities: Portions/Menu High Chairs Food Warming
Nearby: Flamingo Land, Eden Camp, Pickering Steam Railway
Notes: No Dogs (except Assist Dogs) Water and food Garden Food Served Outside Cottage garden seating 32, decking seats 20 Coach parties welcome

LEYBURN   SE19

Sandpiper Inn ♀

Market Place DL8 5AT
☎ 01969 622206 📠 01969 625367
🔵 hsandpiper@aol.com

Dir: From A1 take A684 to Leyburn

The oldest building in Leyburn, dating back to around 1640, has been a pub for just 30 years. In addition to old favourites such as fish and chips in real ale batter and sausage and mash with onion gravy, expect a good choice of starter. This could be followed by breast of chicken on lentils and smoked bacon; Whitby cod with prawns and fennel; or fillet of beef, five onions and shiraz sauce. To finish, the choice includes, bread and butter pudding.

Open: 11.30-3 6.30-11 (Sun 12-3, 6.30-10.30) Closed: 2wks Jan
Bar Meals: L served all week 12-2.30
D served all week 6.30-9 (Fri-Sat 6.30-9.30, Sun 7-9) Av main course £13.95
Restaurant: L served all week 12-2.30
D served all week 6.30-9 Fri-Sat 6.30-9.30, Sun 12-2, 7-9
Brewery/Company: FREE HOUSE
🍺: Black Sheep Best, Black Sheep Special, Daleside, Theakstons Hogshead
Children's Facilities: Fam room High Chairs Food Warming
Nearby: Wensleydale Railway, Forbidden Corner, Leyburn Model Village
Notes: Dogs Allowed in 'snug area' Garden Food Served Outside Terrace area to front Parking 6 Coach parties welcome

LITTON SD97

Queens Arms

Skipton BD23 5QJ
☎ 01756 770208
queensarmslitton@mserve.net

Dir: From Skipton: Northvale Road, 15 miles

Early 16th-century inn in a remote corner of the Yorkshire Dales, now brewing its own Litton Ale with spring water from the neighbouring hillside. Two-foot thick walls, low ceilings, beams and coal fires give the place a traditional, timeless feel. A good range of food incorporates plenty of fish, home-made pies, including rabbit and game, a hefty mixed grill, vegetarian and children's dishes. Only over 14s in bar.

Open: 12-3 7-11
Closed: 3 Jan-1 Feb; Mon ex BHs
Bar Meals: L served Tue-Sun, BH Mon 12-2 D served Tue-Sun, BH Mon 7-9 Av main course £6.95
Restaurant: L served Tue-Sun 12-2 D served Tue-Sun 7-9 Av 3 course - à la carte £17.50
Brewery/Company: FREE HOUSE
: Litton Ale, Tetleys, plus guest ales
Children's Facilities: Fam room Portions/Menu Games High Chairs Food Warming Changing
Nearby: Comistone Stables, Malham Field Centre
Notes: Dogs Allowed Garden Food Served Outside Beer garden, outdoor eating, patio Parking 10 Coach parties welcome

MASHAM SE28

Kings Head Hotel ★★ 🍷

Market Place HG4 4EF
☎ 01765 689295 01765 689070
masham.kingshead@snr.co.uk

Overlooking Masham's spacious market square with its cross and maypole, this 18th-century, three-storey former posting house and excise office is a perfect base for touring the Yorkshire Dales. Pancetta-wrapped chicken breast, cod on lemon and Chardonnay risotto, and glazed pork loin and baked apple will all be found on the menu, plus specials too. Real ales are on tap. A new barn conversion has doubled the number of bedrooms, and includes one fully-fitted for the disabled guest.

Open: 11-11
Bar Meals: L served all week 12-3 D served all week 6-10 Av main course £8
Restaurant: L served all week 12-3 D served all week 6-10
Brewery/Company: SPIRIT GROUP
: Scottish Courage Theakstons Best Bitter, Black Bull & Old Peculier, Guest Ales
Rooms: 23 en suite s£50 d£65
Children's Facilities: Portions/Menu Games High Chairs Food Warming Changing
Nearby: Lightwater Valley Theme Park, Middleham Castle, Leyburn Railway
Notes: Dogs Allowed Water Garden Food Served Outside Georgian style patio

MIDDLEHAM   SE18

Black Swan Hotel 🐾

Market Place DL8 4NP
☎ 01969 622221 📠 01969 622221
✉ blackswanmiddleham@breathe.com

Built in 1640, this grade II listed building is decorated with original oak beams and a log fire. It overlooks Middleham market square, with the beer garden at the rear backing on to the castle. Situated in a famous racing area, horses can be seen passing the front every morning on their way to the gallops. Traditional country cooking results in dishes like local rack of lamb, beef in Old Peculier ale and roast partridge or pheasant. Many circular walks of varying lengths can begin here.

Open: 11-3.30 6-11 (open all day Sat-Sun summer)
Bar Meals: L served all week 12-2 D served all week 6.30-9 Av main course £6
Restaurant: L served all week 12-2 D served all week 6.30-9 Av 3 course - à la carte £17
Brewery/Company: FREE HOUSE 🍺:
Scottish Courage John Smiths, Theakstons Best Bitter, Black Bull, Old Peculier & Guest Beers
Children's Facilities: Fam room Cutlery Games High Chairs Food Warming Changing
Nearby: Forbidden Corner, Middleham Castle, Racing Stable
Notes: Dogs Allowed Dogs by appointment Garden Food Served Outside Patio and lawn with benches, tables Coach parties welcome

PICKERING   SE78

The White Swan ★★ ⊛ 🐾 �

Market Place Ryedale YO18 7AA
☎ 01751 472288 📠 01751 475554
✉ welcome@white-swan.co.uk

Dir: In Market Place between church & steam railway station

The White Swan was built as a four-room cottage in 1532, then extended to become a coaching inn on the York to Whitby road. Seafood comes freshly landed from Whitby, for dishes such as fish pie and real fish and chips with posh mushy peas. Meat-based dinner courses might include Rievaulx venison saddle with cranberry relish, bubble and squeak and sloe gin sauce; or roast belly pork with braised red cabbage, creamed potato and apple sauce.

Open: 10-3 6-11
Bar Meals: L served all week 12-2 D served all week 7-9 Av main course £10.95
Restaurant: L served all week 12-2 D served all week 7-9 Av 3 course · à la carte £27.50
Brewery/Company: FREE HOUSE 🍺: Black Sheep Best & Special, Goldfield Hambleton Ales, Yorkshire Moors Cropton Brewery
Rooms: 12 en suite 2 family s£75 d£130
Children's Facilities: Fam room Portions/ Menu Games High Chairs Food Warming
Nearby: Eden Camp, Flamingo Land, North Yorkshire Moors Railway
Notes: Dogs Allowed Garden Food Served Outside Beautifully planted terrace Parking 35

PICKERING SE78

Fox & Hounds Country Inn

★★

Sinnington YO62 6SQ
☎ 01751 431577 01751 432791
foxhoundsinn@easynet.co.uk

Dir: 3m W of town, off A170

A handsome 18th-century coaching inn with oak-beamed ceilings, old wood panelling and open fires. The lunch-time menu offers soft grain rolls with various fillings; light meals such as salmon and cured cod terrine; and mains like Whitby scampi with salad. For dinner you'll find slow-roasted Goosenargh duck; pan-seared local lamb cutlets; and Charlie Hill's mushroom, garlic and beef sausages and mash. Fish dishes are a strength of the specials board.

Open: 12-2.30 6-11 (Sun 12-2.30, 6-10.30)
Bar Meals: L served all week 12-2 D served all week 6.30-9 (Sun 6.30-8.30) Av main course £8
Restaurant: L served all week 12-2 D served all week 6.30-9 (Sun 6.30-8.30) Av 3 course · à la carte £22
Brewery/Company: FREE HOUSE
: Camerons Bitter, Black Sheep Special, Worthingtons Creamflow
Rooms: 10 en suite 1 family s£49 d£70
Children's Facilities: Portions/Menu Cutlery High Chairs Food Warming Changing
Nearby: Flamingo Land, North York Moors Steam Railway, Eden Camp
Notes: Dogs Allowed Outside kennel if req. Garden Food Served Outside Parking 30

REETH SE09

Charles Bathurst Inn ◆◆◆◆

Arkengarthdale DL11 6EN
☎ 01748 884567 & 884265 01748 884599
info@cbinn.co.uk

This 18th-century inn is ideal for walkers, located close to the halfway point of the Coast-to-Coast Walk. Food is fresh, with the ingredients purchased locally, then prepared and cooked on the premises. The menu is written up daily on a striking mirror. Game comes from the surrounding moors, and fish from Hartlepool is delivered five times a week. Main courses may feature loin of salmon and roast belly pork; to follow try lime cheesecake with winter berries.

Open: 11-11 (Closed Mon-Thurs at lunch)
Closed: End Nov-Feb
Bar Meals: L served all week 12-2
D served all week 6.30-9
Restaurant: L served all week 12-2
D served all week 6.30-9
Brewery/Company: FREE HOUSE
: Scottish Courage Theakstons, John Smiths Bitter & John Smiths Smooth, Black Sheep Best & Riggwelter
Rooms: 18 en suite s£60 d£75
Children's Facilities: Play area (Swings, Climbing Frame & Seesaw) Portions/Menu Cutlery Games High Chairs Food Warming
Nearby: Model Village, Hazel Brow Farm
Notes: Dogs Allowed Garden Parking 50 Coach parties welcome

ROSEDALE ABBEY   SE79

The Milburn Arms Hotel ★★⊛ ⊚

Nr Pickering YO18 8RA
☎ 01751 417312 ▣ 01751 417541
✉ info@millburnarms.co.uk

Dir: A170 W from Pickering 3m, R at sign to Rosedale then 7m N

Dating back to 1776 this charming country house hotel acts as a perfect retreat from the modern world. The family-run hotel offers beautifully furnished en suite bedrooms, with a welcoming bar and log fires in the public rooms. The Priory Restaurant is known for its quality cuisine.

Open: 11.30-3 6-11 Closed: 25 Dec
Bar Meals: L served all week 12-2.15 D served all week 6.30-9 Av main course £8
Restaurant: L served Sun 12-2.30 D served all week 7-9 Av 3 course · à la carte £30
Brewery/Company: FREE HOUSE
🍺: Black Sheep Best, Carlsberg-Tetley Tetely Bitter, John Smith's, Stella, Theakstons
Rooms: 13 en suite 3 family s£47.50 d£40
Children's Facilities: Portions/Menu Cutlery Games High Chairs Food Warming Changing
Nearby: Flamingoland, Pickering Steam Railway, Scarborough seaside
Notes: No Dogs (except Assist Dogs) Garden Food Served Outside Large grassed lawn area Parking 60 Coach parties welcome

THORNTON WATLASS   SE28

The Buck Inn ★ ⊚ ♈

Ripon HG4 4AH
☎ 01677 422461 ▣ 01677 422447
✉ buckwatlass@btconnect.com

Dir: From A1 take A684 to Bedale, then B6268 towards Masham. Village 2m on R, hotel by cricket green

Margaret and Michael Fox offer the warm welcome and relaxed atmosphere that keeps people coming back. Live traditional jazz is a feature on at least two Sundays a month. Five real ales are served, most of them from local independent breweries, and English cooking, freshly prepared on the premises. Specialities are Masham rarebit, deep-fried fresh Whitby cod, and breast of chicken stir-fried in black bean sauce.

Open: 11-11 (Sun 12-10.30)
RS: 25 Dec closed eve
Bar Meals: L served all week 12-2 D served all week 6-9.30 (Sun 12-9.30) Av main course £10
Restaurant: L served all week 12-2 D served all week 6.3-9.3 Av 3 course - à la carte £18.50 Av 3 course fixed price £12.50
Brewery/Company: FREE HOUSE
🍺: Theakston Best, Black Sheep Best, John Smith's & Guest beers **Rooms:** 7 (5 en suite) s£50 d£60 **Children's Facilities:** Play area, Portions/Menu Cutlery Games High Chairs Food Warming Changing **Nearby:** Lightwater Valley, Forbidden Corner **Notes:** Dogs Allowed Water Garden Food served outside Parking 40 Coach parties welcome

NORTH YORKSHIRE

ENGLAND 225

WEST BURTON   SE08

Fox & Hounds

Leyburn DL8 4JY
☎ 01969 663111 📠 01969 663279

Dir: A468 between Hawes and Leyburn, 1/2 mile east of Aysgarth

Overlooking the village green in the unspoilt village of West Burton, this inn offers log fires and home cooking. Hand-pulled ales on offer at the bar include Black Sheep. The new owners continue to provide traditional pub food to accompany your pint: dishes such as steak and kidney pie, curry and lasagne will fortify you for country walks or visits to nearby waterfalls, castles or cheese-tasting at the Wensleydale Creamery.

Open: 11-11 (winter closed 2-6)
Bar Meals: L served all week 12-2 D served all week 6-9 Av main course £6.50
Restaurant: L served all week 12-2 D served all week 6.30-9 Av 3 course - à la carte £15
Brewery/Company: FREE HOUSE
🍺: Black Sheep, Old Peculier, John Smiths
Children's Facilities: Fam room Portions/Menu Cutlery Games High Chairs Food Warming Changing
Nearby: Bolton Castle, Model Village
Notes: Dogs Allowed Parking 6 Coach parties welcome

WIGGLESWORTH   SD85

The Plough Inn ☺

Skipton BD23 4RJ
☎ 01729 840243 📠 01729 840638
✉ sue@ploughinn.info

Dir: From A65 between Skipton & Long Preston take B6478 to Wigglesworth

This traditional 18th-century country inn is ideally placed for exploring the Yorkshire Dales and the Forest of Bowland. The bar has oak beams and an open fire, and the conservatory restaurant has fine views across the hills. The menu includes such dishes as pork chops with apple, cider and black pudding sauce; and vegetable tikka masala with turmeric basmati rice. Also a traditional bar menu.

Open: 11-3 6-11
Bar Meals: L served all week 12-2 D served all week 7-9 (From 6 at busy times) Av main course £8.50
Restaurant: L served all week 12-2 D served all week 7-9 Av 3 course - à la carte £19.50 Av 2 course fixed price £6.50
Brewery/Company: FREE HOUSE
🍺: Tetley Bitter, Black Sheep Best
Rooms: 12 en suite 3 family s£47 d£70 (★★)
Children's Facilities: Fam room Portions/Menu Cutlery Games High Chairs Food Warming
Nearby: Horses health farm, Falconry Centre
Notes: No Dogs (except Assist Dogs) Water Garden Food Served Outside views over Yorkshire Dales Parking 70 Coach parties welcome

HALIFAX SE02

Shibden Mill Inn ◆◆◆◆ ⊛⊛ ⌂ ♀

Shibden Mill Fold HX3 7UL
☎ 01422 365840 🖷 01422 362971
🖃 shibdenmillinn@zoom.co.uk

The 17th-century inn has been sympathetically renovated to retain its original charm. Open fires and soft cushions make the low-beamed bar a cosy place to relax, and there's a wide choice of traditional ales to accompany bar meals like shepherd's pie tart or grilled smoked salmon with bubble and squeak. Meanwhile, crisp napery and candlelit tables give the restaurant a certain rustic elegance. It's the ideal setting in which to sample the contemporary English menu and extensive wine list.

Open: 12-2.30 5.30-11
Bar Meals: L served all week 12-2 D served all week 6-9.30 Av main course £11.50
Restaurant: L served all week 12-2 D served all week 6-9.30
Brewery/Company: FREE HOUSE
🍺: John Smiths, Theakston XB, Shibden Mill
Rooms: 12 en suite s£65 d£80
Children's Facilities: Play area (Colouring materials, board games) Portions/Menu Games High Chairs Food Warming
Notes: No Dogs (ex garden) Garden Food Served Outside Walled garden with heated patio Parking 200 Coach parties welcome

HAWORTH SE03

The Old White Lion Hotel ★★ ⌂ ♀

Main Street Keighley BD22 8DU
☎ 01535 642313 🖷 01535 646222
🖃 enquiries@oldwhitelionhotel.com

Dir: Turn off A629 onto B6142, hotel 0.5m past Haworth Station

300-year-old former coaching inn. Traditionally furnished bars offer a welcome respite from the tourist trail. Theakston ales, and a wide range of generously served snacks and meals. A carte features chicken Italia, champagne halibut, scampi Mediterranean, chicken Rockafella, pork fillet Calvados and crêpe Italiana among others. Jacket potatoes, giant Yorkshire puddings and specials also available.

Open: 11-11
Bar Meals: L served all week 11.30-2.30 D served all week 5.30-9.30 (Sat & Sun 12-9.30) Av main course £6.25
Restaurant: L served Sun 12-2.30 D served all week 7-9.30 Av 3 course - à la carte £19 Av 3 course fixed price £14
Brewery/Company: FREE HOUSE
🍺: Theakstons Best & Green Lable, Tetley Bitter, Scottish Courage John Smith's, Websters
Rooms: 14 en suite 2 family s£48 d£66.50
Children's Facilities: High Chairs Food Warming
Notes: No Dogs (except Assist Dogs) Parking 9 Coach parties welcome

LEDSHAM SE42

The Chequers Inn

Claypit Lane South Milford LS25 5LP
☎ 01977 683135 ▤ 01977 680791

Dir: Between A1 & A656 above Castleford

Quaint creeper-covered inn located in an old estate village in the countryside to the east of Leeds. Unusually, the pub is closed on Sunday because the one-time lady of the manor was offended by drunken farm workers on her way to church more than 160 years ago. Inside are low beams and wooden settles, giving the pub the feel of a traditional village establishment.

Open: 11-3 5-11 (Sat 11-11)
Days closed: Sun
Bar Meals: L served Mon-Sat 12-2.15 D served Mon-Sat 5.30-9.45
Av main course £9.45
Brewery/Company: FREE HOUSE
🍺: Theakston Best, John Smiths, Brown Cow, Timothy Taylor Landlord
Children's Facilities: Fam room
Notes: Dogs Allowed Garden outdoor eating, patio Parking 35

MYTHOLMROYD SE02

Shoulder of Mutton ♀

New Road Halifax HX7 5DZ
☎ 01422 883165

Dir: A646 Halifax to Todmorden, in Mytholmroyd on B6138, opp train station

Character Pennines pub next to a trout stream and ideally placed for the popular 50-mile Calderdale Way. The pub's reputation for real ales and hearty food using locally sourced ingredients remains intact after 30 years of ownership. The menu ranges from beef cooked in Guinness to vegetarian dishes.

Open: 11.30-3 7-11 (Sat 11.30-11, Sun 12-10.30)
Bar Meals: L served all week 11.30-2 D served Wed-Mon 7-8.15 Av main course £3.99 **Restaurant:** L served all week 11.30-2 D served Wed-Mon 7-8.15
🍺: Black Sheep, Boddingtons, Flowers, Taylor Landlord, Castle Eden
Children's Facilities: Fam room Play area Portions/Menu High Chairs Food Warming
Nearby: Jerusalem Farm, Eureka, Hardcastle Crags
Notes: Dogs Allowed Water, Treats Garden Food Served Outside Riverside garden with floral display, seating Parking 25
No credit cards

NEWALL SE14

The Spite Inn

nr Otley LS21 2EY
☎ 01943 463063

'There's nowt but malice and spite at these pubs', said a local who one day did the unthinkable-drank in both village hostelries, renowned for their feuding landlords. The Traveller's Rest, which became The Malice, is long closed, but the Roebuck has survived as The Spite. Salmon mornay, haddock, scampi, steak and ale pie, ostrich fillet and speciality sausages are likely to be on offer.

Open: 12-3 6-11 (Sat 12-11, Sun 12-10.30)
Bar Meals: L served all week 12-5
D served (Tue-Thu 6-8.30, Fri-Sat 6-9)
Av main course £6.50
Restaurant: L served all week 11.30-2
D served (Tue-Thu 6-8.30, Sat 6-9)
Brewery/Company: UNIQUE PUB CO LTD
🍺: John Smiths, Tetleys, Bombardier, Worthington Creamflow, Ruddles, plus guest ales
Children's Facilities: Menu
Notes: Dogs Allowed Water provided Garden Food served outside. Lawned area Parking 50 Coach parties welcome

SHELF SE12

Duke of York ♀

West Street Stone Chair Halifax HX3 7LN
☎ 01422 202056 📠 01422 206618
✉ katrina@dukeofyork.co.uk

> **Dir:** M62 J25 to Brighouse. Take A644 N. Inn 500 yds on R after Stone Chair roundabout

A vast array of brassware and bric-a-brac adorns this 17th-century former coaching inn located between Bradford and Halifax, and the atmosphere is lively and friendly. Expect classic dishes such as beef bourguignon, grilled fillet steak with peppercorn sauce, and braised lamb Henry with orange mashed potatoes and rosemary broth. The pub carries a wide range of cask ales.

Open: 11.30-11.30 (Sun 12-10.30)
Bar Meals: L served all week 12-2.30
D served all week 5-9.30
Restaurant: L served all week 12-2.30
D served all week 5-9.30 Av 3 course fixed price £11.95
Brewery/Company: WHITBREAD
🍺: Landlord, Landlady, J.W Lees, Tetleys & Guest beer
Children's Facilities: High Chairs
Notes: No Dogs (except Assist Dogs) Garden Food Served Outside Patio at front with chairs Parking 30 Coach parties welcome

WEST YORKSHIRE

THORNTON · SE03

Ring O'Bells ♀

212 Hilltop Road Bradford BD13 3QL
☎ 01274 832296 🖷 01274 831707
✆ enquiries@theringobells.com

Dir: From M62 take A58 for 5m, R at crossroads onto A644, after 4.5m follow signs for Denholme, on to Well Head Rd into Hilltop Rd

Pennine pub set high above the village of the Brontë sisters' birth with stunning views over dramatic moorland stretching up to 30 miles on a clear day. The menu is essentially British with an innovative approach and some European and Eastern influences. The range of traditional pies is a house speciality.

Open: 11.30-3.30 5.30-11 (Sun 12-4.30, 6.30-10.30) Closed: 25 Dec
Bar Meals: L served all week 12-2 D served all week 5.30-9.30 Av main course £8.95
Restaurant: L served all week 12-2 D served all week 7-9.30 (Sun 6.15-8.45) Av 2 course fixed price £9.95
Brewery/Company: FREE HOUSE
🍺: Scottish Courage John Smiths & Courage Directors, Black Sheep & Black Sheep Special
Children's Facilities: Portions/Menu High Chairs Food Warming Changing
Nearby: Howarth-Home of Brontë Family, Eureka
Notes: No Dogs (except Assist Dogs) Parking 25

WIDDOP · SD93

Pack Horse Inn

Hebden Bridge HX7 7AT
☎ 01422 842803 🖷 01422 842803

Dir: Off A646 & A6033

A converted laithe farmhouse dating from the 1600s, 300 yards from the Pennine Way and popular with walkers. 130 single malts available.

Open: 12-3 7-11 Days closed: Mon
RS: Oct-Easter Closed lunch during the week
Bar Meals: L served all week summer only 12-2 D served Tue-Sun 7-10 Av main course £6.95
Restaurant: D served Sat 7-9.30
Brewery/Company: FREE HOUSE
🍺: Thwaites, Theakston XB, Morland Old Speckled Hen, Blacksheep Bitter
Notes: Dogs Allowed Parking 40

BALLYGRANT   NR36

Ballygrant Inn & Restaurant ☺

Isle of Islay PA45 7QR
☎ 01496 840277 ▯ 01496 840277
❸ info@ballygrant-inn.co.uk

Dir: NE of Isle of Islay, 3m from ferry terminal at Port Askaig

Set in two and a half acres of grounds and enclosed by heather-clad hills, it's close to two of Islay's seven malt whisky distilleries, and within easy reach of Port Askaig ferry terminal. Food is served all day from breakfast through morning coffee, snacks and lunch, to dinner. Scottish ales and all the island's malts are served in the bar, along with meals such as grilled trout, beef and orange casserole, lamb patia curry, and a vegetarian dish of the day. Fresh Islay crab, oysters and scallops are a must whenever they're available. The restaurant menu features grilled Scottish salmon brochettes, venison and much more.

Open: 11-11 (Wkds 11-1am)
Bar Meals: L served all week 12-3 D served all week 7-10 Av main course £8.95
Restaurant: L served all week 12-3 D served all week 7-10
Brewery/Company: FREE HOUSE
◖: Belhaven Best, calders 80/-, Calders 70/-
Rooms: 3 en suite 1 family s£27.50 d£55 (★★)
Children's Facilities: Fam room Portions/Menu Cutlery Games High Chairs Food Warming Changing
Nearby: Pony trekking, swimming pool
Notes: Dogs Allowed Garden Food Served Outside Patio, grassed area overlooking woodland Parking 35 Coach parties welcome

CLACHAN-SEIL   NM71

Tigh an Truish Inn

Oban PA34 4QZ
☎ 01852 300242

Dir: 14m S of Oban, take A816, 12m turn off B844 toward Atlantic Bridge

The Tigh an Truish offers a good appetising menu based on the best local produce. Homemade seafood pie, moules marinière, salmon steaks, and mussels in garlic cream sauce feature among the fish dishes, while other options might include meat or vegetable lasagne, beef or nut burgers, steak and ale pie, venison in a pepper cream and Drambuie sauce, and chicken curry. Round off your meal by sampling syrup sponge, apple crumble or chocolate puddle pudding.

Open: 11-3 5-11 (May-Sept all day)
Closed: 25 Dec & 1 Jan
Bar Meals: L served all week 12-2 D served all week 6-8.30
Restaurant: L served all week 12-2 D served all week 6-8.30
Brewery/Company: FREE HOUSE
◖: McEwans 80/- plus guest beers
Children's Facilities: Fam room
Notes: Dogs Allowed Garden Food Served Outside Tables beside the sea in garden with lawn Parking 35 Coach parties welcome No credit cards

KILBERRY NR76

Kilberry Inn 🐾

PA29 6YD

☎ 01880 770223 📠 01880 770223

📧 relax@kilberryinn.com

Dir: From Lochgilphead take A83 south.
Take B8024 signposted Kilberry

*An original 'but 'n' ben' cottage with quarried
walls, beams and log fires, the inn was
renovated some 17 years ago. Today it is
renowned for its fine food, which is special
enough to encourage travellers to make the long
journey. The dining room is warmly welcoming
and family friendly, and everything served here,
including bread and cakes, preserves and
chutneys, is home made. Main courses might be
Craignish salmon with lime and parsley butter;
or Ormsary venison and game pie.*

Open: 11-3 6.30-10.30 Closed: Nov-Easter;
Mon, Sun evenings
Bar Meals: L served Tue-Sun 12.30-2
D served Tue-Sat 7-8.30 (Sun 12.30-1.30)
Av main course £6.95
Restaurant: L served Tue-Sun 12.30-2
D served Tue-Sat 6.30-8.30, 12.30-1.30
Av 3 course - à la carte £20
Brewery/Company: FREE HOUSE
🍺: Arran Blonde, Arran Dark, Fyne Ales
Maverick, Tennents Velvet
Rooms: 3 en suite 1 family s£42.50 d£85
(★★★)
Children's Facilities: Fam room
Portions/Menu High Chairs Food Warming
Changing
Notes: Dogs Allowed Water Parking 8 Coach
parties welcome Non-smoking premises

TAYNUILT NN03

Polfearn Hotel 🐾 ♀

PA35 1JQ

☎ 01866 822251 📠 01866 822251

Dir: turn off A85, continue 1.5m through
village down to loch shore

*Close to the shores of Loch Etive, with
stunning all-round views, this friendly family-
run hotel sits at the foot of Ben Cruachen.
Originally a Victorian fishing villa, it was
converted to a hotel in 1960. Whether you're
working, walking, cycling, riding, shooting or
fishing in the area, the proprietors will store
things, dry things, feed, water and warm you
with little formality. Dishes are cooked to
order from fresh local produce, notably
seafood, steak from the local butcher, and
home-made pies.*

Open: 12-2 6-11 Closed: 25-26 Dec
RS: Nov-May closed lunch
Bar Meals: L served all week 12-1.45 D
served all week 6-8.45 Av main course £9
Restaurant: L served 12-1.45 D served all
week 5.30-8.45 Av 3 course - à la carte £22
Brewery/Company: FREE HOUSE
🍺: Weekly changing guest ale
Rooms: 14 en suite 2 family s£30 d£55
Children's Facilities: Food Warming
Nearby: Sea Life Centre, Loch cruises
Notes: Dogs Allowed Water, Food Garden
Food Served Outside Nice lawn, sea view
& mountains Parking 50

KIRKCUDBRIGHT NX65

Selkirk Arms Hotel ♀

Old High Street DG6 4JG
☎ 01557 330402 📄 01557 331639
✉ reception@selkirkarmshotel.co.uk

A traditional white-painted pub on street corner, with nice gardens to the rear. It has associations with the Scottish poet Robert Burns, and T E Lawrence (of Arabia), who lived nearby. Good choice of beers, including Solway Criffel and Youngers Tartan.

Open: 11-12
Bar Meals: L served all week 12-2 D served all week 6-9.30 Av main course £6.50
Restaurant: L served all week 12-2 D served all week 7-9.30 Av 3 course - à la carte £25
🍺: Youngers Tartan, John Smiths Bitter, Criffel, Old Speckled Hen
Children's Facilities: Licence Portions/Menu High Chairs Food Warming Changing
Nearby: Kirkcudbright Wildlife Park
Notes: Dogs Allowed dog bones/biscuits Garden Food Served Outside Beautiful Parking 50 Coach parties welcome

MOFFAT NT00

Black Bull Hotel ♀

Churchgate DG10 9EG
☎ 01683 220206 📄 01683 220483
✉ hotel@blackbullmoffat.co.uk

The main building dates from the 16th century and was used by Graham of Claverhouse as his headquarters. Graham and his dragoons were sent to quell Scottish rebellion in the late 17th century. Scottish bard Robert Burns was a frequent visitor around 1790. The Railway Bar is the place for drinking and pub games, while the Burns Room or restaurant are for eating or relaxation. Traditional fare includes steak pie, seafood platter, macaroni cheese, Black Bull hot pot and Moffat ram pie. Also look out for haggis with tatties and neeps, a selection of tempting sizzlers, and 'Dishes from Around the World.'

Open: 11-11 (Thu-Sat 11-12)
Bar Meals: L served all week 11.30-2.15 D served all week 6-9.15 Av main course £7.25 **Restaurant:** L served all week 11.30-2.15 D served all week 6-9.15
Brewery/Company: FREE HOUSE
🍺: McEwans, Scottish Courage Theakston 80/-
Rooms: 13 en suite 2 family s£39 d£59
(★★★) **Children's Facilities:** Portions/Menu Games High Chairs Food Warming **Nearby:** Station Park, Waterside Walk & Moffatasia **Notes:** Dogs Allowed Garden Food Served Outside Courtyard with eight tables Parking 4 Coach parties welcome

NEW GALLOWAY   NX67

Cross Keys Hotel 🛏

High Street DG7 3RN
☎ 01644 420494 🖷 01644 420672
✉ info@crosskeysng.fsnet.co.uk

Dir: Located at N end of Loch Ken; 10m from Castle Douglas, 40m from Ayr on A713 Galloway Tourist Route

Dates back to 1760, and part of it was once the police station and local jail-you can eat bar meals in the restored stone-walled cell. Alternatively, the à la carte restaurant with its innovative clown theme serves hearty food with a strong Scottish accent-haggis, neeps and tatties; Marbury smoked salmon; Buccleuch steaks; Wigtown lamb; and Loch Arthur organic cheese.

Open: 12-11 Apr-Oct 12-12 all week, Oct-Apr 12-12 Fri-Sat)
Bar Meals: L served all week 12-2 D served all week 6-8 (Oct-Apr no food Mon-Tues. Sun 5.30-7.30) Av main course £7
Restaurant: D served Apr-Oct Tues-Sun 6.30-8.30 (Sun 5.30-7.30. Oct-Apr Thur-Sun) Av 3 course · à la carte £18
🍺: Sulworth real ales, guest real ales
Children's Facilities: Portions/Menu Cutlery High Chairs Food Warming Changing
Nearby: Red Deer Park, Cream of Galloway Fun Park, Loch Ken Watersports
Notes: No Dogs (except Assist Dogs) Kennel available for guest dogs Garden Food Served Outside Small enclosed garden Parking 6

NEWTON STEWART   NX46

Creebridge House Hotel 🛏 ♀

Minnigaff DG8 6NP
☎ 01671 402121 🖷 01671 403258
✉ info@creebridge.co.uk

Dir: From A75 into Newton Stewart, turn right over river bridge, hotel 200yds on left.

This country house hotel dating from 1760, was formerly the Earl of Galloway's shooting lodge. Bridge's Bar and Brasserie offers an interesting menu with an emphasis on fresh Scottish produce. Typical examples are, home-made ravioli filled with local lobster in seafood broth, and steaks cut from Buccluech beef. The Garden Restaurant, overlooking the landscaped grounds, presents a short, fixed-price menu of modern Scottish cooking. The hotel is popular with families, and those who enjoy golfing, fishing, shooting and walking.

Open: 12-2.30 6-11 (Sun, all day)
Bar Meals: L served all week 12-2 D served all week 6-9.30 Av main course £8
Restaurant: D served all week 7-9 Av 3 course · à la carte £25 Av 3 course fixed price £25
Brewery/Company: FREE HOUSE
🍺: Fuller's London Pride, Tenants, Real Ales, Deuchers
Children's Facilities: Licence Portions/Menu High Chairs Food Warming Changing
Nearby: Gem Rock Museum
Notes: Dogs Allowed Kennels, Water Garden Food Served Outside Rose Beds, Fish Pond and Lawns Parking 40 Coach parties welcome

Forest Hills Hotel

23 High Street Cupar KY14 7AP
☎ 01337 828318 ▤ 01337 828318
✉ info@theforesthillshotel.com

Popular inn located in the village square, with an oak-beamed bar, Flemish murals, a cosy lounge, and en suite bedrooms.
The town of Auchtermuchty is well known as home to radio and TV series Dr Finlay's Casebook, acoustic duo The Proclaimers, and accordionist extraordinare Jimmy Shand. A new restaurant boosts the traditional pub food of baguettes and open sandwiches.

Open: 11.30-2.30 5-10
Bar Meals: L served all week 12-2
D served all week 6-9
Restaurant: L served all week 12.30-2
D served Mon-Thu 7-9
Brewery/Company: FREE HOUSE
Children's Facilities: Portions/Menu
Notes: Dogs Allowed

The Golf Hotel 🕾

4 High Street KY10 3TD
☎ 01333 450206 ▤ 01333 450795
✉ enquiries@thegolfhotelcrail.com

Rooted in the 14th century, this is the site of one of Scotland's oldest licensed inns, though the current building dates from the early 18th century. The Crail Golfing Society, formed in the public bar in 1786, is believed to have given the inn its name; it's the seventh oldest club in Scotland. The emphasis here is on traditional Scottish produce, hospitality, and value for money. An entire menu is dedicated to seafood, with dishes such as grilled haddock in a garlic and herb butter; and home-made salmon and smoked haddock fishcakes. Traditional high tea with home baking also a speciality.

Open: 11-12
Bar Meals: L served all week 12-7 D served all week 7-9 Av main course £6
Restaurant: L served all week 12-7 D served all week 7-9
Brewery/Company: FREE HOUSE
🍺: Scottish Courage McEwans 80/-, 70/-, Tetleys, Belhaven Best, real ale
Rooms: 5 en suite 1 family s£37 d£30 (★★★)
Children's Facilities: Portions/Menu High Chairs Food Warming
Nearby: Coastal walk, park, beach
Notes: Dogs Allowed Garden Parking 10 Coach parties welcome

FIFE

DUNFERMLINE NT08

The Hideaway Lodge & Restaurant
♀

Kingseat Road Halbeath KY12 0UB
☎ 01383 725474 📠 01383 622821
✉ enquiries@thehideaway.co.uk

Originally built in the 1930s as a miners' welfare institute, this pleasant country inn enjoys a rural setting on the outskirts of Dunfermline. Each room is named after a Scottish loch, and the extensive menu makes good use of fresh local produce. A typical meal may begin with grilled goats' cheese salad or Oban mussels, then move on to chargrilled tuna steak, Scottish seafood crumble or fillet of Highland venison, and finish with summer fruit pudding or steamed ginger pudding.

Open: 12-3 5-11 (Sun 12-9)
Bar Meals: L served all week 12-2 D served all week 5-9.30
Restaurant: L served all week 12-2 D served all week 5-9.30
Brewery/Company: FREE HOUSE
🍺: John Smith, 80 Special
Notes: No Dogs Garden Parking 35 Coach parties welcome

LOWER LARGO NO40

The Crusoe Hotel

2 Main Street KY8 6BT
☎ 01333 320759 📠 01333 320865

Dir: A92 to Kirkcaldy East, A915 to Lundin Links, then R to Lower Largo

This historic inn is located on the sea wall in Lower Largo, the birthplace of Alexander Selkirk, the real-life castaway immortalised by Daniel Defoe in his novel, Robinson Crusoe. In the past the area was also the heart of the once-thriving herring fishing industry. Today it is a charming bay ideal for a golfing break. A typical menu may include 'freshly shot' haggis, Pittenweem haddock and a variety of steaks.

Open: 12-12 (Fri 11am-1am)
Bar Meals: L served all week 12-3 (Sun 12.30-2.30) D served all week 6-9
Av main course £6
Restaurant: L served 12-3
D served all week 6.30-9 (Sun 7-9)
Av 3 course · à la carte £22
Brewery/Company: FREE HOUSE
🍺: Belhaven 80/-, Best, Caledonian IPA, Deuchars
Children's Facilities: Play area
Notes: Dogs Allowed Parking 30 Coach parties welcome

APPLECROSS NG74

Applecross Inn 🏠 ♀

Shore Street Wester Ross IV54 8LR
☎ 01520 744262 📠 01520 744400
✉ applecrossinn@globalnet.co.uk

Dir: From Lochcarron to Kishorn then L onto unclassified rd to Applecross over 'Bealach Na Ba'

This traditional white-painted inn is set on a sandy cove looking over to Skye and the Cuillins. The kitchen takes its pick of top quality local produce, with the worthy aim of sourcing three-quarters of its ingredients from the surrounding area. Seafood, of course, is a speciality. Alternatives are Applecross Estate venison casserole, on mustard mash with organic green beans; or venison sausages with neeps 'n squeek and a rich onion gravy.

Open: 11-11 (Sun 12.30-11) Closed: 25 Dec, 1 Jan **Bar Meals:** L served all week 12-9 D served all week-Av main course £7.95
Restaurant: L by appointment
D served all week 6-9
Brewery/Company: FREE HOUSE
🍺: Scottish Courage John Smith's, Cask Ale, Red Cullin, Millers
Rooms: 7 bedrooms (3 en suite) (2 family) s£30 d£60 (★★)
Children's Facilities: Licence Play area Portions/Menu Cutlery Games High Chairs Food Warming Changing
Notes: Dogs Allowed Water Garden Food Served Outside Grassed area on beach, six tables Parking 30 Coach parties welcome

ARDVASAR NG60

Ardvasar Hotel ★★ ♀

Sleat IV45 8RS
☎ 01471 844223 📠 01471 844495
✉ richard@ardvasar-hotel.demon.co.uk

Dir: From ferry terminal, 50yds & turn L

The second oldest inn on Skye, this well-appointed white-painted cottage-style hotel offers a warm, friendly welcome and acts as an ideal base for exploring the island, spotting the wildlife and enjoying the stunning scenery. Overlooking the Sound of Sleat, the Ardvasar is within walking distance of the Clan Donald Centre and the ferry at Armadale. Popular menus offers freshly-caught seafood, as well as baked venison in peppers and port wine pie, lamb and leek potato hot pot and savoury vegetable crumble. Straightforward basket meals are a perennial favourite.

Open: 12-12 (Sun 12-11)
Bar Meals: L served all week 12-2.30 D served all week 5.30-9 Av main course £6.50 **Restaurant:** D served all week 7-9
Av 3 course · à la carte £22.50
Brewery/Company: FREE HOUSE
🍺: 80/-, Deuchars, IPA, Isle of Skye Hebridean Gold
Rooms: 6 en suite s£55 d£80
Children's Facilities: Licence
Notes: Dogs Allowed Garden Parking 30

CAWDOR NH85

Cawdor Tavern 🐟 ♀

The Lane IV12 5XP
☎ 01667 404777 📠 01667 404777
✉ cawdortavern@btopenworld.com

Dir: From A96 (Inverness-Aberdeen) take B9006 & follow signs for Cawdor Castle.

The Tavern is located close to the famous castle in a beautiful conservation village. Roaring log fires keep the place cosy and warm on long winter evenings, while the garden patio comes into its own in summer. One menu is offered in the bar or restaurant. The pub has quite a reputation for its food, attracting diners from some distance for great seafood. Another favourite with a thoroughly Scottish flavour is chicken Culloden filled with haggis and served with a Drambuie and mushroom cream sauce.

Open: 11-3 5-11 (May-Oct 11-11)
Closed: 25 Dec, 1 Jan
Bar Meals: L served all week 12-2 D served all week 5.30-9 (Sun 12.30-3, 5.30-9) Av main course £8.95
Restaurant: L (prior arrangement) 12-2 D served all week 6.30-9 (Sun 12.30-3, 5.30-9) Av 3 course · à la carte £19.95
Brewery/Company: FREE HOUSE
🍺: Tennents 80/-, Tomintoul Stag
Children's Facilities: Licence Fam room Play area (Games, Books) Portions/Menu Cutlery Games High Chairs Food Warming Changing
Notes: Dogs Allowed Water provided. Garden Food Served Outside Patio area
Parking 60 Coach parties welcome

DUNDONNELL NH08

Dundonnell Hotel ★★★ ◉

Little Loch Broom IV23 2QR
☎ 01854 633204 📠 01854 633366
✉ selbie@dundonnellhotel.co.uk

Dir: From Inverness W on the A835, at Braemore junct take A382 for Gairloch

Dundonnell is one of the leading hotels in the Northern Highlands. Originally a small inn accommodating the occasional traveller to Wester Ross, it has been considerably extended over the years. The Broom Beg bar and bistro is the 'local', offering a wide range of beers and casual dining, while the Cocktail Bar is the place for a quiet aperitif while mulling over what to eat in the spacious restaurant.

Open: 11-11 (reduced hours Nov-Mar, please phone) **Bar Meals:** L served all week 12-2 D served all week 6-8.30 Av main course £5
Restaurant: D served all week 7-8.30 Av 3 course · à la carte £27.50
Brewery/Company: FREE HOUSE
🍺: John Smith's
Rooms: 28 en suite 3 family s£45 d£90
Children's Facilities: Licence Portions/Menu High Chairs Food Warming
Nearby: Ullapool Leisure Centre, Gairloch pony trekking, beaches
Notes: Dogs Allowed except in eating area Garden Food Served Outside overlooking Little Loch Broom, seating
Parking 60 Coach parties welcome

FORT AUGUSTUS NH30

The Lock Inn

Canalside PH32 4AU
☎ 01320 366302

Dir: On banks of Caledonian Canal

Built in 1820, this former bank and post office building, replete with flagstone floors and original beams, stands on the banks of the Caledonian Canal close to Loch Ness. A thousand Celtic welcomes are extended to regulars and visitors who come to enjoy the regular Scottish folk music evenings. A new team will hopefully retain all the Scottish charm this inn has come to be known for.

Open: 11-11 **Closed:** 25 Dec, 1 Jan
Bar Meals: L served all week 12-3 D served all week 6-9.30 Av main course £6
Restaurant: L served all week 12-3 D served all week 6-10 Av 3 course - à la carte £20
Brewery/Company: FREE HOUSE
🍺: Caledonian 80/-, Orkney Dark Island, Black Isle
Children's Facilities: Fam room
Notes: Dogs in the garden only Food served outside Coach parties welcome

GARVE NH36

Inchbae Lodge Hotel 🐾

IV23 2PH
☎ 01997 455269 📠 01997 455207
✉ stay@inchbae.com

Dir: On A835, hotel 6m W of Garve

Originally a 19th-century hunting lodge, Inchbae Lodge is situated on the banks of the River Blackwater, with an elegant dining room offering panoramic views. An ideal base for those keen walkers wishing to take on Ben Wyvis and the Fannich Hills. Typical dishes include chicken stuffed with pâté, seafood linguine, and lasagne.

Open: 8-11 **Closed:** 2 wks in November, Christmas
Bar Meals: L & D served all week 10.30-9.30
Restaurant: L served all week 12-2 D served all week 7-9.30 Av 3 course - à la carte £15 Av 3 course fixed price £10
Brewery/Company: FREE HOUSE
🍺: Belhaven plus guest ale
Rooms: 15 en suite s£30 d£50 (★★★)
Children's Facilities: Fam room Play area (7 acres, Toy Box, Books, Jigsaws, Puzzles) Games High Chairs Food Warming
Notes: Dogs Allowed Garden Food Served Outside Food served outdoors Parking 30 Coach parties welcome

HIGHLAND

GLENCOE NN15

Clachaig Inn

PH49 4HX
☎ 01855 811252 🖷 01855 812030
❸ inn@clachaig.com

Dir: In the heart of Glen Coe, just off the A82, 20m S of Fort William and 2m E of Glencoe village

Situated in the heart of Glencoe, this 300-year-old inn is hugely popular with mountaineers. Scenes for the third Harry Potter film were shot just 200 yards from the doorstep. The pub is renowned for its real ales, 120 malt whiskies, and warming food which includes such classic local dishes as haggis, Clachaig chicken, venison casserole, and prime Scotch steaks.

Open: 11-11 (Fri 11-12, Sat 11-11.30, Sun 12.30-11) Closed: 24-26 Dec
Bar Meals: L served all week 12-9 D served all week 12-9 Av main course £8.50
Brewery/Company: FREE HOUSE
🍺: Fraoch Heather Ale, Houston Peter's Well, Atlas 3 Sisters, Atlas Brewery-Latitude, Cairngorm Tradewinds
Rooms: 23 en suite 5 family s£32 d£60 (★★)
Children's Facilities: Licence Fam room Portions/Menu High Chairs Food Warming Changing **Nearby:** National Trust Visitor Centre, Glen Coe **Notes:** Dogs Allowed Garden Food Served Outside Grassed area, patio at front Parking 40 Coach parties welcome

GLENELG NG81

Glenelg Inn

by Kyle of Lochalsh IV40 8JR
☎ 01599 522273 🖷 01599 522283
❸ christophermain7@glenelg-inn.com

Dir: From Shiel Bridge (A87) take unclassified road to Glenelg

Very much a home from home, this village inn occupies a 200-year-old stable mews and commands stunning views across the Glenelg Bay from its splendid waterside garden. Folk singers and musicians are frequent visitors to the bar where at times a ceilidh atmosphere prevails. The menu offers traditional Scottish fare based on local produce. The bar and restaurant selection may include chargrilled lemon chicken on courgette fritters, with fresh basil and chilli dressing; fajitas of pan-fried fresh Loch Hourn scallops and coriander, served with an avocado salsa and baby leaves. A choice of vegetarian dishes and home-baked puddings also feature.

Open: 12-11 (Bar closed lunch during winter) Days closed: Sun
Bar Meals: L served all week 12.30-2 D served all week 6-9.30
Restaurant: L served 12.30-2 D served 7.30-9
Brewery/Company: FREE HOUSE
Children's Facilities: Portions/Menu
Notes: Dogs Allowed Garden Food Served Outside Large garden going down to the sea Parking

NORTH BALLACHULISH   NN06

Loch Leven Hotel 🐾 ♀

Old Ferry Road Onich PH33 6SA
☎ 01855 821236 📠 01855 821550
✉ reception@lochlevenhotel.co.uk

Dir: Off A82 N of Ballachulish Bridge

Over 350 years old, this was a working farm up to 50 years ago, as well as accommodating travellers from the Ballachulish ferry. On the northern shore of Loch Leven by the original slipway, it is ideally placed for touring the Western Highlands. A typical menu may include beef lasagne; poached or grilled salmon; haggis, neeps and tatties; pork fillet with rich apple stock sauce; pan-fried chicken breast in wild mushroom jus; or cashew nut roast with leek and cheese cream.

Open: 11-12 (Fri-Sat 11-1, Sun 12.30-11.45)
Bar Meals: L served all week 12-3 D served all week 6-9 Av main course £7.95
Restaurant: L served all week 12-3 D served all week 6-9 Av 3 course - à la carte £16
Brewery/Company: FREE HOUSE
🍺: John Smith's, McEwan's 80/-
Children's Facilities: Fam room Play area Portions/Menu Cutlery Games High Chairs Food Warming Changing
Nearby: Leisure Centre & 9 hole golf course
Notes: Dogs Allowed Water Garden Food Served Outside Terrace with trees & shrubs overlooking loch Parking 30 Coach parties welcome

PLOCKTON   NG83

The Plockton Hotel ★★ 🐾

Harbour Street IV52 8TN
☎ 01599 544274 📠 01599 544475
✉ info@plocktonhotel.co.uk

Dir: On A87 to Kyle of Lochalsh take turn at Balmacara. Plockton 7m N.

The Plockton Hotel overlooks the loch's deep blue waters in a village that has National Trust protection and enjoys stunning views across the bay to Eilean Donan Castle. You can eat prawns from the loch moments after they have been landed. There's fresh pan-fried herring in oatmeal; and monkfish and smoked bacon brochettes. There's meat too - succulent locally-reared beef and lamb; or chicken stuffed with Argyll smoked ham and cheese.

Open: 11-11.45 (Sun 12.30-11)
Bar Meals: L served all week 12-2.15 D served all week 6-9.15 (Sun 12.30-2.15) Av main course £6.25
Restaurant: L served all week 12-2.15 D served all week 6-9.15 Av 3 course · à la carte £23.75
Brewery/Company: FREE HOUSE
🍺: Caledonian Deuchars IPA
Rooms: 15 en suite 1 family s£45 d£60
Children's Facilities: Fam room Play area Portions/Menu High Chairs Food Warming Changing **Nearby:** Eileen Donan Castle, Calums Seal Trips, Reptile Centre
Notes: No Dogs (ex Assist Dogs) Water in garden Food Served Outside Beer garden, summer house Coach parties welcome

PLOCKTON NG83

Plockton Inn & Seafood Restaurant 🕭

Innes Street IV52 8TW
☎ 01599 544222 📠 01599 544487
✉ stay@plocktoninn.co.uk

Dir: On A87 to Kyle of Lochalsh take turn at Balmacara. Plockton 7m N

Formerly a church manse, the Plockton Inn is today run by a local family. Local produce takes pride of place on the menu, and locally caught fish and shellfish are a speciality-look for Plockton prawns and Queenie scallops. A purpose-built smokehouse behind the hotel adds to the variety of seafood on offer. Vegetarians too are assured of an excellent choice.

Open: 11-1am (Sun 12.30-11pm)
Bar Meals: L served all week 12-2.30 D served all week 5.30-9.30 Av main course £10
Restaurant: L served N all 12-2.30 D served all week 5.30-9.30 Av 3 course - à la carte £15
Brewery/Company: FREE HOUSE
🍺: Greene King Abbot Ale & Old Speckled Hen, Fuller's London Pride, Isle Of Skye Blaven, Caledonian 80/-
Rooms: 14 bedrooms (13 en suite) (4 family) s£38 d£70 (★★★)
Children's Facilities: Licence Play area Portions/Menu Cutlery Games High Chairs Food Warming Changing
Nearby: Rare Animal Farm, Seal Boat Trips
Notes: Dogs Allowed Garden Food Served Outside 2 gardens, sloping grass space at rear, trees Parking 10 Coach parties welcome

SHIELDAIG NG85

Shieldaig Bar ★ 🏵🏵 ⚲

IV54 8XN
☎ 01520 755251 📠 01520 755321
✉ tighaneileanhotel@shieldaig.fsnet.co.uk

Dir: 5m S of Torridon off A896 on to village road signposted Shieldaig, bar on Loch front

All the seafood in this popular loch-front bar in a charming fishing village is caught locally. You can expect a friendly welcome here, the views across Loch Torridon to the sea beyond are stunning, and on a summer Friday night the bar is likely to be alive with the sound of local musicians, among them owner Chris Field, playing guitar, banjo, or pipes. The pub has a fine reputation for its bar snacks, such as sandwiches, home-made soups, and salads, and for its daily-changing specials such as fresh crab bisque, local seafood stew, Hebridean scallop Mornay, venison, hare and other game in season, steak and ale pie, and Tuscan-style leek tart with home-made bread.

Open: 11-11 (Sun 12.30-10)
Closed: Dec 25 & Jan 1 **Bar Meals:** L served all week 12-2.30 D served all week 6-8.30 Av main course £6.50 **Restaurant:** D served all week 7-8.30 Av 3 course fixed price £32
Brewery/Company: FREE HOUSE
🍺: Black Isle Ales, Tenants Superior Ale
Rooms: 11 en suite 1 family s£52.5 d£115
Children's Facilities: Licence
Notes: No Dogs In the garden only. Water provided Open courtyard on Lochside with umbrellas Parking Coach parties welcome

ALMONDBANK NO02

The Almondbank Inn

31 Main Street Perth PH1 3NJ
☎ 01738 583242 ≣ 01738 582471

Dir: From Perth take A85 towards Crieff.
3m to Almondbank

*A family-run pub a little way out of Perth.
From its neat rear garden the views are
wonderful. As well as snacks and high teas,
there's a dinner menu featuring steaks,
chicken, fish, pastas and Mexican dishes, and
specials such as duck with wild berries. Owner
Tommy Campbell, a retired Scottish football
manager, has decorated his bar with football
strips bearing famous players' signatures.*

Open: 11-3 5-11 (Thu-Sun 11-12.30)
Bar Meals: L served all week 12-2 D served
Wed-Sun 5-10 Av main course £4
Restaurant: L served all week 12-3
D served Wed-Sun 5-10 Av 3 course -
à la carte £12
Brewery/Company: BELHAVEN BREWERY
🍺: Belhaven Best, Tennants
Children's Facilities: Licence Fam room
Notes: Dogs Allowed Water, biscuits Garden
Food Served Outside 6 tables, water fountain
Coach parties welcome

BURRELTON NO23

The Burrelton Park Inn

High Street Blairgowrie PH13 9NX
☎ 01828 670206 ≣ 01828 670676

*Ideally situated for touring the highlands, this
long roadside inn is characterised by its
typical Scottish vernacular style. Spacious
lounge bar and conservatory offering steamed
mussels, braised lambs' liver and farmhouse
mixed grill, and a well appointed restaurant
featuring stuffed supreme of chicken and
venison fillet-among other more elaborate
dishes. Fresh catch of the day and special high
teas served.*

Open: 12-2.30 5-11 (Sat-Sun 12-11.45)
Bar Meals: L served all week 12-8.30 D
served all week 12-8.30 (No meals 2.30-5)
Restaurant: L served all week 12-8.30
D served all week 12-8.30
Brewery/Company: FREE HOUSE
🍺: Tennents, Guinness, Bellhaven Best &
Guest ales
Rooms: s£30 d£45
Children's Facilities:
Notes: Dogs Allowed Parking 30 Coach
parties welcome

PITLOCHRY NN95

The Old Mill Inn ♀

Mill Lane PH16 5BH
☎ 01796 474020
✉ r@old-mill-inn.com

Dir: In the centre of Pitlochry, along Mill Lane. Behind the post office.

Set at the gateway to the Highlands, this converted old mill still boasts a working water wheel, now with a patio overlooking it. Visitors are assured of a good choice of real ales, malts and wine by the glass to accompany an eclectic cuisine ∴ smoked haddock chowder, Stornaway black pudding, steamed mussels, salmon stir-fry, plus burgers, bacon and brie ciabatta, and smoked salmon bagel.

Open: 10-11
Bar Meals: L served all week 10-10 D served all week-Av main course £7.95
Restaurant: L served all week 10-10 D served all week-Av 3 course - à la carte £15
Brewery/Company: FREE HOUSE
🍺: Carlsberg-Tetley Tetley Bitter, Orkney Dark Island, Kettle Ale
Rooms: s£55 d£45
Children's Facilities: Menu
Notes: No Dogs Garden Food served outside Parking 10 Coach parties welcome

POWMILL NT09

Gartwhinzean Hotel

FK14 7NW
☎ 01577 840595 🖷 01577 840779

Dir: A977 to Kincardine Bridge road, for approx 7m to the village of Powmill, hotel at the end of village

Located between two of Scotland's finest cities, Edinburgh and Perth, and handy for exploring the nearby Ochil and Cleish Hills, this attractive hotel overlooks Perthshire's picturesque countryside. A large selection of malt whiskies and a cosy open fire add to the attractions. Traditional steak pie, lightly grilled fillet of salmon and noisettes of lamb feature among the dishes on the interesting, regularly changing menu.

Open: 11-11 (Sun 12.30-10.30)
Bar Meals: L served all week 12-1.45 D served all week 5-8.45 Av main course £8
Restaurant: L served all week 12-1.45 D served all week 5-8.45 Av 3 course - à la carte £20 Av 3 course fixed price £17.5
Brewery/Company: FREE HOUSE
🍺: Tetley Smoothflow, 70/-
Rooms: 23 en suite s£50 d£70 (★★★)
Children's Facilities: Menu, High Chairs
Notes: Dogs Allowed Garden Food served outside Parking 100 Coach parties welcome

GALASHIELS NT43

Abbotsford Arms Hotel ★★ ☺

63 Stirling Street TD1 1BY
☎ 01896 752517 🖷 01896 750744
✉ roberts750@aol.com

Dir: Turn off A7 down Ladhope Vale,
turn L opposite the bus station

*Handy for salmon fishing in the nearby Tweed
and visiting Melrose Abbey, this family-run,
stone-built 19th-century coaching inn offers
comfortable accommodation and traditional
bar food. The lunchtime choice runs from
filled croissants, salads and baked potatoes to
breaded haddock, chicken curry and sirloin
steak, bolstered in the evening by roast lamb
shank, duck and orange sausages, and quails
in cranberry and port. A function room holds
up to 150, and there are plenty of good local
golf courses.*

Open: 11.30-11
Bar Meals: L served all week 2-6
D served all week 6-9 (Sun 12-6, 6-8)
Av main course £6.50
Restaurant: L served all week 12-6
D served all week 6-9 (Sun 12-6, 6-8)
Av 3 course - à la carte £12.50
Brewery/Company: FOX TAVERNS
🍺: John Smith's, Miller, McEwans 70/-
Rooms: 14 en suite 3 family s£10 d£60
Children's Facilities: Portions/Menu Cutlery
Games High Chairs Food Warming Changing
Notes: No Dogs (except Assist Dogs) Garden
Food Served Outside Paved area with grass
Parking 10 Coach parties welcome

INNERLEITHEN NT33

Traquair Arms Hotel ◆◆◆

Traquair Road EH44 6PD
☎ 01896 830229
✉ traquair.arms@scotborders.com

Dir: 6m E of Peebles on A72. Hotel
100metres from junc with B709

*This traditional stone-built inn is in a village
setting close to the River Tweed, surrounded
by lovely Borders countryside and offering en
suite bedrooms, a dining room and cosy bar.
Real ales include Traquair Ale from nearby
Traquair House, and the food has a distinctive
Scottish flavour with dishes of Finnan savoury,
salmon with ginger and coriander, and fillet of
beef Traquair. Also a selection of omelettes,
salads, and baked potatoes are available.*

Open: 11-12 (Sun 12-12) Closed: 25 & 26
Dec, 1-3 Jan
Bar Meals: L served all week 12-9 D served
all week-Av main course £6.50
Restaurant: L served all week-D served all
week 12-9 Av 3 course · à la carte £18 Av 4
course fixed price £20
Brewery/Company: FREE HOUSE
🍺: Traquair Bear, Broughton Greenmantle,
plus seasonal guest
Rooms: 15 en suite s£45 d£58
Notes: Dogs Allowed Garden Parking 75
Coach parties welcome

SWINTON NT84

Wheatsheaf Hotel ★ ◎◎ 🛏 ♈

Main St Duns TD11 3JJ
☎ 01890 860257 📠 01890 860688
✉ reception@wheatsheaf-swinton.co.uk

Dir: 6m N of Duns on A6112

Owners Chris and Jan Winson are continuing to create gastronomic delights at the Wheatsheaf with locally-reared meats, salmon from the Tweed, game from the Borders and seafood from the coast. Dinner is served in either the pine conservatory or more traditional dining room. Main dishes include roast rack of border lamb with a mustard crust on roast butternut squash and rosemary. Light lunches, such as Greenland prawns in a lemon and chive mayonnaise with avocado, are available on ciabatta or panini bread. There are plenty of places to visit including Kelso Racecourse, Paxton House, and Abbotsfield, the home of Sir Walter Scott.

Open: 11-2.30 6-11 (Closed Sun eve in winter) **Closed:** 24-26, 31 Dec, 1 Jan
Bar Meals: L served all week 12-2
D served all week 6-9 (Sun 6-8.30)
Restaurant: L served all week 12-2
D served all week 6-9
Brewery/Company: FREE HOUSE
🍺: Caledonian 80/- & Deuchars IPA, Broughton Greenmantle Ale, Caledonian 70/-
Rooms: 7 en suite s£62 d£95
Children's Facilities: Licence Play area (In garden) Portions/Menu High Chairs Food Warming
Notes: Dogs Allowed Parking 6

TWEEDSMUIR NT12

The Crook Inn ♈

Scottish Borders ML12 6QN
☎ 01899 880272 📠 01899 880294
✉ thecrookinn@btinternet.com

First licensed in 1604 and transformed into the art deco style in the 1930s, the Crook nestles deep in the Tweed Valley. Once a haunt of Rabbie Burns, the pub is an ideal base for country pursuits. Broad Law, the second highest peak in southern Scotland, is only five miles away. Good range of bar meals includes Crook haggis, Cumberland sausages, Borders shepherd's pie and Arbroath haddock. Ice cream honeypot and banana split feature among the puddings.

Open: 9-12 **Closed:** Dec 25, 3rd week in Jan
Bar Meals: L served all week 12-2.30
D served all week 5.30-8.30 Av main course £7
Restaurant: L served all week 12-2.30
D served all week 7-9 Av 3 course -
à la carte £16
Brewery/Company: FREE HOUSE
🍺: Broughton Greenmantle & Best, Scottish Courage John Smith's
Children's Facilities: Fam room Portions/Menu High Chairs Food Warming Changing
Nearby: Dawyck Gardens, New Lanark Visitor Centre, Traquair House
Notes: Dogs Allowed Water bowls Garden Food Served Outside Large grass area Parking 60 Coach parties welcome

WAUNFAWR SH55

Snowdonia Parc Hotel & Brewpub
🐾

Caernarfon LL55 4AQ
☎ 01286 650409 & 650218 📠 01286 650409
✉ karen@snowdonia-park.co.uk

A village brewpub and campsite in an idyllic mountain setting, 400 feet above sea level with a river running by. It's situated at Waunfawr Station on the Welsh Highland Railway, with steam trains on site (the pub was originally the station master's house). The pub offers home-brewed beer and home-made food prepared from local produce-Welsh lamb casserole and roast Welsh beef. Children and dogs are welcome and a children's playground is provided.

Open: 11-11
Bar Meals: L served all week 11-8.30 D served all week 5-8.30 Av main course £6
Restaurant: Av 3 course - à la carte £10.50
🍺: Marston's Bitter & Pedigree, Welsh Highand Bitter (ownbrew), Mansfield Dark Mild
Children's Facilities: Fam room Play area (Swings, Roundabout, Bouncy Castle Apr-Sep) Cutlery Games High Chairs Food Warming Changing
Nearby: Welsh Highland Railway, Sygum Copper Mines, The Greenwood Centre
Notes: Dogs Allowed Food Served Outside Parking 100

BEAUMARIS SH67

Ye Olde Bulls Head Inn ★★ 🏵🏵

Castle Street LL58 8AP
☎ 01248 810329 📠 01248 811294
✉ info@bullsheadinn.co.uk

Dir: From Brittannia Road Bridge follow A545

A short walk from Beaumaris Castle and the Menai Straits, this traditional watering hole dates back to 1472. Famous guests have included Samuel Johnson and Charles Dickens. There's a traditional bar leading on to the popular brasserie which offers lighter pasta and vegetarian dishes and the occasional spatchcocked poussin or grilled mullet. Or it's up the stairs to the smartly decorated, first-floor restaurant which offers a more formal menu.

Open: 10-11 (Sun-12-10.30)
Closed: 25 Dec
Bar Meals: L served all week 12-2 D served all week 6-9 Av main course £8
Restaurant: D served Mon-Sat 7.30-9.30 Av 3 course - à la carte £30
Brewery/Company: FREE HOUSE
🍺: Bass, Hancocks, Worthington
Rooms: 13 en suite s£67 d£95
Notes: No Dogs Parking 10

BETWS-Y-COED   SH75

White Horse Inn ◆◆◆◆ ♀

Capel Garmon LL26 0RW
☎ 01690 710271 🖷 01690 710721
📧 whitehorse@supanet.com

Picturesque Capel Garmon perches high above Betws-y-Coed, with spectacular views of the Snowdon Range, a good 20 kilometres away. To make a detour to find this cosy 400-year-old inn is to be rewarded not just by a striking collection of Victorian pottery and china, but by a menu featuring fresh local produce such as shoulder of Welsh lamb, traditional cottage pie, and horseshoe gammon steak. No children under 12 overnight.

Open: 11-3 6-11 **Closed:** 2 wks Jan
Bar Meals: L served Sat-Sun 12-2
D served all week 6.30-9.30 (Sun 7-9)
Av main course £7.50
Restaurant: L served Sat-Sun 12-2
D served all week 6.30-9.30 (Sun 7-9)
Av 3 course - à la carte £7.50
Brewery/Company: FREE HOUSE
🍺: Tetley Imperial, Tetley Smoothflow, Greene King, Abbot Ale
Rooms: 6 en suite s£35 d£58
Children's Facilities: Fam room Portions/Menu High Chairs Changing
Nearby: Electric Mountain, Snowdon Railway, Slate Caverns
Notes: Dogs Allowed Water Parking 30 Coach parties welcome

BETWS-YN-RHOS   SH97

The Wheatsheaf Inn ⌂

LL22 8AW
☎ 01492 680218 🖷 01492 680666
📧 perry@jonnyp.fsnet.co.uk

Dir: A55 to Abergele, take A548 to Llanrwst from the High St. 2m turn R-B5381, 1m to Betws-yn-Rhos

Built in the 13th century as an alehouse, the Wheatsheaf became licensed in 1640 as a coaching inn on the Conwy to Chester road. Splendid oak beams studded with horse brasses, old stone pillars and an original hayloft ladder add to its cosy charm. Food in the lounge bar or restaurant is good British traditional, with starters like garlic mushrooms, mains like the speciality Welsh lamb joint slow-roasted with rosemary and thyme, and several home-made sweets.

Open: 12-3 6-11
Bar Meals: L served all week 12-2 D served all week 6-9 (Sun 12-3)
Restaurant: L served all week 12-2 D served all week 6-9 (Sun 12-3) Av 3 course - à la carte £14.20
🍺:Greene King IPA, Wadworth 6X, Courage Directors, Worthington Smooth
Children's Facilities: Portions/Menu Cutlery Games High Chairs Food Warming
Nearby: Castle & Marina at Conway
Notes: No Dogs (except Assist Dogs) Garden Food Served Outside Paved beer garden with Wendy house & BBQ Parking 30 Coach parties welcome

CAPEL CURIG SH75

Cobdens Hotel ★★ 🐾

Snowdonia LL24 0EE
☎ 01690 720243 📠 01690 720354
📧 info@cobdens.co.uk

Dir: On A5, 4m N of Betws-Y-Coed

Situated in a beautiful mountain village in the heart of Snowdonia, this 250-year-old inn is a popular centre for outdoor pursuits. Wholesome food prepared from fresh local ingredients satisfies the needs of the mountaineer as well as the tourist. Welsh lamb and beef is well represented, as are fish and pasta dishes. Light bites and sandwiches are also available plus real ales and guest beers. A Mountain Bar and sauna are new attractions.

Open: 11-11 (Sun 12-10.30)
Closed: 6-26 Jan
Bar Meals: L served all week 12-2.30
D served all week 6-9 Av main course £8
Restaurant: L served all week 12-2
D served all week 6-9 Av 3 course -
à la carte £15
Brewery/Company: FREE HOUSE
🍺: Greene King Old Speckled Hen, Brains, Tetley's cold, Rev James Tetleys, plus guest beers
Rooms: 17 en suite 3 family s£29.50 d£59
Children's Facilities: Cutlery Games Food Warming
Notes: Dogs Allowed Garden Food Served Outside Parking 35

COLWYN BAY SH87

Pen-y-Bryn 🐾 ♀

Pen-y-Bren Road LL29 6DD
☎ 01492 533360 & 535808 📠 01492 536127
📧 pen.y.bryn@brunningandprice.co.uk

The wonderful view to the headlands and sea was a major selling point when this large 1970s-built pub came on the market. It reopened in June 2001 after a substantial refit, juke boxes and fruit machines having been banished (as have children in the evenings). Now it offers old furniture, open fires, oak floors, rugs and newspapers to provide an ambience conducive to the enjoyment of excellent real ales and good food. Reasonably priced fare ranges from sandwiches and light bites through to mains such as twice-roasted pork with Colcannon mash, black pudding and honey.

Open: 11.30-11 (Sun 12-10.30)
Bar Meals: L served all week 12-9.30
D served all week-Av main course £8.95
🍺: Timothy Taylors Landlord, Fullers London Pride, Thwaites Best Bitter, Phoenix Arizona, Oakham JHB
Children's Facilities: Food Warming
Nearby: Welsh Mountain Zoo, Colwyn Bay sea front, Llandudno sea front
Notes: No Dogs (except Assist Dogs) Dog park outside Garden Food Served Outside Terraced garden, views over Rhos on Sea Parking 80

LLANBEDR SH52

Victoria Inn ◆◆◆◆

LL45 2LD
☎ 01341 241213 🖨 01341 241644
✉ junebarry@lineone.net

Heavily beamed and richly atmospheric, the Victoria is ideal for the pub enthusiast seeking authentic features like flagged floors, an ancient stove, and unusual circular wooden settle. Good food is served in the bars and restaurant, including tasty filled baguettes, and lamb shoulder shank, fish pie, steak and kidney pie, and Welsh dragon pie. A well-kept garden is inviting on warmer days.

Open: 11-11 (Sun 12-10.30)
Bar Meals: L served all week 12-9 D served all week 6-9 Av main course £7
Restaurant: L served all week 12-3 D served all week 6-9 Av 3 course · à la carte £15
Brewery/Company: FREDERIC ROBINSON
🍺: Robinson`s Best Bitter, Hartleys XB, Carling Black Label
Rooms: 5 en suite 1 family s£42.50 d£72.50
Children's Facilities: Play area (Climbing frame and slide)
Notes: Dogs Allowed Garden Food Served Outside Riverside garden, pond, trees & plants Parking 50

LLANDWROG SH45

The Harp Inn

Tyn'llan Nr Caernarvon LL54 5SY
☎ 01286 831071 🖨 01286 830239
✉ management@theharp.globalnet.co.uk

Dir: A55 from Chester bypass, signed off A487 Pwllheli rd

A long established haven for travellers, in the historic home village of the nearby Glynllifon Estate. A proudly Welsh menu offers lob scouse with roll and red cabbage, Welsh mackerel rarebit on toast, trio of local bangers and mash, Welsh lamb steaks with a laverbread and citrus sauce, local sea bass with ginger and sesame seeds, and Glamorgan sausages with red onion marmalade. Welsh language menu supplied.

Open: 12-3 6-11 (Times vary, ring for details, Sat 12-11) Closed: 1 Jan
RS: 1 Oct - Easter Closed Sun, Mon
Bar Meals: L served Tue-Sun 12-2 D served Tue-Sun 6.30-8.30 Av main course £7.95
Restaurant: L served Tue-Sun 12-2 D served Tue-Sun 6.30-8.30 Av 3 course - à la carte £15 Av 3 course fixed price £9.95
Brewery/Company: FREE HOUSE
🍺: Interbrew Bass, Black Sheep Best, Wyre Piddle Piddle in the Wind, Plassey Bitter, Spinning Dog Chase Your Tail
Rooms: 4 bedrooms (1 en suite) (1 family) s£25 d£50 (★★★)
Children's Facilities: Fam room Play area (for all ages)
Notes: Dogs Allowed Water Garden Food Served Outside 6 tables Parking 20 Coach parties welcome

BETTWS-NEWYDD   SO30

Black Bear Inn ☺

Nr Usk NP15 1JN
☎ 01873 880701

Dir: Off B4598 N of Usk

*Dating back to the 16th century, the Black
Bear retains many of its original features. The
bar has a welcoming, informal atmosphere,
with its oak beams, a quarry tiled floor and a
large fireplace. Local produce is used almost
entirely in the dining rooms, includes fish,
pheasant, venison and duck when available.
Welsh beef and lamb also feature on the
menu and the Black Bear is known for
specialising in seafood and home-made
sauces and dressings. The constantly changing
menu offers plenty of choice.*

Open: 12-2 6-12 Days closed: Mon Lunch
Bar Meals: L served Tue-Sun 12-2 D served
Mon-Sat 6-10 Av main course £10
Restaurant: L served Tue-Sun 12-2
D served Mon-Sat 6-10
Brewery/Company: FREE HOUSE
🍺: Fuller's London Pride, Timothy Taylor
Landlord, Interbrew Bass, Greene King Old
Speckled Hen
Children's Facilities: Portions/Menu
Food Warming
Nearby: Raglan Castle, Abergavenny Leisure
Centre, Caerleon Roman Museum
Notes: Dogs Allowed Water tap Garden Food
Served Outside Shrubs, fruit trees, hen house,
seating Parking 20 Coach parties welcome
No credit cards

SKENFRITH   SO42

The Bell at Skenfrith ★ ◉◉ ♀

MONMOUTHSHIRE NP7 8UH
☎ 01600 750235 📠 01600 750525
✉ enquiries@skenfrith.co.uk

*This 17th-century coaching inn is located just
inside the Welsh border, on what is now a
mere B road, but which was once a main
route from England into the Principality.
Standing on the banks of the water by the
historic arched bridge over the River Monnow,
it has beautiful views across to Skenfrith
Castle. An oak bar, flagstones, and old settles
provide character. Locally sourced and mainly
organic ingredients are used in most dishes.*

Open: 11-11 (Sun 12-10.30) Closed: 1st 2
wks of Feb RS: Closed Mon Nov-Mar
Bar Meals: L served all week 12-2.30
D served all week 7-9.30 (Sun 7-9)
Av main course £14
Restaurant: L served all week 12-2.30
D served all week 7-9.30 Sun 7-9 Av 3 course
- à la carte £27
Brewery/Company: FREE HOUSE
🍺: Freeminer Best Bitter, Hook Norton Best
Bitter, Timothy Taylor Landlord
Rooms: 8 en suite s£70 d£90
Children's Facilities: Portions/Menu Cutlery
Games High Chairs Food Warming Changing
Nearby: Puzzle Wood, Fairy Tale Land &
Maze, Perry Grove Railway
Notes: Dogs Allowed Garden Food Served
Outside Lawn, terrace, tables & chairs
Parking 36

TINTERN PARVA SO50

Fountain Inn ♦♦♦ ⓨ

Trellech Grange NP16 6QW
☎ 01291 689303 📠 01291 689303
📧 dmaachi@aol.com

Dir: J2, M48 (8 miles), Grid Ref: SO 502013

A fire nearly destroyed this fine old inn, but
the thick 17th-century walls survived the
flames, and its character remains unspoilt. It
enjoys open views of the Wye Valley, and is
close to Tintern Abbey. Food in the bar ranges
from sandwiches and pies to Hungarian
goulash, grills and steaks, and asparagus
lasagne, with specials like beef Stroganoff,
and duck à l'orange. A couple of well-kept
ales are always on tap, plus a good selection
of lagers.

Open: 12-3 6-10.30 **Days closed:**
Mon(except BH), Sun evenings
Bar Meals: L served all week 12-2 D served
all week 7-10 Av main course £7
Restaurant: L served all week 12-2
D served all week 7-10 Av 3 course
fixed price £15
Brewery/Company: FREE HOUSE
🍺: Wye Valley Butter Bach, Freeminers,
Interbrew Flowers, Timothy Taylor Landlord
Rooms: 5 bedrooms (2 en suite) s£32 d£48
Children's Facilities: Fam room
Notes: Dogs Allowed Water, open fields for
walks Garden Food Served Outside Open
views of Wye Valley countryside Parking 30
Coach parties welcome

USK SO30

The Nags Head Inn ⓨ

Twyn Square NP15 1BH
☎ 01291 672820 📠 01291 672720

Dir: On A472

A warm welcome is assured in this 15th-
century coaching inn, where the same family
has been in charge for nearly forty years.
Overlooking the square and just a short stroll
from the River Usk, the flower-adorned pub
has undoubtedly played a key role in the town
winning Wales in Bloom awards for the last
three years. Friendly staff work in the
traditional bar with polished tables and chairs;
lots of horse brasses, farming tools and
lanterns hang from exposed oak beams. You
know you're in for a treat when you see the
hearty dishes of local game in season,
including wild boar steak in an apricot and
brandy sauce; pheasant cooked in port; whole
stuffed partridge; and rabbit pie. Vegetarian
options include Glamorgan sausage, filled with
cheese and leek and served with a chilli relish.

Open: 10-3 5.30-11 **Closed:** 25 Dec
Bar Meals: L served all week 10-2 D served
all week 5.30-10.30 Av main course £7.50
Restaurant: L served all week 11.30-2
D served all week 5.30-10.30
Brewery/Company: FREE HOUSE
🍺: Brains Bitter, Dark, Buckleys Best
& Reverend James
Children's Facilities: Portions/Menu Cutlery
Games High Chairs Food Warming
Notes: No Dogs (except Assist Dogs) Garden
Parking Coach parties welcome

LAMPHEY SN00

The Dial Inn ☜ ♟

Ridgeway Road nr Pembroke SA71 5NU
☎ 01646 672426 ▤ 01646 672426

Dir: Just off A4139 (Tenby to Pembroke rd)

The Dial started life around 1830 as the Dower House for nearby Lamphey Court, and was converted into a pub in 1966. It immediately established itself as a popular village local, and in recent years the owners have extended the dining areas. You can choose from traditional bar food, the imaginative restaurant menu, or the daily blackboard. There's a family room, with darts, pool and other pub games; and a patio for al fresco dining when the weather permits.

Open: 11-3 6-12
Bar Meals: L served all week 12-3 D served all week 6.30-10 Av main course £10.50
Restaurant: L served all week 12-3 D served all week 6.30-10
Brewery/Company: FREE HOUSE
🍺: Hancocks, Interbrew Bass, Worthington
Children's Facilities: Licence Fam room Play area (Family room, games (darts/pool)) Portions/Menu Cutlery Games High Chairs Food Warming
Nearby: Folly Farm, Oakwood, Manor Park
Notes: No Dogs (except Assist Dogs) Water Garden Food Served Outside Patio area Parking 50 Coach parties welcome

LANDSHIPPING SN01

The Stanley Arms ♟

Narberth SA67 8BE
☎ 01834 860447

Dir: Off A40 at Canaston Bridge onto A4075, R at Cross Hands, next to Canaston Bowls

Built as a farmhouse around 1765, first licensed in 1875, the pub has its own mooring on the Cleddau Estuary and is popular with sailors. There's an attractive garden with fine views across the water to Picton Castle, and the area is good for walking. Freshly-cooked pub food includes marinated chicken breast, gammon with egg or pineapple, grilled Milford plaice, Welsh dragon sausage in mustard sauce and Welsh steaks, as well as salads and a children's menu.

Open: 12-3 6-11 (Sun 7-10.30, all day Thur-Sun, Jul-Sept) RS: Mon-Tue (winter) Closed Lunch
Bar Meals: L served all week 12-2.30 D served all week 6-9.30 Av main course £7
Restaurant: L served all week 12-2.30 D served all week 6-9.30
Brewery/Company: FREE HOUSE
🍺: Worthington, Fuller's London Pride, Everards Tiger, Hancocks HB
Children's Facilities: Menu Licence Play area (Slide and play centre)
Notes: Dogs Allowed Water Garden Food Served Outside Large garden with swings annd sandpit Parking 20 Coach parties welcome

PORTHGAIN SM83

The Sloop Inn ☜

SA62 5BN
☎ 01348 831449 📠 01348 831388
✉ matthew@sloop-inn.freeserve.co.uk

From the outside, this family-friendly harbourside pub doesn't look particularly large, but just like the Tardis, appearances are deceptive. The large interior has brick, slate, quarry-tile and carpet on the floors, comfy seating, a large warming stove, and a collection of maritime photos and artefacts. The bar menu has sandwiches, baguettes, light snacks and an evening menu. There's also an all-year lunch and evening menu.

Open: 11-11 (Sun 12-4 5.30-10.30)
RS: 25 Dec No food, limited bar
Bar Meals: L served all week 12-2.30
D served all week 6-9.30 Av main course £7
Restaurant: L served all week 12-2.30
D served all week 6-9.30 Av 3 course -
à la carte £20

Brewery/Company: FREE HOUSE
🍺: Interbrew Worthingtons, Felinfoel, Brains Reverend James
Children's Facilities: Licence Portions/Menu
Notes: No Dogs (except Assist Dogs) Outside water drinker Garden y Food Served Outside Raised patio area, sun trap Parking 50 Coach parties welcome

BERRIEW SJ10

The Lion Hotel & Bistro ☜

nr Welshpool SY21 8PQ
☎ 01686 640452 📠 01686 640604

Dir: 5m from Welshpool on A483,
R to Berriew. Centre of village next to church.

17th-century black and white inn with exposed beams throughout and plenty of character. Welcoming and friendly atmosphere inside. Food options include a variety of starters or light meals and main courses ranging from fillet of salmon to baked goats' cheese salad, steak, mushroom and ale pie, and curry. A range of specials, sandwiches and home-made puddings is also available.

Open: 12-3 6-11 (Fri 5.30-11, Sat 7-11,
Sun 7-10.30) Closed: 25 Dec
Bar Meals: L served all week 12-2 D served all week 7-9 Av main course £9.95
Restaurant: L served all week 12-2
D served Mon-Sat 7-9
Brewery/Company: FREE HOUSE
🍺: Worthington Bitter, Woods Shropshire Lad, Brains Reverend James, Woods Wonderful
Rooms: 7 en suite 1 family s£55 d£70
(★★★) **Children's Facilities:** Licence Fam room Portions/Menu High Chairs Food Warming Changing
Nearby: Powys Castle, River Rhew, Welshpool-Llanfair Light Railway
Notes: Dogs Allowed Water Garden Food Served Outside Patio area surrounded by plants Parking 6 Coach parties welcome

COEDWAY SJ31

The Old Hand and Diamond

nr Shrewsbury SY5 9AR
☎ 01743 884379 📄 01743 884267

*Close to the Shropshire border and the River
Severn, this 17th-century inn still retains much
of its original character. Large open log fires
burn in the winter and autumn. Typical menu
includes chicken in mushroom and Stilton
cream sauce, pork chops with cider and apple
sauce, fresh sea bass, roast beef and
Yorkshire pudding, and vegetable cannelloni.*

Open: 11-11
Bar Meals: L served all week 12-10
D served all week-Av main course £6.95
Restaurant: L served all week 12-10
D served all week
Brewery/Company: FREE HOUSE
🍺: Bass, Worthington, Shropshire Lad,
Guest beers
Rooms: s£40 d£54
Children's Facilities: Play area
Notes: Dogs Allowed Guide Dogs Only
Garden Food served outside Parking 90
Coach parties welcome

LLOWES SO14

The Radnor Arms 🐾

HR3 5JA
☎ 01497 847460 📄 01497 847460

Dir: A438 Brecon-Hereford Rd between
Glasbury & Clyro

*This 400-year-old former drovers' inn provides
outstanding views from the garden, looking
over the Wye Valley to the Black Mountains,
to the west of the Brecon Beacons. Local
Felinfoel bitter is amongst the superb range of
beers served beside blazing winter fires in the
cosy bar, and the extensive blackboard menus
offer plenty of variety, with good vegetarian
options. Expect steak pie, loin of pork and
braised lamb, as well as a selection of fish
dishes, including swordfish and tiger prawns.*

Open: 11-2.3 6.30-10 (Sun 12-3)
Days closed: Mon (ex BHs)
Bar Meals: L served Tue-Sun 12-2.30 D
served Tue-Sun 6.30-9 Av main course £8.95
Restaurant: L served Tue-Sun 12-2.30 D
served Tue-Sun 6.30-9 (Sun 12-2.30)
Brewery/Company: FREE HOUSE
🍺: Felinfoel, Worthington, Bitburger
Notes: No Dogs (except Assist Dogs) Garden
Food Served Outside Parking 50

OLD RADNOR   SO25

The Harp Inn

Presteigne LD8 2RH
☎ 01544 350655 📄 01544 350655

Dir: A44 from Leominster to Gore,
then L to Old Radnor

This charming inn dates back to the 15th-century, yet has been sympathetically renovated, taking great care to retain as much of its original period character as possible. The slate-flagged floor, exposed stone walls and ancient bread oven still remain, as do traditional standards of hospitality and good food. Charles I complained about the food here centuries ago, but he could scarcely do so today. A typical menu includes 10oz Herefordshire steaks, steak and mushroom pie and pork steak in mustard sauce. Vegetarian options always available.

Open: 12-2 6-11 (Sat-Sun 12-3, 6-10.30)
Days closed: Monday
Bar Meals: L served Sat-Sun 12-2 D served
Tue-Sun 6-9
Restaurant: L served Sat-Sun 12-2 D served
Tue-Sun 7-9
Brewery/Company: FREE HOUSE
🍺: Shepherd Neame, Six Bells Brewery,
Bishops Castle, Big Nevs, Duck and Dive
Children's Facilities: Play area
Portions/Menu Cutlery Food Warming
Notes: No Dogs (except Assist Dogs) Garden
Food Served Outside Large lawn in front of
pub Parking 18 Coach parties welcome

TRECASTLE   SN82

The Castle Coaching Inn ♀

nr Brecon LD3 8UH
☎ 01874 636354 📄 01874 636457
✉ guest@castle-coaching-inn.co.uk

Dir: On A40 W of Brecon

Family-owned and run, the hotel has been carefully restored in recent years. Food is served in the bar or more formally in the restaurant. Bar lunches consist of sandwiches (roast beef, turkey, Stilton or tuna), ploughman's with tuna, duck and port pâté perhaps, and hot filled baguettes (steak with melted Stilton, bacon with mushrooms and melted mature Cheddar). A separate children's list runs through the usual favourites. Specialities include mature Welsh 12oz sirloin steak served with mushrooms and onion rings.

Open: 12-3 6-11
Bar Meals: L served Mon-Sun 12-2 D served
Mon-Sat 6.30-9 (Sun 7-9) Av main course £7
Restaurant: L served Mon-Sun 12-2 D served
Mon-Sat 6.30-9 (Sun 7-9) Av 3 course - à la
carte £16
Brewery/Company: FREE HOUSE
🍺: Fuller's London Pride, Breconshire Brewery
Red Dragon, Timothy Taylor Landlords
Rooms: 10 en suite 2 family s£45 d£60
(★★★)
Children's Facilities: Licence Portions/Menu
Cutlery High Chairs Food Warming Changing
Notes: No Dogs (except Assist Dogs) Garden
Food Served Outside Paved sun terrace
Parking 25 Coach parties welcome